Contents

Unit 3 Physical and Inorganic Chemistry

Unit 4 Organic Chemistry and Analysis

Unit 5 Practical

How to use this book

What this book contains

The contents of this book match the specification for WJEC A2 Level Chemistry. It provides you with information and practice examination questions that will help you to prepare for the examinations at the end of the year.

This book covers all three of the Assessment Objectives required for your WJEC Chemistry course. The main text covers the three Assessment Objectives:

- AO1 Knowledge and Understanding
- AO2 Application of Knowledge and Understanding
- AO3 Analyse, interpret and evaluate information, ideas and evidence

This book also addresses

- The mathematics of chemistry, which will represent a minimum of 20% of your assessment, with explanations and worked examples.
- Practical work. The assessment of your practical skills and understanding of experimental chemistry represents a minimum of 10% and will also be developed by your use of this book. Some practical details are mentioned in the chapters of Units 3 and 4. Further comments about the required experimental task and the practical methods and analysis task, are given in the details for Unit 5.

The book content is clearly divided into the units of this course. These are Unit 3 – Physical and Inorganic Chemistry, Unit 4 – Organic Chemistry and Analysis and Unit 5 – Practical.

Each chapter covers one topic. Each topic is divided into a number of sub-topics, which are listed at the start of each chapter, as a list of learning objectives. Following this, there are a number of practice exam questions designed to help you to practise for the examinations and to reinforce what you have learned. Answers to these questions are given at the end of the book.

Marginal features

The margins of each page hold a variety of features to support your learning:

Key Terms

These are terms that you need know how to define. They are **highlighted in blue** in the body of the text.

Knowledge check

These are short questions for you to check whether you have followed the material in the text as you go along, and allow you to apply the knowledge you have acquired. Answers are given at the back of the book.

▼ Study point

These contain advice that may help to clarify certain points or aspects of each topic, or help you understand and use the knowledge content.

 Stretch & Challenge

This may provide material that while it might not be in the main text, or strictly in the specification and the exam, it will still be relevant to it. It may provide new material that is of interest, and helps to broaden your understanding overall.

 From time to time facts and points appear that are relevant to different parts of the specification, so it will broaden your understanding overall if these connections are made.

 **YOU SHOULD KNOW ›››**

Learning objectives are provided for each main sub-topic.

PRACTICAL CHECK

Occasionally a topic covers an experiment or a practical that is a **specified practical task**. This feature appears alongside in the margin to highlight its importance and to give you some extra information and hints on understanding it fully.

❗ Extra Help

These are helpful hints or extra explanations of key points.

MATHS

An assessment of your mathematical skills is very important, this feature demonstrates some common uses of mathematics in chemistry. You are preparing for a chemistry examination not a maths exam, but it is still important to apply numerical analysis, and these features will help you to do so. Mathematical requirements are given in Appendix C, at the end of the specification course content. The level of understanding is greater at the A2 level and some requirements are equivalent to Level 3 (post GCSE).

HOW SCIENCE WORKS

In some cases it helps you to see how chemistry itself has evolved, the interaction between theory and experiments as well as their limitations. Science works by using theories and ideas, knowledge and understanding, IT and ICT and experimental investigations to obtain, analyse, interpret and evaluate data. Also by considering the applications of science, benefits, risks and ethical issues it evaluates how society may use science to inform decision making.

A2 Chemistry – a summary of assessment

Assessment in the A2 specification consists of two written papers of 1 hour 45 minutes each, and there is one paper for each of two units that are themselves 25% of the A level qualification. There are 80 marks available on each paper. In addition, practical work at A2 is assessed through Unit 5. This consists of an experimental task, of up to three hours in duration and a one hour written practical methods and analysis task. Both parts carry 30 marks each and the overall mark counts 10% of the marks towards the overall qualification.

Unit 3 deals with Physical and Inorganic Chemistry

Unit 4 deals with Organic Chemistry and Analysis

Unit 5 deals with the Practical aspects of chemistry

Each of the papers in Units 3 and 4 consists of Section A short answer questions (for 10 marks), and Section B structured and extended response answer questions. Section B questions are worth 70 marks.

There are no multiple choice questions in these papers.

Assessment objectives (AOs) and weightings

Assessment objectives

Examination questions are written to reflect the assessment objectives described in the specification. You must meet the following assessment objectives in the context of the subject content, which is given in detail in the specification.

AO1 Covers showing knowledge and understanding of all aspects of the subject.

AO2 Covers applying this knowledge and understanding theoretically, practically and qualitatively and quantitatively.

AO3 Covers analysis, interpretation and evaluation of scientific information and evidence, making judgements, reaching conclusions and developing practical design and procedures.

The weightings of these objectives – which are the same for Units 3 and 4 – are as follows (for the whole A level qualification):

AO1 – 7.2% (or for each paper 28.8%)

AO2 – 10.6% (or for each paper 42.4%)

AO3 – 7.2% (or for each paper 28.8%)

For Unit 5

AO1 – 2.0% (or for this unit 20%)

AO2 – 5.0% (or for this unit 50%)

AO3 – 3.0% (or for this unit 30%)

Mathematical skills

These will be tested across all three papers and have a total weighting of at least 20%. The skills include those tested at AS level and some extra skills, which include the use of logarithms. The specification lists these requirements in more detail.

Practical work

The practical work at A2 level is tested through Unit 5 and details of this are given later in the book.

Suggested practical exercises

There are many opportunities for practical work during the A2 year and the specification mentions some that should be done. These are

Unit 3, Topic 3.1

- Construction of electrochemical cells and measurement of E_{cell}

Unit 3, Topic 3.2

- Simple redox titration
- Estimation of copper in copper(II) salts

Unit 3, Topic 3.5

- Determination of the order of a reaction, for example, the oxidation of iodide ions by hydrogen peroxide in acid solution

Unit 3, Topic 3.8

- Determination of an equilibrium constant, for example, for the equilibrium established when ethanol reacts with ethanoic acid

Unit 3, Topic 3.9

- Titration using a pH probe, for example, titration of a weak acid against a weak base

Unit 4, Topic 4.4

- Identification of aldehydes/ketones by their reaction with 2,4-dinitrophenylhydrazine

Unit 4, Topic 4.8

- Synthesis of a liquid organic product, including separation using a separating funnel
- Synthesis of a solid organic product, including recrystallisation and determination of melting temperature
- Two-step organic synthesis, including purification and determination of melting temperature of product
- Planning a sequence of tests to identify organic compounds from a given list
- Paper chromatography separation, including two-way separation

The examinations

As well as being able to recall facts, name structures and describe their functions, you also need to appreciate the underlying principles of the subject and understand associated concepts and ideas. In other words, you need to develop skills so that you can apply what you have learned, perhaps to situations not previously encountered. For example, the inter-conversion of numerical data and graph form; the analysis and evaluation of numerical data or written information; the interpretation of data; and the explanation of experimental results.

You will be expected to answer different styles of question, in each paper, for example:

- **Section A** Short answer questions – these often require a one-word answer or are a simple calculation.
- **Section B** Structured questions may be in several parts usually about a common theme. They become more difficult as you work your way through. Structured questions can be short, requiring a one-word response, or may include the opportunity for extended writing. The number of lined spaces and the mark allocation at the end of each part question are there to help you. They indicate the length of answer expected. If three marks are allocated then you must give three separate points.
- In each of the papers for Units 3 and 4 there will be ONE longer six-mark question that will be assessed using a banded level of response mark scheme. What is required is a piece of writing that answers the question directly using well-constructed sentences and suitable chemical terminology. Often candidates rush into such questions. You should take time to read it carefully to discover exactly what the examiner requires in the answer, and then construct a plan. This will not only help you organise your thoughts logically but will also give you a checklist to which you can refer when writing your answer. In this way you will be less likely to repeat yourself, wander off the subject or omit important points.

Further notes on the papers

- There will be no multiple choice questions.
- A maximum of 10% will rely on recall only, i.e. no understanding.
- A minimum of 15% will be related to practical work and a minimum of 20% to Level 2/3 mathematical skills.

Examination questions are worded very carefully to be clear and concise. It is essential not to penalise yourself by reading questions too quickly or too superficially. Take time to think about the precise meaning of each word in the question so that you can construct a concise, relevant and unambiguous response. To access all the available marks it is essential that you follow the instructions accurately. Here are some words that are commonly used in examinations:

- *Complete:* You may be asked to complete a comparison table. This is straightforward and, if you know your work, you may pick up easy marks. For example: Complete the table to show the number of bonding electrons and the molecular shape. Follow the instructions carefully. If you leave a space blank in such a question, your examiner will not assume that this is equivalent to a cross. Similarly, if you put a tick and change your mind, do not put a line through the tick to convert it to a cross. Cross it out and write a cross.

- *Describe* This term may be used where you need to give a step-by-step account of what is taking place.

- *Explain* A question may ask you to describe and also explain. You will not be given a mark for merely describing what happens – a chemical explanation is also needed.

- *Suggest* This action word often occurs at the end of a question. There may not be a definite answer to the question but you are expected to put forward a sensible idea based on your chemical knowledge.

- *Name* You must give no more than a one-word answer. You do not have to repeat the question or put your answer into a sentence. That would be wasting time.

- *State* Give a brief, concise answer with no explanation.

- *Compare* If you are asked to make a comparison do so. Make an explicit comparison in each sentence, rather than writing separate paragraphs about what you are comparing.

- *Deduce* Use the information provided and your knowledge to answer the question.

- *Calculate* Work out the answer required using the information provided and your mathematical knowledge.

- *Predict* Evaluate the information provided and use your judgement to give an answer.

- *Write or Balance an equation* To write you will need to know the reactants and products, to balance you will need to apply the ideas of valency and the laws of conservation of atoms.

How to maximise your score

We all vary in speed and natural ability but by attacking the challenge of A2 Chemistry in the right way the best possible outcome can be achieved. This book has been written by examiners who have had many years of experience of candidates' performance with the aim of pointing students in the right direction. Here are some of the best tips we have gathered over many years of teaching and examining:

1 Give yourself time. Take each topic slowly, clear up any uncertainties then try the exam practice questions. If you need to then make sure you return to each topic after an interval of time to ensure that you still have it mastered. This may take more than one return trip. It is known that the unconscious mind continues to work and sort learned material so you must give it time. Last-minute cramming is of little use.

2 Be careful to understand what the question is really asking for. Candidates sometimes rush ahead down the wrong track and lose both time and marks. Questions on AO1 will ask you to show that you know and/or understand something; those on AO2 will ask you to apply these and AO3 to analyse, interpret and evaluate something.

   The actual lead words in the questions may include, 'state', 'describe', 'draw', 'name' and 'explain' for AO1, 'calculate', for AO2 and 'suggest' and 'analyse data' for AO3.

3 There is no substitute for work and concentration.

Chris Froome did many very long training runs on his bicycle. Practice trains the mind and produces understanding and enjoyment in mastery of the subject.

Unit 3

Overview
Physical and Inorganic Chemistry

3.1 Redox and standard electrode potential — p10

- The ideas of reduction and oxidation.
- Produce and use ion/electron half-equations.
- Half-cells and how they can be used to produce electrochemical cells.
- Standard electrode potentials to calculate EMF values.
- Apply these principles to the hydrogen fuel cell and balance its advantages and disadvantages.

3.2 Redox reactions — p19

- Recall and use common ion/electron half-equations.
- Combine half-equations to give an overall redox equation.
- Practical techniques of titration with redox reactions.
- Analyse the copper content of solutions using indirect redox titrations.

3.3 Chemistry of the p-block — p27

- The pattern in metallic character on going down groups and its effect on bonding and acid-base character of compounds.
- The inert pair effect and its effect on the redox properties of compounds.
- The ideas of electron deficiency and octet expansion to explain compounds with different numbers of electrons in their outer shells.
- The bonding in donor-acceptor compounds and Al_2Cl_6.
- The reactions of group 4 chlorides with water.
- The reactions of chlorine with sodium hydroxide.
- The reactions of concentrated sulfuric acid with sodium halides.

3.4 Chemistry of the d-block transition metals — p39

- Variable oxidation states in the d-block elements.
- The bonding in tetrahedral and octahedral complexes.
- The origin of colour in complexes.
- Examples of complexes containing copper (II) and cobalt (II).
- The catalytic properties of transition metals and their compounds.
- The aqueous reactions of sodium hydroxide with Cr^{3+}, Fe^{2+}, Fe^{3+} and Cu^{2+}.

3.5 Chemical kinetics — p49

- Measuring reaction rates, including sampling and quenching.
- Using experimental data to find reaction orders and rate equations.
- Rate-determining steps and reaction mechanism.
- The link between temperature, activation energy and rate using the Arrhenius equation.

3.6 Enthalpy changes for solids and solutions

p58

- Standard enthalpy changes including atomisation, hydration, solution, lattice formation and breaking.
- Linking the solubility of ionic compounds to enthalpy changes of lattice breaking and hydration.
- Building and using Born–Haber cycles for ionic compounds.
- Linking the stability of compounds to the sign of the standard enthalpy of formation.

3.8 Equilibrium constants

p71

- Write expressions for K_c and K_p and relate the values of these to the position of equilibrium.
- The effect of temperature of the values of K_c and K_p.
- Calculating the values of K_c and K_p from the concentrations or partial pressures of substances.
- Calculating the concentrations or partial pressures of substances using the values of K_c and K_p.

3.7 Entropy and feasibility of reactions

p67

- The meaning of entropy.
- How the entropy of a material depends on its physical state.
- Calculating entropy changes for chemical reactions.
- Calculating Gibbs free energy values and using these to identify whether reactions are feasible.

3.9 Acid-base equilibria

p77

- The Lowry–Bronsted theory of acids and bases.
- Strong and weak acids and bases and the values of K_a for these.
- The ionic product of water, K_w, and its use in calculations.
- Calculating pH for strong and weak acids and for strong bases.
- The shapes of titration curves for strong and weak acids and bases.
- How buffers work and their importance in living things and industry.
- Calculating the pH of a buffer solution.
- The hydrolysis of salts of weak acids or bases.
- The selection of appropriate indicators for acid-base titrations.

Unit 3

3.1
Redox and standard electrode potential

Chemists organise the properties and reactions of materials to see patterns and make predictions. One way to classify reactions is as oxidation with the name linked to the original definitions as processes that gained oxygen. The opposite reaction, reduction, referred to the loss of mass when oxygen was removed from a compound.

Over time chemists have adjusted their ideas of oxidation and reduction as their understanding of the processes have developed, so the focus is now on electrons in the definitions of these terms. The harnessing of flows of electrons between compounds is key to the function of the batteries used to power all the mobile devices used today.

Content

You should be able to demonstrate and apply your knowledge and understanding of:

- The definitions of redox reactions in terms of electron transfer.

- Using ion/electron half-equations to represent redox systems.

- Building half-cells into cells and showing these as cell diagrams.

- The concept of standard electrode potentials and the role of the standard hydrogen electrode in finding these.

- Half-cells based on metal/metal ion electrodes and electrodes based on different oxidation states of the same element.

- How simple electrochemical cells are formed by combining electrodes.

- The concept of cell EMF and how it can be used to deduce the feasibility of reactions.

- The principles of the hydrogen fuel cell and its benefits and drawbacks.

Redox reactions

Redox reactions are reactions where are electrons are transferred from one species to another. They are combinations of Oxidation and Reduction:

Oxidation is a process where *electrons are lost*.　　**OIL (Oxidation is Loss of electrons)**

Reduction is a process where *electrons are gained*.　**RIG (Reduction is Gain of electrons)**

These two processes always occur together, giving a redox reaction (**Red**uction-**Ox**idation). They must occur at the same time, as the electrons gained during reduction must have come from a different material. We call the material that donates the electrons the reducing agent, and as it loses electrons in the process the reducing agent is oxidised.

- An **oxidising agent** is a species that oxidises another species, and is itself reduced in the process.

- A **reducing agent** is a species that reduces another species, and is itself oxidised in the process.

Oxidation and reduction half-equations

A full equation describes what happens to all the substances in a chemical reaction; however, it can be useful to focus on what happens to each substance separately. To do this we can split a full ionic equation into two ion-electron half-equations which separately describe what happens to each of the substances present. One half-equation represents electrons being lost (oxidation) and one half-equation represents electrons being gained (reduction).

Worked example

The ionic equation for the reduction of Cu^{2+} by metallic zinc is:

$$Zn\ (s) + Cu^{2+}\ (aq) \rightarrow Cu\ (s) + Zn^{2+}\ (aq)$$

In this reaction we can split the changes into what happens to the zinc and what happens to the copper:

The zinc changes from $Zn\ (s)$ to $Zn^{2+}\ (aq)$. To do this it must lose two electrons.

$$Zn\ (s) \rightarrow Zn^{2+}\ (aq) + 2e^- \qquad \text{OXIDATION}$$

The copper changes from $Cu^{2+}\ (aq)$ to $Cu\ (s)$. To do this it must gain two electrons.

$$Cu^{2+}\ (aq) + 2e^- \rightarrow Cu\ (s) \qquad \text{REDUCTION}$$

The half-equations must be balanced in terms of atoms and charge, so it is important to remember that each electron has a negative charge.

Key Terms

An **oxidising agent** is a substance that takes electrons from another substance and so it is reduced.

A **reducing agent** is a substance that gives electrons to another substance and so it is oxidised.

YOU SHOULD KNOW › › ›

›› oxidation is the loss of electrons

›› reduction is the gain of electrons

Link Oxidation numbers in AS Topic 1.1 on page 12 of the AS book.

◀ The zinc placed into copper sulfate solution rapidly changes from a silvery surface to brown as copper metal covers the zinc.

Knowledge check ⌐1

Write ion-electron half-equations for the oxidation and reduction processes in these reactions.

1. $Mg\ (s) + Fe^{2+}\ (aq) \rightarrow Mg^{2+}\ (aq) + Fe\ (s)$
2. $Zn\ (s) + 2\ H^+(aq) \rightarrow Zn^{2+}\ (aq) + H_2\ (g)$

Cells and half-cells

YOU SHOULD KNOW › › ›

››› the type of half-cell needed for any half-equation

››› platinum is used as an electrode in many cases as it is unreactive and doesn't affect the chemical reaction occurring

Stretch & Challenge

The electrochemical cells always use high-resistance voltmeters. The resistance is important as it prevents the flow of electrons. If the electrons were flowing this would cause the redox reactions to occur in each half-cell, which would change the concentrations of the solutions. This would affect the potential difference reading on the voltmeter and it would not be possible to obtain a steady value.

PRACTICAL CHECK

The construction of electrochemical half-cells and full cells, and the measurement of cell EMF values is a **specified practical task**. These can include a range of different types of half-cell. Although you do not need to perform practical tasks involving the standard hydrogen electrode you will need to be able to recall how this is constructed and used.

Key Term

A **salt bridge** is a piece of apparatus that connects the solutions in two half-cells so that the circuit can be complete and the current can flow without the solutions mixing.

Writing redox reactions as two half-equations is not a theoretical process – it is possible to physically separate the two processes so that oxidation happens in one place and reduction happens somewhere else. To do this we need to set up two half-cells, one for the oxidation and one for the reduction. We join them together to complete the circuit:

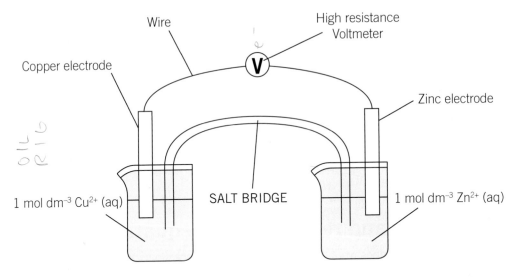

- The wire allows electrons to flow from the half-cell where oxidation occurs to the half-cell where reduction occurs. We often include a high resistance voltmeter if we are measuring the potential difference in the cell.

- The **salt bridge** completes the circuit and allows ions to flow without the solutions mixing. A typical salt bridge is made of a gel soaked in a solution of potassium nitrate. A simpler salt bridge that you may use in your experimental work is made of filter paper soaked in the same solution.

- The entire apparatus is called a cell, with the two parts called half-cells.

Half-cells

Each cell is made up of two half-cells, each of which must contain both the reactants and products of the half-equation. This means the half-cell for the reduction of Cu^{2+} ions to copper atoms must contain both of these. It must also contain a metal to allow electrons to flow into or out of the half-cell. There are various types of half-cell depending on the physical states of each substance in the reaction.

There are three key types of electrochemical half-cell that you need to be aware of:

1. Metal / metal ions

The half-cells described so far have consisted of metals in contact with metal ions, with two key examples being Zn (s) with Zn^{2+} (aq) and the Cu (s) with Cu^{2+} (aq) half-cells. In both cases we have a piece of metal as the electrode, with a solution containing a 1 mol dm^{-3} solution of the metal ions. In the case of zinc, there is no apparent colour change, but for copper the blue solution may lose colour as the copper ions are reduced.

2. A gas in contact with a solution of non-metal ions, with an inert metal electrode

Since non-metals are not conductors, we must use an <u>inert</u> platinum electrode to allow electrons to flow in or out of the half-cell. This is typically used for a hydrogen electrode ($H_2(g)$ I $H^+(aq)$) or oxygen ($O_2(g)$ I $OH^-(aq)$) half-cells. The gas is bubbled over the inert electrode which is dipping into a solution of the ions. These changes do not cause any apparent colour change.

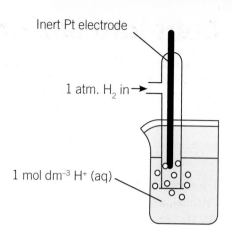

Inert Pt electrode

1 atm. H_2 in →

1 mol dm^{-3} H^+ (aq)

3. A solution containing ions of a metal in two different oxidation states, again using an inert metal electrode

Again there is no conductor in the system so we must use an inert platinum electrode to allow electrons to flow in or out of the half-cell. This is typically used for the transition metals, where the metal may have several oxidation states. Good examples are Fe^{2+}/Fe^{3+} and Mn^{2+}/MnO_4^-. Both these half-cells cause colour changes when oxidation or reduction occurs. Fe^{2+} is pale green and Fe^{3+} is yellow/orange; Mn^{2+} is colourless, MnO_4^- is purple.

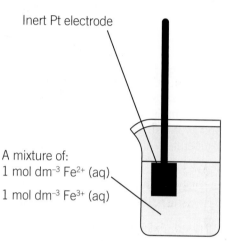

Inert Pt electrode

A mixture of:
1 mol dm^{-3} Fe^{2+} (aq)
1 mol dm^{-3} Fe^{3+} (aq)

Representing half-cells

We can show half-cells using cell diagrams. These list all the essential substances present in a half-cell, starting with the metal that is used to conduct electrons into or out of the half-cell. Each substance is then listed, with vertical lines separating substances in different physical states (solid, liquid, gas or solution) and commas separating substances in the same physical state.

Mg (s) I Mg^{2+} (aq)	This is the metal/metal ion half-cell for magnesium.
Pt (s) I H_2 (g) I H^+ (aq)	This is a gas/solution half-cell containing an inert platinum electrode. As this is for hydrogen, it is the standard hydrogen electrode if it is under standard conditions.
Pt (s) I Mn^{2+} (aq), MnO_4^- (aq)	This is a mixed solution half-cell containing an inert platinum electrode. In this case a comma separates the two manganese-containing ions in aqueous solution as they are in the same physical state.

◀ The cell involving copper and zinc electrodes is called the Daniell cell after its inventor John Daniell.

Standard electrode potentials

Although the chemical reactions that occur in electrochemical cells can be performed directly, using these cells can allow us to obtain detailed information about the reaction. We can measure the EMF of the reaction, and this tells us a lot about the ease of oxidising or reducing the substances in each half-cell. The EMF measured is the difference in the redox power of the two half-cells, with the largest EMF values when a half-cell containing a species that is easy to oxidise, such as magnesium, is connected to a half-cell with a species that is easy to reduce, such as manganate (VII).

The ability of a half-cell to gain or lose electrons is measured using the **Standard Electrode Potential, E^θ**. The scale of the standard electrode potential uses hydrogen as zero, and any species that is easier to reduce has a negative E^θ value, with ones that are easier to oxidise having a positive E^θ value. The hydrogen half-cell is called the **standard hydrogen electrode**.

The standard hydrogen electrode

This consists of a platinum electrode coated with fine platinum grains, called platinum black. This is dipped into a 1.0 mol dm^{-3} solution of H$^+$ (aq), used as hydrochloric acid, and hydrogen gas is slowly passed over the electrode at a pressure of 1 atmosphere and a temperature of 298K.

YOU SHOULD KNOW › › ›

››› the definitions of the standard hydrogen electrode and standard electrode potential

Exam tip

When describing any standard cell then standard states must be stated clearly: 1 atm pressure for any gas; 1 mol dm^{-3} for any solution; 298K for temperature.

2 Knowledge check

Draw a labelled diagram that shows the cell represented by: Pt (s) I Fe^{2+}, Fe^{3+} (aq) II Mg^{2+} (aq) I Mg (s).

Exam tip

Don't draw a vertical line between two different ions that are present in the same solution.

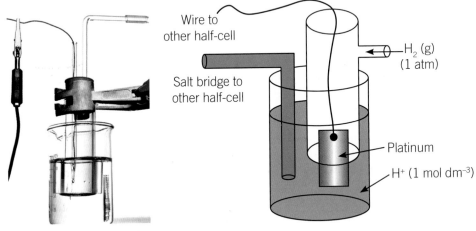

Wire to other half-cell

H$_2$ (g) (1 atm)

Salt bridge to other half-cell

Platinum

H$^+$ (1 mol dm^{-3})

▲ Standard hydrogen electrode

The standard electrode potential for a half-cell is measured by joining it to the standard hydrogen electrode. This creates a system like the one shown below:

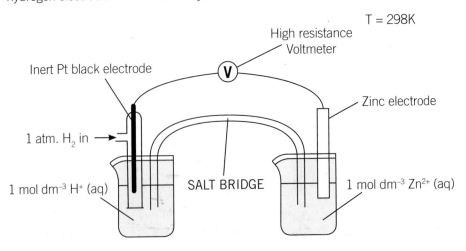

T = 298K

High resistance Voltmeter

Inert Pt black electrode

Zinc electrode

1 atm. H$_2$ in

1 mol dm^{-3} H$^+$ (aq)

SALT BRIDGE

1 mol dm^{-3} Zn^{2+} (aq)

Standard electrode potential

This is the potential difference between the standard hydrogen electrode and any other system in which the concentration of all the active ions in solution is 1.0 mol dm^{-3} and all gases are at 1 atm. pressure at 298K (25°C). Its symbol is E^θ.

To measure a standard electrode potential, we must set up a half-cell under standard conditions, and connect it to the standard hydrogen electrode, e.g. $Zn^{2+}(aq) \mid Zn(s)$ connected to $H^+ \mid H_2 \mid Pt$. The lines in each of these systems represent a change of physical state. If combining two half-cells together we use a double line between them to represent a salt bridge and place the metals at both ends, such as:

$$Pt(s) \mid H_2(g) \mid H^+(aq) \parallel Zn^{2+}(aq) \mid Zn(s)$$

Using standard electrode potentials

The E^θ value for the zinc half-cell is –0.76V. The negative sign signifies that the electrode potential of $Zn^{2+} \mid Zn$ is more negative than the potential of the standard hydrogen electrode. Electrons thus flow along the wire from the zinc half-cell to the standard hydrogen electrode and the hydrogen electrode becomes the positive electrode. (i.e. Zn loses electrons more readily than the H_2).

- The positive electrode has the more positive E^θ.

- The electrons flow to the half-cell with the more positive E^θ.

The E^θ value for the copper half-cell ($Cu^{2+} \mid Cu$) is +0.34 V. The plus sign signifies that the standard hydrogen electrode has the more negative potential. Electrons therefore flow along the wire from the standard hydrogen electrode to the copper and the hydrogen electrode becomes the negative electrode. (i.e. H_2 loses electrons more readily than the Cu).

We can use this method to put the reducing power of any set of half-cells in order. These are always quoted as reduction potentials, and it is noticeable that the order of these potentials for metals reflects the reactivity series, so this is sometimes called the electrochemical series. The most reactive metals have the most negative E^θ, with the most reactive non-metals having the most positive E^θ, so the electrochemical series has the same order as the reactivity series.

Reaction			E^θ / Volts
$Na^+(aq) + e^-$	$\rightleftharpoons$	$Na(s)$	−2.71
$Mg^{2+}(aq) + 2e^-$	$\rightleftharpoons$	$Mg(s)$	−2.36
$Zn^{2+}(aq) + 2e^-$	$\rightleftharpoons$	$Zn(s)$	−0.76
$2H^+(aq) + 2e^-$	$\rightleftharpoons$	$H_2(g)$	0.00
$Cu^{2+}(aq) + 2e^-$	$\rightleftharpoons$	$Cu(s)$	+0.34
$I_2(s) + 2e^-$	$\rightleftharpoons$	$2I^-(aq)$	+0.54
$Fe^{3+}(aq) + e^-$	$\rightleftharpoons$	$Fe^{2+}(aq)$	+0.77
$Br_2(l) + 2e^-$	$\rightleftharpoons$	$2Br^-(aq)$	+1.09
$Cr_2O_7^{2-}(aq) + 14H^+(aq) + 6e^-$	$\rightleftharpoons$	$2Cr^{3+}(aq) + 7H_2O(l)$	+1.33
$Cl_2(g) + 2e^-$	$\rightleftharpoons$	$2Cl^-(aq)$	+1.36
$MnO_4^-(aq) + 8H^+(aq) + 5e^-$	$\rightleftharpoons$	$Mn^{2+}(aq) + 4H_2O(l)$	+1.51

Stretch & Challenge

If electrons are allowed to flow, this will affect the concentrations of each species. It is possible to use Le Chatelier's principle to predict the effect of the changing concentration on the standard electrode potential. If we consider the $Fe^{3+}(aq) + e^- \rightleftharpoons Fe^{2+}(aq)$ which has a standard electrode potential of +0.77V, this means it will have a greater tendency to gain electrons than the standard hydrogen electrode. If electrons flow then reduction will occur in this half-cell, increasing the concentration of Fe^{2+} and reducing the concentration of Fe^{3+}. Le Chatelier's principle would suggest that this would attempt to shift the equilibrium to the left, decreasing the tendency of the half-cell to gain electrons and hence making the electrode potential less positive. Note that this is not the standard electrode potential any more as it is not under standard conditions.

Knowledge check **3**

Draw a labelled diagram that shows the cell represented by: $Mg(s) \mid Mg^{2+}(aq) \parallel Zn^{2+}(aq) \mid Zn(s)$ labelling the positive and negative electrode, and the direction of flow of electrons in the wire. Calculate the EMF of this cell.

Knowledge check **4**

Classify the following species as reducing agents or oxidising agents. Place the oxidising agents in order of decreasing oxidising power:

Na^+, Cu, I_2, Cl^-, H_2, MnO_4^-, Mg.

▼ Study point

When calculating the standard electrode potential for a full cell you should always obtain a positive value.

YOU SHOULD KNOW ›››

>›› how to use standard electrode potentials to identify whether a reaction is feasible or not

5 **Knowledge check**

Write the equation for the reaction that occurs when the following pairs of half-cells are connected together:

a. Zn I Zn²⁺ with Fe²⁺,Fe³⁺ I Pt

b. Cl₂ I Cl⁻ I Pt and Cu²⁺ I Cu

You will need to refer to the table of standard electrode potentials.

6  **Knowledge check**

Are the following reactions feasible?

a. $2 H^+ (aq) + Zn (s) \rightarrow Zn^{2+} (aq) + H_2 (g)$

b. $Cu (s) + Mg^{2+} (aq) \rightarrow Cu^{2+} (aq) + Mg (s)$

You will need to refer to the table of standard electrode potentials.

In these equations the oxidising agents are the substances that are being reduced such as Cl_2, I_2 or Zn^{2+}. The strongest oxidising agents are those that have the most positive standard electrode potentials. The strongest reducing agents are present in the half-equations with the most negative standard electrode potentials, such as Mg, Zn or H_2.

Calculating the EMF of an electrochemical cell

When two half-cells are connected, the high resistance voltmeter will give a reading showing the EMF of the cell. The value of the EMF is given by the difference between the standard electrode potentials of the two half-cells. The EMF value is positive.

Worked example

Calculate the EMF for a cell represented by the cell diagram below:

$$Zn (s) \text{ I } Zn^{2+} (aq) \text{ II } Cu^{2+} (aq) \text{ I } Cu (s)$$

The two standard electrode potentials are −0.76 V and +0.34 V.

$$EMF = +0.34 - (-0.76) = +1.10V$$

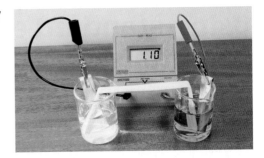

Feasibility of reactions

When an oxidising agent and reducing agent are mixed, a redox reaction may occur but this will not always be the case. The oxidising agent needs to be strong enough to oxidise the reducing agent. The standard electrode potentials give information about the strength of oxidising agents and reducing agent and allow you to work out if a reaction is feasible. A feasible reaction is one that can occur spontaneously. Most of these reactions will happen easily, but the standard electrode potentials do not give any information about the rate of reaction so for a few reactions the rate may be too slow to be effective.

Comparing the standard electrode potentials

If a piece of magnesium metal is placed in a solution containing Zn^{2+} ions, a redox reaction occurs with the magnesium forming Mg^{2+} ions and the Zn^{2+} being reduced to zinc metal. This can be proved using standard electrode potential values.

			E^θ / V
$Mg^{2+} (aq) + 2e^-$	$\rightleftharpoons$	Mg (s)	−2.36
$Zn^{2+} (aq) + 2e^-$	$\rightleftharpoons$	Zn (s)	−0.76

In this case we have one reactant from the left-hand side of a half-equation (the Zn^{2+} ions) and one from the right-hand side of a half-equation (the magnesium metal). For the overall reaction to occur the Zn^{2+} must be a stronger oxidising agent than Mg^{2+} so it can oxidise magnesium metal to form Mg^{2+} ions. In this case the Zn^{2+} is a stronger oxidising agent as it has a more positive standard electrode potential than the Mg^{2+} half-cell.

It can be easier to remember this as the 'anticlockwise rule':

1. Write the two half-equations in order of increasing standard electrode potentials, with the most negative value first.

2. Start in the top right-hand corner, and move anticlockwise around the equations. This means that in the feasible reaction the top reaction goes in reverse and the bottom goes in the direction is written.

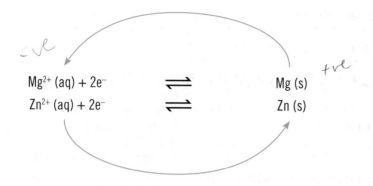

The feasible reaction is therefore $Mg (s) + Zn^{2+} (aq) + 2e^- \rightarrow Mg^{2+} + 2e^- + Zn (s)$

Cancelling out the electrons that are present on both sides of the equation gives the following feasible reaction.

$$Mg (s) + Zn^{2+} (aq) \rightarrow Mg^{2+} + Zn (s)$$

Calculating the EMF

A chemical reaction is feasible if the EMF for the redox process is positive. The EMF can be calculated from the standard electrode potentials for two half-cells. To assess the feasibility of the reaction between $Zn^{2+} (aq)$ and $Cu (s)$ we need the two standard electrode potentials below.

			E^θ / Volts
$Zn^{2+} (aq) + 2e^-$	$\rightleftharpoons$	$Zn (s)$	−0.76
$Cu^{2+} (aq) + 2e^-$	$\rightleftharpoons$	$Cu (s)$	+0.34

The reaction between $Zn^{2+} (aq)$ and $Cu (s)$ would need the first reaction to occur as written and the second to occur in reverse. This makes the first equation a reduction and the second an oxidation.

$Zn^{2+} (aq) + 2e^-$	$\rightleftharpoons$	$Zn (s)$	REDUCTION
$Cu (s)$	$\rightleftharpoons$	$Cu^{2+} (aq) + 2e^-$	OXIDATION

EMF for the reaction = $E^\theta_{REDUCTION} - E^\theta_{OXIDATION}$ = $-0.76 - (+0.34) = -1.10V$

As this value is negative the reaction is not feasible.

Fuel cells

Fuel cells are being developed as a method of releasing energy very efficiently from fuels such as hydrogen, methane or methanol. They are an electrochemical method of releasing the energy which avoids the need to burn the fuel, followed by using this heat to cause an expansion which is used to move a motor. Energy is lost at each stage of the traditional process, with much of the energy released from the fuel being lost as heat out of the exhaust.

▲ Hydrogen fuel cell car

YOU SHOULD KNOW › › ›

› › › at least two advantages and drawbacks of hydrogen fuel cells

Exam tip

When you are discussing the advantages and drawbacks you should link these to chemical concepts and specific reasons. Avoid overgeneralisations such as 'cheaper' or 'better for the environment'.

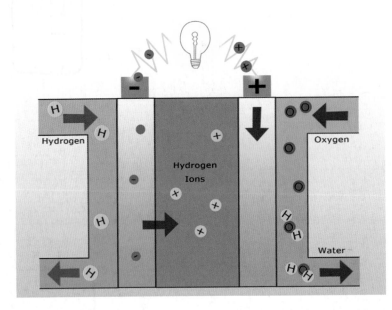

The fuel cell system passes the fuel over platinum metal which acts as a catalyst, but also as an electrode for the electrochemical system. Electrons are removed from hydrogen atoms at one electrode:

$$H_2 \rightarrow 2H^+ + 2e^-$$

The protons (H^+) diffuse through a semi-permeable membrane to the other electrode where they receive electrons and oxygen molecules to form water molecules:

$$O_2 + 4H^+ + 4e^- \rightarrow 2H_2O$$

The overall reaction is $2H_2 + O_2 \rightarrow 2H_2O$ and the voltage produced is 1.23 V.

These cells have been particularly studied as ways of storing energy to be released as electricity or heat, for instance in the development of 'zero emissions' cars which use hydrogen fuel and release no carbon dioxide.

Benefits:

- These are a convenient way of storing and releasing energy.

- The energy efficiency is much higher than standard fuel systems (e.g. 36–45% for fuel cell compared to 22% for diesel).

- Emissions from fuel cells are less damaging than the carbon dioxide from traditional engines.

Drawbacks:

- The hydrogen fuel must be generated elsewhere and this is likely to use fossil fuel energy sources which will cause their own carbon dioxide emissions. There is also an energy loss here as the conversion process is not 100% efficient.

- The gases needed are difficult to store compared to liquid fuels.

- The fuel cells operate at lower temperatures (about 80°C) so need very efficient catalysts which use expensive metals.

Redox reactions

Redox reactions can be used in the synthesis of a range of organic and inorganic substances. Once any substance is produced it is important to ensure that it is pure, and that the levels of any impurity can be measured to make sure they do not affect the use of the material. The labels on many chemical substances that are sold will show the amounts of impurities – you will see similar labels on bottles of mineral water.

The measurement of purity for a range of substances was an early use of chemical reactions, with methods of qualitatively ensuring the purity of precious metals being particularly important. We can now use redox reactions to analyse metals and their compounds quantitatively using redox titrations. In this chapter you will see how the copper content of compounds can be derived, but similar approaches can be used for a range of metals due to the versatility of redox reactions. These methods allow very accurate values to be obtained, which is very important when the value of the metal involved is high.

You should be able to demonstrate and apply your knowledge and understanding of:

- Constructing ion/electron half-equations to represent reduction and oxidation processes.

- Combining ion/electron half-equations to produce full redox equations.

- Carrying out titrations involving a range of redox reactions.

- Using the reaction of copper ions with iodide ions as a step in the analysis for copper.

Content

20 Ion/electron half-equations

21 Redox titrations

Link Half-equations and half-cells. Page 14

Exam tip

When you are given ion-electron equations these will always be written as reduction processes, with electrons being gained. When you are using ion/electron half-equations you can write them as reduction or oxidation, depending on the reaction occurring. Each reaction will have one oxidation and one reduction.

Exam tip

You can calculate the numbers of electrons in these ion-electron equations by using oxidation states. In the reduction of MnO_4^- to Mn^{2+} the oxidation state changes from +7 to +2. A change of 5 in the oxidation state means that five electrons will be needed in the half-equation. The reduction of $Cr_2O_7^{2-}$ to $2 Cr^{3+}$ will need six electrons in the half-equation, as each chromium changes its oxidation state by 3.

7

Knowledge check

Write ion/electron half-equations for the processes below:

a. The reduction of an acidified solution of perchlorate (VII), ClO_4^-, to chlorine gas.

b. The reduction of acidified manganate (VII) to manganese dioxide, MnO_2.

Ion/electron half-equations

The use of simple ion/electron half-equations has been discussed in the last topic; however, it is important to be able to construct these for a range of simple and compound ions. In the case of elements where the oxidation state of a single atom is changing, such as a magnesium atom becoming an Mg^{2+} ion or an Fe^{3+} ion becoming an Fe^{2+} ion, then a half-equation will only need electrons to be included to balance.

$$Mg\ (s) \rightarrow Mg^{2+}\ (aq) + 2e^-$$

$$Fe^{3+}\ (aq) + e^- \rightarrow Fe^{2+}\ (aq)$$

When compound ions are involved in an ion/electron half-equation it can be more complex. Ions such as dichromate (VI) and manganate (VII) include oxygen atoms, and each oxygen requires two hydrogen ions to contribute to the formation of water in the products:

$$MnO_4^- + 8H^+ + 5e^- \rightarrow Mn^{2+} + 4H_2O$$

$$Cr_2O_7^{2-} + 14H^+ + 6e^- \rightarrow 2Cr^{3+} + 7H_2O$$

The electrons are needed to ensure each half-equation is balanced in terms of charge, and so the numbers of electrons can be calculated by counting the charges on each side of the half-equation.

Worked example

The bromate (V) ion, BrO_3^-, can be reduced to bromine, Br_2, in acid solution. Write the ion-electron half-equation for this process.

STEP 1: Write the reagents and products:

$$BrO_3^- \rightarrow Br_2$$

STEP 2: Balance the atoms present:

$$2BrO_3^- \rightarrow Br_2$$

STEP 3: Add two hydrogen ions to combine with each oxygen to form water.

$$2BrO_3^- + 12H^+ \rightarrow Br_2 + 6H_2O$$

STEP 4: Find the total charges on both sides to find the number of electrons needed:

Total charge at the start $= 2- + 12+ = 10+$

Total charge at the end $= 0 + 0 = 0$

Change in charge = 10, so there needs to be 10 electrons in the ion-electron half-equation.

$$\mathbf{2BrO_3^- + 12H^+ + 10e^- \rightarrow Br_2 + 6H_2O}$$

Combining half-equations

When undertaking a redox reaction, the overall reaction combines the ion/electron half-equation for the oxidation process and the one for the reduction process. These must be combined in the correct ratio to have the same numbers of electrons in each half-equation.

Link Combining standard electrode potentials on page 17.

Worked example

Bromate (V) ions can act as an oxidising agent, with the half-equation for this process given below. This can be used to oxidise bromide ions to form bromine molecules, Br_2.

$$2BrO_3^- + 12H^+ + 10e^- \rightarrow Br_2 + 6H_2O$$

$$2Br^- \rightarrow Br_2 + 2e^-$$

To combine the two half-equations above, we need to multiply the second by five to give ten electrons.

$$2BrO_3^- + 12H^+ + 10e^- \rightarrow Br_2 + 6H_2O$$

$$10Br^- \rightarrow 5Br_2 + 10e^-$$

These two half-equations are now added together:

$$2BrO_3^- + 12H^+ + 10e^- + 10Br^- \rightarrow Br_2 + 6H_2O + 5Br_2 + 10e^-$$

We now cancel out the electrons on both sides of the equation, and add the two sets of bromine molecules in the product together:

$$2BrO_3^- + 12H^+ + 10Br^- \rightarrow 6Br_2 + 6H_2O$$

As there are even numbers of each species we can halve the equation to give the final answer below.

$$BrO_3^- + 6H^+ + 5Br^- \rightarrow 3Br_2 + 3H_2O$$

Redox titrations

Redox titrations are carried out in the same way as acid-base titrations. This involves 25.0 cm³ of a solution being measured using a volumetric pipette and placed in a conical flask. A second solution is added a little at a time from a burette, swirling the mixture during addition. This is continued until the desired colour change is seen. Many redox titrations do not need an indicator as the colours of the reactants frequently allow the end point to be seen. The volume of solution added is measured using initial and final burette readings.

As in all titrations, the procedure is repeated until the readings taken are sufficiently close together.

YOU SHOULD KNOW › › ›

› › › how to perform a redox titration

› › › how to calculate concentrations using redox titration data

Link The redox titrations use the same techniques as acid-base titrations found in AS Topic 1.7 described on pages 71–74 of the AS book.

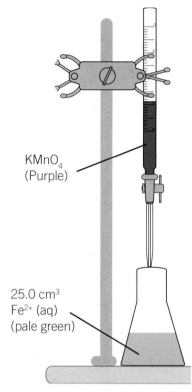

KMnO$_4$
(Purple)

25.0 cm^3
Fe^{2+} (aq)
(pale green)

Examples of redox titrations

Acidified manganate (VII) ions with iron (II) ions

In the case of a titration involving potassium manganate (VII), the purple solution of this oxidising agent is added from the burette. When it reacts with the species to be oxidised, it forms Mn^{2+}, which is almost colourless. The end point is reached when the solution goes pale pink. This is because a very small amount of the purple MnO$_4^-$ remains, which appears pink when dilute in the conical flask. The half-equation for the reduction of the manganate (VII) is:

$$① \quad MnO_4^- \text{ (aq)} + 8H^+ \text{ (aq)} + 5e^- \rightarrow Mn^{2+} \text{ (aq)} + 4H_2O \text{ (l)}$$

The colour change of the solution as Fe^{2+} (pale green) is oxidised to Fe^{3+} (yellow) is usually difficult to see as the solutions are generally dilute, and so the colour change associated with the manganate is used for the end point. The iron ions are oxidised according to the half-equation:

$$② \quad Fe^{2+} \text{ (aq)} \rightarrow Fe^{3+} \text{ (aq)} + e^-$$

To obtain the overall equation we need combine these two half-equations to balance the electrons. In this case, we combine equation ① + 5 × equation ② giving:

$$MnO_4^- \text{ (aq)} + 8H^+ \text{ (aq)} + 5Fe^{2+} \text{ (aq)} \rightarrow Mn^{2+} \text{ (aq)} + 4H_2O \text{ (l)} + 5Fe^{3+} \text{ (aq)}$$

The 5 electrons on each side of the equation have balanced out and so do not appear in the overall equation. The acid **must** be present for this reaction to occur, and this is usually added as H$_2$SO$_4$.

Calculations

The calculations are worked out in the same way as for other titrations. From the chemical equation we can see that 1 MnO$_4^-$ reacts with 5Fe^{2+}. The calculations are therefore:

$$\frac{\text{Number of moles of Fe}^{2+}}{\text{Number of moles of MnO}_4^-} = \frac{5}{1}$$

Giving:

$$\frac{C_{Fe^{2+}} \times V_{Fe^{2+}}}{C_{MnO_4^-} \times V_{MnO_4^-}} = \frac{5}{1}$$

This can be rearranged to calculate the concentration of one specific solution, so for the concentration of Fe^{2+} this would be:

$$C_{Fe^{2+}} = \frac{5 \times C_{MnO_4^-} \times V_{MnO_4^-}}{1 \times V_{Fe^{2+}}}$$

Worked example

Samples of 25.0 cm³ of a solution of acidified iron (II) sulfate were titrated using a solution of potassium manganate (VII) of concentration 0.0200 mol dm⁻³. The results obtained are shown in the table below. Calculate the concentration of the iron (II) sulfate solution, giving your answer to an appropriate number of significant figures.

	1	2	3	4
Initial reading / cm³	0.00	0.55	0.20	0.75
Final reading / cm³	30.40	30.35	30.10	30.60

First calculate the volumes used in each titration:

Volume used / cm³	30.40	29.80	29.90	29.85

The first volume is anomalous and so the average volume is (29.80 + 29.90 + 29.85) ÷ 3 = 29.85 cm³.

The reacting ratio is $5Fe^{2+}$ reacting with $1MnO_4^-$, so the relationships can be written as:

$$\frac{C_{Fe^{2+}} \times V_{Fe^{2+}}}{C_{MnO_4^-} \times V_{MnO_4^-}} = \frac{5}{1}$$

Rearranging gives:

$$C_{Fe^{2+}} = \frac{5 \times C_{MnO_4^-} \times V_{MnO_4^-}}{1 \times V_{Fe^{2+}}}$$

So

$$C_{Fe^{2+}} = \frac{5 \times 0.0200 \times 29.85}{1 \times 25.0}$$

$$C_{Fe^{2+}} = 0.1194 \text{ mol dm}^{-3}$$

As the lowest numbers of significant figures in the measurements are three (25.0 and 0.0200) then the answer should be given to three significant figures:

$$C_{Fe^{2+}} = 0.119 \text{ mol dm}^{-3}$$

Acidified dichromate (VI) ions with iron (II) ions

Potassium dichromate (VI) in acid solution will oxidise Fe^{2+} to Fe^{3+}, with a colour change from dark orange $Cr_2O_7^{2-}$ to a green solution of Cr^{3+} according to the half-equation:

① $Cr_2O_7^{2-} (aq) + 14H^+ (aq) + 6e^- \rightarrow 2Cr^{3+} (aq) + 7H_2O (l)$

The iron is again oxidised according to the half-equation:

② $Fe^{2+} (aq) \rightarrow Fe^{3+} (aq) + e^-$

To obtain the overall equation we need combine these two half-equations to balance the electrons. In this case, we combine equation ① + 6 × equation ② giving:

$Cr_2O_7^{2-} (aq) + 14H^+ (aq) + 6Fe^{2+} (aq) \rightarrow 2Cr^{3+} (aq) + 7H_2O (l) + 6Fe^{3+} (aq)$

Knowledge check 8

Write an ionic equation for the oxidation of oxalic acid (ethanedioic acid), $C_2O_4H_2$, to carbon dioxide by acidified potassium manganate (VII).

▼ **Study point**

When combining half-equations then any species appearing on both sides of the equation should be cancelled out, not just electrons. Other species that may be affected are H^+ ions and H_2O molecules.

PRACTICAL CHECK

A redox titration is a **specified practical task**. These can include a range of oxidising agents and reducing agents, and you should be familiar with the colour change in each case. You should be aware that an indicator is not needed in most cases.

Knowledge check 9

A metal nail is made of an alloy containing iron. A sample of 1.740g of the alloy is dissolved in acid which converts all the iron to Fe^{2+}. The mixture is diluted to form a 250 cm³ solution and samples of 25.0 cm³ are taken for titration using 0.0200 mol dm⁻³ acidified potassium manganate (VII) and 23.30 cm³ of the potassium manganate (VII) is needed for complete reaction. Calculate the percentage of iron in the original alloy.

▼ Study point

For each common redox titration, you need to learn the colours of the species involved. This is because the colour changes take the place of indicators.

Exam tip

When using oxidation states to identify whether a reaction is a redox reaction, you should calculate the oxidation states of each atom at the start and end. If any of these oxidation states changes then the reaction is a redox reaction – one oxidation state must become more negative (reduction) and one more positive (oxidation).

Link Copper (II) ions in solution are blue whilst copper (I) ions in CuI are colourless. The reasons for these differences in colour are discussed on pages 45 and 46.

The 6 electrons on each side of the equation have balanced out and so do not appear in the overall equation.

Calculations

From the equation above,

$$\frac{\text{Number of moles of } Fe^{2+}}{\text{Number of moles of } Cr_2O_7^{2-}} = \frac{6}{1}$$

Giving:

$$\frac{C_{Fe^{2+}} \times V_{Fe^{2+}}}{C_{Cr_2O_7^{2-}} \times V_{Cr_2O_7^{2-}}} = \frac{6}{1}$$

NOTE:

The acid **must** be present for this reaction to occur, and this is usually added as H_2SO_4. If the pH of a solution rises too high, then the dichromate (VI) ion is broken up into two chromate (VI) ions.

$$Cr_2O_7^{2-} \text{ (aq)} + H_2O \text{ (l)} \rightleftharpoons 2CrO_4^{2-} \text{ (aq)} + 2H^+ \text{ (aq)}$$

Dark orange   Yellow

The chromium always has an oxidation state of +6, so there is no change in oxidation state: **this is not a redox reaction.**

By Le Chatelier's principle, this equilibrium will shift to the left-hand side if acid is added, and to the right-hand side if base is added. This can be seen as a change of the colour of the solution.

Redox titration for copper (II) ions

It is not straightforward to analyse a solution for copper (II) ions directly, so an indirect route is used. Addition of a colourless solution containing iodide ions, such as potassium iodide, to a blue solution containing copper (II) ions leads to the formation of a cloudy brown solution. Cu^{2+} ions in solution react with iodide ions to generate a brown solution of iodine, and are reduced to copper (I) in a precipitate of CuI. The equation for this process is:

$$2Cu^{2+} \text{ (aq)} + 4I^- \text{ (aq)} \rightarrow 2CuI \text{ (s)} + I_2 \text{ (aq)}$$

We can titrate this iodine with sodium thiosulfate, to work out how much copper was present originally. Sodium thiosulfate is a common reducing agent, working according to the half-equation:

$$2S_2O_3^{2-} \text{ (aq)} \rightarrow S_4O_6^{2-} \text{ (aq)} + 2e^-$$

A common reaction of thiosulfate ions is with iodine molecules (I_2), to form iodide ions (I^-):

$$I_2 \text{ (aq)} + 2e^- \rightarrow 2I^- \text{ (aq)}$$

Brown   Colourless

This gives an overall equation of:

$$2S_2O_3^{2-} \text{ (aq)} + I_2 \text{ (aq)} \rightarrow S_4O_6^{2-} \text{ (aq)} + 2I^- \text{ (aq)}$$

Experimental details

- Add excess iodide ions (e.g. KI) to Cu^{2+} (aq) to ensure all Cu^{2+} reacts to produce I_2. The mixture formed is a cloudy brown solution.

▲ Copper (II) ions in solution

▲ Mixture after addition of potassium iodide

- Titrate the brown I_2 (aq) against sodium thiosulfate ($Na_2S_2O_3$), until the mixture is straw-coloured.

- Add starch indicator which goes blue-black, and continue until the colour vanishes. The mixture is often describes as flesh-coloured.

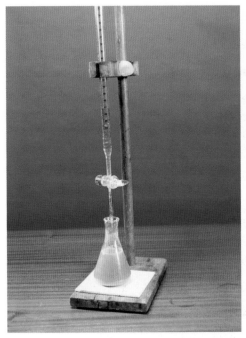

▲ Titration until straw coloured

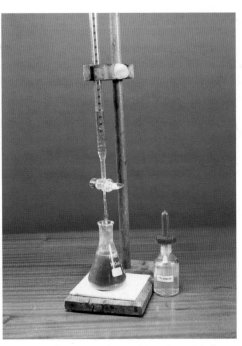

▲ Mixture after addition of starch indicator

PRACTICAL CHECK

The insoluble CuI precipitate formed when KI is added to the copper (II) ions in solution remains throughout the experiment. This makes the mixture cloudy throughout the experiment. In some cases, it is better to let the solid settle to see the colour of the solution.

▼ **Study point**

Even when you are not asked to prove the relationship between moles of thiosulfate and moles of copper, you should recall the $1\ Cu^{2+} \equiv 1$ thiosulfate relationship.

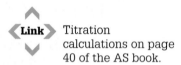

Link Titration calculations on page 40 of the AS book.

Calculations

Looking at the equations above we see that two copper (II) ions make one iodine molecule: $2Cu^{2+} \equiv 1I_2$

We can also see that one iodine molecule reacts with two thiosulfate ions: $1I_2 \equiv 2S_2O_3^{2-}$

Combining this gives $2Cu^{2+} \equiv I_2 \equiv 2S_2O_3^{2-}$ so $1Cu^{2+} \equiv 1S_2O_3^{2-}$

The titration calculations therefore use:

$$\frac{C_{Cu^{2+}} \times V_{Cu^{2+}}}{C_{S_2O_3^{2-}} \times V_{S_2O_3^{2-}}} = \frac{1}{1}$$

Worked example

A transition metal complex contains copper (II) ions. A sample of 4.242g of the complex was dissolved in 250 cm³ of deionised water, and samples of 25.0 cm³ were taken and excess potassium iodide was added to each. This was titrated against sodium thiosulfate solution of concentration 0.0500 mol dm⁻³ and 28.35 cm³ was needed for complete reaction. Find the M_r of the complex.

The number of moles of sodium thiosulfate used in the reaction are given by:

Moles thiosulfate = $0.0500 \times 28.35 \div 1000 = 14.175 \times 10^{-4}$ moles

Since 1 thiosulfate $\equiv 1Cu^{2+}$ then the number of moles of $Cu^{2+} = 14.175 \times 10^{-4}$ moles in 25.0 cm³.

The full volume was 250 cm³, which would contain ten times the number of moles = 0.014175 moles.

Since moles = mass $\div M_r$ then M_r = mass $\div$ moles

$$M_r = 4.242 \div 0.014175$$

$$= 299.3$$

Chemistry of the p-block

The periodic table is the greatest tool available to a chemist. Patterns and similarities in behaviour across periods and down groups allow chemists to make predictions. The explanations for these patterns have led to many of the significant ideas in chemistry.

The p-block makes up a significant part of the periodic table, from group 3 to group 0. Like all groups in the periodic table, there are similarities between the elements in a group; however, the p-block also shows patterns with significant differences. The differences we see in some fundamental properties of these elements, such as the metal/non-metal behaviour or their common oxidation states can make elements in the same group behave very differently.

You should be able to demonstrate and apply your knowledge and understanding of:

- Acid/base properties of the elements and oxides, including amphoteric behaviour.

- The variations in oxidation states on going down groups, including octet expansion and the inert pair effect.

- Electron deficiency in group 3 compounds, and the formation of coordinate bonds involving these.

- The bonding and structure in hexagonal and cubic boron nitride and how these relate to their properties and uses.

- The bonding, physical properties and redox behaviour of lead and carbon oxides.

- Changes in the types of bonding down group 4 as shown by the chlorides CCl_4, $SiCl_4$ and $PbCl_2$ and their reactions with water.

- The reactions of $Pb^{2+}(aq)$ with aqueous NaOH, Cl^- and I^-.

- The different reactions of Cl_2 with both cold and warm aqueous NaOH and the various disproportionation reactions involved, and the uses of the products of the reactions.

- The differences in behaviour of NaCl, NaBr and NaI with concentrated sulfuric acid.

Content

Link The chemistry of group 7, part of the p-block, was discussed in AS Topic 1.6 on pages 59–60 of the AS book.

YOU SHOULD KNOW › › ›

››› the most common oxidation states for the p-block elements in groups 3, 4 and 5

››› the most stable oxidation state for the p-block elements, especially those in group 4

▼ **Study point**

It is easier to learn the patterns in oxidation states rather than learn each element separately. For all elements, the highest oxidation state equals the group number, with a second oxidation state two lower in many cases.

Key ideas in p-block chemistry

The p-block elements are called this as their outer electrons are located in p sub-shells (2p, 3p, 4p, etc.). You need to be able to write the electronic configurations for these p-block elements in the second and third periods, i.e. those with outer electrons in the 2p or 3p sub-shells.

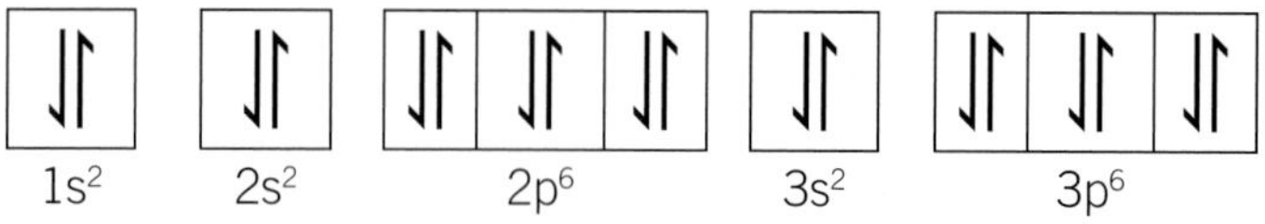

$1s^2 \qquad 2s^2 \qquad 2p^6 \qquad 3s^2 \qquad 3p^6$

Every p-block element has a full s sub-shell in their outer shell, with between 1 and 6 further electrons in their p sub-shell.

- Group 3 atoms have 1 electron in their p sub-shells, i.e. outer electrons are s^2p^1.

- Group 4 atoms have 2 electrons in their p sub-shells, i.e. outer electrons are s^2p^2.

- Group 5 atoms have 3 electrons in their p sub-shells, i.e. outer electrons are s^2p^3.

- Group 6 atoms have 4 electrons in their p sub-shells, i.e. outer electrons are s^2p^4.

- Group 7 atoms have 5 electrons in their p sub-shells, i.e. outer electrons are s^2p^5.

The division of the outer electrons into s-electrons and p-electrons has a substantial effect on the chemistry of these elements, and so it is important that you can differentiate between these sets of electrons.

Oxidation states

Elements in the p-block typically show two oxidation states – the maximum oxidation state which equals the group number, and a lower oxidation state which is two less.

Group 3		Group 4		Group 5	
B	**3**	C	2, **4**	N	**3**, 5
Al	**3**	Si	**4**	P	**3**, 5
Ga	1, **3**	Ge	2, **4**	As	**3**, 5
In	**1**, 3	Sn	**2**, 4	Sb	**3**, 5
Tl	**1**, 3	Pb	**2**, 4	Bi	**3**, 5

(Most stable oxidation state shown in **bold**)

Inert pair effect

The stability of the lower oxidation states becomes greater down the group, as is shown above. This tendency of the heavier elements to form the lower oxidation state is called the **inert pair effect**. For an element in group 4, the outer electronic configuration is:

- When the element has an oxidation state of 4, it involves all four electrons.

- When the element has an oxidation state of 2, the inner two electrons do not become involved, and this ns^2 pair is called the *inert pair*.

The trend for the ns^2 electron pair to become an inert pair occurs in groups 3, 4 and 5 of the periodic table. It is only the lower members of these groups that show this tendency to lower oxidation states: +1 for group 3; +2 for group 4 and +3 for group 5. In groups 3 and 4, the lower oxidation state is not observed in the first two members of each group (with the exception of +2 in carbon monoxide), but in group 5 the upper members (nitrogen and phosphorus) exhibit the lower oxidation state more frequently.

Octet expansion

There are significant differences seen between the first members of the p-block groups and the lower members of these groups. The maximum number of outer shell electrons that can surround the atoms in the first members of each group (Boron to Neon, 2nd period elements) is eight – four pairs of electrons. This limits the numbers of bonds that can be formed in the first row elements:

- Boron: Can form 3 covalent bonds and is electron deficient.

- Carbon: Can form 4 covalent bonds.

- Nitrogen: Can form 3 covalent bonds and one lone pair.

- Oxygen: Can form 2 covalent bonds and two lone pairs.

The other members of each group (3rd period and below) have access to d-orbitals that are not present in the second shell. This allows them to 'expand their octet' which means every electron in the outer shell can be used to form a covalent bond as there is no longer a limit of 8 electrons in the outer shell. This affects the numbers of bonds that can be formed for elements in groups 5, 6 and 7:

- Phosphorus: can form 5 covalent bonds, e.g. PCl_5.

- Sulfur: can form 6 covalent bonds, e.g. SF_6.

- Chlorine: can form up to 7 covalent bonds, e.g. ClO_4^-.

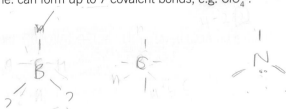

Stretch & Challenge

What causes the inert pair effect?

For a group 4 atom to form four bonds, the pair of s electrons must be unpaired, which requires energy to move an electron from the s to p sub-shell. This becomes more difficult down the group.

The unpairing energy must come from the energy released when bonds are formed and as you go down the group, the bonds get weaker, so less energy is released as they form. For the lowest members of the group, the energy released by making two extra bonds is not enough to balance the energy needed to move an electron from the s to p sub-shell.

Stretch & Challenge

The change from non-metal to metal on going down the group is linked to the ionisation energy of the elements. Ionisation energy decreases on going down a group so it is easier for the atoms to form positive ions. This allows the atoms to contribute to ionic bonding with non-metals and helps the elements form metallic bonding, as the atoms form positive ions and a sea of delocalised electrons easily.

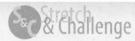

Key Term

Amphoteric materials react with both acids and bases.

Study point

When learning the equations for the reactions of acids and alkalis with amphoteric metals, remember that the equations for all metals forming +2 ions have similar formulae and the same balancing numbers. You do not need to learn each metal separately, as zinc, lead (II) and tin (II) will behave similarly

Stretch & Challenge

All acid-base reactions can be treated as reversible reactions, so a reaction written as
$Pb^{2+}(aq) + 2OH^-(aq) \rightarrow Pb(OH)_2(s)$
can be treated as showing Pb^{2+} acting as an acid, as it is reacting with hydroxide ions. It can also be treated as
$Pb(OH)_2 \rightarrow Pb^{2+} + 2OH^-$, which shows $Pb(OH)_2$ acting as a base.

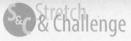

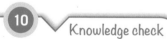

10 Knowledge check

Write two chemical equations to show that zinc oxide is an amphoteric oxide.

Metallic properties

In the p-block the elements at the top of each group are non-metals, such as boron, carbon or nitrogen, whilst the elements at the bottom of each group are metals such as thallium, lead or bismuth. This change in properties leads to the characteristic zig-zag line between metals and non-metals.

1	2											3	4	5	6	7	0
				H													He
Li	Be											B	C	N	O	F	Ne
Na	Mg											Al	Si	P	S	Cl	Ar
K	Ca	Sc	Ti	V	Cr	Mn	Fe	Co	Ni	Cu	Zn	Ga	Ge	As	Se	Br	Kr
Rb	Sr	Y	Zr	Nb	Mo	Tc	Ru	Rh	Pd	Ag	Cd	In	Sn	Sb	Te	I	Xe
Cs	Ba	La	Hf	Ta	W	Re	Os	Ir	Pt	Au	Hg	Tl	Pb	Bi	Po	At	Rn
Metals												*Some metals and non-metals*				*Non-metals*	

This change in metallic character has a significant effect on the bonding and properties of the p-block compounds.

Amphoteric behaviour

Many p-block elements form **amphoteric** oxides, and these are typically metals close to the line separating metals and non-metals. They show both acidic and basic properties. To show amphoteric behaviour, we must show that an element or its compounds react with both acids and bases. Typically this would be to show the material reacting with an acid such as hydrochloric or nitric acid and sodium hydroxide:

For aluminium oxide or hydroxide:

$$Al_2O_3 + 6HCl \rightarrow 2AlCl_3 + 3H_2O \quad \text{or} \quad Al(OH)_3 + 3H^+ \rightarrow Al^{3+} + 3H_2O$$

$$Al_2O_3 + 2NaOH + 3H_2O \rightarrow 2Na[Al(OH)_4] \quad \text{or} \quad Al(OH)_3 + OH^- \rightarrow [Al(OH)_4]^-$$

For lead (II) oxide or hydroxide:

$$PbO + 2HNO_3 \rightarrow Pb(NO_3)_2 + 2H_2O \quad \text{or} \quad Pb(OH)_2 + 2H^+ \rightarrow Pb^{2+} + 2H_2O$$

$$PbO + 2NaOH + H_2O \rightarrow Na_2[Pb(OH)_4] \quad \text{or} \quad Pb(OH)_2 + 2OH^- \rightarrow [Pb(OH)_4]^{2-}$$

Solutions containing amphoteric metal compounds form precipitates when sodium hydroxide is added to their solutions. These precipitates are metal hydroxides. Since the hydroxides can react with more sodium hydroxide, these precipitates will then redissolve:

For aluminium:

$Al^{3+}(aq) + 3OH^-(aq) \rightarrow Al(OH)_3(s)$ then $Al(OH)_3(s) + OH^-(aq) \rightarrow [Al(OH)_4]^-(aq)$

For lead:

$Pb^{2+}(aq) + 2OH^-(aq) \rightarrow Pb(OH)_2(s)$ then $Pb(OH)_2(s) + 2OH^-(aq) \rightarrow [Pb(OH)_4]^{2-}(aq)$

Group 3 chemistry

The two most common elements in group 3 are the first two in this group: boron and aluminium. These elements have very different physical properties as one is a non-metal and the other is a metal. Although aluminium is a metal, it has a relatively high electronegativity so some of its compounds are covalent and show some similarities to analogous compounds of boron.

YOU SHOULD KNOW › › ›

››› the effects of electron deficiency on the compounds of group 3 elements

››› the bonding, structure and properties of the allotropes of boron nitride

Electron deficiency

An electron-deficient atom is one that does not have a full outer shell, i.e. has fewer than eight electrons in its outer shell. When elements in group 3 form compounds, they commonly form three covalent bonds such as in BF_3, BCl_3 and $AlCl_3$. In each of these cases the three electrons from the group 3 atom (shown as dots below) form covalent bonds with halogen atoms.

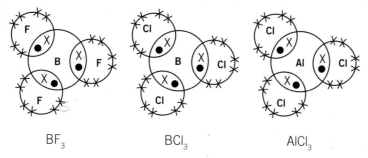

BF_3 BCl_3 $AlCl_3$

To fill their outer shell, these atoms will often form co-ordinate bonds to gain extra electron pairs (they are **electron acceptors**). This may be done by reacting with other compounds, or by forming dimers, as in the case of $AlCl_3$ in the gas phase, which forms Al_2Cl_6 dimers:

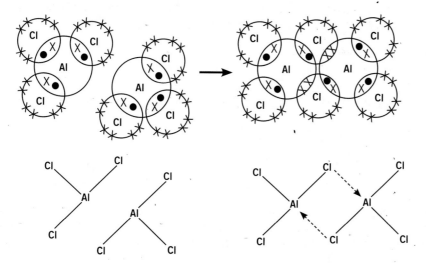

In this case, each electron deficient aluminium atom uses a lone pair on a chlorine atom to form a coordinate bond.

The aluminium chloride dimer no longer has any electron-deficient atoms as each aluminium atom has eight electrons in its outer shell. Other molecules can also form co-ordinate bonds to remove their electron deficiency. These compounds are classified as donor-acceptor compounds, where one molecule donates a lone pair and the other accepts it. A typical example is the compound formed between electron-deficient BF_3 and the lone pair on NH_3. Once again the compound formed is no longer electron deficient.

Exam tip

When discussing electron deficiency in group 3 compounds, always be specific about the atom that is electron deficient. Writing 'Aluminium chloride is electron deficient' does not identify the aluminium atom as the source of the electron deficiency.

‹Link› The formation of coordinate bonds in compounds such as these is included in AS Topic 1.4 on page 47 of the AS book.

Knowledge check ⑪

Draw a dot-and-cross diagram to show the bonding in the compound formed when boron trichloride (BCl_3) is mixed with phosphine (PH_3).

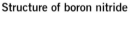

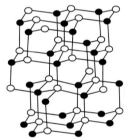

Exam tip

When discussing the structures of BN and the allotropes of carbon, focus on the requirements of the question. These may ask you to focus on similarities or differences in structures or properties, and if you try to simply repeat everything you know about these substances, you may not address the specific points required.

Link The structures of diamond and graphite are included in AS Topic 1.5 on page 54 of the AS book.

diamond

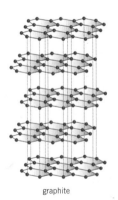

graphite

Boron nitride

Boron forms a large variety of compounds with nitrogen, and these have been of great interest due to the analogy between the B–N bond and the C–C bond. In each case there are a total of 12 electrons on the two atoms. The atomic radii of all the atoms are similar with carbon being almost exactly the average of the radii of boron and nitrogen, with a similar relationship in their electronegativities. This leads to boron nitride, BN, having several forms which are similar to the several different forms of carbon.

Structure of boron nitride

(a) Hexagonal boron nitride

Layers where nitrogen and boron atoms combined in a hexagonal network are superimposed and have a structure similar to graphite.

(b) Cubic boron nitride

Boron and nitrogen atoms combine three-dimensionally replacing carbon atoms in diamond.

Hexagonal boron nitride ('graphite structure')

Boron nitride can form hexagonal sheets similar to those found in graphite, but in this case the atoms in different layers lie directly above one another, with each boron having a nitrogen atom directly above and below it. This differs from graphite as the layers in graphite are arranged so that atoms on adjoining layers are not directly above one another. The forces between layers are weak so boron nitride shares the ability for layers to slip over one another with graphite, so it is used as a lubricant.

The electrical properties of boron nitride are very different from graphite as there are no delocalised electrons present, with electrons localised as lone pairs on nitrogen atoms. The B–N bonds are polar due to the different electronegativities of the two atoms. This makes BN an insulator and leads to its use in electronics as a substrate for semiconductors, microwave-transparent windows, and a structural material for seals, electrodes and catalyst carriers in fuel cells and batteries.

Cubic boron nitride ('diamond structure')

Like diamond, cubic boron nitride is extremely hard with a high melting point as covalent bonds must be broken to break or melt the solid. This leads to its use as a wear-resistant coating or an industrial abrasive.

Group 4 chemistry

Group 4 contains a range of metals and non-metals, with most being familiar names to chemists and non-chemists alike. Indeed most of the elements in this group have been known for a very long time with carbon, tin and lead known for thousands of years. The changes from the top to the bottom of the group are amongst the most significant of all the groups in the periodic table. The first element, carbon, is a non-metal which forms a huge range of covalent compounds with the carbon showing a +4 oxidation state, whilst the heaviest stable member of the group, lead, is a metal which generally forms ionic compounds with the +2 oxidation state being most stable.

The oxides of carbon and lead: redox properties

The oxidation states shown in group 4 are +2 and +4, with the stability of the +2 oxidation state increasing down the group as the inert pair effect becomes more significant. The most stable oxidation state for all the elements in the group is +4 apart from lead where the +2 oxidation state is most stable. The stability of these oxidation states governs the redox properties of the compounds, and the oxides of carbon and lead exemplify this.

Carbon

Carbon dioxide, CO_2, is the most stable oxide of carbon. Carbon monoxide, CO, is the only stable compound to contain carbon in the +2 oxidation state. CO will act as a reducing agent as it easily becomes oxidised from +2 to +4. Carbon monoxide is used as a reducing agent, especially for extracting metals from their oxides. For example:

Iron $\quad\quad Fe_2O_3 \text{ (s)} + 3CO \text{ (g)} \rightarrow 2Fe \text{ (s)} + 3CO_2 \text{ (g)}$

Copper $\quad\quad CuO \text{ (s)} + CO \text{ (g)} \rightarrow Cu \text{ (s)} + CO_2 \text{ (g)}$

This method can only be used for the oxides of the less reactive metals. The oxides of the more reactive metals (anything above zinc in the reactivity series) are too stable, and so will not react.

Lead

Lead (II) oxide, PbO, is the most stable oxide of lead. Lead (IV) oxide, PbO_2, will act as an oxidising agent as it easily becomes reduced from +4 to +2. All lead (IV) compounds are oxidising agents, so PbO_2 may be used for this purpose:

$$PbO_2 \text{ (s)} + 4HCl \text{ (conc)} \rightarrow PbCl_2 \text{ (s)} + Cl_2 \text{ (g)} + 2H_2O \text{ (l)}$$

The oxides of carbon and lead: acid-base properties

In general we can classify metal oxides as basic oxides and non-metal oxides as acidic oxides. Some metals form amphoteric oxides that can show both acidic and basic properties. The change from non-metal at the top of group 4 to metals at the bottom of the group is reflected in the acid-base properties of the oxides.

Exam tip

When discussing any of the oxides of carbon or lead you must make it totally clear which one you mean. Any reference to lead oxide is unlikely to be specific enough.

[handwritten notes:]
$Fe_2O_3 + 3CO \rightarrow 2Fe_{(s)} + 3CO_2$
$CuO + CO \rightarrow Cu + CO_2$

▼ **Study point**

Make sure you are able to write equations to show the redox behaviour of any oxide.

[handwritten note:]
$Fe_2O_3 + CO \rightarrow 2Al_{(s)} + CO_2 + O_2$

Exam tip

It is not enough to say that an oxide is acidic as it forms acidic solutions, you need to show it reacts with bases. Similarly basic oxides react with acids. You will need to be able to write equations for these reactions.

Stretch & Challenge

Although we focus on carbon and lead here, the patterns are still relevant for the elements in between. The stability of the +2 oxidation state increases down the group; however, it is only lead that has +2 as the most stable oxidation state. In terms of the acid-base properties, both carbon dioxide and silicon dioxide are acidic; however, oxides of germanium, tin and lead are amphoteric.

Carbon

Carbon dioxide is a colourless gas made up of small covalent molecules. This is an acidic oxide as the oxide is soluble in water to give the very weak acid, carbonic acid:

$$CO_2 \text{ (g)} + H_2O \text{ (l)} \rightleftharpoons H^+ \text{ (aq)} + HCO_3^- \text{ (aq)}$$

Like all acidic oxides, carbon dioxide will react with alkalis to form a salt. All salts produced in this way are carbonates or hydrogencarbonates:

$$CO_2 \text{ (g)} + 2NaOH \text{ (aq)} \rightarrow Na_2CO_3 \text{ (aq)} + H_2O \text{ (l)}$$

$$CO_2 \text{ (g)} + NaOH \text{ (aq)} \rightarrow NaHCO_3 \text{ (aq)}$$

Lead

Lead (II) oxide, PbO, is an orange solid which contains bonding which is mainly ionic. Lead (II) oxide is an amphoteric oxide, so it reacts with acids and bases:

$$PbO \text{ (s)} + 2HNO_3 \text{ (aq)} \rightarrow Pb(NO_3)_2 \text{ (aq)} + H_2O \text{ (l)} \qquad \text{Acting as base}$$

$$PbO \text{ (s)} + 2NaOH \text{ (aq)} + 2H_2O \text{ (l)} \rightarrow Na_2[Pb(OH)_4] \text{ (aq)} \qquad \text{Acting as an acid}$$

The chlorides of carbon, silicon and lead

Carbon and silicon

The stable chlorides of carbon and silicon are the tetrachlorides, CCl_4 and $SiCl_4$. These are both colourless liquids containing individual covalent molecules. The molecules found in both are tetrahedral, due to the 8 electrons in the valence shell. For CCl_4, the electronic configuration is as shown:

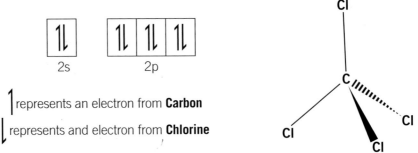

↑ represents an electron from **Carbon**

↓ represents and electron from **Chlorine**

Reactions with water

CCl_4 does not react with water as it merely forms a separate layer under the water. The carbon atom cannot combine easily with water molecules. This lack of reactivity is due to the absence of available d-orbitals in the valence shell meaning that the octet cannot be expanded to allow the water molecules to combine with the carbon atom.

Silicon tetrachloride, $SiCl_4$, reacts very quickly with water in a hydrolysis reaction. This reaction produces fumes of hydrogen chloride gas, and silicon dioxide, SiO_2, as a solid precipitate. The reaction becomes more vigorous down the group as the bonds in the compound become weaker.

$$SiCl_4 \text{ (l)} + 2H_2O \text{ (l)} \rightarrow SiO_2 \text{ (s)} + 4HCl \text{ (g)}$$

The reason for the increased reactivity is that silicon possesses available 3d-orbitals in addition to the 3s and 3p orbitals involved in bonding to the chlorine atoms. The lone pairs of the water can form co-ordinate bonds with these empty d-orbitals, giving a complex molecule that can then eliminate two HCl molecules.

▲ Silicon chloride fumes in moist air as water reacts with it to release acidic HCl fumes.

Key Term

Octet expansion is the ability of an atom to form species with more than eight electrons in the valence shell. These may be stable compounds, such as SF_6, or intermediate stages in a reaction mechanism such as the coordinate bonding of water to $SiCl_4$.

Stretch & Challenge

Energy calculations suggest that carbon tetrachloride should react easily with water to form carbon dioxide; however, the reaction does not occur as it would be too slow – we say that the carbon tetrachloride shows **kinetic stability**.

This molecule can then eliminate two more molecules of HCl to leave SiO_2.

You may also see the product of the reaction written as $Si(OH)_4$, with the overall reaction written as:

$$SiCl_4 \text{ (l)} + 4H_2O \text{ (l)} \rightarrow Si(OH)_4 \text{ (s)} + 4HCl \text{ (g)}$$

Both of these alternatives are acceptable, as the nature of the product formed is not well defined. Hydrated silicon dioxide ($SiO_2.2H_2O$) has the same overall composition as silicon hydroxide ($Si(OH)_4$) and spectroscopic analysis does not distinguish between these.

Lead

Lead (II) chloride is the most stable chloride of lead. It is a white ionic solid made up of Pb^{2+} and Cl^- ions. As it is an ionic compound, it does not react with water, but neither does it dissolve in cold water, although it can be dissolved in hot water. This is in common with most lead (II) compounds, which are insoluble in cold water.

Reactions of solutions of lead (II) compounds, Pb^{2+} (aq)

Lead (II) compounds are ionic compounds and practically all of them are insoluble in water. The only two common compounds which dissolve readily in cold water are lead nitrate, $Pb(NO_3)_2$, and lead ethanoate, $Pb(CH_3COO)_2$. The reactions of solutions of these salts with various anions produces a range of precipitates:

Solution added	Anions present	Observation/explanation
NaOH (aq)	OH⁻ (aq)	An initial white precipitate of $Pb(OH)_2$ is formed: $$Pb^{2+} \text{ (aq)} + 2OH^- \text{ (aq)} \rightarrow Pb(OH)_2 \text{ (s)}$$
excess NaOH (aq)	OH⁻ (aq)	The white precipitate redissolves in excess OH^- (aq) to form the tetrahydroxoplumbate (II) ion: $$Pb(OH)_2 \text{ (s)} + 2OH^- \text{ (aq)} \rightarrow [Pb(OH)_4]^{2-} \text{ (aq)}$$
HCl (aq)	Cl⁻ (aq)	A dense white precipitate of lead chloride, $PbCl_2$ is formed: $$Pb^{2+} \text{ (aq)} + 2Cl^- \text{ (aq)} \rightarrow PbCl_2 \text{ (s)}$$
KI (aq)	I⁻ (aq)	A dense bright yellow precipitate of lead iodide, PbI_2 is formed: $$Pb^{2+} \text{ (aq)} + 2I^- \text{ (aq)} \rightarrow PbI_2 \text{ (s)}$$ **THIS IS A KEY OBSERVATION TO IDENTIFY Pb^{2+} IONS**

<Link> The reasons for the solubility, or lack of solubility, of ionic compounds are covered in Topic 3.6 on page 62

Exam tip

There are two yellow precipitates that are commonly seen in qualitative analysis. These are silver iodide and lead iodide; however, they are very different colours. The precipitate of lead iodide is often described as bright yellow or canary yellow whilst the precipitate for silver iodide is pale yellow. Whenever a bright yellow precipitate is mentioned in qualitative analysis, this is a good starting point for identifying all solutions present.

▲ Lead iodide precipitate is bright yellow.

YOU SHOULD KNOW ›››

››› how the oxidising power of the halogens governs their reactions

››› the reactions of sodium halides with concentrated sulfuric acid

››› the reactions of chlorine with sodium hydroxide

Group 7

The group 7 elements are familiar to chemists as a set of diatomic molecules, containing elements in all three physical states. The chemical properties of the elements are very similar, with all the elements being non-metals although the range and stability of oxidation states shows clear patterns on descending the group.

The oxidising power of halogens

The halogens have different strengths as oxidising agents, with their oxidising power decreasing down the group. This ability to remove electrons from other species can be measured using the standard electrode potentials for the halogens. The values for chlorine, bromine and iodine are given below.

Reaction			$E^\ominus$ / Volts
$Cl_2\ (g) + 2e^-$	$\rightleftharpoons$	$2Cl^-\ (aq)$	+1.36
$Br_2\ (l) + 2e^-$	$\rightleftharpoons$	$2Br^-\ (aq)$	+1.09
$I_2\ (s) + 2e^-$	$\rightleftharpoons$	$2I^-\ (aq)$	+0.54

- As the value for chlorine is the most positive, it readily gains electrons to form chloride ions, Cl^-. This also shows that it is difficult to oxidise chloride ions to chlorine molecules.

- As the value for iodine is the least positive, it gains electrons less readily than bromine and chlorine. This also shows that it is easier to oxidise iodide ions than it is to oxidise bromide or chloride ions.

Example

If we bubble chlorine gas into a solution containing bromide ions, the solution goes orange, showing bromine is being formed.

$$Cl_2\ (g) + 2Br^-\ (aq) \rightarrow Br_2\ (aq) + 2Cl^-\ (aq)$$

This occurs because chlorine is a stronger oxidising agent than bromine (it has a more positive standard electrode potential). This means that chlorine is able to oxidise bromide to form bromine molecules.

Reactions of concentrated sulfuric acid with sodium halides

Concentrated sulfuric acid is a strong acid and an oxidising agent. The different ease of oxidising the halide ions means that the reactions undertaken by the different sodium halides are very different. When any sodium halide is added to concentrated sulfuric acid, the hydrogen halide is formed as a steamy gas.

The sulfuric acid or products formed from it may oxidise the halide in the hydrogen halide to form the halogen if the halide is relatively easy to oxidise. This process becomes easier lower down the group.

Exam tip

When discussing the chemistry of the halogens, it is essential to distinguish between a halogen and a halide. Students frequently use these terms interchangeably and they mean different things – a halide is always a negative ion whilst a halogen ion is a positive ion such as I^+. If in doubt use the formula each time to make your answer clear.

Link Standard electrode potentials are covered in Topic 3.1 on page 14.

Exam tip

Whenever you are comparing standard electrode potentials use the terms more positive or less negative rather than larger or higher as many standard electrode potentials are negative. It is possible to write that −1.27 V is larger than −0.54 V; however, stating that −1.27 V is more negative than −0.54 V avoids ambiguity.

Sodium chloride, NaCl

Addition of sulfuric acid to sodium chloride produces HCl gas. The hydrochloric acid is difficult to oxidise ($E^\theta = + 1.36$ V), and so the sulfuric acid doesn't cause any redox reaction.

$$NaCl \text{ (s)} + H_2SO_4 \text{ (conc.)} \rightarrow NaHSO_4 \text{ (s)} + HCl \text{ (g)}$$

Observations: Steamy fumes of HCl

Sodium bromide, NaBr

Addition of sulfuric acid to sodium bromide produces HBr gas.

$$NaBr \text{ (s)} + H_2SO_4 \text{ (conc.)} \rightarrow NaHSO_4 \text{ (s)} + HBr \text{ (g)}$$

The sulfuric acid oxidises some of the HBr to form brown fumes of Br_2, and SO_2 gas. The hydrobromic acid is slightly easier to oxidise ($E^\theta = + 1.09$ V), and so the sulfuric acid causes the redox reaction below:

$$2HBr \text{ (s)} + H_2SO_4 \text{ (conc.)} \rightarrow SO_2 \text{ (g)} + Br_2 \text{ (g)} + 2H_2O \text{ (l)}$$

Sulfur is reduced from $+ 6$ in H_2SO_4 to $+4$ in SO_2.

Bromine is oxidised from -1 in Br^- to 0 in Br_2. conc e⁻ BIG OIL

Observations: Steamy fumes of HBr; Orange fumes of Br_2.

$$2H\overset{+1}{\underset{4}{B}}\overset{-1}{r} + H_2\overset{+6}{S}\overset{-8}{O_4} \rightarrow \overset{0}{Br_2}{}_{(g)} + \overset{+8-4}{SO_2} + 2H_2O$$

Sodium iodide, NaI

Addition of sulfuric acid to sodium iodide initially produces HI gas.

$$NaI \text{ (s)} + H_2SO_4 \text{ (conc.)} \rightarrow NaHSO_4 \text{ (s)} + HI \text{ (g)}$$

The sulfuric acid easily oxidises the HI ($E^\theta = + 0.54$ V) to form a complex mixture of products including I_2 (s), SO_2 (g) and H_2S (g). The reaction below occurs:

$$2HI \text{ (s)} + H_2SO_4 \text{ (conc.)} \rightarrow SO_2 \text{ (g)} + I_2 \text{ (s)} + 2H_2O \text{ (l)} + H_2S$$

S is reduced from $+ 6$ in H_2SO_4 to $+4$ in SO_2.

I is oxidised from -1 in I^- to 0 in I_2.

Further reduction of the sulfuric acid to S (O.S. = 0) and H_2S (O.S. = −2) can occur as the HI is a better reducing agent than HBr or HCl.

Observations: Steamy fumes of HI, Purple fumes of I_2 or black solid/brown solution; Smell of rotten eggs (H_2S), yellow solid (S).

Reactions of chlorine with sodium hydroxide

We have already seen the most common oxidation states of the halogens, which are 0 in the element and −1 in the halide ions, but there are many other oxidation states possible including +1 and +5. The higher oxidation states become more stable as you go down the group. Fluorine cannot achieve any of the high oxidation states, but all the other members of the group can form compounds with oxidation states up to +5 with very electronegative elements like oxygen or fluorine. We will examine the chemistry of the ions ClO^- (chlorate (I), + 1 oxidation state) and ClO_3^- (chlorate (V), + 5 oxidation state). These ions are formed by reaction of the elements with an alkali.

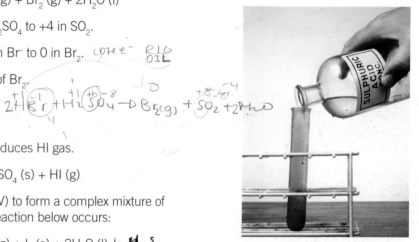
▲ The addition of concentrated sulfuric acid to sodium bromide.

Key Term

A **disproportionation reaction** is one in which the same element is both oxidised and reduced, forming products containing the element in two different oxidation states.

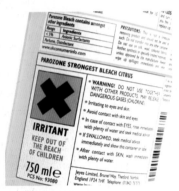

▲ Bleach is usually a solution of sodium chlorate (I) in water.

Link The use of chlorine in the sterilisation of water on page 60 of the AS book.

When chlorine is bubbled through water, a reversible reaction occurs:

$$Cl_2 (g) + H_2O (l) \rightleftharpoons HCl (aq) + HOCl (aq)$$

In this reaction, the chlorine is being both oxidised and reduced: the element at the start has an oxidation state of 0. The chlorine in the end has an oxidation state of –1 in HCl, and +1 in HOCl. A process where an element ends up in two different compounds, one with a higher oxidation state and one with a lower is called a **disproportionation reaction**.

This is an equilibrium reaction, and the products are both acids. If we use the alkali sodium hydroxide instead of water, this will force the equilibrium over to the right-hand side:

$$Cl_2 (g) + 2OH^- (aq) \rightarrow Cl^- (aq) + OCl^- (aq) + H_2O (l)$$

The ClO^- ion is stable in the solution at room temperature, but on heating with concentrated sodium hydroxide a further disproportionation reaction occurs:

$$3Cl_2 (g) + 6OH^- (aq) \rightarrow 5Cl^- (aq) + ClO_3^- (aq) + 3H_2O (l)$$

This gives the chlorate (V) ion, where chlorine is in the +5 oxidation state, and to balance this change from 0 → +5 there must be five chlorine atoms undergoing the 0 → –1 change in oxidation state.

Uses of chlorine and chlorate ions

The ions formed above are oxidising agents, being reduced in the process:

$$ClO^- (aq) + 2H^+ (aq) + 2e^- \rightarrow Cl^- (aq) + H_2O (l)$$

Similarly, elemental chlorine is an oxidising agent:

$$Cl_2 + 2e^- \rightarrow 2Cl^-$$

The oxidising power of chlorine and of chlorate ions is the basis of their use in bleaches, which are often labelled with the old name of this chemical, sodium hypochlorite. Bleaching is an oxidation reaction, with the oxidised form of the coloured material or dye being colourless. Similarly the oxidising ability of ClO^- leads to its ability to kill bacteria, as the microbe cells are oxidised. This is the basis of chlorination of water supplies to disinfect them.

Chemistry of the d-block transition metals

The periodic table can be divided into the main group elements (s-block and p-block) and the transition elements found in the d-block and f-block. The transition elements show key similarities with other elements in the same block, as well as the expected similarities with those in the same group. The similarity is greatest in the lanthanides, a set of f-block transition elements, but this chapter focuses on the first period of the d-block. These exemplify some key ideas such as variable oxidation states, coloured compounds and the formation of complexes which help us understand the chemistry of the entire d-block.

You should be able to demonstrate and apply your knowledge and understanding of:

- Variable oxidation states in the d-block elements, including the important oxidation states of Cr, Mn, Fe, Co and Cu and the colours of key species containing these ions.

- The bonding in tetrahedral and octahedral complexes.

- The origin of colour in octahedral complexes such as $[Cu(H_2O)_6]^{2+}$ and $[Fe(H_2O)_6]^{3+}$

- Examples of tetrahedral and octahedral complexes containing copper (II) and cobalt (II) and how ligand exchange can interconvert these.

- The origin of the catalytic properties of transition metals and their compounds, including both homogeneous and heterogeneous examples.

- The aqueous reactions of sodium hydroxide with Cr^{3+}, Fe^{2+}, Fe^{3+} and Cu^{2+}.

Content

d-block transition elements

The **d-block** consists of the elements scandium to zinc, along with similar elements in the next two periods; however, this topic focuses on the first row of the d-block alone, showing how the chemistry of these elements is very different from the metals of the s-block. The elements contain some of the most familiar metals, such as iron, copper and zinc. These elements are hard, dense metals with some of the highest melting and boiling points out of all the elements.

YOU SHOULD KNOW › › ›

››› how electrons are arranged in transition metal atoms and ions

Atomic No.	21	22	23	24	25	26	27	28	29	30
Symbol	Sc	Ti	V	Cr	Mn	Fe	Co	Ni	Cu	Zn
Name	Scandium	Titanium	Vanadium	Chromium	Manganese	Iron	Cobalt	Nickel	Copper	Zinc

Key Terms

The **d-block** is the groups of elements whose outer electrons are found in d-orbitals.

A transition element is a metal that possesses a partially filled d sub-shell in its atom or stable ions.

Transition elements are considered to be the metals with partially filled d-orbitals. These include all the elements from scandium to nickel as they have partially filled d-orbitals in the unreacted metals. Copper has a full set of d-orbitals as a metal but is considered to be a transition metal as it has partially filled d-orbitals in most of its compounds. Zinc has a filled d sub-shell in a zinc atom, and maintains this in its compounds. As its d sub-shell is never partially filled, it is not a transition element; however, all the other elements in the d-block can all be classified as transition elements.

Electronic configurations for the elements

When working out the electronic configurations of elements beyond argon, we need to fill 3*d* and 4*s* orbitals. As studied in the AS units, the 3d-orbitals are filled before the 4s orbitals. Despite this, the 'arrows in boxes' are usually written with the 3d-orbitals first. The order of filling orbitals for these elements is: 4*s* then 3*d* then 4*p*. So we have the following electronic configurations, with 4*s* filled first:

Stretch & Challenge

The definitions of transition elements have varied over the years; however, all focus on the need for partially filled d-orbitals. The traditional definition is that transition metals have partially filled d-orbitals in their stable compounds. Under this definition neither scandium nor zinc would be transition elements. A more recent adjustment by IUPAC, the governing body of chemistry, includes atoms with partially filled d-orbitals into the group of transition elements as well. This would include scandium as a transition element but zinc would still not be in this category. This is the definition used here.

Potassium (Atomic Number 19)

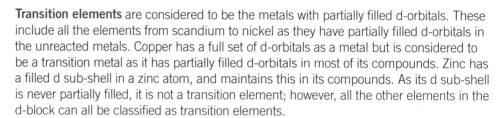

Calcium (Atomic Number 20)

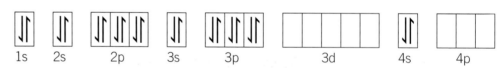

Then the d-orbitals are filled, with one electron going into each:

Link Electronic structures in AS Topic 1.2 on pages 23 and 24 of the AS book.

Scandium (Atomic Number 21)

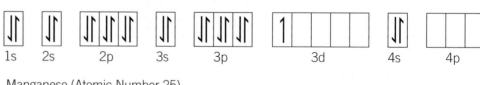

Manganese (Atomic Number 25)

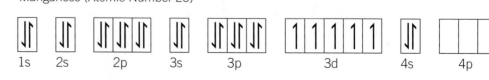

Then the electrons pair up in the d-orbitals:

Zinc (Atomic Number 30)

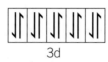

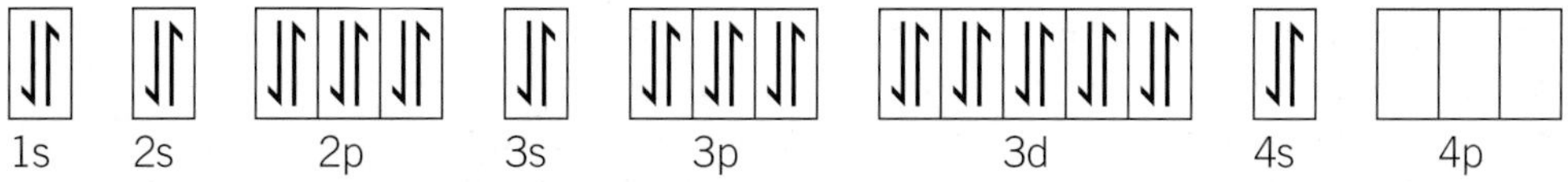

1s 2s 2p 3s 3p 3d 4s 4p

And finally, we fill the 4p orbitals:

Gallium (Atomic Number 31)

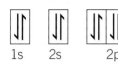

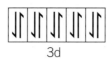

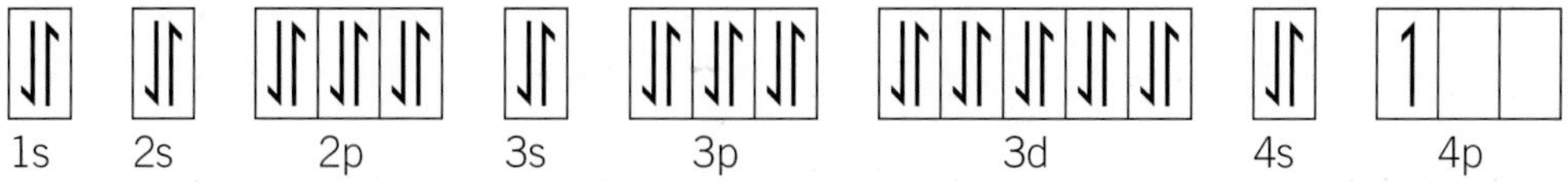

1s 2s 2p 3s 3p 3d 4s 4p

Exceptions to the rules

Two transition elements do not obey the rules given above. *You must know these exceptions.* These elements are Chromium (Cr) and Copper (Cu), whose electronic configurations are given below:

Chromium, Atomic Number 24, $1s^2\ 2s^2\ 2p^6\ 3s^2\ 3p^6\ 3d^5\ 4s^1$.

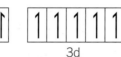

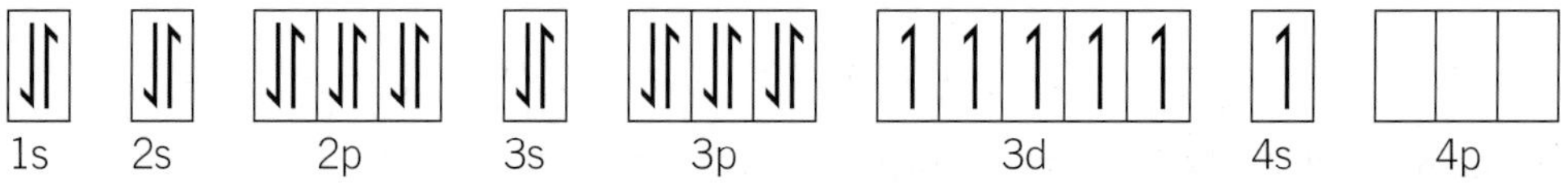

1s 2s 2p 3s 3p 3d 4s 4p

Copper, Atomic Number 29, $1s^2\ 2s^2\ 2p^6\ 3s^2\ 3p^6\ 3d^{10}\ 4s^1$.

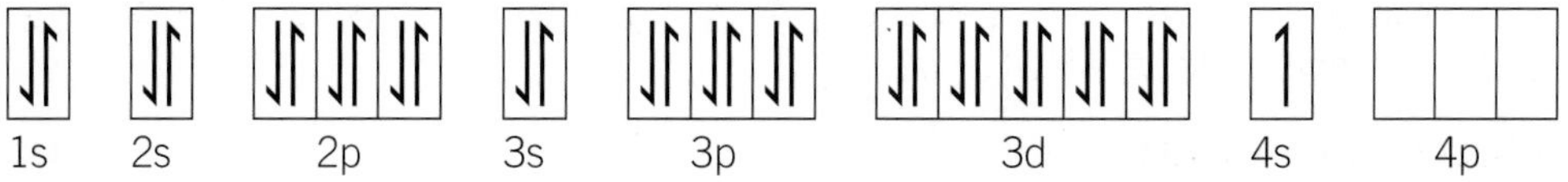

1s 2s 2p 3s 3p 3d 4s 4p

In these cases, we see that we have one electron in the 4s orbital, even though it is slightly lower in energy than the 3d orbitals. The small difference between the energy of the 3d and 4s orbitals, and the extra energy required to pair up electrons, leads to these configurations being more stable than the alternative $3d^4\ 4s^2$ and $3d^9\ 4s^2$ configurations. **You can remember these exceptions by thinking that shells are more stable if they are filled or half-filled.**

Stretch & Challenge

The idea that chromium and copper adopt unexpected electronic configurations due to the stability of filled or half-filled d sub-shells is a simplification that reminds us of the pattern, but does not truly explain it. Due to the similar energy of the 3d and 4s sub-shells, it does not take much to move electrons between them and so factors such as repulsion between electrons in the same sub-shell and pairing energy for electrons in the same orbital are enough to change the stable electronic configuration.

Electronic configurations for the ions

When the electronic configurations of the transition metal atoms are filled, the electronic configurations suggest that the 4*s* orbital is filled before the 3d-orbitals. When electrons are removed to form positive ions, the **4s electrons are lost first**. This is because the 4s and 3d-orbitals are very close together in energy, so on balance it is more energetically favourable to lose these 4s electrons before the 3d electrons. If we examine an atom of iron, the electronic structure is:

[Ar]
3d 4s 4p

Knowledge check 14

Write the electronic configurations of the transition elements Ti, V, Fe.

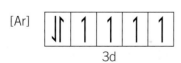

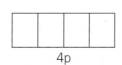

Common iron ions are therefore Fe^{2+} and Fe^{3+}. To work out the electronic configurations of these ions, we need to remember to remove the 4s electrons first:

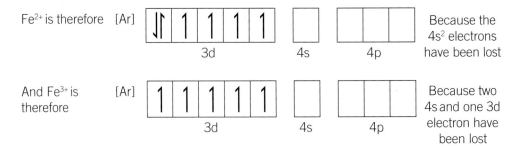

Fe^{2+} is therefore   [Ar]   3d   4s   4p   Because the $4s^2$ electrons have been lost

And Fe^{3+} is therefore   [Ar]   3d   4s   4p   Because two 4s and one 3d electron have been lost

Oxidation states for the transition elements

Although we have already observed metals showing more than one oxidation state when we studied the p-block, the range of oxidation states seen in the transition metals is much greater. Manganese shows the most, with 7 different positive oxidation states, ranging from +1 to +7. The table below lists all the possible oxidation states of the first row of transition metals, with the most common stable oxidation states shown in **bold**.

Sc	Ti	V	Cr	Mn	Fe	Co	Ni	Cu	Zn
	+1	+1	+1	+1	+1	+1	+1	**+1**	
	+2	**+2**	+2	**+2**	**+2**	**+2**	**+2**	**+2**	**+2**
+3	**+3**	+3	**+3**	**+3**	**+3**	**+3**	+3	+3	
	+4	**+4**	+4	**+4**	+4	+4	+4		
		+5	+5	+5	+5	+5			
			+6	**+6**	+6				
				+7					

[You do not need to remember all these oxidation states, but should be familiar with the common oxidation states for the elements highlighted in yellow.]

These elements can form these different oxidation states because the energies of the 4s and 3d-orbitals are very similar so the energy required to remove any of these electrons is similar. As the elements form compounds energy is released, either through the formation of covalent bonds or when the ionic lattice forms. The energy needed to reach higher oxidation states and the energy released in compound formation is finely balanced allowing a range of oxidation states to form.

The oxidation state favoured by each metal depends on many factors. The oxidising power of the other atoms in the compound is one factor, so when iron metal reacts with chlorine gas the product is iron (III) chloride but when it reacts with iodine vapour the product is iron (II) iodide. The iodine is a much weaker oxidising agent than chlorine and so it cannot oxidise the iron to the +3 oxidation state.

Transition metal complexes

Transition metal ions are small and can have large positive charges. They have many orbitals available for bonding, many of which are empty. Electron-rich molecules have lone pairs, so these can form coordinate bonds with the empty orbitals on the transition metal ions:

 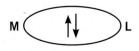

The Metal (M) has an empty orbital, and the ligand has a lone pair of electrons.

The two atomic orbitals overlap to form a molecular orbital

A co-ordinate bond is formed.

A *ligand* is a small molecule with a lone pair that can form a bond to a transition metal, e.g. H_2O, NH_3, Cl^-, CN^-.

A combination of the transition metal ion and the ligands is called a *complex*.

Most of the ions we have written as simple ions are actually complexes with water molecules as ligands around the transition metal atom or ion.

Typically the transition metal complexes have either:

6 ligands arranged octahedrally around the metal atom. [MOST COMMON]

OR

4 ligands arranged tetrahedrally around the metal atom [LESS COMMON]

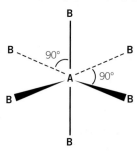 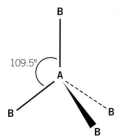

Examples in solution:

$[Fe(H_2O)_6]^{2+}$, a pale green complex

$[Fe(H_2O)_6]^{3+}$, a yellow complex

$[Cu(H_2O)_6]^{2+}$, a blue complex

$[Cr(H_2O)_6]^{3+}$, a dark green complex

$[Co(H_2O)_6]^{2+}$, a pink complex

Examples:

$[CuCl_4]^{2-}$, a yellow or green complex.

$[CoCl_4]^{2-}$, a blue complex.

Both shapes can be seen for the same transition metal ion with different ligands. The shape found is dependent on the metal, the oxidation state of the metal and the ligands, and these factors often favour the octahedral complex with six ligands around the metal atom.

Exam tip

You need to know the colours of the complexes formed by the following ions in aqueous solution: Fe^{2+}, Fe^{3+}, Co^{2+}, Cu^{2+} or Cr^{3+}. These may be written as the ions themselves or as their complexes containing six water molecules as ligands. If the question specifies there are no ligands then the compounds are often colourless, although Co^{2+} in the absence of water is blue.

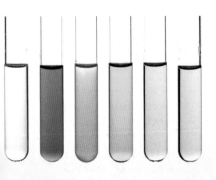

Solutions of zinc sulfate ($ZnSO_4$), cobalt(II) chloride ($CoCl_2$), iron(II) sulfate ($FeSO_4$), iron(III) chloride ($FeCl_3$), copper(II) sulfate ($CuSO_4$), copper(II) chloride ($CuCl_2$).

 Link In Topic 3.1 on pages 20–21 the colours of the oxoanions MnO_4^- (dark purple), $Cr_2O_7^{2-}$ (orange) and CrO_4^{2-} (yellow) were discussed. You should be able to recall these colours as well as the colours discussed in this topic.

Typical transition metal complexes

The complexes of copper can be used to demonstrate the variation in transition metal complexes. The three complexes $[Cu(H_2O)_6]^{2+}$, $[Cu(NH_3)_4(H_2O)_2]^{2+}$ and $[CuCl_4]^{2-}$ all contain Cu^{2+} ions, but their different structures and properties are due to their different ligands. Similarly cobalt can form $[Co(H_2O)_6]^{2+}$ and $[CoCl_4]^{2-}$ both containing Co^{2+} ions.

$[Cu(H_2O)_6]^{2+}$ and $[Co(H_2O)_6]^{2+}$

These are the complexes present in most aqueous solutions of Cu^{2+} and Co^{2+} giving the familiar colours of these solutions and many copper (II) and cobalt (II) compounds. The complexes are octahedral, with one lone pair of each oxygen atom of the water molecules used for bonding to the metal ion.

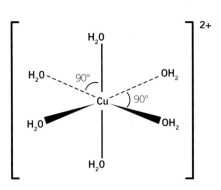

$[Cu(NH_3)_4(H_2O)_2]^{2+}$

Addition of ammonia to a solution containing $[Cu(H_2O)_6]^{2+}$ causes four ammonia molecules to replace water molecules, forming a royal blue solution containing $[Cu(NH_3)_4(H_2O)_2]^{2+}$ ions. This complex is octahedral, but because it contains two different ligands, there could be two different arrangements of ligands:

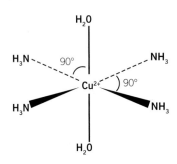

Trans *isomer*	Cis *isomer*
Two water molecules opposite each other.	*Two water molecules next to each other.*
THIS IS THE COMMON ISOMER	

$[CuCl_4]^{2-}$ and $[CoCl_4]^{2-}$

These are tetrahedral complexes, with all four chlorides at 109.5° to each other. The complexes are formed when copper (II) or cobalt (II) ions react with concentrated hydrochloric acid, which displaces the water molecules. There are distinct colour changes as the change in ligands and coordination geometry both contribute to changes in the light absorbed. The colour changes are:

- Copper (II) goes from pale blue to yellow/green.
- Cobalt (II) goes from pink to blue.

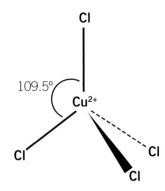

Ligand exchange

When a transition metal ion is exposed to a mixture of ligands, such as an aqueous solution containing chloride ions, ligands can be exchanged to form a new complex. This is an equilibrium process, so the concentrations of the metal ions and any possible ligands are key to identifying the species that will be present in solution.

$$[Cu(H_2O)_6]^{2+} + 4NH_3 \rightleftharpoons [Cu(H_2O)_2(NH_3)_4]^{2+} + 4H_2O$$

According to Le Chatelier's principle, addition of extra ammonia forces the equilibrium to the left, producing more of the $[Cu(H_2O)_2(NH_3)_4]^{2+}$ Addition of extra water forces the equilibrium to the right, producing more of the $[Cu(H_2O)_6]^{2+}$ complex. This is associated with a colour change, with the ammonia-containing complex being royal blue compared to the pale blue of the original complex.

The equilibrium between complexes can lead to a change in geometry depending on the ligands used. The equilibrium below shows the interconversion between two complexes of cobalt. If a large amount of chloride is used, such as by adding concentrated hydrochloric acid, then the equilibrium shifts from the octahedral complex to the tetrahedral chloro-complex.

$$[Co(H_2O)_6]^{2+} + 4Cl^- \rightleftharpoons [CoCl_4]^{2-} + 6H_2O$$

Colour in transition metal ions and complexes

Transition metal complexes are almost always coloured, with almost every colour being seen in the wide range of transition metal complexes. Although we are familiar with these colours, it is important to remember that *transition metal atoms are only coloured in* **complexes**. In the absence of any ligands around the metal ion, the compound would be colourless.

When ligands are introduced around a transition metal ion, they have a dramatic effect on the orbitals in the atom. Without the ligands, the transition metal atom has 5 degenerate d-orbitals, that is 5 d-orbitals with the same energy. The shapes of these are shown below.

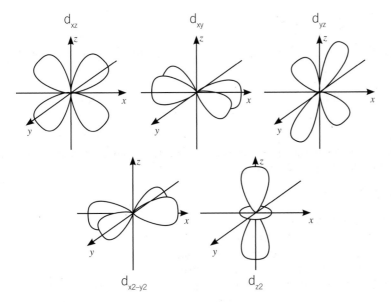

The first three orbitals d_{xz}, d_{xy} and d_{yz}, point between a pair of axes: the first orbital points between the x and z axes.

The last two orbitals d_{x2-y2} and d_{z2} point along the axes: the first along the x and y axes, the last along the z axis.

In an octahedral complex, six negatively charged ligands approach the transition metal ion along the directions of the three axes. These negative charges repel the electrons in the orbitals that point along these axes, which makes these orbitals less stable. The orbitals that do not point along the axes are not made less stable. This means that the energies of the orbitals are no longer the same, i.e. they are no longer degenerate.

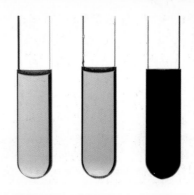

▲ Copper (II) ions (tube 1) change colour when concentrated hydrochloric acid (tube 2) or ammonia (tube 3) are added.

Stretch & Challenge

The equilibrium constant, K_c, for any ligand exchange equilibrium gives a guide to the relative stability of the complex and the free ligands and metal ions. If the value of K_c is large then the complex is more stable than the free ion and ligands.

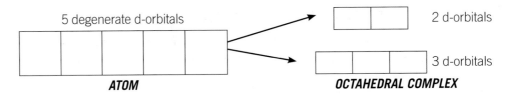

5 degenerate d-orbitals

2 d-orbitals

3 d-orbitals

ATOM

OCTAHEDRAL COMPLEX

16 Knowledge check

Explain why the complex $[Cr(H_2O)_6]^{3+}$ is dark green.

H₂O ligand approaches
the Cr ion and
the electrons in the
d orbital repel
it causing the
d orbital to
split into 2
one of higher e⁻ 3 one
lower. The electron
moving absorbs all
light e⁻ bar darkgreen
to move to higher
e⁻ level thus
showing darkgreen

This splitting of the d-orbitals gives two sets of orbitals close together in energy. An electron in one of the d-orbitals can move from the lower to the upper of these sets of orbitals, but to do this it needs to gain energy which is absorbed in the form of light. It is only one frequency (colour) of light that is absorbed, which corresponds to the energy gap between the orbitals. The relationship between the energy and the frequency absorbed is given by the equation $E = hf$. The light that remains gives the complex its characteristic colour.

Light absorbed of energy hf

OCTAHEDRAL COMPLEX

OCTAHEDRAL COMPLEX

These d–d transitions depend on the amount of splitting between the d-orbitals, and this varies between ions of different transition metal complexes. As the splitting varies, so does the frequency (colour) of the light absorbed and this leads to different colours for different complexes. Compounds containing the complex $[Cu(H_2O)_6]^{2+}$ are typically blue as they absorb all colours apart from blue, whilst those containing $[Fe(H_2O)_6]^{3+}$ are yellow as they absorb other colours.

Different ligands give different splitting of orbitals, and so give different colours.

What is the effect of splitting on electronic structure?

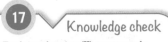

17 Knowledge check

Explain why zinc (II) compounds form colourless solutions.

To work out how the electrons are arranged in these orbitals, we must follow the same rules as for all other electronic structures. In the split orbitals, the lower three orbitals are filled first with one electron each, before the electrons pair up. Once these three orbitals are filled with six electrons, the higher two orbitals are filled.

Why are some complexes colourless?

Copper (I) complexes have an electronic configuration with a full d sub-shell (d^{10}), which means that there are no empty orbitals to allow electrons to move between energy levels. As a consequence, Cu(I) complexes do not absorb light in the visible range, and appear colourless. Similarly Sc^{3+} ions have an empty d sub-shell so there are no electrons to move between d-orbitals.

Transition metals as catalysts

Transition metals and their compounds are used in industry as catalysts for a large range of chemical processes. Examples of where the metals themselves are used include:

Iron	The Haber process, to produce ammonia from nitrogen and hydrogen.
Nickel	The hydrogenation of vegetable oils to form margarine.
Platinum	The oxidation of ammonia to form nitric acid.

Transition metal compounds are used in the following processes:

| Vanadium oxide, V_2O_5 | The Contact process for the production of sulfuric acid. |
| Manganese dioxide, MnO_2 | The catalytic decomposition of hydrogen peroxide. |

Transition metal **catalysts** are used in many industrial processes that would be uneconomical without them, and these catalysts are therefore essential to our current economy: they are needed to make almost all plastics, artificial fibres, fertilisers, explosives, ethanoic acid and most other acids and solvents, including ethanal.

The ability of transition metals to acts as catalysts depends on their unique properties. Catalysts act as intermediaries in chemical reactions, and provide an alternative, lower energy route for the reaction. They can do this due to their:

Partially filled d-orbitals, which have enough empty orbitals to combine with other molecules. Molecules with lone pairs can form co-ordinate bonds to the metal atom to form complexes, and this can increase the reactivity of the species bonded to the metal, or bring two reacting molecules closer together. This makes a reaction more likely, especially when a solid surface can provide an area where molecules are adsorbed and brought close together for reaction

Variable oxidation states of the transition metal ions allow the metal ion to act as a catalyst in redox reactions. It can act as an oxidising or reducing agent, by oxidising or reducing one of the reactants. The transition metal can then be returned to its original oxidation state by reaction with another molecule. It therefore appears unchanged at the end of the reaction.

The key factors depend on whether the catalyst is homogeneous or heterogeneous. **Heterogeneous catalysts** are typically solids that provide a surface for molecules to be adsorbed and come together in an advantageous arrangement. **Homogeneous catalysts** typically use their variable oxidation states to oxidise/reduce a reactant which makes it much more reactive.

Link Catalysts and their functions are discussed in AS Topic 2.2 on pages 112–113 of the AS book.

Key Terms

Catalysts are substances which increase the rate of a chemical reaction by providing an alternative pathway with a lower activation energy.

Homogeneous catalysts are catalysts that are in the same physical state as the reactions that they catalyse.

Heterogeneous catalysts are catalysts that are in a different physical state from the reactions that they catalyse.

▼ **Study point**

You will need to recall the examples of catalysts listed on this page. These are all heterogeneous so adsorption is a key stage in the alternative reaction route they provide.

◄ Manganese dioxide catalyses the decomposition of hydrogen peroxide.

18 Knowledge check

Write an equation for the formation of a precipitate on addition of sodium hydroxide solution to $[Cu(H_2O)_6]^{2+}$ (aq).

▲ Addition of sodium hydroxide solution to Cr^{3+} (aq) causes a grey-green precipitate to form.

Reactions of transition metal ions with hydroxide ions

Transition metal ions in aqueous solution are present as the hydrated complexes, $[M(H_2O)_6]^{n+}$. Due to the high positive charge density on the complex ion, such metal ions are often acidic, readily losing H^+ ions, e.g.:

$$[Cr(H_2O)_6]^{3+} \rightleftharpoons [Cr(H_2O)_5(OH)]^{2+} + H^+$$

Addition of alkali removes the H^+ as H_2O, and the reaction can progress further to the metal hydroxide, which is insoluble:

$$[Cr(H_2O)_6]^{3+} + OH^- \rightleftharpoons [Cr(H_2O)_5(OH)]^{2+} + H_2O$$

$$[Cr(H_2O)_5(OH)]^{2+} + OH^- \rightleftharpoons [Cr(H_2O)_4(OH)_2]^+ + H_2O$$

$$[Cr(H_2O)_4(OH)_2]^+ + OH^- \rightleftharpoons [Cr(H_2O)_3(OH)_3] + H_2O$$

This behaviour is typical of transition metal ions such as Cr^{3+}, Fe^{2+}, Fe^{3+} and Cu^{2+}. All these reactions are reversible so addition of acid can reverse them to regenerate the complex ions in solution.

For chromium (III) addition of excess alkali removes the H^+ from some of the remaining water molecules, forming an anionic hydroxide complex:

$$[Cr(H_2O)_3(OH)_3] + 3OH^- \rightleftharpoons [Cr(OH)_6]^{3-} + 3H_2O$$

We say that chromium (III) hydroxide is amphoteric: it can react as both an acid and a base. The reaction above shows the reaction of this hydroxide as an acid as it is donating H^+ to the hydroxide ions. It reacts as a base in the reverse of the earlier reactions:

$$[Cr(H_2O)_3(OH)_3] + H_2O \rightleftharpoons [Cr(H_2O)_4(OH)_2]^+ + OH^-$$

In this equation the hydroxide acts as a base by accepting H^+ from the water.

The observations seen on addition of sodium hydroxide to solutions containing each complex are given below.

Transition metal ion	Addition of some OH^-	Addition of excess OH^-
$[Cr(H_2O)_6]^{3+}$	Grey-green precipitate of $[Cr(H_2O)_3(OH)_3]$	Precipitate dissolves giving a deep green solution of $[Cr(OH)_6]^{3-}$.
$[Fe(H_2O)_6]^{2+}$	Dark green precipitate of $[Fe(H_2O)_4(OH)_2]$	No further reaction for the bulk. (Some red-brown colour seen at the surface due to oxidation by the air.)
$[Fe(H_2O)_6]^{3+}$	Red-brown precipitate of $[Fe(H_2O)_3(OH)_3]$	No further reaction
$[Cu(H_2O)_6]^{2+}$	Pale blue precipitate of $[Cu(H_2O)_4(OH)_2]$	No further reaction

3.5
Chemical kinetics

Chemists have many ways of working out whether or not chemical reactions are possible, but it is also important to know about the rate of a reaction. If a reaction is possible in terms of energy, it may be too slow to be useful, or need too high a temperature to be effective. This topic includes more information on methods to study the rate of a chemical reaction and how temperature affects the rate.

Studying the way reaction rates change as concentrations change can also give information about the mechanism of a reaction. This topic includes methods of producing a rate equation and how this can be used to distinguish between different proposed mechanisms.

You should be able to demonstrate and apply your knowledge and understanding of:

- Principles underlying the measurement of reaction rate, including by sampling and quenching.

- The meaning of order of reaction and how this is found from experimental results.

- Rate equations and how these are found and used.

- Rate-determining steps for reactions and how this links the kinetics to the mechanism.

- The effect of temperature and catalysts on reaction rate, and the use of the Arrhenius equation to link these.

Content

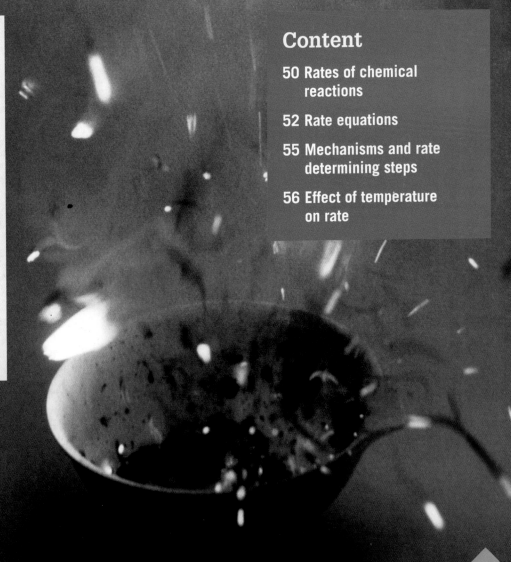

Rates of chemical reactions

Chemical kinetics is the study of rates of chemical reactions. In Unit 2 of the course the fundamental ideas of reaction rates were introduced, as well as some methods of studying the rates of chemical reactions. In this topic alternative approaches to studying the rates of reactions are explored, as well as using the measured rates to give key information about the mechanism of chemical reactions.

YOU SHOULD KNOW › › ›

› › › how to measure the rate of a range of chemical reactions

› › › how to obtain initial rates from experimental data

Link Rates of reaction in AS Topic 2.2 on page 106 of the AS book.

Exam tip

When discussing the ways of measuring the rate of a chemical reaction, it is important to refer to the measurement of time, as this is often forgotten.

Key Terms

Quenching is the sudden stopping or significant slowing of a chemical reaction to allow for analysis to occur without the reaction proceeding further. It is usually undertaken by cooling and diluting, such as by adding the sample to iced water.

Activation energy is the minimum amount of energy required for a collision to be successful.

Measuring rates of reaction

To measure the rate of a reaction, we need to work out how much of a reactant has been used up, or how much of a product has been produced in a set period of time. This is conveniently done by looking at a property of the reaction that changes with time, such as mass of reactants, volume or pressure of gas, colour or other electromagnetic absorption. A specific example is the iodine clock reaction which shows a distinct colour change after a set amount of compound has reacted.

Sampling and quenching

Many of the methods discussed in Topic 2.2 allow data to be collected on the progress of reaction throughout the entire chemical reaction. This is not always possible and sometimes a more labour-intensive approach is required. This is sampling and **quenching**, where a small amount of the reaction mixture is removed at regular time intervals (sampling) and immediately placed into iced water. This cools and dilutes the reaction mixture, which slows the reaction down and effectively stops it. This is the quenching stage.

When sampling and quenching is used the samples collected must be analysed by an appropriate method, with titration being a common approach. Each sample must be analysed individually to attain information on the progress of the reaction.

Advantages and disadvantages:

- Sampling and quenching can be used for a large range of reactions.

- Sampling and quenching is labour and time intensive as each sample must be analysed individually, so the time intervals used between measurements tend to be longer than in colorimetric methods, which can be automated.

- Sampling is only appropriate when a reaction mixture is homogeneous, such as reactions that are all in solution. If a reaction mixture is not homogeneous then the sample taken may not be representative of the overall mixture.

If a reaction uses a heterogeneous catalyst then sampling can be undertaken without quenching. When a solid catalyst is used in a gas or liquid mixture, the catalyst speeds up the reaction significantly. Removing a sample of the gas or liquid takes it away from the catalyst so the reaction rate is immediately reduced.

If a reaction uses a homogeneous catalyst then taking a sample also takes a sample of the catalyst with the reactants, so the reaction will continue. Quenching is needed in this case, and it can be undertaken using cooling and dilution like any other reaction. It can also be quenched by destroying the catalyst, for instance an acid catalyst can be neutralised using alkali.

Calculating rates of reaction

Once data is collected, a rate must be calculated. In most methods, the rate is calculated by using the equation:

$$\text{Rate} = \frac{\text{Change in concentration}}{\text{Time taken}}$$

The rate calculated in this manner is the average rate over the time period. The concentrations change as the reaction progresses so it is likely that the rate will also change, with the rate decreasing as the concentrations of reactants decreases. To find the initial rate the results should be plotted as a graph and a tangent drawn to the curve at time = 0, as shown in the graph below which shows how the concentration of the product of a reaction changes with time.

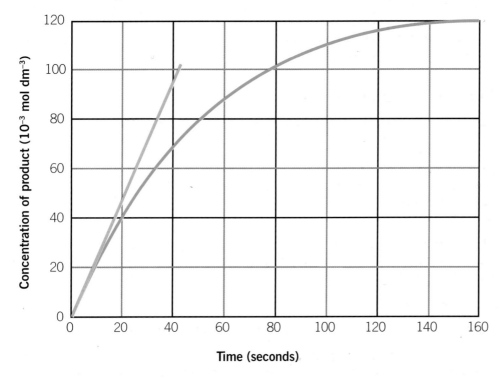

The tangent when time = 0 seconds gives us:

$$\text{reaction rate} = \frac{44 \times 10^{-3} \text{ mol dm}^{-3}}{20\text{s}} = 2.2 \times 10^{-3} \text{ mol dm}^{-3} \text{ s}^{-1}$$

Rates can be measured at different times by plotting a tangent at different places on the curve. The same method can be used when provided with a graph showing how the concentration of a reactant changes although in this case the concentration will be decreasing.

Exam tip

When explaining any changes in rates, collision theory should be used. This means that rate should be linked to the **frequency of successful collisions**. Rate decreases when the frequency of collisions decreases or when fewer collisions have more than the **activation energy**.

Exam tip

When calculating rate it is important that the units of rate match the units of the measurements. For example, time can be given in alternative units such as minutes, which may give rate units of mol dm⁻³ min⁻¹.

YOU SHOULD KNOW ›››

››› the meaning of reaction order

››› how to obtain reaction orders, and hence rate equations, from experimental data

Study point

An alternative way of identifying a first order reaction is to measure the half-life of the reaction. The half-life is the time taken for the concentration of a reactant to halve, and it is commonly used when discussing radioactivity. A first order reaction has a constant half-life, so if the concentration of a reactant drops from 2 mol dm^{-3} to 1 mol dm^{-3} in 85 seconds then it will drop from 1 mol dm^{-3} to 0.5 mol dm^{-3} in a further 85 seconds.

Rate equations

The rate of a chemical reaction in solution depends on the concentration of the reactants. When the concentration of one reactant (shown as [A]) is doubled, scientists have found that the rate of the reaction may:

Stay the same	Rate is not proportional to concentration	rate $\propto [A]^0$
Double	Rate is proportional to concentration	rate $\propto [A]^1$
Increase by four times	Rate is proportional to concentration squared	rate $\propto [A]^2$

This has led scientists to produce a rate equation that gives the rate of a chemical reaction at different concentrations of reactants.

For a general reaction:

$$A + B \rightarrow \text{products}$$

The rate equation is:

$$\text{Rate} = k\,[A]^m[B]^n$$

k is called the rate constant

m is the order of the reaction with respect to A

n is the order of the reaction with respect to B

Meanings of words

Rate: This is the rate of change of the concentration, or of the amount, of a particular reactant or product.

Rate constant: This is a constant in the rate equation. It is constant for a given reaction at a particular temperature, and is not affected by changing the concentrations of the reactants. It is not constant if we change the temperature.

Order of reaction: The order of a reaction with respect to a particular reactant is the power to which the concentration is raised in the rate equations (m or n in the equation above).

The overall order of a reaction is the sum of all these orders of reactions, i.e. m+n for the reaction above.

- We describe reactions as being **zeroth order** if the total is 0.
- We describe reactions as being **first order** if the total is 1.
- We describe reactions as being **second order** if the total is 2.
- We describe reactions as being **third order** if the total is 3.

Units of the rate constant

The rate of a reaction in solution is typically quoted as mol dm^{-3} s^{-1}: This is the change in concentration (mol dm^{-3}) per second. The rate constant has to have units for the units in the equation to balance.

Zeroth order reaction, e.g. Rate = k	The units of rate are mol dm^{-3} s^{-1}.	Units of k are mol dm^{-3} s^{-1}
First order reaction, e.g. Rate = k [A]	The units of rate are mol dm^{-3} s^{-1}, The units of concentration are mol dm^{-3}.	Units of k are s^{-1}
Second order reaction, e.g. Rate = k [A]^2	The units of rate are mol dm^{-3} s^{-1}, The units of concentration are mol dm^{-3}.	Units of k are mol^{-1} dm^3 s^{-1}

Obtaining rate equations

Rate equations can only be found experimentally, by studying the effects of changing the concentration of each individual reactant. **There is no way of obtaining this rate equation from the overall equation of the reaction.**

How to derive a rate equation from experimental data

1. Look at the given information to find two experiments that differ only in the concentration of one reactant.

2. If doubling this reactant concentration does not affect the reaction rate, the order with respect to this reactant is zero.

3. If doubling this reactant concentration doubles the rate of reaction, the order with respect to this reactant is one.

4. If doubling this reactant concentration increases the reaction rate by a factor of four, the order with respect to this reactant is two.

5. Repeat this process for each reactant, to find the order with respect to each one.

6. The order of the reaction is the sum of each of these orders.

Worked example 1

Derive a rate equation for the reaction of Br_2 with butadiene, C_4H_6 in solution.

Experiment number	Initial concentration of Br_2/ mol dm^{-3}	Initial concentration of butadiene/ mol dm^{-3}	Initial rate of formation of product/ mol dm^{-3} s^{-1}
1	6×10^{-3}	1×10^{-3}	3×10^{-3}
2	6×10^{-3}	2×10^{-3}	6×10^{-3}
3	6×10^{-3}	3×10^{-3}	9×10^{-3}
4	1×10^{-3}	6×10^{-3}	0.5×10^{-3}
5	2×10^{-3}	6×10^{-3}	2.0×10^{-3}
6	3×10^{-3}	6×10^{-3}	4.5×10^{-3}

Handwritten annotations: "1st order", "2nd order", "×4", "$k\bar{7}$", "$R : k[Br_2]^2$"

Knowledge check 19

What is the order of the following reactions?

a) Rate = k [H$_2$]^1[I$_2$]^1

b) Rate = k [CH$_3$I]^1[Br$^-$]^0

c) Rate = k [CH$_3$COOH]^1

d) Rate = k [CH$_3$CHO]

e) Rate = k [C$_2$H$_4$]^1[Br$_2$]^2

What are the units of the rate constant in (a) to (d) above.

Stretch & Challenge

Rate data does not always contain pairs of data sets with only one concentration doubled. There may be cases where data sets match with one concentration changed in a different way, such as tripled, quadrupled or increased tenfold. In this case first order reactions will show a similar increase in reaction rate, as rate is proportional to concentration. Those that are second order will increase by the change in concentration squared: when concentration quadruples the rate will increase by a factor of 16.

Link The effects of changing concentration on rate in AS Topic 2.2 on page 108 of the AS book.

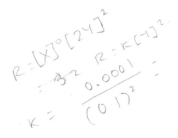

To find the order with respect to $[Br_2]$, two sets of data where the concentration of Br_2 changes but the concentration of butadiene stays the same are needed. In this case, experiment numbers 4 and 5 are suitable. In these the concentration of Br_2 doubles, and the rate quadruples. This shows that the reaction is second order with respect to Br_2.

To find the order with respect to $[C_4H_6]$, two sets of data where the concentration of C_4H_6 changes but the concentration of bromine stays the same are needed. In this case, experiment numbers 1 and 2 are suitable. In these the concentration of butadiene doubles, and the rate doubles. This shows that the reaction is first order with respect to butadiene.

The rate equation is therefore: Rate = $k[Br_2]^2[C_4H_6]^1$

The overall order of reaction is: Third order

After working out the rate equation, work out a value for the rate equation, k. To do this select any one set of data and put in these values to the rate equation.

$$k = \frac{Rate}{[Br_2]^2[C_4H_6]} = \frac{4.5 \times 10^{-3}}{(3 \times 10^{-3})^2 \times (6 \times 10^{-3})}$$

$$k = 83.3 \times 10^3 \text{ mol}^{-2} \text{ dm}^6 \text{ s}^{-1}$$

Worked example 2

Derive a rate equation for the reaction of X with Y to produce XY_2.

$$X \text{ (aq)} + 2Y \text{ (aq)} \rightarrow XY_2 \text{ (aq)}$$

Experiment number	Initial concentration of X / mol dm^{-3}	Initial concentration of Y / mol dm^{-3}	Initial rate of formation of XY$_2$ / mol dm^{-3} s^{-1}
1	0.10	0.10	0.0001
2	0.10	0.20	0.0004
3	0.10	0.30	0.0009
4	0.20	0.10	0.0001
5	0.30	0.10	0.0001

Find the order of the reaction with respect to X. *The order is zero.*

Find the order of the reaction with respect to Y. *The order is 2.*

Write an overall rate equation. *Rate = $k[X]^0[Y]^2 = k[Y]^2$*

Find the value and units of the rate constant.
$k = Rate \div [Y]^2 = 0.0001 \div (0.1)^2 = 0.01$ mol^{-1} dm^3 s^{-1}

20 Knowledge check

Write a rate equation for the reaction:

$$H_2O_2 \text{ (aq)} + 2 I^- \text{ (aq)} + 2 H^+ \text{ (aq)} \rightarrow I_2 \text{ (aq)} + 2 H_2O \text{ (l)}$$

Use the following information:

Concentration of H$_2$O$_2$ (aq) / mol dm^{-3}	Initial concentration of I$^-$ (aq) / mol dm^{-3}	Initial concentration of H$^+$ (aq) / mol dm^{-3}	Initial rate / 10^{-6} mol dm^{-3} s^{-1}
0.0010	0.10	0.10	2.8
0.0020	0.10	0.10	5.6
0.0020	0.10	0.20	5.6
0.0010	0.40	0.10	11.2

Determine the value of k in this reaction.

Mechanisms and rate-determining steps

A mechanism is a description of the series of steps that occur during a chemical reaction. Each step in a mechanism will occur at a different rate, with its own rate equation. The rate of the slowest step limits the rate of the overall reaction, and this step is called the **rate-determining step**. From a study of the kinetics of a reaction, we are effectively studying the kinetics of the rate-determining step.

The rate-determining step is the slowest step in the mechanism.

What information do we obtain about the rate-determining step?

Collision theory says that for a reaction to occur:

1. The reacting particles must collide.

2. The particles must have sufficient energy for reaction (the activation energy).

The rate equation tells us how many particles must collide in the rate-determining step:

- In a second order reaction, two particles must collide.

- In a third order reaction, three particles must collide.

- In a first order reaction, there is only one particle in the rate-determining step.

So if the rate equation is:	The rate-determining step has the following reactants:
Rate = k [C_3H_7I][Br^-]	$C_3H_7I + Br^- \rightarrow$ products
Rate = k [C_4H_9I]	$C_4H_9I \rightarrow$ products
Rate = k [CH_3COOCH_3][H^+]	$CH_3COOCH_3 + H^+ \rightarrow$ products

It is not possible to identify conclusively the products of the rate-determining step in every case; however, it is possible to suggest products. These must balance like any other equation, such as:

$$C_3H_7I + Br^- \rightarrow C_3H_7Br + I^-$$

All the steps in the mechanism, including the rate-determining step, must combine to form the overall equation.

If the rate-determining step has the following reactants:	The rate equation is:
$C_3H_7I + Br^- \rightarrow$ products	Rate = k [C_3H_7I][Br^-]
$CH_3I \rightarrow$ products	Rate = k [CH_3I]

We can use the information derived from the kinetics of a reaction to prove or disprove a reaction mechanism. From the kinetics, we can work out what the reactants are for the rate-determining step. If our proposed mechanism does not have a step with these reactants, then it cannot be the correct mechanism.

Key Term

The **rate-determining step** is the slowest step in a reaction mechanism.

Knowledge check 21

Write equations for the rate-determining steps of the chemical reactions that have the following rate equations:

a) Rate = k [C_2H_4][Br_2]

b) Rate = k [I_2]

c) Rate = k [H_2O_2][I^-][H^+]

a) $C_2H_4 + Br_2 \rightarrow$ products.

b) $I_2 \rightarrow$ products

c) $H_2O_2 + I^- + H^+ \rightarrow$ products

▲ Svante Arrhenius

Link The effects of temperature on rate are explained qualitatively in the AS course, Topic 2.2, on page 112 of the AS book. This uses the Boltzmann distribution.

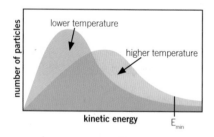

Exam tip

Take care with the units you use in your calculations. The units of activation energy are usually given in kJ mol^{-1}, with the value of R often given as J mol^{-1} K^{-1}. When calculating you must convert both to the same energy units, either multiply the activation energy by 1000 to convert to J mol^{-1} or divide the value of R by 1000 to give kJ mol^{-1} K^{-1}.

The units of $Ae^{(-E_a/RT)}$ all cancel out so there are no units for this expression. This means that the units of A must be the same as the units of the rate constant.

Effect of temperature on rate

Increasing the temperature of a reaction causes the rate of a reaction to increase. This can be explained by collision theory, as particles will react when they collide with sufficient energy. Increasing the temperature means that more of the collisions will have sufficient energy to react, called the activation energy.

Arrhenius equation

In terms of the rate equation, temperature does not affect the concentrations of each substance, so it is the rate constant that is affected when we heat or cool a reaction mixture. We can quantify the effect of temperature on the rate constant using the Arrhenius equation:

$$k = Ae^{(-E_a/RT)}$$

k = Rate constant

A = Frequency factor, related to the frequency of collisions between particles. It can be treated as a constant over a limited range of temperatures, although it does vary if temperature varies significantly. In many cases the value of the frequency factor is calculated from a given set of data at one temperature prior to its use in calculating the rate constant at a different temperature.

e = Mathematical constant, found on all scientific calculators.

E_a = Activation energy, used in J mol^{-1}

R = Gas constant, given on the data sheet in units of J K^{-1} mol^{-1}. The value of this is 8.314 J K^{-1} mol^{-1}.

T = Temperature in Kelvin

Overall the expression $e^{(-E_a/RT)}$ is considered to show the fraction of collisions that possess an energy level above the activation energy. As the expression includes two constants (e, R) three out of the four remaining factors (k, A, E_a and T) must be known to calculate a value for the final factor. In many cases the value of the frequency factor is calculated from a given set of data at one temperature

Worked example

The reaction between iodine and hydrogen to produce HI has a rate constant of 1.37×10^{-4} mol^{-1} dm^3 s^{-1} at a temperature of 575 K. The activation energy for this reaction is 157 kJ mol^{-1}. Calculate the value of the frequency factor giving its units. Use this to find the rate constant at a temperature of 600 K.

STEP 1: Find the value of A by rearranging the expression.

$$k = Ae^{(-E_a/RT)} \quad so \quad A = k \div e^{(-E_a/RT)}$$

The energy terms are converted to J so A = $1.37 \times 10^{-4} \div e^{(-157 \times 10^3/8.314 \times 575)}$
$$= 1.37 \times 10^{-4} \div e^{-32.84}$$
$$= 2.51 \times 10^{10} \text{ mol}^{-1} \text{ dm}^3 \text{ s}^{-1}$$

The units of the frequency factor are the same as the units of the rate constant.

STEP 2: Find the value of the rate constant at 600 K.

$$k = Ae^{(-E_a/RT)}$$

Fill in the values for A, E_a, R and T at 600 K.

$$k = 2.51 \times 10^{10} \times e^{(-157 \times 10^3/8.314 \times 600)}$$
$$k = 5.38 \times 10^{-4} \text{ mol}^{-1} \text{ dm}^3 \text{ s}^{-1}$$

Finding the activation energy

The activation energy can be found by rearranging the Arrhenius equation if we have information about the frequency factor; however, it is more common to find information regarding the rate constant at different temperatures. These can be used to find both frequency factor and activation energy. The Arrhenius equation can be rearranged to give:

$$\ln k = \ln A - \frac{E_a}{RT}$$

The structure of this version of the Arrhenius equation can be used to plot a straight line graph of ln k against 1/T, and the intercept of this graph gives ln A with the gradient equal to $\frac{-E_a}{R}$.

- In k is the log of the rate constant – the logarithm adjusts well for the range of values seen in the rate constant at different temperatures.

- 1/T uses the temperatures in Kelvin in all cases.

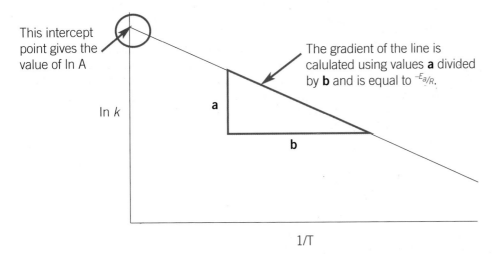

This intercept point gives the value of ln A

The gradient of the line is calulated using values **a** divided by **b** and is equal to $\frac{-E_a}{R}$.

ln k

a

b

1/T

The gradient is calculated at any point along the straight line. The value of the gradient is $\frac{-E_a}{R}$ so needs to be multiplied by -8.314 J K^{-1} mol^{-1} to find a value for the activation energy. E_a is calculated in J mol^{-1} in this case, and needs to be converted to kJ mol^{-1} for use by dividing by 1000.

The intercept on the vertical axis gives a value for ln A. To find the value for A the calculation is e$^{\text{intercept value}}$. The units of this are the same as the units of the rate constant.

Effect on catalysts on rate

Catalysts increase the rate of chemical reactions by providing alternative routes with lower activation energies. This does not affect the concentrations in a rate equation, so it is the rate constant that is changed. Looking at the Arrhenius equation, we can see that reducing the activation energy will increase the value of $e^{(-E_a/RT)}$ and hence increase the rate constant. As the route of reaction changes it is likely that the value of the frequency factor will also change, but the combination of both changes is likely to lead to a significant increase in reaction rate.

Stretch & Challenge

Chemists often use the concept that the rate of a chemical reaction doubles when the temperature increases by 10 K (which also equals 10°C). This is a simplification, as it depends on the activation energy, and the temperatures involved. For temperatures around room temperature, this rule of thumb is only true for activation energies of around 50 kJ mol^{-1}. If the activation energy is less than this then the effects of temperature change are less. If the activation energy is greater then the effects of temperature change are greater.

Knowledge check **22**

The rate of a first order chemical reaction at 300 K is 0.0345 mol dm^{-3} s^{-1} when the initial concentration is 0.100 mol dm^{-3}. The activation energy of this reaction is 42 kJ mol^{-1}. Calculate the rate of this reaction at 320K with an initial concentration of 0.150 mol dm^{-3}.

3.6
Enthalpy changes for solids and solutions

When substances are formed or changed, either physically or chemically, there are energy changes. In chemistry, we are often concerned with the changes between chemical energy and heat energy, and the classification of changes as exothermic and endothermic is one that is fundamental to how chemists expect reactions to behave.

Chemists have many ways of describing specific energy changes, and the need for precise naming of these is as important as the precise naming of chemical substances. Changes such as those associated with standard enthalpies of formation and combustion should already be familiar but in this section a wider range of changes are discussed. These allow predictions about the physical and chemical properties of the substances involved, such as the solubility of ionic compounds.

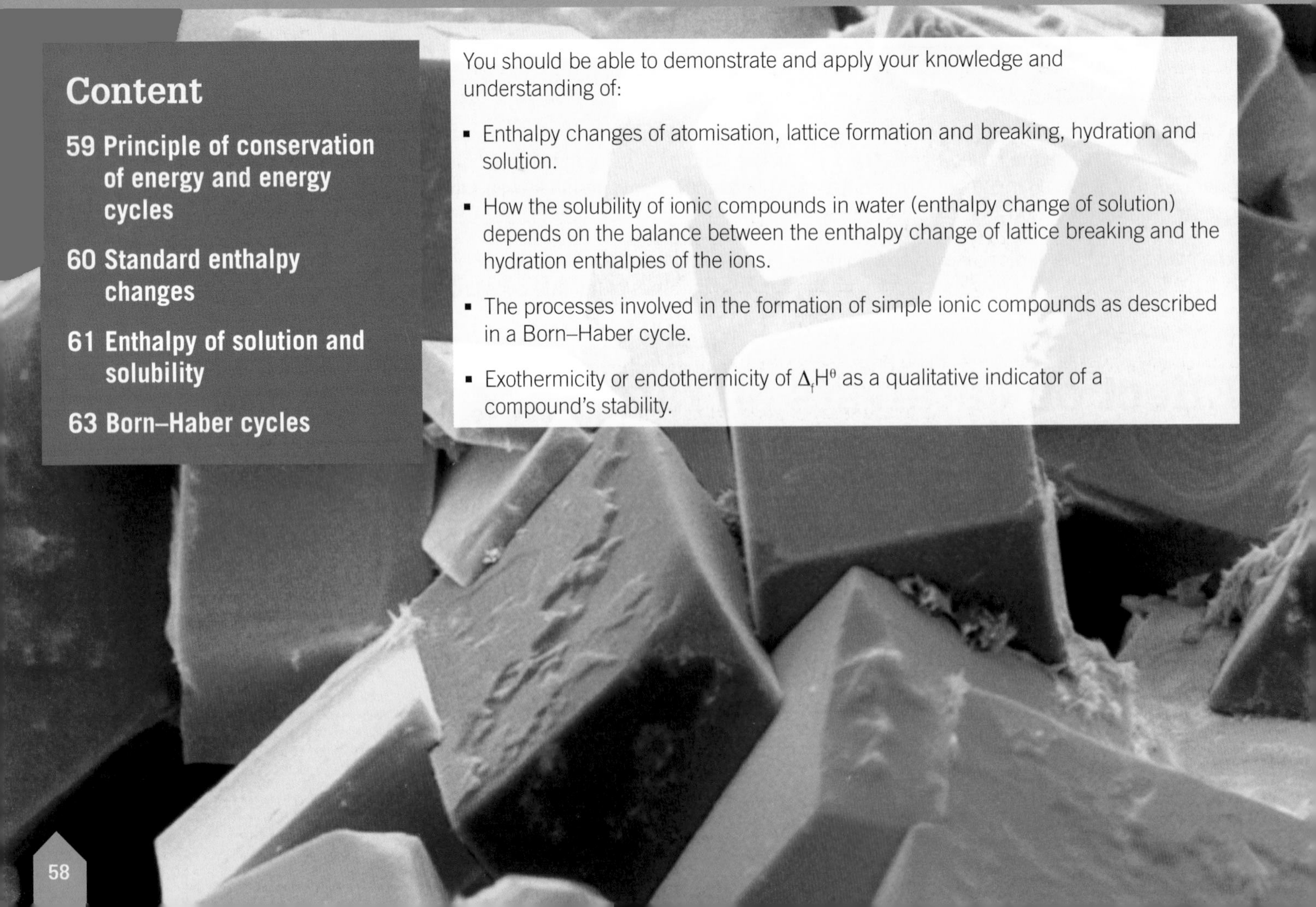

Content

You should be able to demonstrate and apply your knowledge and understanding of:

- Enthalpy changes of atomisation, lattice formation and breaking, hydration and solution.

- How the solubility of ionic compounds in water (enthalpy change of solution) depends on the balance between the enthalpy change of lattice breaking and the hydration enthalpies of the ions.

- The processes involved in the formation of simple ionic compounds as described in a Born–Haber cycle.

- Exothermicity or endothermicity of $\Delta_f H^\theta$ as a qualitative indicator of a compound's stability.

Enthalpy changes are a way of measuring the changes in energy during any chemical or physical change. At A-level, enthalpy and energy can be treated as being the same. Knowledge of the energy needed or released during a chemical reaction is key when planning a chemical process in a laboratory, and even more important when undertaking chemical reactions on an industrial scale.

Principle of conservation of energy

Link Thermochemistry in AS Topic 2.1 on pages 94–105 of the AS book.

All the ideas regarding energy changes in chemistry and all other sciences are based on the principle of conservation of energy:

Energy cannot be created or destroyed, but may only be converted from one form to another.

In terms of chemical changes, this has two main consequences:

- To measure the energy change of a chemical reaction we can measure the energy given off in the reaction. The energy of the chemicals has decreased by the same amount of energy as has been given out as heat or other energy types.

- Hess's law: The energy change of any chemical reaction is the same regardless of the route taken.

Energy cycles

It is often difficult to measure the enthalpies of formation directly, but it is possible to use the principle of conservation of energy to calculate these enthalpies from values we can measure more easily. This method is based on *Hess's law*, which can be expressed as:

'If a reaction can take place by more than one route, then the total energy change for each route will be the same.'

This allows us to construct energy cycles like this one:

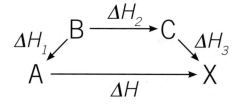

- If we have a chemical reaction that changes A to X, the energy shown above is ΔH.

- If we change A to B to C to X, the total energy change is the same i.e.
  $\Delta H = -\Delta H_1 + \Delta H_2 + \Delta H_3$.

- If we know three out of the four terms in the energy cycle above, we can use this information to calculate the fourth energy change using this equation.

It is possible to undertake calculations involving enthalpies of formation without drawing an energy cycle. If you are given enthalpies of formation **only**, and need to work out the enthalpy of a reaction, there is a more straightforward method of working out the enthalpy change. As a consequence of the energy cycle, the enthalpy change of any reaction is:

Enthalpy change = $\Delta_f H^\theta$ (for all products) $-\Delta_f H^\theta$ (for all reactants)

REMEMBER:

- The enthalpy change is calculated using Products – Reactants

- If you have balancing numbers in the equation, you must include these. For example, if a reaction forms 2NaCl you need to include 2× the enthalpy of formation of NaCl.

Standard enthalpy changes

The **enthalpy change of reaction**, with the symbol ΔH, is a measure of the energy change of a reaction. It is more common to see standard enthalpy changes of reaction, ΔH^θ, which represent the energy change under standard conditions.

Standard conditions are: A temperature of 298K (25°C)
A concentration of 1 mol dm⁻³ for solutions.
A pressure of 101 kPa, or one atmosphere (1 atm), for gases.

Standard state is the physical state of a substance under standard conditions, such as oxygen gas, liquid water or sodium chloride solid.

The **standard enthalpy change of reaction, ΔH^θ**, is the enthalpy change that occurs in a reaction between molar quantities of reactants in their standard states under standard conditions.

The enthalpy changes of some specific reactions are given special names, and the standard enthalpies of formation and combustion were covered in the AS work. In many of the calculations undertaken for ionic compounds, the energy cycles are constructed with the alternative route going via the gaseous state. This means that energy terms associated with converting substances to and from gaseous atoms or ions are commonly used.

Standard enthalpy change of atomisation, $\Delta_{at}H^\theta$

This is the enthalpy change that occurs when one mole of atoms of an element in the gas phase are formed from in the element in its standard state under standard conditions.

e.g. $Na\,(s) \rightarrow Na\,(g)$ or $\frac{1}{2}\,Cl_2\,(g) \rightarrow Cl\,(g)$ or $\frac{1}{4}\,P_4\,(s) \rightarrow P\,(g)$

Standard enthalpy change of lattice formation, $\Delta_{latt}H^\theta$

This is the enthalpy change that occurs when one mole of an ionic compound is formed from ions of the elements in the gas phase.

e.g. $Na^+\,(g) + Cl^-\,(g) \rightarrow NaCl\,(s)$ or $Ca^{2+}\,(g) + 2Cl^-\,(g) \rightarrow CaCl_2\,(s)$

You may also see the enthalpy of lattice breaking, which is the reverse of this process – the energy change that occurs when one mole of an ionic compound is broken up into ions of the elements in the gas phase.

e.g. $NaCl\,(s) \rightarrow Na^+\,(g) + Cl^-\,(g)$ or $CaCl_2\,(s) \rightarrow Ca^{2+}\,(g) + 2Cl^-\,(g)$

Standard enthalpy change of hydration, $\Delta_{hyd}H^\theta$

This is the enthalpy change that occurs when one mole of an ionic compound in solution is formed from ions of the elements in the gas phase.

e.g. $Na^+\,(g) + Cl^-\,(g) + aq \rightarrow NaCl\,(aq)$ or $Ca^{2+}\,(g) + 2Cl^-\,(g) + aq \rightarrow CaCl_2\,(aq)$

Electron affinity

This is the enthalpy change that occurs when one mole of gaseous negative ions are formed from gaseous atoms of a substance by gaining an electron.

$$Cl\ (g) + e^- \rightarrow Cl^-\ (g) \quad \text{or} \quad O\ (g) + e^- \rightarrow O^-\ (g)$$

Ionisation energy

This is the enthalpy change that occurs when one mole of gaseous positive ions are formed from gaseous atoms a substance by losing an electron.

$$Na\ (g) \rightarrow Na^+\ (g) + e^- \quad \text{or} \quad Cu\ (g) \rightarrow Cu^+\ (g) + e^-$$

Enthalpy of solution and solubility

Ionic substances consist of a lattice of positive and negative ions held together by electrostatic forces. To dissolve, the forces between the ions must be broken, and this can only happen if they are replaced by other forces. The water molecules are dipolar – the oxygen atoms are δ– and the hydrogen atoms are δ+. The oxygen atoms surround the positive ions and the hydrogen atoms surround the negative ions – we say the ions become hydrated. In the case of sodium chloride the ions are Na^+ and Cl^- as shown below.

YOU SHOULD KNOW ›››

››› how enthalpy changes control the solubility of ionic compounds

Knowledge check 23

The standard enthalpy change of hydration of calcium ions are –1650 kJ mol^{-1} and chloride ions are –364 kJ mol^{-1}. If the enthalpy change of lattice breaking for calcium chloride, $CaCl_2$, is 2237 kJ mol^{-1} find the standard enthalpy change of solution and explain whether you expect calcium chloride to be soluble.

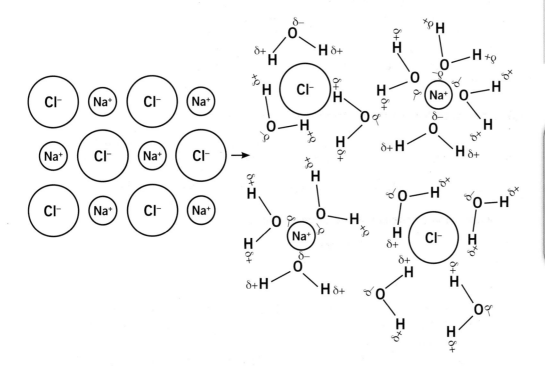

The enthalpy change during this process is called the enthalpy change of solution.

Stretch & Challenge

The idea that an exothermic change is needed for a substance to dissolve is a simplification. In general, all exothermic changes will occur; however, some endothermic changes will also occur. The factor that is not considered in these is entropy, and the effects of entropy are covered in Topic 3.7 on pages 67–70. The increase in entropy when a solid dissolves can balance out a change that is slightly endothermic. A common example is the enthalpy of solution of sodium chloride which is +4 kJ mol^{-1}.

Exam tip

As it is not easy to predict the solubility of compounds, so you should recall the common patterns seen throughout the course. These include the fact that the following compounds are soluble:

all group 1 compounds,
all ammonium compounds,
all metal nitrates.

The following are insoluble, except when the rules above say that they would be soluble:

all metal carbonates,
all metal hydroxides,
all lead compounds.

Standard enthalpy change of solution $\Delta_{sol} H^{\theta}$

This is the enthalpy change that occurs when one mole of a substance dissolves completely in a solvent under standard conditions to form a solution.

The enthalpy of solution is the sum of the enthalpy of lattice breaking and enthalpy of hydration:

$$M^+X^- (s) \rightarrow M^+ (g) + X^- (g) \rightarrow M^+ (aq) + X^- (aq)$$

- The enthalpy of lattice breaking is endothermic.

- The lattice of hydration is exothermic.

If the lattice of hydration is greater than the enthalpy of lattice breaking, the salt dissolves; however, if the lattice of hydration is less than the enthalpy of lattice breaking, the salt will not usually dissolve. The more exothermic the total of these values, the more soluble a salt is likely to be. The same factors affect both the enthalpy of lattice breaking and enthalpy of solution:

- Both are increased by increasing charge on the ions.

- Both are increased by decreasing size of the ions.

This makes it very difficult to predict solubility from first principles, and so patterns in solubility are used to predict whether particular salts are soluble or not.

Worked example

Use the data below to explain why the silver chloride is insoluble:

Standard enthalpy of hydration of silver ions, Ag$^+$	–464 kJ mol^{-1}
Standard enthalpy of hydration of chloride ions, Cl$^-$	–364 kJ mol^{-1}
Standard enthalpy of lattice breaking for AgCl	905 kJ mol^{-1}

The standard enthalpy of solution is given by:

Standard enthalpy of solution = Standard enthalpy of hydration + Enthalpy of lattice breaking

$$= -464 - 364 + 905 = 77 \text{ kJ mol}^{-1}$$

The process of dissolving is highly endothermic and so the silver chloride will not dissolve.

Born–Haber cycles

Born–Haber cycles are energy cycles similar to those seen for other processes; however, there are many more steps. The energy cycle involves turning all the initial elements into gas phase atoms, then ions and then combining these back to form a solid (using a lattice enthalpy term) or a solution (using a solution enthalpy term). The energy changes associated with these can be broken down into a series of small steps. These are shown on the Born–Haber cycle (energy cycle) below.

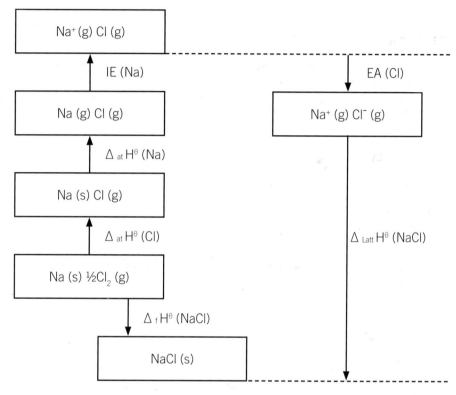

The ease of formation of an ionic compound depends on the energy changes associated with each step of the process. These steps are:

Formation of gas phase atoms: The enthalpy of atomisation

This is the energy required to form one mole of atoms of an element in the gas phase from the element in its standard state.

$$Na\ (s) \rightarrow Na\ (g)\quad \text{and}\quad \tfrac{1}{2}\ Cl_2\ (g) \rightarrow Cl\ (g)$$

Formation of a cation: ionization energy

Formation of a metal cation requires the atom to lose one or more electrons, and this requires energy to be put into the atom.

$$\text{Ionisation energy:}\quad Na\ (g) \rightarrow Na^+\ (g) + e^-$$

This process is always endothermic as you need energy to remove an electron from an atom.

▲ Max Born and Fritz Haber, the scientists that give the Born–Haber cycle its name

▼ **Study point**

The enthalpy of atomisation of a diatomic gas is half the bond enthalpy.

Exam tip

When ions are formed with multiple charges (2+, 3+, 2– or 3–) then there will be several ionisation energies or several electron affinities in the calculation as each one represents the loss or gain of one electron.

24 ⌄ Knowledge check

Write chemical equations that correspond to the following standard enthalpy changes:

(a) First ionisation energy of copper.

(b) The bond energy of Cl_2.

(c) The atomisation of O_2

(d) The lattice formation of Na_2O

(e) The electron affinity of fluorine.

Formation of anions

When a non-metal atom gains an electron to form an anion with a charge of –1, the energy change is called the electron affinity.

$$\text{Electron affinity:} \quad Cl\,(g) + e^- \rightarrow Cl^-\,(g)$$

This process is sometimes exothermic, but second and third electron affinities (to form ions with –2 and –3 charge) are usually endothermic.

Enthalpy of lattice formation

Lattice enthalpies represent the energy released when the positive and negative ions in an ionic compound come together to form a solid. This process always releases energy, and it is this lattice energy that is the energy that drives the formation of ionic compounds. Since the formation of cations is always endothermic, and the formation of anions is often endothermic, there would not be any ionic compounds formed without any other energy to balance this out. This energy change is caused by the oppositely charged ions coming together to form the crystal lattice:

$$Na^+\,(g) + Cl^-\,(g) \rightarrow NaCl\,(s)$$

This is always exothermic, and the more exothermic it is, the more stable the ionic compound.

Calculations using given Born–Haber cycles

Looking at the Born–Haber cycle for sodium chloride, the term that is usually 'unknown' is the enthalpy of lattice formation. This is the change from Na^+ (g) and Cl^- (g) to form NaCl (s), the longest arrow on the diagram. We can calculate this value by using an alternative route around the cycle, The calculation is:

$$\Delta_{Latt}H^\theta = -EA\,(Cl) - IE\,(Na) - \Delta_{at}H^\theta\,(Cl) - \Delta_{at}H^\theta\,(Na) + \Delta_f H^\theta\,(NaCl)$$

In writing this equation any time the path goes against the direction of the arrow the value is subtracted, and when it goes with the arrow this value is added.

Producing and using simple Born–Haber cycles

If a Born–Haber cycle is not provided then one can be constructed using equations provided in a question. In this case look for equations that contain any of the substances listed in the chemical equation and link these together to form an overall cycle.

Exam tip

Make sure you include the physical state for every substance when working though these calculations as the enthalpy for a substance is different in different physical states.

Worked example

Calculate the enthalpy of lattice formation for calcium hydride, CaH_2 using the data provided.

$$Ca\,(s) + H_2\,(g) \rightarrow CaH_2\,(s) \quad \Delta_f H^\theta = -189 \text{ kJ mol}^{-1}$$

	Enthalpy change / kJ mol⁻¹
$Ca\,(s) \rightarrow Ca\,(g)$	193
$Ca\,(g) \rightarrow Ca^+\,(g) + e$	590
$Ca^+\,(g) \rightarrow Ca^{2+}\,(g) + e$	1150
$H_2\,(g) \rightarrow 2H\,(g)$	436
$H\,(g) + e \rightarrow H^-\,(g)$	–72

In this case start with the equation provided, and add the unknown value:

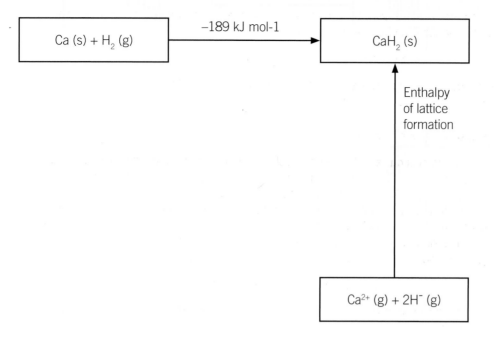

Next, identify any changes that you can link to this skeletal Born–Haber cycle. Looking at the reactants Ca (s) and H_2 (g) it is possible to identify atomisation reactions for both substances from the table of data. These can be added to the cycle.

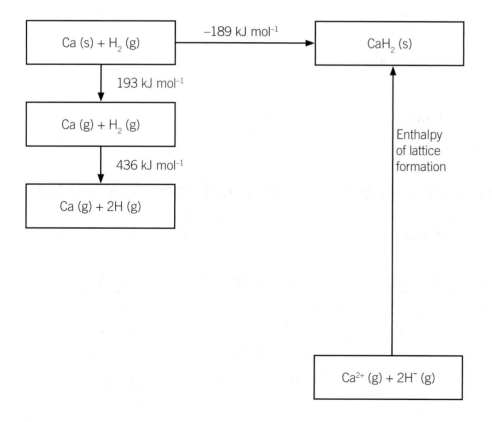

Next, we can see that the table of data includes steps to form the ions Ca^{2+} and H^- from these atoms; however, we need to make sure that the values for H are doubled as there are two of them. This allows us to complete the cycle.

Exam tip

Make sure you always state the physical state for all substances in your Born–Haber cycle.

Exam tip

When transferring your information to the calculation, the most common errors are forgetting the multiplication numbers when two atoms are involved in any of the changes, and incorrectly transferring the direction of any arrows into + and – signs.

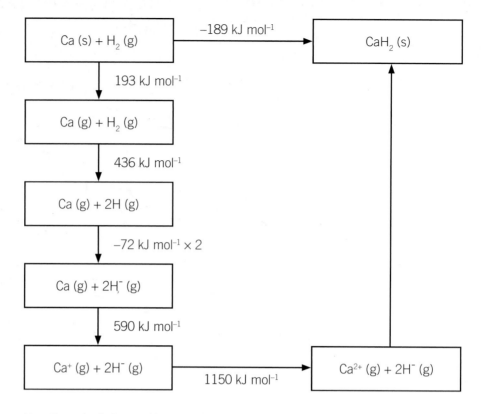

Now the calculation can be completed:

Enthalpy of lattice formation = – (1150) –(590) – (2 × –72) – (436) – (193) + (–189)
= –2414 kJ mol^{-1}

Stability of compounds

Exam tip

When discussing the stability of compounds in terms of enthalpy of formation, it is important to emphasise that this is the stability **relative to the elements.**

If the enthalpy change of formation of a compound is negative, then energy is given out as the compound is formed from its elements. This tells us that the compound is stable compared with the elements. The more negative the enthalpy change of formation of a compound, the more stable it is.

If the enthalpy change of formation is positive, then the compound is unstable compared with the elements that make it up. This does not mean the compound cannot exist, but it means that energy is needed to change the elements into the compound. Many compounds that exist have a positive enthalpy change of formation, but they do not decompose because the process is too slow.

Entropy and feasibility of reactions

Chemists need to be able to predict whether a reaction is feasible without having to try every one. They use a range of theories and ideas to predict feasibility and some of the ones seen so far, such as enthalpy change of reaction, only give a guide to whether a reaction is feasible.

Entropy is one of the fundamental concepts of science. It is described in many different ways; however, the second law of thermodynamics states that the overall entropy in any system will increase during any spontaneous change. This makes an understanding of entropy essential in predicting whether reactions are feasible.

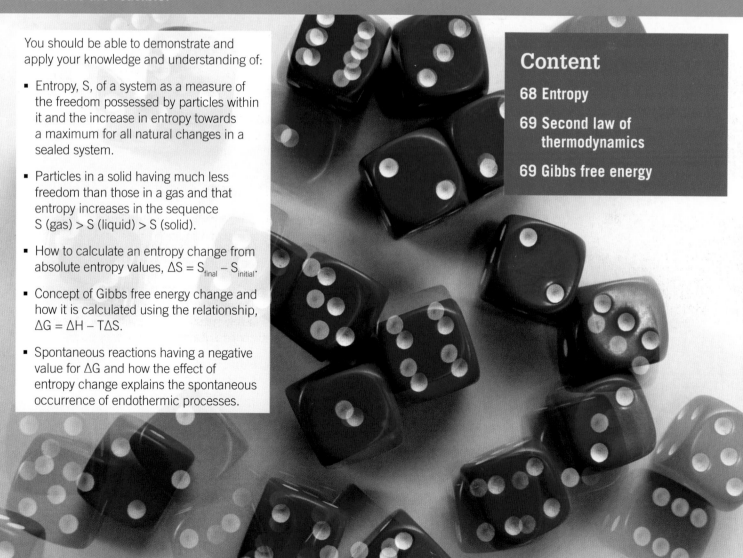

You should be able to demonstrate and apply your knowledge and understanding of:

- Entropy, S, of a system as a measure of the freedom possessed by particles within it and the increase in entropy towards a maximum for all natural changes in a sealed system.

- Particles in a solid having much less freedom than those in a gas and that entropy increases in the sequence S (gas) > S (liquid) > S (solid).

- How to calculate an entropy change from absolute entropy values, $\Delta S = S_{final} - S_{initial}$.

- Concept of Gibbs free energy change and how it is calculated using the relationship, $\Delta G = \Delta H - T\Delta S$.

- Spontaneous reactions having a negative value for ΔG and how the effect of entropy change explains the spontaneous occurrence of endothermic processes.

Stretch & Challenge

When considering the entropy of a single substance in different physical states, the pattern of S (solid) < S (liquid) < S (gas) remains true; however, when considering different substances, there are degrees of freedom within the molecule. A large molecule such as hexane in the liquid state will have a larger entropy than a small molecule such as methane in the gas state. This is because the hexane can bend and fold in many ways, and these increase the entropy of the molecule even though it is a liquid.

Entropy

Entropy is often described as the disorder in a system. The first beaker below has low entropy and the second has a much higher entropy.

This definition of entropy is not the main one used in chemistry. Chemists view entropy as the degree of freedom of a system – particles that can move freely in any direction have a much higher entropy than particles that are constrained.

- If a system has the atoms in fixed positions, without any freedom to move, then the entropy is low. This is typical of a solid.

- If a system has the atoms free to move in any direction and but must stay close together, then the entropy is greater. This is typical of a liquid.

- If a system has the atoms free to move in any direction and to move to any position, then the entropy is high. This is typical of a gas.

The entropy is represented by the symbol S, and has units of Joules per Kelvin ($J\ K^{-1}$), with standard entropies given as $J\ K^{-1}\ mol^{-1}$. For any substance in its different physical states the entropy of the gas is greatest and the solid is least:

$$S\ (\text{solid}) < S\ (\text{liquid}) < S\ (\text{gas})$$

Entropy changes

In a chemical reaction the entropy change can be calculated from the standard entropy of the substances involved. The standard entropy of a substance is the entropy of one mole in a given physical state under standard conditions. There are tables of data that list these for a range of substances. The calculation is:

$$\Delta S = S\ (\text{all products}) - S\ (\text{all reactants})$$

Worked example

Calculate the entropy change for the combustion of methane.

$$CH_4 (g) + 2O_2 (g) \rightarrow CO_2 (g) + 2H_2O (l)$$

Substance	Physical state	Standard entropy / $J\ K^{-1}\ mol^{-1}$
Methane, CH_4	Gas	186
Hexane, C_6H_{14}	Liquid	204
Oxygen, O_2	Gas	205
Carbon dioxide, CO_2	Gas	214
Water, H_2O	Liquid	70
Water, H_2O	Gas	189

The entropy change is given by:

$$\Delta S = S(CO_2) + 2 \times S(H_2O) - S(CH_4) - 2 \times S(O_2)$$

$$= 214 + 140 - 186 - 410$$

$$= -4\ J\ K^{-1}\ mol^{-1}$$

Note that the value for water used is the liquid phase as this matches the chemical equation.

Knowledge check 25

Calculate the entropy change for the combustion of hexane, assuming that the water is produced in the liquid phase.

Second law of thermodynamics

The second law of thermodynamics states:

Entropy will always tend to increase in any isolated system that is not in equilibrium.

In simple terms this means that if you take any ordered system that is not in equilibrium, it will tend to increase its degree of freedom unless work is done to it. It is important that we are discussing overall entropy in this case – parts of a system may have entropy decreasing but this is because entropy has increased elsewhere.

In the combustion of methane, the entropy change calculated for the substances involved is negative – the entropy of the substances decreases. This appears to go against the second law of thermodynamics; however, the combustion releases a significant amount of heat energy to the surroundings. This increases the entropy of the surroundings, which more than compensates for the decrease in the entropy of the substances in the reaction.

Gibbs free energy, ΔG

In the previous topic, it is implied that chemical reactions tend to occur when the energy change is negative, i.e. they are exothermic. It is true that most chemical reactions are exothermic, but some endothermic reactions also occur. To explain this, both enthalpy and entropy need to be considered together, and these may be combined into the Gibbs free energy, ΔG. The relationship is:

$$\Delta G = \Delta H - T\Delta S$$

YOU SHOULD KNOW ›››

››› how entropy changes govern the feasibility of any changes

YOU SHOULD KNOW ›››

››› how to calculate Gibbs free energy

››› how Gibbs free energy can identify reactions that are feasible or not

▼ Study point

When undertaking calculations of Gibbs free energy the units of enthalpy and entropy must always be the same. As Gibbs free energy is usually quoted in kJ mol^{-1}, it is usually best to convert entropy values into kJ by dividing entropy values by 1000.

- ΔG is the change in the Gibbs free energy in kJ mol^{-1} or J mol^{-1}.

- ΔH is the enthalpy change in kJ mol^{-1} or J mol^{-1}.

- ΔS is the entropy change in kJ mol^{-1} K^{-1} or J mol^{-1} K^{-1}. The same units of energy (J or kJ) must be used throughout.

- T is the temperature in Kelvin (K).

If the free energy change is negative then a reaction will occur spontaneously, but if the free energy change is positive, the reaction will not occur spontaneously. If a reaction has a positive free energy change, we may be able to cause the reaction to occur by changing the temperature:

- If ΔS is positive (an increase in entropy) such as a gas being produced, then increasing the temperature will cause –TΔS to become more negative until the overall change is negative.

- If ΔS is negative (a decrease in entropy) such as a precipitation, then decreasing the temperature will cause –TΔS to become smaller and less positive until the overall change is negative.

Because the reaction will occur spontaneously if the free energy is negative, this means that a change that has a great increase in entropy will occur even though it is endothermic, as the entropy will be enough to make the Gibbs free energy change negative. Endothermic change can be physical changes, such as boiling or dissolving or chemical changes such as the thermal decomposition of some salts where gases are produced.

Worked example

The enthalpy change of combustion of methane is –890 kJ mol^{-1} with an entropy change of –4 J K^{-1} mol^{-1}. Show that the reaction is feasible at 298 K.

$$\Delta G = \Delta H - T\Delta S$$
$$= -890 - (298 \times -4 \div 1000) \qquad \text{The} \div 1000 \text{ converts J into kJ}$$
$$= -889 \text{ kJ mol}^{-1}$$

As the value is negative the reaction is feasible at 298K.

Some reactions are feasible at some temperatures but not at others. The temperature when the reaction becomes feasible is when the value of ΔG changes from positive to negative. At this point ΔG = 0. We can use this to find the minimum temperature when a reaction becomes feasible.

$$\Delta G = \Delta H - T\Delta S = 0 \qquad \text{so} \qquad \Delta H = T\Delta S$$

This rearranges to $\qquad\qquad T = \Delta H \div \Delta S$

Worked example

Find the minimum temperature at which a reaction will occur when ΔH is 46.0 kJ mol^{-1} and ΔS is 140 J K mol^{-1}.

$$T = 46 \div 0.140 = 329 \text{ K}$$

The reaction is feasible at temperatures above 329 K.

Equilibrium constants

Not all chemical reactions convert 100% of reactants into products. Many reactions are reversible and in these cases the systems reach equilibrium with a mixture of reactants and products formed. In the laboratory and in industry it is important to know how much product will be formed in a mixture to maximise this and to know whether a reaction is economically worthwhile. Changes in temperature affect the equilibrium mixture and using equilibrium constants allow chemists to quantify the contents of the equilibrium mixtures.

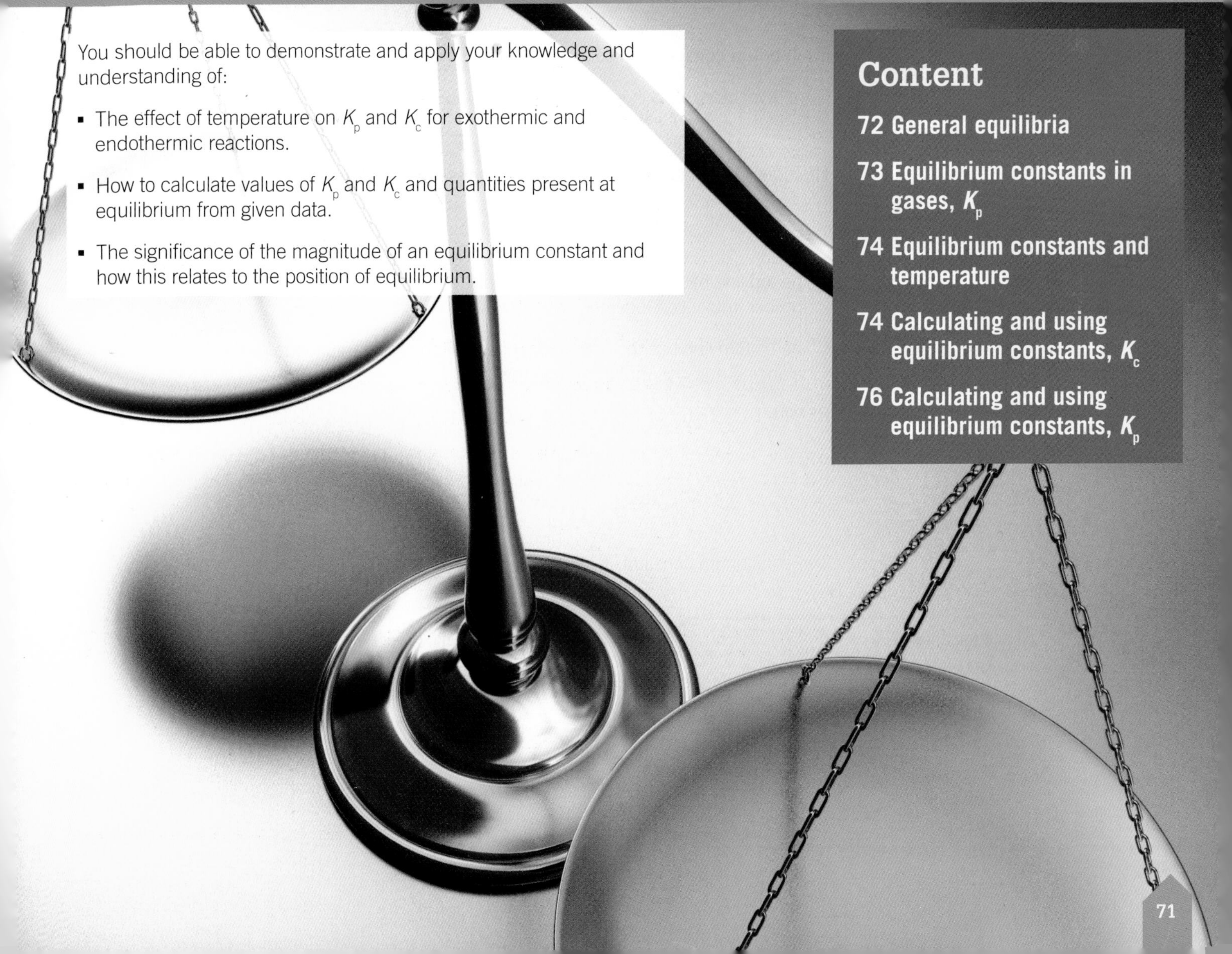

You should be able to demonstrate and apply your knowledge and understanding of:

- The effect of temperature on K_p and K_c for exothermic and endothermic reactions.

- How to calculate values of K_p and K_c and quantities present at equilibrium from given data.

- The significance of the magnitude of an equilibrium constant and how this relates to the position of equilibrium.

Content

PRACTICAL CHECK

The determination of an equilibrium
constant for a reaction is a **specified
practical task**. To do this you
need to measure or calculate the
concentrations of all species involved
in a system at equilibrium.

Link Equilibria and
equilibrium
constants were
covered initially in
AS Topic 1.7.

Key Term

A **dynamic equilibrium** is a
reversible reaction where the
rates of the forward and reverse
reactions are equal, so the
quantities of each substance stay
the same.

▼ **Study point**

You need to ensure that you are
confident using Le Chatelier's
principle to identify the way an
equilibrium shifts when temperature
or pressure changes. This was part
of the AS course.

General equilibria

A system in which none of the concentrations of reactants or products are changing is
described as being in equilibrium, with chemical equilibria being **dynamic equilibria** as
both forward and reverse reactions are occurring all the time. The equilibrium mixture
stays the same as long as the conditions stay the same, but may change when the
conditions change. Le Chatelier's principle gives a qualitative method of identifying the
effects of changing the conditions.

*Le Chatelier's principle states that if a system at dynamic equilibrium experiences a
change in its conditions then the equilibrium will shift to try to minimise change.*

Equilibrium constants

To work out the exact amount of reactants and products in a mixture at dynamic
equilibrium, we can use the equilibrium constant. In AS the equilibrium constant K_c was
introduced, but there is also a second equilibrium constant K_p:

- K_c is the equilibrium constant in terms of concentration, and is usually used for
reactions in solution, although it can be used for any reaction.

- K_p is the equilibrium constant in terms of partial gas pressures, and is used for reactions
only involving gases.

Equilibrium constants in solution, K_c

For a reversible reaction in solution of the type:

$$a\text{ A (aq)} \quad + \quad b\text{ B (aq)} \quad \rightleftharpoons \quad x\text{ X (aq)} \quad + \quad y\text{ Y (aq)}$$

The equilibrium constant for reactions in solution is:

$$K_c = \frac{[X]^x[Y]^y}{[A]^a[B]^b} \qquad \text{where [X] represents the concentration of X}$$

- The top line has the concentrations of all the products to the powers of the balancing
number, multiplied together.

- The bottom line has the concentrations of all the reactants to the powers of the
balancing number, multiplied together.

REMEMBER THE FORMULA HAS PRODUCTS OVER REACTANTS.

e.g. For the reaction below:

$$\text{Sn}^{4+}\text{ (aq)} \quad + \quad 2\text{Fe}^{2+}\text{ (aq)} \quad \rightleftharpoons \quad 2\text{Fe}^{3+}\text{ (aq)} + \text{Sn}^{2+}\text{ (aq)}$$

The equilibrium constant, K_c is given by: $K_c = \dfrac{[\text{Fe}^{3+}]^2[\text{Sn}^{2+}]}{[\text{Sn}^{4+}][\text{Fe}^{2+}]^2}$

26 Knowledge check

Write equilibrium constants K_c for these equilibria.

Reaction 1 H_2CO_3 (aq) $\rightleftharpoons$ $2\,H^+$ (aq) + $CO_3{}^{2-}$ (aq)

Reaction 2 $NH_4{}^+$ (aq)   + OH^- (aq) $\rightleftharpoons$ NH_4OH (aq)

Reaction 3 H_2O (aq)   + Cl_2 (aq) $\rightleftharpoons$ HCl(aq) + HOCl(aq)

Reaction 4 Fe^{3+} (aq)   + NCS^- (aq) $\rightleftharpoons$ $FeNCS^{2+}$ (aq)

Equilibrium constants in gases, K_p

In gases, we do not usually talk about the 'concentration of a gas', although it is possible to do this. We usually refer to the pressure of a gas, and we can do this for mixtures of gases as well. In a mixture of gases, the total pressure of the gas is the sum of the pressure exerted by each of the gases in the mixture. In the production of ammonia, there is a mixture of three gases: hydrogen, nitrogen and ammonia. In this case:

Pressure of gas mixture	=	pressure exerted by nitrogen	+	pressure exerted by hydrogen	+	pressure exerted by ammonia

We call the pressure exerted by an individual gas the partial pressure, and it is directly proportional to the concentration of the gas in the mixture. We write the partial pressure of an individual gas as p_{NH_3}. So the equation above can be written as:

$$pTOTAL = pH_2 + pN_2 + pNH_3$$

Because the partial pressures are related to the concentrations of each gas, we can use them in place of concentrations in an equilibrium constant. This equilibrium constant is called K_p. For a reversible reaction between gases of the type:

$$a\,A\,(g) \quad + \quad b\,B\,(g) \quad \rightleftharpoons \quad x\,X\,(g) \quad + \quad y\,Y\,(g)$$

The equilibrium constant for reactions in gases is:

$$K_p = \frac{p_X{}^x\, p_Y{}^y}{p_A{}^a\, p_B{}^b} \quad \text{where } p_X \text{ represents the partial pressure of X}$$

- The top line has the partial pressures of all the products to the powers of their balancing numbers, multiplied together.

- The bottom line has the partial pressures of all the reactants to the powers of their balancing numbers, multiplied together.

The equilibrium constant has products over reactants.

Interpreting equilibrium constants

Equilibrium constants can give us a guide to the degree that an equilibrium lies towards products or starting materials. An equilibrium that has equal amounts of starting materials and products would have $K_c = 1$.

- If K_c is a lot less than 1, then very few products are formed, and most of the mixture is starting materials. This is typically the case when ΔG for the reaction is positive, as the reaction will not occur spontaneously.

- If K_c is a lot more than 1, then most of the reactants have been converted into products. This is typically the case when ΔG for the reaction is negative, as the reaction will occur spontaneously.

Equilibrium and kinetic data can both give us a lot of information about chemical reactions; however, they tell us very different things:

Equilibrium data tells us about the relative stability of the reactants and products, and the free energy changes that occur between them. It tells us nothing about how the reaction occurs.

Reaction rates give us information about the changes that occur between the reactants and transition state. This allows us to deduce what is happening <u>during</u> the reaction, and the order in which individual bonds are broken and made, called the **reaction mechanism**. It tells us nothing about the relative stability of reactants and products.

YOU SHOULD KNOW › › ›

› › › the differences and similarities between K_c and K_p

Exam tip

Square brackets represent concentrations so these must not be used in any form in an expression of K_p as the values here are not concentrations.

Knowledge check 27

Write equilibrium constants K_p for these equilibria.

Reaction 1 $2\,SO_2\,(g) + O_2\,(g) \rightleftharpoons 2\,SO_3\,(g)$

Reaction 2 $CH_4\,(g) + H_2O\,(g) \rightleftharpoons CO\,(g) + 3\,H_2\,(g)$

Reaction 3 $H_2\,(g) + I_2\,(g) \rightleftharpoons 2\,HI\,(g)$

Reaction 4 $COCl_2\,(g) \rightleftharpoons CO\,(g) + Cl_2\,(g)$

Reaction 5 $PCl_5\,(g) \rightleftharpoons PCl_3\,(g) + Cl_2\,(g)$

Stretch & Challenge

Although pressure changes do not affect the value of the equilibrium constant, they may affect the position of equilibrium. If there are the same number of molecules of gas on both sides of the equilibrium then the effects of pressure cancel out and there is no effect on the position of equilibrium. If there are different numbers of molecules on both sides of the equilibrium then a change in pressure will affect the position of equilibrium even though the constant stays the same.

28 Knowledge check

Work out the value of K_c in the following system.

A mixture of Fe^{3+} and NCS^- which has 0.2 mol dm^{-3} of each at the start produces a mixture containing 0.15 mol dm^{-3} FeNCS^{2+}.

Fe^{3+} (aq) + NCS^- (aq) $\rightleftharpoons$ FeNCS^{2+} (aq)

Key Term

An **equimolar mixture** is one that has equal amounts of moles (and hence equal concentrations) of each substance.

Kinetic, energetic and equilibrium data are all considered for any industrial process. Any reaction must aim to produce the maximum amount of product as quickly as possible with the efficient use of energy to reduce costs. Often these factors cannot all be at their ideal values at the same time, and so a compromise must be reached which gets as close to each ideal value as possible.

- Equilibrium yield of product can be changed by altering concentration, pressure or temperature. The equilibrium constant will allow us to identify which concentration or pressure values favour high yield, and the energetics can allow us to identify what temperature will favour a higher yield.

- Rates may be maximised by increasing temperature, increasing pressure or adding a catalyst. In industry, these factors would be altered to increase rate, unless that factor would decrease yield.

- Energy calculations will identify how much energy needs to be input into the system for a reaction to occur, minimising the input of excess energy. Similarly the energy generated by an exothermic reaction may be calculated and this allows a company to decide whether it is economical to harness this energy or whether it merely needs to be removed as waste.

Equilibrium constants and temperature

Both types of equilibrium constant remain the same as long as the temperature is constant:

Temperature is the only thing that affects equilibrium constants.

The way temperature affects the equilibrium constants can be deduced using Le Chatelier's principle. For any exothermic reaction an increase in temperature will cause the equilibrium to shift in the endothermic direction, which will reduce the amount of products and increase the amount of reactants. This will decrease the value of the equilibrium constant.

For any endothermic reaction an increase in temperature will cause the equilibrium to shift in the endothermic direction which will increase the amount of products and decrease the amount of reactants. This will increase the value of the equilibrium constant.

- Exothermic reaction: Increasing temperature decreases K_c and K_p.
- Endothermic reaction: Increasing temperature increases K_c and K_p.

Calculating and using equilibrium constants, K_c

From information about the amounts of each substance in an equilibrium mixture, we can obtain values for the equilibrium constant.

Example:
An equilibrium mixture of the reactants H_2 and I_2 and product HI contains 0.0035 mol dm^{-3} of each reactant and 0.0235 mol dm^{-3} HI. Calculate the value of K_c.

Answer:
The reaction is:

$$H_2 \text{ (g)} + I_2 \text{ (g)} \rightleftharpoons 2HI \text{ (g)}$$

So the equilibrium constant is: $K_c = \dfrac{[HI]^2}{[H_2][I_2]}$

And putting the values in gives: $K_c = (0.0235)^2 / (0.0035 \times 0.0035) = 45.1$

Because there are two concentrations on the top of the formula and two on the bottom, they cancel out and K_c **has no units.**

If the information given does not list the concentrations of every reactant and product at equilibrium, then you need to work these out. A common situation is to give the concentrations of each reactant at the start of the reaction and then give the concentration of *one* product at equilibrium.

Exam tip

When calculating the values of concentrations at equilibrium, remember that the numbers of moles of compounds are not conserved in a reaction. It is possible to get more moles of products than there are of reactants.

Worked example

If an equimolar solution of A and B where the concentration of each is 0.5 mol dm^{-3} is allowed to reach equilibrium then the equilibrium mixture contains 0.2 mol dm^{-3} of D. Calculate the value of K_c.

$$A + B \rightarrow 2C + D$$

	[A]	[B]	[C]	[D]
At start	0.5	0.5	0	0
At equilibrium	0.3	0.3	0.4	0.2

At the start we only have A and B, both with concentration 0.5 mol dm^{-3}.

At equilibrium we have [D] = 0.2, but since 2C are made when each D is made then [C] = 0.4 mol dm^{-3}.

To make 0.2 D we must use up 0.2 A and 0.2 B, leaving 0.3 of each behind.

We now must write an expression for K_c and put these values into it to get the value of K_c.

$$K_c = \frac{[C]^2[D]}{[A][B]} = \frac{0.4^2 \times 0.2}{0.3 \times 0.3} = \textbf{0.36 mol dm}^{-3}$$

There are three concentration terms in the numerator and two in the denominator. These cancel leaving one set of concentration units for the equilibrium constant.

Exam tip

When writing equilibrium constants, include all charges within the square brackets. It is common to see charges incorrectly placed outside, such as $[NH_4]^+$.

Using values of K_c

Equilibrium constants can be used to calculate the amounts of different reactants in a mixture. If given the value of an equilibrium constant, it is possible to calculate the percentage of each substance at equilibrium.

Worked example

The equilibrium constant, K_c, for the reaction below is 8 mol dm^{-3}. If there is 2 mol dm^{-3} of N_2O_4 in an equilibrium mixture, what concentration of NO_2 is present?

$$N_2O_4 \text{ (g)} \rightleftharpoons 2NO_2 \text{ (g)}$$

Step 1: Work out the expression for K_c in terms of concentration.

$$K_c = \frac{[NO_2]^2}{[N_2O_4]}$$

Step 2: Put the numbers into the equation:

$$8 = \frac{[NO_2]^2}{2} \quad \text{so } [NO_2]^2 = 16 \quad \text{giving } \textbf{[NO}_2\textbf{] = 4 mol dm}^{-3}$$

YOU SHOULD KNOW › › ›

› › › how to calculate the value of K_p

› › › how to find the units of K_p

▼ **Study point**

Pressure can be measured in Pa, kPa or in atmospheres. These calculations work for all three, but the final unit must match the units used. If pressure values are given in units different to those required in the answer then do the conversion prior to placing the numbers in an expression for K_p

29 Knowledge check

An equimolar mixture of H_2 and I_2 has a total pressure of 101000 Pa. The mixture reaches dynamic equilibrium, which contains HI with a partial pressure of 37500 Pa. Calculate the value of K_p.

$$H_2\,(g) + I_2\,(g) \rightleftharpoons 2HI\,(g)$$

▼ **Study point**

The units of the equilibrium constant depend on the units of pressure used. If the pressure is in Pascals then the units of K_p will be in multiples of Pa – they may commonly be Pa^{-2}, Pa^{-1}, Pa or Pa^2. The units for each partial pressure on the top of the expression can cancel with any on the bottom to leave the units of the expression. If there are the same number of molecules on both sides of the reversible reaction then there are the same numbers on the top and bottom, which all cancel and leave no units .

Calculating and using equilibrium constants, K_p

From information about the partial pressures of each gas in an equilibrium mixture, it is possible to obtain values for the equilibrium constant K_p as well. The partial pressures represent the part of the total pressure exerted by a particular gas.

$$\text{Partial pressure} = \%\ \text{of a particular gas} \times \text{pressure}$$

$$\text{Partial pressure} = \text{Pressure of a particular gas in a mixture}$$

In a straightforward calculation, the partial pressures of all the substances present in an equilibrium mixture are provided and these simply need to be placed into the expression for the equilibrium constant.

Worked example

Ammonia is produced from hydrogen and nitrogen gases in the Haber process. A mixture is found to contain 300 Pa partial pressure of both nitrogen and hydrogen gases and 4230 Pa partial pressure of ammonia. Calculate the value of K_p under these conditions.

$$K_p = \frac{p_{NH_3}^2}{p_{N_2}\,p_{H_2}^3} \quad \text{where } p_x \text{ represents the partial pressure of X}$$

Substituting the values above gives:

$$K_p = = \frac{4230^2}{300 \times 300^3} = 2.2 \times 10^{-3}\ Pa^{-2}$$

When measuring and calculating a value for K_p experimentally, it is more likely that you will know the initial pressures of the gas(es) as these can be easily measured. Measurement of one gas in the equilibrium mixture will then allow the partial pressures of all to be found and hence K_p can be calculated.

Worked example

A sample of pure PCl_5 with a partial pressure of 1.01×10^6 Pa was introduced into a vessel. The equilibrium below occurred, producing a partial pressure of 4.02×10^4 Pa of PCl_3.

$$PCl_5\,(g) \rightleftharpoons PCl_3\,(g) + Cl_2\,(g)$$

Calculate the value of K_p at this temperature.

First, the values for the partial pressures of PCl_5 and Cl_2 must be calculated.

Cl_2: When one mole of PCl_3 is produced, 1 mole of Cl_2 is also produced so a partial pressure of 4.02×10^4 for PCl_3 means the partial pressure of Cl_2 will be the same.

PCl_5: When 4.02×10^4 Pa of PCl_3 is produced, then 4.02×10^4 Pa of PCl_5 must have decomposed, leaving $1.01 \times 10^6 - 4.02 \times 10^4$ Pa $= 9.698 \times 10^5$ Pa.

Next we place these in the expression for K_p:

$$K_p = \frac{p_{Cl_2} \times p_{PCl_3}}{p_{PCl_5}} = \frac{4.02 \times 10^4 \times 4.02 \times 10^4}{9.698 \times 10^5} = 1666\ Pa$$

Acid-base equilibria

Some acids and bases are amongst the most familiar compounds; however, the range of acidic and basic compounds is very large. These include both strong and weak acids and bases and the properties of these can be very different. Weak acids such as ethanoic acid form a common part of our diet, but strong acids such as sulfuric acid can be very corrosive and harmful to living things.

Acid-base reactions can be reversible and set up dynamic equilibria. The concepts of general equilibria can be applied to acids and bases to find how these substances will behave. In this topic equilibria from weak acids, weak bases and buffers are studied.

You should be able to demonstrate and apply your knowledge and understanding of:

- Lowry–Brønsted theory of acids and bases and the differences in behaviour between strong and weak acids and bases explained in terms of the acid dissociation constant, K_a.

- The significance of the ionic product of water, K_w and how to use pH, K_w, K_a and pK_a in calculations involving strong and weak acids and pH and K_w in calculations involving strong bases.

- The shapes of the titration curves for strong acid/strong base, strong acid/weak base, weak acid/strong base and weak acid/weak base systems and how suitable indicators are selected for acid-base titrations.

- The mode of action of buffer solutions and how to use pH, K_w, K_a and pK_a in buffer calculations.

- The importance of buffer solutions in living systems and industrial processes.

- The acidity and basicity of some salt solutions and the concept of hydrolysis of salts of a strong acid/strong base, a strong acid/weak base and a weak acid/ strong base.

Content

Acids and bases

There are a few definitions of acids and bases in chemistry; however, one of the most common and most useful is the Lowry–Brønsted definition.

> An acid is a substance that releases or provides H$^+$ ions, i.e. it is an H$^+$ donor.

A base in the same theory is:

> A base is any substance that removes or accepts H$^+$ ions, i.e. it is an H$^+$ acceptor.

Strong and weak acids and bases

The differences between strong and weak acids were first noted in terms of pH, but a better approach is to work with the degree of dissociation of the acid.

A strong acid is one that almost totally dissociates (splits up) into H$^+$ ions and negative ions in solution in water, e.g. hydrochloric acid, HCl:

$$HCl\ (aq) \rightarrow H^+\ (aq) + Cl^-\ (aq)$$

A weak acid is one that only partially dissociates into H$^+$ ions and negative ions in water. The free ions are in equilibrium with the undissociated acid molecule, e.g. ethanoic acid, CH_3COOH:

$$CH_3COOH\ (aq) \rightleftharpoons H^+\ (aq) + CH_3COO^-\ (aq)$$

This leads to the differences in pH, so a 1 mol dm^{-3} solution of a strong acid has a pH of 0, whilst a 1 mol dm^{-3} solution of a particular weak acid has a pH of 4.0, which represents 10000 times fewer free H$^+$ ions.

Reviewing pH

The strengths of acids are usually quoted on the pH scale. This ranges from 0 (strong acid) to 14 (strong alkali) through 7, which is neutral. We can measure the pH by using a pH probe, which will give a value for the pH for the solution, or more simply we can use an indicator or pH paper to obtain a guide to the pH value.

| 0 | 1 | 2 | 3 | 4 | 5 | 6 | 7 | 8 | 9 | 10 | 11 | 12 | 13 | 14 |

Strong acid   **Weak acid**   **Neutral**   **Weak alkali**   **Strong alkali**

Acids have pH values below 7.
In simple terms, the further a solution's pH value is below neutral (7), the stronger the acid.

Alkalis have pH values above 7.
In simple terms, the further a solution's pH value is above neutral (7), the stronger the alkali.

The numbers on the pH scale are obtained from the concentration of H$^+$ (aq) ions.

$$pH = -\log[H^+(aq)] \qquad \text{where log means } \log_{10}$$

Note: the value of $\log[10^x]$ is x, so if $[H^+] = 10^{-7}$, as it is for water, then $pH = -\log[10^{-7}] = 7$

Therefore:

- A change of one pH unit is equivalent to a 10 times change in H$^+$ concentration, so 2 pH units are 100 times, 3 represent 1000 times.

- The minus sign means that a higher pH means a lower H$^+$ concentration.

Acid dissociation constants, K_a

When an acid dissociates, it is an equilibrium process, and so it has an equilibrium constant.

$$HA\ (aq) \rightleftharpoons H^+(aq) + A^-\ (aq)$$

For the equilibrium above, $K_c = \dfrac{[H^+(aq)][A^-(aq)]}{[HA(aq)]}$ The units of this are always mol dm^{-3}

If we ignore the water involved we can produce the acid dissociation constant, K_a:

$$K_a = \frac{[H^+][A^-]}{[HA]}$$

The more dissociated the acid is, the more hydrogen ions and anions there will be, so the larger the value of K_a.

A weak acid will have a low value of K_a.

A strong acid will have a high value of K_a.

We can use the value of K_a for an acid to work out whether an acid is strong or weak. The table gives values of K_a for some acids:

Acid	Formula	K_a / mol dm^{-3}
Nitric acid	HNO_3	24
Sulfurous acid	H_2SO_3	1.4×10^{-2}
Methanoic acid	$HCOOH$	1.8×10^{-4}
Ethanoic acid	CH_3COOH	1.7×10^{-5}
Carbonic acid	H_2CO_3	4.5×10^{-7}

The range of values of K_a is large and so these values are often reported as pK_a values. The method of calculating this is similar to that used to calculate pH:

$$pK_a = -\log_{10}(K_a)$$

For some of the acids above this gives pK_a values of -1.38 for nitric acid, 1.85 for sulfurous acid and 4.77 for ethanoic acid.

Ionic product of water, K_w, and neutralisation

Water can be purified to remove all the impurities in it, to attempt to obtain 100% pure water. Even after all purification processes, water can still conduct a small amount of electricity, showing that there are still ions dissolved in it. We cannot remove these ions, as they are produced by the water itself. There is an equilibrium process in the water, where the water dissociates (breaks down) to form H^+ and OH^- ions:

$$H_2O\ (l) \rightleftharpoons H^+\ (aq) + OH^-\ (aq)$$

The reaction lies mainly to the left-hand side, so almost all the water exists as water molecules, with a very small amount of ions. The equilibrium constant of this reaction is:

$$K_c = \frac{[H^+][OH^-]}{[H_2O]}$$

Knowledge check 30

Work out the pH of the following solutions:

a) A solution that contains 0.2 mol.dm^{-3} H$^+$ ions.

b) A solution that contains 0.03 mol.dm^{-3} H$^+$ ions.

c) A solution that contains 10^{-9} mol.dm^{-3} H$^+$ ions.

d) A solution that contains 3×10^{-11} mol.dm^{-3} H$^+$ ions.

Exam tip

When describing weak and strong acids in an exam it is important to link the strength to dissociation or the value of K_a. Linking acid strength to pH is not sufficient.

Knowledge check 31

Work out the concentration of H$^+$ ions in the following solutions:

a) pH = 0.0

b) pH = 2.7

c) pH = 6.3

d) pH = 10.5

e) pH = 14.0

Knowledge check 32

Write expressions for the acid dissociation constants, K_a, for HClO and HCN.

Knowledge check

The value of K_w at 25°C is 1.0×10^{-14} mol^2 dm^{-6} and at 50°C is 5.5×10^{-14} mol^2 dm^{-6}. Explain what information this provides about the enthalpy change of the reaction.

Exam tip

Whenever you write a value for K_a and K_w you must include the correct units. These are always the same. These equilibrium constants are different from K_c and K_p as the units for K_c and K_p are different for different equilibria.

YOU SHOULD KNOW ›››

››› that the concentration of H$^+$ ions in a strong monobasic acid equals the concentration of the acid

››› how to calculate the concentration of H$^+$ ions for weak acids and strong bases

››› how to use pH = - log [H$^+$] to calculate the pH for any solution

Stretch & Challenge

A dibasic acid can donate two H$^+$ ions (H$_2$SO$_4$ for example) and a tribasic acid can donate three H$^+$ ions (H$_3$PO$_4$ for example). In these cases the concentration of H$^+$ ions will be higher than the concentration of the acid. If all the H$^+$ ions in a dibasic acid were released then the concentration of H$^+$ would be two times the concentration of the acid so [H$^+$] = 2 × [dibasic acid]. This is not always the case as the degree of dissociation of each H$^+$ can become lower with each one lost. This means the K_a for each proton gets smaller. In the case of H$_2$SO$_4$ the K_a for the first H$^+$ is 1×10^3 mol dm^{-3} and the second is 1×10^{-2} mol dm^{-3}.

Because the amount of water that dissociates is tiny, the concentration of water can be considered to be constant and we can combine it into the equilibrium constant and rename this K_w, the *ionic product of water*:

$$K_w = [H^+][OH^-] \qquad \text{Ionic product of water}$$

The value of K_w is a constant at a particular temperature, and at 25°C the value of K_w is approximately 10^{-14} mol^2 dm^{-6}. Since the amount of H$^+$ and OH$^-$ must be the same in pure water, we can work out the concentration of H$^+$ in the pure water.

Since $\qquad [H^+] = [OH^-], \qquad$ and $\qquad K_w = [H^+][OH^-]$

We can write: $\qquad\qquad\qquad\qquad\qquad\qquad K_w = [H^+]^2 = 10^{-14}$

Therefore $\qquad\qquad\qquad\qquad\qquad\qquad [H^+] = 10^{-7}$ mol dm^{-3}

When an acid reacts with a base, the reaction is the reverse of the equilibrium above and a neutral solution is produced in a neutralisation reaction. During the reaction, the free H$^+$ ions react with free OH$^-$ to produce water:

$$H^+ (aq) + OH^- (aq) \rightarrow H_2O (l)$$

This is the ionic equation for the reaction occurring in all neutralisation reactions. Ionic equations only list the ions actually involved in the reaction, and ions that remain unchanged at the end are not included. Because the neutralisation reaction is the same in all cases, the energy change is the same in every case, so all neutralisation reactions involving strong acids and bases cause the same temperature rise of the solutions.

Calculating pH

To calculate the pH of any solution, the concentration of H$^+$ ions must be found, and then the equation for pH must be applied to this. For all solutions whether they are acidic or basic, pH is defined as:

$$pH = -\log_{10}[H^+]$$

pH of strong acids

For a strong acid, all the hydrogen ions are released from the acid molecules, so the concentration of the acid gives the concentration of H$^+$ ions.

e.g. In 1.0 mol dm^{-3} hydrochloric acid, [H$^+$] = 1.0 mol dm^{-3}

In 0.2 mol dm^{-3} nitric acid, [H$^+$] = 0.2 mol dm^{-3}

This can then be used directly with the formula for pH.

Worked example

What is the pH of a 0.05 mol dm^{-3} solution of hydrochloric acid?

A solution of 0.05 mol dm^{-3} HCl will have the same concentration of H$^+$ ions, so [H$^+$] = 0.05.

$$pH = -\log_{10}[H^+] = -\log_{10}(0.05) = 1.30$$

pH of weak acids

In weak acids, not all the hydrogen ions are free, but we can use the K_a values to work out the concentration of H^+ ions. For ethanoic acid, the K_a value is 1.7×10^{-5} mol dm^{-3}, so to calculate the concentration of H^+ ions in a solution we see that:

$$K_a = \frac{[H^+][CH_3COO^-]}{[CH_3COOH]}$$

Since each CH_3COOH molecule that dissociates produces one CH_3COO^- and one H^+, then the concentrations of each must be equal. In the expression above we can state that $[H^+]$ = $[CH_3COOH]$ giving,

$$K_a = \frac{[H^+]^2}{[CH_3COOH]}$$

For a weak acid very little dissociation occurs, so it is possible to assume that the concentration of the acid molecules (CH_3COOH) present is the same as the concentration we put in. This allows us to rearrange the equation to give:

$$[H^+] = \sqrt[2]{K_a \times [acid]}$$

Worked example

What is the pH of a 0.5 mol dm^{-3} solution of ethanoic acid? ($K_a = 1.7 \times 10^{-5}$ mol dm^{-3})

$$[H^+] = \sqrt[2]{K_a \times [acid]}$$

$$[H^+] = \sqrt[2]{1.7 \times 10^{-5} \times 0.5}$$

$$[H^+] = 0.00292 \text{ mol dm}^{-3}$$

Applying the expression for pH $= -\log_{10}[H^+] = -\log_{10}(0.00292) = \underline{2.53}$

Study point

You need to be aware of some familiar strong acids such as nitric acid, sulfuric acid and hydrochloric acid and some weak acids such as ethanoic acid and other carboxylic acids. If you are provided with any other acids you will need to identify whether these are strong or weak by looking at the K_a value or by being told as part of a question.

Knowledge check 34

1. Work out the pH of the following solutions of ethanoic acid ($K_a = 1.7 \times 10^{-5}$ mol dm^{-3})
   (a) 0.05 mol dm^{-3}
   (b) 2 mol dm^{-3}
   (c) 0.01 mol dm^{-3}

2. Work out the pH of these solutions of chloric (I) acid, HClO ($K_a = 2.9 \times 10^{-8}$ mol dm^{-3})
   (a) 1 mol dm^{-3}
   (b) 0.5 mol dm^{-3}
   (c) 5 mol dm^{-3}

3. Which of these two acids is the stronger? Explain your answer in terms of K_a.

Working out K_a values for weak acids

Given the pH of a solution of known concentration, we can work out the value of K_a. This involves rearranging the expression for K_a in a similar manner to above.

Worked example

What is the K_a of an unknown monobasic acid if a 2.0 mol dm^{-3} solution has a pH of 4.5?

First convert the pH into a concentration of H^+ ions:

$$pH = -\log[H^+] \rightarrow [H^+] = 10^{(-pH)}$$

In this case: $[H^+] = 10^{-4.5} = 3.2 \times 10^{-5}$ mol dm^{-3}

Then use the formula for K_a, remembering that each acid molecule that dissociates produces one hydrogen ion and one anion, so $[A^-] = [H^+]$.

$$K_a = \frac{[H^+][A^-]}{[HA]}$$

$$K_a = (3.2 \times 10^{-5})^2 / 2$$

$$K_a = 5.12 \times 10^{-10} \text{ mol dm}^{-3}$$

Exam tip

The strength of an acid may be provided in the form of K_a or pK_a. K_a can be found from pK_a by using $K_a = 10^{-pKa}$.

Knowledge check 35

Work out the K_a values for the following weak acids:

a) HB where a 0.5 mol dm^{-3} solution has a pH of 2.9

b) HC which has a pH of 2.2 for a 1 mol dm^{-3} solution.

c) HD where a 0.5 mol dm^{-3} solution has a pH of 3.5

pH for strong bases

When a strong base dissolves in water, all the possible OH^- ions are produced so the concentration of the base gives the concentration of OH^-.

e.g.   In 1.0 mol dm^{-3} sodium hydroxide, $[OH^-] = 1.0$ mol dm^{-3}

         In 0.2 mol dm^{-3} potassium hydroxide, $[OH^-] = 0.2$ mol dm^{-3}

Using the ionic product of water, K_w, we can use this information to work out the concentration of H^+ ions in the same solution.

$$K_w = [H^+] \times [OH^-] \quad \text{so} \quad [H^+] = K_w \div [OH^-]$$

This provides a value for the concentration of H^+, which can then be used in the expression for pH.

Worked example

What is the pH of a solution of NaOH of concentration 0.1 mol dm^{-3}?

In this solution of NaOH, the concentration of OH^- ions is 0.1 mol dm^{-3}. Using K_w we can say:

$$[H^+][OH^-] = 10^{-14}$$

so $[H^+] \times 0.1 = 10^{-14}$

so $[H^+] = 10^{-13}$ mol dm^{-3}

We can work out the pH from this value, with pH $= -\log_{10}[H^+] = -\log(10^{-13}) = 13$

Buffers

Buffers are solutions whose pH stays relatively constant as a small amount of an acid or alkali is added. The buffer solution maintains a nearly constant pH by removing any added H^+ or OH^-.

How buffers work

Typically, a buffer solution is made from a mixture of:

- A weak acid, HA e.g. CH_3COOH.

- A salt of the same acid with a strong base, NaA e.g. CH_3COONa. This acts as a source of the anion A^-.

In the buffer solution, there is a high concentration of the anion as the sodium salt will dissociate completely:

$$CH_3COONa \rightarrow CH_3COO^- + Na^+$$

The weak acid dissociates partially, and the reversible reaction below sets up an equilibrium.

$$CH_3COOH \text{ (aq)} \rightleftharpoons H^+ \text{ (aq)} + CH_3COO^- \text{ (aq)}$$

36   **Knowledge check**

Work out the pH of the following concentration NaOH solutions:

(a) 1.0 mol dm^{-3}

(b) 0.2 mol dm^{-3}

(c) 0.05 mol dm^{-3}

(d) 0.003 mol dm^{-3}

YOU SHOULD KNOW › › ›

››› that buffers keep the pH constant when small amounts of acid or base are added

››› how to calculate the pH of any given buffer solution

Key Term

A **buffer** resists changes in pH as small amounts of acid and alkali are added.

▼ Study point

Buffers only resist changes in pH when SMALL amounts of acid or alkali are added. Addition of large amounts of acid or alkali does not allow the pH to remain constant.

The ethanoic acid is almost all in the undissociated form, as all the CH_3COO^- ions released from the sodium ethanoate dissociation forces the equilibrium to the left.

When an acid is added to a buffer

The amount of H^+ is increased, and this causes the equilibrium to shift to the left, removing the H^+ ions by reaction with CH_3COO^-.

$$CH_3COOH\ (aq) \rightleftharpoons H^+\ (aq) + CH_3COO^-\ (aq)$$

⬅ **H⁺ ions removed**

When an alkali is added to a buffer

The amount of OH^- is increased, and this removes some of the H^+ ions present. This causes the equilibrium to shift to the right, producing H^+ ions and CH_3COO^- from CH_3COOH. The H^+ ions replace those removed by reaction with the hydroxide ions.

$$CH_3COOH\ (aq) \rightleftharpoons H^+\ (aq) + CH_3COO^-\ (aq)$$

H⁺ ions replaced ➡

In both cases, the pH of the solution does not stay totally constant, but the buffer minimises any change when H^+ or OH^- are added with the change in pH being insignificant. If a larger amount of acid or alkali is added, these may react with a significant amount of the ethanoate ions or ethanoic acid molecules which then causes pH to change by a measurable amount.

Buffers are used where pH is very important, which is common for biological systems. They are therefore used for:

- Using or storing enzymes, to ensure the pH remains at the optimum value.

- Storage of biological molecules, such as pharmaceuticals, which will be denatured at the incorrect pH.

Some industrial processes rely on biological molecules. The fermentation processes during baking and brewing can use buffers to keep the conditions appropriate for the living things to survive. This buffering often uses the weakly acidic solutions formed when carbon dioxide dissolves in water. The process of dyeing also uses buffers as the pH of the system can affect the colour and absorption of a dye.

Basic buffers

A similar buffer system for maintaining alkaline pH is based on a mixture of ammonium chloride and ammonia solution. The ammonium chloride dissociates completely, releasing all the ammonium ions.

$$NH_4Cl\ (aq) \rightarrow NH_4^+\ (aq) + Cl^-\ (aq)$$

The key equilibrium is:

$$NH_4^+ \rightleftharpoons NH_3 + H^+$$

- Addition of base removes H^+ ions and this causes the equilibrium to shift to the right to produce more H^+ ions.

- Addition of acid causes the equilibrium to shift to the left, and this removes the additional H^+ provided by the acid.

Knowledge check 37

Calculate the pH of the following buffer solutions:

(a) A mixture of 0.20 mol dm⁻³ CH_3COOH ($K_a = 1.7 \times 10^{-5}$ mol dm⁻³) and 0.10 mol dm⁻³ CH_3COONa.

(b) A mixture of 0.20 mol dm⁻³ CH_3COOH and 0.40 mol dm⁻³ CH_3COONa.

(c) A mixture of 1.0 mol dm⁻³ CH_3COOH and 0.2 mol dm⁻³ CH_3COONa.

(d) A mixture of 0.20 mol dm⁻³ H_2SO_3 ($K_a = 1.6 \times 10^{-2}$ mol dm⁻³) and 0.10 mol dm⁻³ $NaHSO_3$

▼ **Study point**

When a strong base is added gradually to a weak acid, such as during a titration, a salt forms. For example, adding sodium hydroxide to ethanoic acid produces sodium ethanoate. This means that a mixture of weak acid and a salt of a weak acid has been formed. This is a buffer being created as part of the reaction.

pH for buffers

To calculate the pH of a buffer, we need to know:

- The K_a value for the weak acid.

- The ratio of the concentrations of the acid and the salt.

We use the expression:

$$K_a = \frac{[H^+][A^-]}{[HA]}$$

By substituting for the values of K_a and the ratio of $[A^-]/[HA]$ we can work out the concentration of $[H^+]$ ions. This can then be converted into a value of pH.

In the buffer mixture, all the salt will dissociate and almost none of the acid will be dissociated. This means that it can be assumed that $[HA]$ is equal to the concentration of acid used, and $[A^-]$ is equal to the concentration of the salt.

Worked example

Work out the pH of a buffer that contains equal concentrations of ethanoic acid ($K_a = 1.7 \times 10^{-5}$ mol dm^{-3}) and sodium ethanoate.

Answer

Using the formula above, we substitute in the values above:

$$K_a = [H^+]\frac{[CH_3COO^-]}{[CH_3COOH]} \qquad \frac{[CH_3COO^-]}{[CH_3COOH]} = 1 \text{ as the two concentrations are the same}$$

$1.7 \times 10^{-5} = [H^+] \times 1$
$[H^+] = 1.7 \times 10^{-5}$ mol dm^{-3}

Convert this to pH using   pH $= -\log[H^+]$
$ = -\log(1.7 \times 10^{-5})$
pH $= \mathbf{4.77}$

Stretch & Challenge

Although the Henderson–Hasselbalch equation and the other approaches to calculate pH for buffers contain approximations, the same approximations are present in each. These are that all the anions come from the salt, and that none of the acid is dissociated. These are very good approximations and, although they are present, the answers calculated using them are generally very close to the true values. Deviations become significant when the weak acid is replaced by a stronger (but still 'weak' acid) or when the concentrations of the acid and salt are very low.

Henderson–Hasselbalch equation

It is possible to combine all the calculation steps for buffers into one expression. This is called the Henderson–Hasselbalch equation:

$$pH_{buffer} = pK_a + \log\frac{[SALT]}{[ACID]}$$

In this case the value of K_a (or pK_a) and the concentrations of both the salt and acid allow the pH of the buffer to be found. When the concentration of the salt is equal to the concentration of the salt then the log term can be simplified to log (1) which equals zero.

When the concentration of the salt equals the concentration of the acid, then pH $= -\log_{10}K_a = pK_a$

When the concentrations of the salt and acid are different we can use the same method as above. It is always the ratios of these two concentrations that is key, rather than the absolute values of the concentrations. If the concentration of the sodium ethanoate salt was double that of the ethanoic acid then the calculation gives:

$$1.7 \times 10^{-5} = [H^+] \times 2$$
$$[H^+] = 0.85 \times 10^{-5} \text{ mol dm}^{-3}$$

This can then be converted to pH giving a value of 5.07.

pH of salts

When salts are dissolved in water, many form neutral solutions; however, some salts are acidic salts, and others are basic salts.

- A salt produced from a strong acid and a strong alkali will form neutral solutions, e.g. NaCl. This is a neutral salt.

- A salt produced from a strong acid and a weak alkali will be an acidic salt, e.g. NH_4Cl.

- A salt produced by a weak acid and a strong alkali will be a basic salt, e.g. CH_3COONa.

YOU SHOULD KNOW › › ›

››› which salts are neutral and which are acidic or basic

››› how to explain why some salts do not form neutral solutions

Knowledge check 38

Ammonium sulfate is used as a fertiliser. Suggest a pH for a solution of ammonium sulfate explaining your reasons.

Why do we see these effects?

When ammonium chloride, NH_4Cl, dissolves, it produces free NH_4^+ and Cl^- ions. Since ammonia is a weak base, the following equilibrium will occur in solution:

$$NH_4^+ \text{ (aq)} \rightleftharpoons NH_3 \text{ (aq)} + H^+ \text{ (aq)}$$

This releases free H^+ ions in solution, making the solution slightly acidic. As the concentration of H^+ ions is increased, the pH of the solution is decreased so that it is slightly lower than 7.

When sodium ethanoate, CH_3COONa, dissolves it produces free CH_3COO^- and Na^+. Since the ethanoic acid is a weak acid, the following equilibrium is always present when the ethanoate ion is in aqueous solution.

$$H^+ \text{ (aq)} + CH_3COO^- \text{ (aq)} \rightleftharpoons CH_3COOH \text{ (aq)}$$

In this case, the equilibrium removes some H^+ ions from the water, producing a slightly alkaline solution. As the concentration of H^+ ions is decreased, the pH increases slightly above 7.

▲ The acidic salt ammonium chloride is formed immediately when the weakly basic gas ammonia mixes with the strongly acidic hydrogen chloride gas.

Acid-base titration curves

When a base is added to an acid, a neutralisation reaction occurs, according to the equation:

$$H^+ (aq) + OH^- (aq) \rightarrow H_2O (l)$$

This is the reaction that occurs during acid-base titrations. The effect of this is to reduce the concentration of H^+ ions, and therefore increase the pH. The increase in pH is not a straight line, however, and it depends on whether the acid and alkali are strong or weak.

YOU SHOULD KNOW › › ›

››› how to undertake an acid-base titration.

Exam tip

All the curves shown here are for bases added to acids. This means that the pH starts low (acidic) and increases to a high value (bases). Titrations can also be undertaken by adding acid to alkali. In these cases the curves will appear similar but in reverse, with the initial pH high and decreasing in a similar pattern to that seen in the curves here

Strong acid–strong base

The titration curve for a strong acid with a strong alkali, e.g. HCl with NaOH of the same concentration, is shown in the graph below.

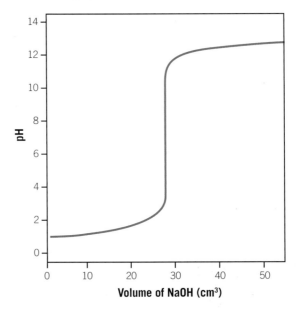

In this case, a 0.1 mol dm^{-3} solution of NaOH is added to 25 cm^3 of a solution of 0.1 mol dm^{-3} hydrochloric acid.

- The graph starts at pH 1, the pH of 0.1 mol dm^{-3} solution of a strong acid.

- There is a slow gradual increase in pH as the first 20 cm^3 is added.

- There is a sudden increase from about pH 2 to pH 12 as a very small volume of base is added around 25 cm^3, which is approximately vertical – use a ruler for this.

- There is then a slow gradual increase in pH as the last 20 cm^3 of base is added.

- The graph ends at just below pH 13.

The vertical region of the curve occurs when the number of moles of alkali added equals the number of moles of acid in the original solution. This is called the equivalence point – when the concentrations of the two solutions are the same it will occur when the volume of alkali added is equal to the volume of acid.

The pattern is always similar to this for a strong acid with a strong base, but when a weak acid is used the acid quadrant (from pH 0–7) is changed and when a weak alkali is used the alkali quadrant (pH 7–14) is changed. The pattern is changed by the fact that the molecules are not totally dissociated. These give different patterns, with the sudden increase in pH being much smaller.

Weak acid–strong base

The titration curve for a weak acid with a strong alkali, e.g. ethanoic acid with NaOH of the same concentration, is shown in the graph below.

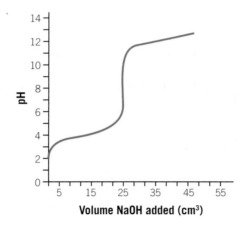

Key points

The pH increases gradually to about 4, as the base is added. When the volume of sodium hydroxide is about half the volume of acid, and hence the number of moles of sodium hydroxide is half the number of moles of acid, the pH levels off. This is because a mixture is formed containing the unreacted acid and the salt formed by neutralisation of the acid, and this acts as a buffer. The pH therefore levels out slightly over a volume range of about 5 cm^3.

The pH then increases gradually towards pH 7, when volume of base added equals volume of acid before increasing vertically to about pH 12. The pH gradually increases up to about between 13 and 14.

Strong acid–weak base

The titration curve for a strong acid with a weak alkali, e.g. hydrochloric acid with ammonia of the same concentration, is shown in the graph below.

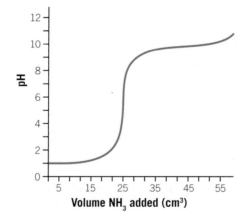

Key points

The pH up to 7 mirrors the original strong acid–strong base titration curve. After pH 7, the line becomes smoother and then levels off at a volume of about 35–45 cm^3 due to the buffer effect. The pH then increases gradually up to a pH of about 12.

Exam tip

It is often useful to label the buffer region of the weak acid–strong base titration curve so that it is clear to any examiner.

Study point

The terms equivalence point and end point are used interchangeably in many texts. Although both very similar, they are not the same. The **equivalence point** is the point when the number of moles of alkali added is equal to the number of moles of acid. The **end point** is the point at which an indicator changes colour in a titration.

Exam tip

When sketching any of the titration curves, it is important to start by noting any points that are known. These include:

The pH of the initial acid (at a volume of alkali of 0 cm^3).

The pH at half neutralisation (for weak acid–strong base calculations).

The pH at the equivalence point (7 for a strong acid–strong alkali titration).

Weak acid–weak base

The titration curve for a weak acid with a weak alkali, e.g. ethanoic acid with ammonia of the same concentration, is shown in the graph below.

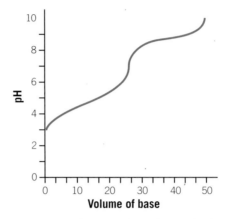

Titration of a weak base into a weak acid

The graph for weak acids with weak bases lacks the clear vertical region that is present in the other graphs. This makes it much harder to study using an indicator in titration. In place of an indicator a pH probe is used, measuring the pH throughout the titration. A plot of the data is then used to identify the equivalence point, as this is the point of inflection.

Study point

All these diagrams are plotted for concentrations of acid and base that are the same. If a titration is undertaken with different concentrations of acid and base, the shape of the plot will be unchanged but the graph will be compressed along the volume axis (when the base has a higher concentration) or extended along the volume axis (when the acid has a higher concentration). Use the volume when the vertical region occurs to find the equivalence point and this will tell you whether the concentrations of the two are the same, as it will occur at the same volume of base as the original volume of acid.

Stretch & Challenge

The curves already seen are drawn for monobasic acids only, such as HCl or HNO_3. Dibasic acids such as H_2SO_4 lose each hydrogen in turn and so there are two equivalence points, with tribasic acids showing three equivalence points. The graph below shows what this pattern would look like for a tribasic acid.

This graph allows us to check our calculations as the volume needed for the first equivalence point should be half that for the second, with the third value being three times the original.

Obtaining data from titration curves

Equivalence points

Titration curves can be used to find the volume of alkali needed to neutralise the acid. For titration curves where there are vertical regions these mark the volume required for neutralisation. The value obtained can be used in the titration calculations to find the concentration of one solution.

pH of salt formed

The pH at the end point of each of these titrations can be found from the midpoint of the vertical region. In the case of strong acid–strong base this will be 7; however, this will shift away from neutral when we use a weak acid or a weak base. At the end point the solution only includes a salt, and the salts formed from weak acids are basic whilst those formed from weak alkalis are acidic. The pH at neutralisation is equal to the pH of the salt solution.

pK_a of a weak acid

In the discussion of buffers the pH of a buffer was expressed as:

$$pH_{buffer} = pK_a + \log \frac{[SALT]}{[ACID]}$$

When half the volume of base needed for neutralisation is added to the acid, half the acid will have been converted into salt. This means that the concentration of the salt will equal the concentration of the acid, and so the log term would be log (1) which equals zero. This simplifies the equation above to:

$$pH_{buffer} = pK_a$$

So the pK_a equals the pH at the point that half the alkali has been added for neutralisation.

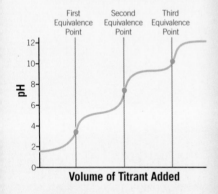

Indicators

Indicators are substances that change colour as the pH changes. To do this they must be weak acids, with the original molecule and dissociated ions having different colours.

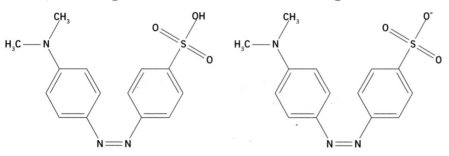

Methyl orange (red form)
In acid

Methyl orange (orange form)
In alkali

The solutions of these ions change colour as the pH of the solution changes, due to the relative amounts of the two forms changing.

- In acid, most of the indicator exists as the neutral form (HInd).

- In alkali, most of the indicator exists as the anion (Ind⁻).

The indicator does not suddenly change from one form to another at a specific pH – it changes over a range of pH values. This range is different for each indicator. The reason we see a sharp colour change in a titration is that the pH of the solution changes sharply at the end point. To make sure that the indicator is suitable, we have to check that the range that the indicator changes colour lies within this sharp increase in pH value.

Indicator	Approximate colour change range
Phenolphthalein	8.3–10.0
Bromothymol blue	6.0–7.5
Litmus	4.0–6.5
Methyl orange	3.2–4.4

Strong acid – strong base

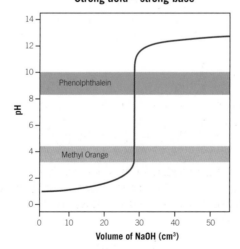

For a strong acid–strong base the pH increases sharply from 2 to 12. All the indicators change fully in this range, so any of them could be used, although the colour change of phenolphthalein means it is frequently the one chosen.

Key Terms

An **indicator** is a substance that has different colours in low and high pH solutions. This can be used to differentiate between an acid and an alkali but cannot distinguish between acids of different pH or alkalis of different pH.

Universal indicator is a solution that shows a range of colours as the pH changes, so it can be used to find the pH of a particular solution.

Link Acid-base titrations in AS Topic 1.7

Stretch & Challenge

Dibasic acids and bases show two different equivalence points, both having small vertical regions. Indicators can be selected that match each separate vertical region, which allows a titration to be performed with one indicator to find the first equivalence point, and then a second indicator can be added to find the second equivalence point. A similar approach can be used to analyse a mixture of a strong and weak acid (or a strong and weak alkali).

Weak acid – strong base

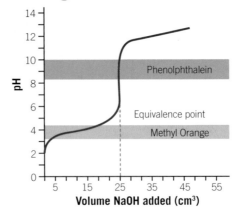

The pH titration curve of weak acid (CH$_3$COOH) and strong base (NaOH)

For a weak acid–strong base the pH increases sharply from 5 to 12 so phenolphthalein or bromothymol blue can be used as they change colour completely in the right pH range. Methyl orange would not change colour at all in this vertical range – it would have changed colour before reaching this point. Phenolphthalein is the most commonly used indicator for this type of titration.

Strong acid – weak base

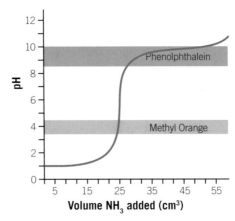

For a strong acid–weak base the pH increases sharply from 2 to 8. Methyl orange, litmus and bromothymol blue change fully in this range. Phenolphthalein starts to change at the end of this range, but it will not change fully, so we can't use it for a titration using a weak alkali. Methyl orange is the most commonly used indicator for this type of titration.

PRACTICAL CHECK

The titration of a weak acid–weak base using a pH probe is a specified practical task. This section explains why a pH probe is used rather than an indicator as is the case for all other types of titration. A weak acid–weak base titration is only used when no other method is available as the technique is more challenging than titration using an indicator.

Weak acid–weak base

There is no significant vertical area showing a significant and sudden change in pH. No indicator would therefore work and alternative methods must be used for titration. This is usually by using a pH probe.

3.1

1 Define the term oxidation. [1]

2 Show that the reaction between chlorine and Fe^{2+} is a redox reaction. [2]

$$2Fe^{2+}(aq) + Cl_2(g) \rightarrow 2Fe^{3+}(aq) + 2Cl^-(aq)$$

3 Identify the oxidising agent in the reaction below, giving a reason for your answer. [1]

$$2Na(s) + Br_2(g) \rightarrow 2NaBr(s)$$

4 Explain what is meant by the standard hydrogen electrode. [2]

5 Define the standard electrode potential. [2]

6 What is the function of the salt bridge? [1]

7 **(a)** Draw a diagram showing the apparatus required to measure the standard electrode potential for $Ni^{2+}(aq)|Ni(s)$. [3]

The standard electrode potential for this cell is given in the table below.

(b) Label the direction of electron flow on your diagram. [1]

(c) Label the positive electrode on your diagram. [1]

8 The table below gives **standard electrode potentials**, E^θ, for some systems for which the ion/electron half-equations are given.

Half-equation	E^θ / V
$Fe^{2+}(aq) + 2e^- \rightleftharpoons Fe(s)$	−0.44
$Ni^{2+}(aq) + 2e^- \rightleftharpoons Ni(s)$	−0.25
$H^+(aq) + e^- \rightleftharpoons \frac{1}{2}H_2(g)$	0.00
$Cu^{2+}(aq) + 2e^- \rightleftharpoons Cu(s)$	0.34
$\frac{1}{2}I_2(aq) + e^- \rightleftharpoons I^-(aq)$	0.54
$Ag^+(aq) + e^- \rightleftharpoons Ag(s)$	0.80

Using the information from the table, answer the following questions:

(a) State the strongest reducing agent. [1]

(b) Find the EMF measured when the $Fe^{2+}(aq)|Fe(s)$ and $Ni^{2+}(aq)|Ni(s)$ are connected. [1]

(c) State all the species that can be oxidised by aqueous iodine. [1]

(d) State, giving a reason, whether you would expect a reaction to occur if a piece of nickel were placed in an aqueous solution of copper(II) sulfate. [2]

(e) State, giving a reason, whether acid will corrode nickel metal. [2]

9 Iron metal can corrode in water in the presence of air by a redox reaction.

$$2Fe \text{ (s)} + O_2 \text{ (g)} + 2H_2O \text{ (l)} \rightarrow 2Fe^{2+} \text{ (aq)} + 4OH^- \text{ (aq)}$$

(a) Use the changes in oxidation numbers (states) to determine which reactant is being oxidised and which reduced in the above equation. [2]

(b) An equivalent corrosion reaction could be written for silver, Ag:

$$4Ag \text{ (s)} + O_2 \text{ (g)} + 2H_2O \text{ (l)} \rightarrow 4Ag^+ \text{ (aq)} + 4OH^- \text{ (aq)}$$

Given the standard electrode potentials below, explain why the corrosion reaction for iron occurs but silver does not corrode. [2]

$$Fe^{2+} \text{ (aq)} + 2e^- \rightarrow Fe \text{ (s)} \qquad E = -0.44V$$
$$O_2 \text{ (g)} + 2H_2O \text{ (l)} + 4e^- \rightarrow 4OH^- \text{ (aq)} \qquad E = +0.40V$$
$$Ag^+ \text{ (aq)} + e^- \rightarrow Ag \text{ (s)} \qquad E = +0.80V$$

10 Hydrogen fuel cells are used in some vehicles and these are advertised as being good for the environment. Give a reason why the use of fuel cells is good for the environment and one environmental disadvantage of their use. [2]

11 Dichromate(VI) ions, $Cr_2O_7^{2-}$, react with iron(II) ions in acid solution according to the following equation.

$$Cr_2O_7^{2-} \text{ (aq)} + 14H^+ \text{ (aq)} + 6Fe^{2+} \text{ (aq)} \rightleftharpoons 2Cr^{3+} \text{ (aq)} + 7H_2O \text{ (l)} + 6Fe^{3+} \text{ (aq)}$$

This reaction can be used as the basis of an electrochemical cell where the standard electrode potentials of the two half-reactions are shown below.

$$Fe^{3+} \text{ (aq)} + e^- \rightleftharpoons Fe^{2+} \text{ (aq)} \qquad +0.77V$$
$$Cr_2O_7^{2-} \text{ (aq)} + 14H^+ \text{ (aq)} + 6e^- \rightleftharpoons 2Cr^{3+} \text{ (aq)} + 7H_2O \text{ (l)} \qquad +1.33V$$

(a) Calculate the EMF of the cell. [1]

(b) Platinum electrodes are used in the cell. Explain the purpose of these platinum electrodes. [1]

(c) Draw a labelled diagram to show a possible construction for the cell. Your labels should include:

- The apparatus used
- The reagents
- The positive and negative electrodes
- The direction of electron flow in the circuit. [5]

12 Vanadium(V)(aq), as VO_3^-, is yellow and can be reduced by zinc and aqueous acid producing a series of coloured solutions until the reduction stops with the formation of a violet solution. The reducing agent involves the Zn^{2+}(aq) / Zn(s) equilibrium.

Oxidation state of vanadium at start of reaction	Reaction	E^0 / V
+5	VO_3^- (aq) + 4H$^+$ (aq) + e $\rightleftharpoons$ VO^{2+} (aq) + 2H$_2$O (l)	+1.00
+4	VO^{2+} (aq) + 2H$^+$ (aq) + e $\rightleftharpoons$ V^{3+} (aq) + H$_2$O (l)	+0.34
+3	V^{3+} (aq) + e $\rightleftharpoons$ V^{2+} (aq)	−0.26
+2	V^{2+} (aq) + 2e $\rightleftharpoons$ V (s)	−1.13
	Zn^{2+} (aq) + 2e $\rightleftharpoons$ Zn (s)	−0.76
	Cu^{2+} (aq) + 2e $\rightleftharpoons$ Cu (s)	+0.34

(i) State the identity of the violet vanadium-containing solution produced in this reduction. Use standard electrode potentials to explain your answer. [3]

(ii) What is the standard potential of a cell formed from a standard $Zn^{2+}(aq)$ / $Zn(s)$ electrode and a standard $Cu^{2+}(aq)$ / $Cu(s)$ electrode? [1]

(iii) Write the equilibrium equation for the change occurring at the zinc electrode showing the direction in which the reaction proceeds. [1]

(iv) Use Le Chatelier's principle to predict the effect on the electrode potential of the zinc electrode of increasing the concentration of $Zn^{2+}(aq)$ in the electrode. Explain your answer. [2]

3.2

1 Write an ion-electron half-equation for the reduction of dichromate (VI) ions in acid solution, stating any colour change. [2]

2 Acidified potassium manganate(VII) can be used to oxidise ethanedioate ions, $C_2O_4^{2-}$. Use the two ion-electron half-equations below to write an ionic equation for the reaction. [1]

$$MnO_4^- + 8H^+ + 5e^- \rightleftharpoons Mn^{2+} + 4H_2O \quad \times 2$$
$$2CO_2 + 2e^- \rightleftharpoons C_2O_4^{2-} \quad \times 5$$

3 An alloy containing iron was analysed by redox titration. A sample of 0.190 g of the alloy was converted to a solution of iron(II) ions, Fe^{2+}, by dissolving in acid. The solution required 26.80 cm³ of a solution containing dichromate(VI) ions, $Cr_2O_7^{2-}$, of concentration 0.0162 mol dm⁻³, for oxidation of all the Fe^{2+} to iron(III) ions, Fe^{3+}.

(a) The ion/electron half–equation for the oxidation of iron(II) is

$$Fe^{3+}(aq) + e^- \rightarrow Fe^{2+}(aq)$$

Write the ion/electron half-equation for the reduction of the oxidising agent $Cr_2O_7^{2-}$ in acid solution. [1]

(b) Calculate the percentage by mass of iron in the alloy to an appropriate number of significant figures. [4]

4 Arsenic is a toxic element that in the past has been used in the form of the oxide As_4O_6 as a poison. Analysis of a sample containing arsenic oxides amongst other materials was undertaken by attempting to dissolve 50.0 g in water, which dissolved the arsenic oxide leaving the remainder as an undissolved solid.

(a) Give a method for separating the solution from the undissolved solids. [1]

(b) The solution containing the arsenic was made up to 250 cm³ and samples were titrated against a standard solution containing iodine. Arsenic(III) oxide reacts with iodine according to the following equation, giving an acidic solution.

$$As_4O_6(aq) + 4I_2(aq) + 4H_2O(l) \rightarrow 2As_2O_5(aq) + 8HI(aq)$$

(i) 20.0cm³ of a standard iodine solution of concentration 0.0500 mol dm⁻³ reacted with 25.0 cm³ of the arsenic containing solution. Calculate the number of moles of arsenic (III) oxide, As_4O_6, present in 25.0 cm³ of the solution. [2]

(ii) Use the answer to part (i) to calculate the total number of moles of arsenic(III) oxide, As_4O_6 present and hence the percentage, by mass, of arsenic(III) oxide in the original sample of mass 50.0 g. Give your answer to an appropriate number of significant figures. [3]

5 The concentration of $Fe^{2+}(aq)$ can be determined by titrating against standard potassium dichromate(VI) solution. In one experiment, a 25.0 cm³ sample of a solution containing Fe^{2+} was titrated against 0.0250 mol dm⁻³ potassium dichromate(VI) solution in excess acid, when 12.5 cm³ potassium dichromate(VI) solution was required to reach the end-point.

$$Cr_2O_7^{2-}(aq) + 14H^+(aq) + 6Fe^{2+}(aq) \rightarrow 2Cr^{3+}(aq) + 7H_2O(l) + 6Fe^{3+}(aq)$$

Calculate, to an appropriate number of significant figures, the concentration of the $Fe^{2+}(aq)$ solution. [3]

6 Sodium chlorate(I) is used in bleach. The concentration of sodium chlorate(I) in domestic bleach can be found by reacting the bleach with an acidified iodide solution to form iodine and then titrating with a thiosulfate solution.

(a) Name a suitable indicator for this reaction. [1]

(b) The equation for this reaction is given below.

$$ClO^-(aq) + 2H^+(aq) + 2I^-(aq) \rightarrow I_2(aq) + Cl^-(aq) + H_2O(l)$$

A 25.00 cm³ sample of domestic bleach was diluted to 250.0 cm³ in a volumetric flask. 25.00 cm³ of this solution was added to an excess of acidified potassium iodide and the iodine produced reacted with 20.40 cm³ of aqueous sodium thiosulfate of concentration 0.09200 mol dm⁻³.

(i) Write an equation for the reaction of I_2 with sodium thiosulfate solution. [1]

(ii) Use the equation above, together with your equation in (b)(i), to calculate the concentration of sodium chlorate(I) in the original bleach sample to an appropriate number of significant figures. [4]

7 A sample of a copper-containing fungicide was analysed to determine its copper content. Firstly, it was reacted with excess potassium iodide:

$$2Cu^{2+} + 4I^- \rightarrow 2CuI + I_2$$

and the iodine produced was then titrated against sodium thiosulfate solution.

$$I_2 + 2Na_2S_2O_3 \rightarrow 2NaI + Na_2S_4O_6$$

(i) Name the indicator used for the titration and state the colour change at the end-point. [2]

(ii) If a 31.2 g sample of the fungicide required 12.25 cm³ of sodium thiosulfate solution with concentration 0.100 mol dm⁻³ $Na_2S_2O_3$ to react with the liberated iodine, calculate the mass of copper in the sample and hence the %Cu by mass in the fungicide. [3]

8 The iron content of an alloy can be determined by a redox titration using acidified potassium dichromate(VI) solution, $K_2Cr_2O_7$. A piece of alloy of mass 1.870 g was dissolved completely in acid to form Fe^{2+} ions, and the solution made up to 250.0 cm³. A 25.00 cm³ sample of this solution was titrated against acidified $K_2Cr_2O_7$. This required 23.80 cm³ of $K_2Cr_2O_7$ solution of concentration 0.0200 mol dm⁻³ for complete reaction.

(i) The half-equations for the processes occurring are:

$$Cr_2O_7^{2-} + 14H^+ + 6e \rightarrow 2Cr^{3+} + 7H_2O$$
$$Fe^{3+} + e^- \rightarrow Fe^{2+}$$

Write an **ionic** equation for the reaction between Fe^{2+} ions and $Cr_2O_7^{2-}$ ions in acid solution. [1]

(ii) Calculate the number of moles of Fe^{2+} ions present in the 25.00 cm³ sample used in the titration. [2]

(iii) Calculate the percentage of iron in the original alloy sample. [2]

9 Halogens can also form compounds with a variety of oxidation states. Some of these including compounds of iodate(V), IO_3^-, behave as oxidising agents.

A student was investigating the reaction that occurs when iodate(V) oxidises iodide ions to produce iodine. Two possible equations were suggested.

$$IO_3^- + 6H^+ + 5I^- \rightarrow 3I_2 + 3H_2O \qquad \textbf{equation 1}$$
$$IO_3^- + 4H^+ + 4I^- \rightarrow IO^- + 2H_2O + 2I_2 \qquad \textbf{equation 2}$$

He prepared a solution of potassium iodate(V) by dissolving 0.978 g of KIO_3 in 250 cm³ of solution. He pipetted 25.0 cm³ of this solution into a conical flask, added excess potassium iodide and titrated the iodine produced with 0.100 mol dm⁻³ sodium thiosulfate solution, $Na_2S_2O_3$. A volume of 27.40 cm³ of this solution was needed to react with the iodate(V).

The equation for the reaction of thiosulfate with iodine is shown below.

$$2S_2O_3^{2-} + I_2 \rightarrow S_4O_6^{2-} + 2I^-$$

(i) Calculate the number of moles of thiosulfate used to react with the iodine. [1]

(ii) Deduce the number of moles of iodine present in the 25.0 cm³ sample. [1]

(iii) Calculate the number of moles of KIO_3 present in 250 cm³ of the original solution and hence the number of moles present in 25.0 cm³. [1]

(iv) Use your results from (ii) and (iii) to deduce which of equation 1 and equation 2 suggested above, correctly shows what happens when iodate(V) ions oxidise iodide ions. Show, by calculation, how you came to this conclusion. [2]

3.3

1 The table shows a section of the Periodic Table together with the maximum covalency for each element. Maximum covalency is the highest number of covalent bonds formed by each element, **excluding** coordinate covalent bonds.

Group 3	Group 4	Group 5	Group 6
B	C	N	O
3	4	3	2
Al	Si	P	S
3	4	5	6

(a) Explain why B and Al are both limited to a maximum covalency of 3 and why their compounds are **electron deficient**. [2]

(b) Explain why N has a maximum covalency of 3 but P in the same group has a maximum of 5. [2]

2 Aluminium oxide, Al_2O_3, is an **amphoteric** oxide. Explain the meaning of the term **amphoteric** and give **two** reactions, including equations, which demonstrate the amphoteric behaviour of aluminium oxide. [4]

3 Group IV elements can show oxidation states of +2 and +4 in their compounds. State, giving examples, how the relative stability of these oxidation states changes as the group is descended and give a reason for this trend. [3]

4 Write balanced equations for the following:

(a) **One** reaction in which lead(IV) oxide is an oxidising agent. [1]

(b) **Two** reactions which show the amphoteric behaviour of lead or one of its compounds. [2]

(c) **One** reaction in which carbon monoxide is a reducing agent. [1]

5   State what is observed in **each** of the following:

(a) Tetrachloromethane, CCl_4, is added to water.

(b) Silicon(IV) chloride, $SiCl_4$, is added to water.

Explain the difference in behaviour. [3]

6   Both boron nitride, BN, and carbon, C, form hexagonal graphite-type structures. Explain why:

- BN and C can both adopt the same hexagonal structure.

- both BN and C exhibit lubricating properties.

- C is an electrical conductor but BN is an insulator at room temperature. [6]

7   Both sodium chloride and sodium iodide react with concentrated sulfuric acid. The observations made during both reactions are very different. Discuss the reactions occurring. Your answer should include:

- The observations made during both reactions

- The identities of any products

- The reasons for any differences in the reactions that occur. [5]

8   Iron is usually extracted from iron(III) oxide, Fe_2O_3, in a blast furnace using carbon monoxide, CO, as a reducing agent, releasing metallic iron and the gas carbon dioxide.

(i)   Write the overall equation for this reaction. [1]

(ii) Explain in terms of oxidation states why carbon monoxide is considered to be the reducing agent in this reaction. [2]

(iii) Explain why carbon monoxide, CO, can be used as a reducing agent but the corresponding oxide of lead, PbO, cannot. [2]

9   (a) The diagram shows some of the reactions of lead compounds.

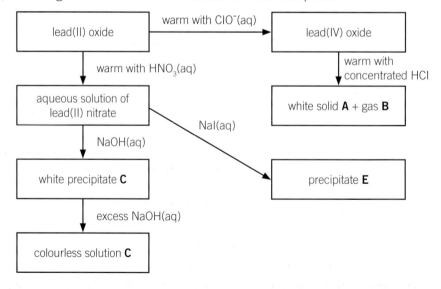

(a) (i) State the role of lead(IV) oxide in the reaction with concentrated hydrochloric acid. [1]

(ii) Name white solid A and gas B. [2]

(iii) Give the formula of the lead-containing species present in colourless solution D. [1]

(iv) Give the colour of precipitate E. [1]

(v) Write the equation for the formation of lead(II) nitrate from lead(II) oxide. [1]

(b) Carbon is the first element in Group 4. Two of its allotropes are diamond and graphite. A compound that forms structures corresponding to diamond and graphite is boron nitride.

(i) Describe the structure of graphite and explain why hexagonal boron nitride can adopt the same structure yet have different electrical conductivity properties. [4]

(ii) State one use for the cubic boron nitride structure. [1]

3.4

1 (a) State the full electron configurations of

(i) Chromium metal, Cr (ii) Chromium(III) ion, Cr^{3+} [2]

(b) The octahedral complex ion $[Cr(H_2O)_6]^{3+}$ is violet. Explain how the colour arises in this complex ion. [4]

2 A characteristic of these metals is the ability to form coloured ions.

(i) Give the electronic configuration of copper(I) ions, Cu^+, and state why copper(I) compounds are not usually coloured. [2]

(ii) Copper(II) ions can form the following coloured complexes:

$[Cu(H_2O)_6]^{2+}$ and $[CuCl_4]^{2-}$

I State the shape and colour for **each** complex. [4]

II Describe the bonding in copper(II) complexes. [2]

3 (a) Using the convention of representing electrons by arrows in boxes, give the outer electronic configuration of an iron(III) ion, Fe^{3+}. [1]

(b) Hydrated crystals of iron(III) chloride contain the purple $[Fe(H_2O)_6]^{3+}$ ion, which has the same shape as the $[Cu(H_2O)_6]^{2+}$ ion. Sketch the shape of the $[Fe(H_2O)_6]^{3+}$ ion. [1]

(c) Explain why aqueous ions such as $[Fe(H_2O)_6]^{3+}$ and $[Cu(H_2O)_6]^{2+}$ are coloured. [3]

(d) Describe what is **seen** when an aqueous solution of sodium hydroxide is added, dropwise, to a solution containing Fe^{3+} (aq) ions until an **excess** of sodium hydroxide is present.

You should give an equation for any reaction that occurs. [3]

4 (a) Give the **full** electron configuration of

(i) an iron atom, Fe,   (ii) an iron(II) cation, Fe^{2+}. [2]

(b) Iron forms Fe^{3+} as well as Fe^{2+} ions. Explain why transition metals such as iron form compounds with more than one oxidation state. [2]

(c) Iron forms a green octahedral complex ion $[Fe(H_2O)_6]^{2+}$. Describe the bonding between a water molecule, H_2O, and the Fe^{2+} cation in the complex ion. [2]

5 Bordeaux Mixture is one of the earliest fungicides, first used about 1885. It can be prepared by mixing copper sulfate solution with excess limewater (calcium hydroxide solution).

(i) State what you would observe when copper sulfate solution is mixed with limewater. [2]

(ii) Write an equation for the reaction that occurs. [1]

6 (a) (i) State what is meant by the term transition element. [1]

(ii) Explain why both iron and copper are classed as transition elements, whilst zinc is not. [1]

(b) Transition elements such as copper frequently form coloured complexes. Copper(II) complexes are usually blue, but the exact colour can vary, with $[Cu(H_2O)_6]^{2+}$ being pale blue and $[Cu(NH_3)_4(H_2O)_2]^{2+}$ being royal blue. Copper(I) complexes are usually colourless. Explain why transition metal complexes are usually coloured.

Your answer should include details of:

• The origin of colour in transition metal complexes

• Why the copper(II) species above are coloured blue

• Why the colours seen in different copper(II) complexes are different

• Why copper(I) complexes do not form coloured compounds. [6]

7 When concentrated hydrochloric acid is added to a pink aqueous solution of cobalt(II) chloride, the colour changes to blue. Cobalt takes part in an equilibrium reaction.

$$[Co(H_2O)_6]^{2+} (aq) + 4Cl^- (aq) \rightleftharpoons [CoCl_4]^{2-} (aq) + 6H_2O (l)$$

(i) What is the oxidation state of cobalt in $[CoCl_4]^{2-}$? [1]

(ii) What type of bonding is present in $[CoCl_4]^{2-}$? [1]

(iii) Use the equation to identify the ions responsible for the pink and blue colours described above. Explain why the colour change occurs when concentrated hydrochloric acid is added to the pink solution. [3]

(iv) Draw diagrams to clearly show the shape of the $[Co(H_2O)_6]^{2+}$ ion and the $[CoCl_4]^{2-}$ ion. [2]

3.5

1 The gaseous reaction between carbon monoxide, CO, and nitrogen dioxide, NO_2, is shown by the equation below.

$$CO (g) + NO_2 (g) \rightarrow CO_2 (g) + NO (g)$$

(a) At temperatures below 500 K, experiments have shown the rate equation to be given by

$$Rate = k [NO_2]^2$$

The mechanism can be represented as two stages, one of which is the **rate-determining step**:

Stage 1 $NO_2 (g) + NO_2 (g) \rightarrow$ Intermediates

Stage 2   Intermediates + CO (g) $\rightarrow$ NO (g) + CO_2 (g) + NO_2 (g)

Explain the term **rate-determining step** and, giving your reasoning, state which of the above two stages is the rate-determining step in this reaction. [2]

(b) At higher temperatures, the products are the same but the reaction proceeds by a different mechanism. Experiments at a temperature of 600 K produced the following results.

Initial rate of reaction / mol dm^{-3} s^{-1}	Initial concentration of NO_2 $[NO_2]$ / mol dm^{-3}	Initial concentration of CO [CO] / mol dm^{-3}
1.12×10^{-4}	0.050	0.050
2.24×10^{-4}	0.050	0.100
4.48×10^{-4}	0.100	0.100
8.96×10^{-4}	0.100	0.200

(i) Determine the order of reaction with respect to NO_2 and the order with respect to CO and state the rate equation for this reaction at 600 K. [3]

(ii) Calculate the value of the rate constant, k, at 600 K, and give its units. [2]

(iii) Suggest a rate-determining step which fits the rate equation at 600 K. [1]

2 The thermal decomposition of ozone is shown in the equation below.

$$2O_3 (g) \rightarrow 2O_3 (g)$$

Kinetic studies have shown that the reaction is second order with respect to ozone.

(a) Write the rate equation for the reaction and use it to explain the term **order of reaction**. [2]

(b) The value of the rate constant at 298 K is 3.4×10^{-5} dm^3 mol^{-1} s^{-1}. If the concentration of ozone is 0.023 mol dm^{-3}, calculate the rate of reaction at 298 K and state its units. [2]

(c) In the stratosphere, chlorine radicals act as catalysts and speed up the decomposition of ozone. Explain how catalysts increase the rate of reaction. [2]

3 The ester methyl ethanoate, CH_3COOCH_3, hydrolyses slowly when dissolved in dilute hydrochloric acid.

$$CH_3COOCH_3 + H_2O \rightarrow CH_3COOH + CH_3OH$$

It has been shown by experiments that, at constant room temperature, the rate of the reaction is given by the rate equation

$$Rate = k [CH_3COOCH_3]^x [HCl]^y$$

(a) The rate of reaction at constant temperature was measured for different concentrations of methyl ethanoate in hydrochloric acid. The results are shown in the following table.

Methyl Ethanoate concentration / mol dm^{-3}	Hydrochloric Acid concentration / mol dm^{-3}	Rate of Reaction / mol dm^{-3} s^{-1}
0.0100	0.0500	0.560×10^{-6}
0.0200	0.0500	1.12×10^{-6}
0.0300	0.0500	1.68×10^{-6}
0.0100	0.100	1.12×10^{-6}
0.0200	0.100	2.24×10^{-6}
0.0300	0.100	3.36×10^{-6}

(i) Explain the term **rate of reaction** for a chemical reaction. [1]

(ii) From the results in the table, determine x, the order of reaction with respect to methyl ethanoate, and y, the order of reaction with respect to hydrochloric acid. [2]

(iii) Giving your reasons, explain the role of hydrochloric acid in the hydrolysis of methyl ethanoate. [2]

(b) **(i)** Write out the rate equation for the reaction, calculate the value of the rate constant, k, to an appropriate number of significant figures and give its units. [3]

(ii) Giving your reasons, state which **one** of the following three mechanisms is compatible with the rate equation. [2]

Mechanism 1

$$CH_3COOCH_3 \xrightarrow{\text{slow}} CH_3COO^- + CH_3^+$$

$$CH_3COO^- + CH_3^+ + H^+ + OH^- \xrightarrow{\text{fast}} CH_3COOH + CH_3OH$$

Mechanism 2

$$CH_3COOCH_3 + H^+ \xrightarrow{\text{slow}} CH_3COOHCH_3^+$$

$$CH_3COOHCH_3^+ + H_2O \xrightarrow{\text{fast}} CH_3COOH + CH_3OH + H^+$$

Mechanism 3

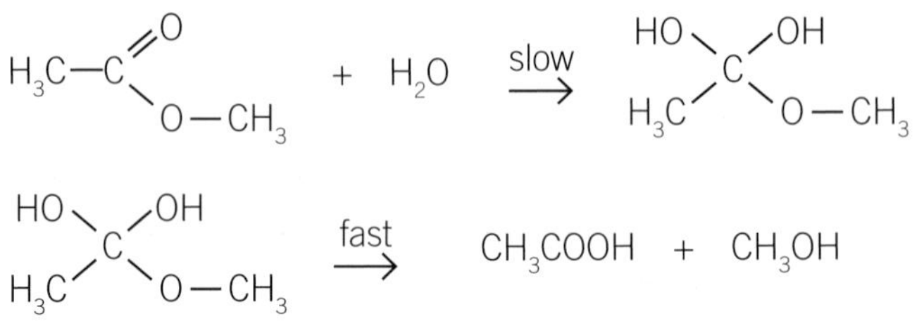

4   Bromine, Br_2, reacts with propanone, CH_3COCH_3, in aqueous solution.

$$Br_2 \text{ (aq)} + CH_3COCH_3 \text{ (aq)} \rightarrow HBr \text{ (aq)} + CH_3COCH_2Br \text{ (aq)}$$

(i) If the initial bromine concentration, [Br_2 (aq)], was 0.0020 mol dm^{-3} and the Br_2 was completely used up in 17min 30seconds, calculate the rate of the reaction (including units). [2]

(ii) Outline one method which could be used to determine the rate for this reaction. [2]

(iii) The following results were obtained when propanone and bromine were reacted in acid solution.

Reaction rate / mol dm^{-3} min^{-1}	[Br_2 (aq)] / mol dm^{-3}	[CH_3COCH_3 (aq)] / mol dm^{-3}
6.80×10^{-5}	0.10	0.40
1.36×10^{-4}	0.10	0.80
1.36×10^{-4}	0.20	0.80

Determine the orders of reaction with respect to Br_2 (aq) and with respect to CH_3COCH_3 (aq). [2]

(iv) A separate experiment was carried out to determine the effect of pH on the rate of reaction.

Reaction rate / mol dm^{-3} min^{-1}	[Br$_2$ (aq)] / mol dm^{-3}	[CH$_3$COCH$_3$ (aq)] / mol dm^{-3}	pH
1.36×10^{-3}	0.10	0.80	0
1.36×10^{-4}	0.10	0.80	1
1.36×10^{-5}	0.10	0.80	2

  I   State how the rate of reaction varies with change in pH. [1]

  II   Using the table, show that the reaction is first order with respect to H$^+$ ions. [1]

  III State the role of H$^+$ ions in the reaction. [1]

  IV Write the full rate equation for the reaction, giving the units for the rate constant. [2]

5 Dinitrogen pentoxide, N$_2$O$_5$, decomposes in the gas phase according to the equation shown.

$$2N_2O_5 \rightarrow 4NO_2 + O_2$$

The initial rates of this reaction for different concentrations of N$_2$O$_5$ were measured and are given in the table below.

Concentration of N$_2$O$_5$ / mol dm^{-3}	Initial rate / mol dm^{-3} s^{-1}
4.00×10^{-3}	3.00×10^{-5}
6.00×10^{-3}	4.50×10^{-5}
8.00×10^{-3}	6.00×10^{-5}

The rate equation for this reaction is: Rate = $k[N_2O_5]^1$

(a) Show that the rate equation is consistent with the data above. [2]

(b) Calculate the value of the rate constant under these conditions. Give your answer to an appropriate number of significant figures and state its units.

(c) Two possible mechanisms have been suggested for this reaction. These are shown below.

Mechanism A	Mechanism B
N$_2$O$_5$ → NO$_2$ + NO$_3^{\cdot}$	2N$_2$O$_5$ → 2NO$_3^{\cdot}$ + N$_2$O$_4$
NO$_3^{\cdot}$ → NO$^{\cdot}$ + O$_2$	NO$_3^{\cdot}$ + N$_2$O$_4$ → NO$^{\cdot}$ + 2NO$_2$ + O$_2$
NO$^{\cdot}$ + N$_2$O$_5$ → 3NO$_2$	NO$^{\cdot}$ + NO$_3^{\cdot}$ → 2NO$_2$

Giving your reasons, state which of the mechanisms is compatible with the rate equation. [2]

6 The reaction between persulfate ions and iodide ions in aqueous solution is

$$S_2O_8^{2-} + 2I^- \rightarrow 2SO_4^{2-} + I_2$$

In an experiment to follow the rate of this reaction, the values below were obtained.

Experiment	Initial rate / mol dm^{-3} s^{-1}	Initial concentration of S$_2$O$_8^{2-}$ / mol dm^{-3}	Initial concentration of I$^-$ / mol dm^{-3}
1	8.64×10^{-6}	0.0400	0.0100
2	3.46×10^{-5}	0.0800	0.0200

(i) The reaction is first order with respect to iodide ions. Use both the initial rate values and the concentrations to show that the order with respect to persulfate ions is also first order. [2]

(ii) Write the rate equation for this reaction and use it to calculate the value of the rate constant, k, giving its units. [3]

(iii) It is suggested that this reaction occurs in two steps.

Step 1 $S_2O_8^{2-} + I^- + H_2O \rightarrow 2SO_4^{2-} + HOI + H^+$

Step 2 $HOI + H^+ + I^- \rightarrow H_2O + I_2$

State, using your answer to (ii), why Step 1 is the rate-determining step. [1]

7   Ammonium chloride and sodium nitrite react together in aqueous solution to produce nitrogen gas. This can be represented by the ionic equation:

$$NH_4^+ (aq) + NO_2^- (aq) \rightarrow N_2 (g) + 2H_2O (l)$$

The rate equation for the reaction is given below.

$$\text{Rate} = k[NH_4^+][NO_2^-]$$

(i) Complete the table of data for the above reaction. All experiments were carried out at the same temperature. [3]

	$[NH_4^+ (aq)]$ / mol dm^{-3}	$[NO_2^- (aq)]$ / mol dm^{-3}	initial rate / mol dm^{-3} s^{-1}
1	0.200	0.010	4.00×10^{-7}
2		0.010	2.00×10^{-7}
3	0.200		1.20×10^{-6}
4	0.100	0.020	

(ii) Calculate the value of the rate constant, k, giving its units. [2]

(iii) State how the value of k will alter, if at all, if the concentration of NH_4^+ ions is increased. [1]

(iv) State, giving a reason, how the value of k will alter, if at all, if the temperature is increased. [2]

8   A chemical reaction has a rate constant, k, of 3×10^7 mol^{-1} dm^3 s^{-1} at 350K.

(a) Identify the order of this reaction, giving a reason for your answer. [1]

(b) The activation energy of this reaction is 23 kJ mol^{-1}.

(i) State what is meant by the activation energy. [1]

(ii) Find the frequency factor, A, for this reaction, giving its units. [3]

(iii) Calculate the value of the rate constant at 400K. [2]

(c) **(i)** A catalyst for the reaction halves the activation energy to 11.5 kJ mol^{-1}. Calculate the rate constant at a temperature of 350K. [2]

(ii) Explain why the use of catalysts is often preferred to the use of very high temperatures for reactions such as these. [2]

3.6

1   **(a)** Showing your working, use the data in the table to construct a Born–Haber energy cycle and hence calculate (in kJ mol^{-1}) the standard enthalpy of formation, $\Delta_f H$, of the ionic solid sodium hydride, NaH. [4]

$$Na (s) + \tfrac{1}{2} H_2 (g) \rightarrow NaH (s)$$

Process	Enthalpy change, ΔH^θ / kJ mol^{-1}
NaH (s) $\rightarrow$ Na$^+$ (g) + H$^-$ (g)	806
H$_2$ (g) $\rightarrow$ 2H (g)	436
H (g) $\rightarrow$ H$^-$ (g)	-72
Na (s) $\rightarrow$ Na (g)	107
Na (g) $\rightarrow$ Na$^+$ (g)	496

(b) Giving your reasons, use your answer to part (a) to predict the stability of sodium hydride, NaH(s). [1]

2 The enthalpy of formation of copper(II) fluoride, CuF$_2$, can be determined indirectly using a Born–Haber cycle.

Use the data given below to calculate the enthalpy of formation of copper(II) fluoride in kJ mol^{-1}. [4]

Process	ΔH^θ / kJ mol^{-1}
Cu (s) $\rightarrow$ Cu (g)	339
½F$_2$ (g) $\rightarrow$ F (g)	79
Cu (g) $\rightarrow$ Cu$^+$ (g) + e$^-$	745
Cu$^+$ (g) $\rightarrow$ Cu^{2+} (g) + e$^-$	1960
F (g) + e$^-$ $\rightarrow$ F$^-$ (g)	-348
Cu^{2+} (g) + 2F$^-$ (g) $\rightarrow$ CuF$_2$ (s)	-3037

3 (a) The diagram shows an outline of the Born–Haber cycle for the formation of sodium iodide (NaI) from its elements.

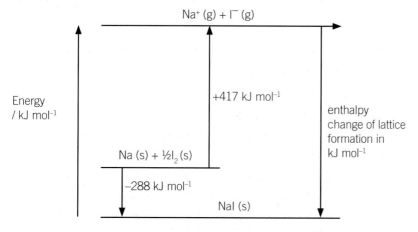

Use the information given to calculate the enthalpy change of lattice formation (in kJ mol^{-1}) of sodium iodide. [2]

(b) Sodium iodide is very soluble in water at room temperature.

Complete the sentence below using the relevant enthalpy terms.

For a compound to be very soluble in water the value of the enthalpy of

.... will be greater than the

enthalpy of .... [1]

4   Magnesium oxide, MgO, is a white solid with a very high melting temperature and it is used as the refractory lining in furnaces.

The following Born–Haber cycle shows the enthalpy changes involved in the formation of magnesium oxide. All enthalpy changes are in kJ mol^{-1}. The cycle is not drawn to scale.

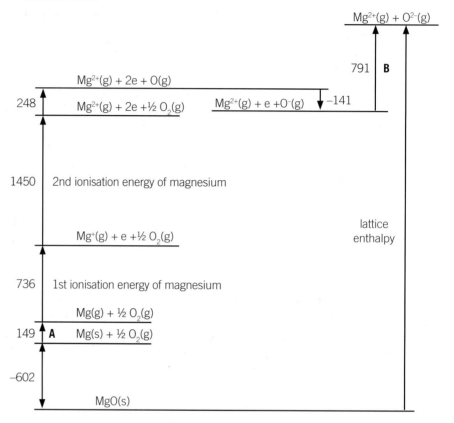

(i)   What is the name given to the enthalpy change labelled A?   [1]

(ii) State why the second ionisation energy of magnesium is greater than its first ionisation energy.   [1]

(iii) Suggest why the second electron affinity of oxygen, labelled B, is positive.   [1]

(iv) Calculate the value of the lattice enthalpy for magnesium oxide.   [2]

3.7

1   The enthalpy of solution of sodium chloride is +3.87 kJ mol^{-1}. Explain why this endothermic change is feasible at room temperature.   [2]

2   Magnesium carbonate decomposes on heating.

$$MgCO_3(s) \rightarrow MgO(s) + CO_2(g)$$

(a) Given the enthalpy change of formation, $\Delta_f H^\theta$, values below, calculate the enthalpy change, ΔH^θ, for the decomposition of magnesium carbonate.   [1]

Species	Enthalpy change of formation $\Delta_f H^\theta$ / kJ mol^{-1}
CO_2 (g)	−393.5
$MgCO_3$ (s)	−1095.8
MgO (s)	−601.7

(b) The entropy change, ΔS, for the decomposition is 174.8 J mol^{-1} K^{-1}. Explain why there is an increase in entropy for this reaction. [1]

(c) Using your answers above determine, in degrees K, the temperature above which magnesium carbonate would decompose spontaneously. [4]

3 One fuel for use in fuel cells is methanol, CH_3OH, which would undergo the following reaction with oxygen.

$$CH_3OH(l) + 1\tfrac{1}{2}O_2(g) \rightarrow CO_2(g) + 2H_2O(l)$$

Compound	Standard enthalpy change of formation, Δ_fH^θ / kJ mol^{-1}
CH_3OH	−239
CO_2	−394
H_2O	−286

(i) Calculate the standard enthalpy change of combustion for methanol. [2]

(ii) The entropy change of this reaction is calculated as follows.

ΔS = (Sum of all entropies for products) – (Sum of all entropies for reactants)

$\Delta S = 354 - 435$

$\Delta S = -81$ J K^{-1} mol^{-1}

The reaction was repeated using gaseous methanol, $CH_3OH(g)$, in place of the liquid methanol, $CH_3OH(l)$, used above. What effect, if any, would this have on the value of the entropy change ΔS given above? Explain your answer. [2]

(iii) Use the values in parts (i) and (ii) of this question to calculate the value of the Gibbs free energy, ΔG, for this reaction at 298K and state what information this gives about the feasibility of the reaction. [2]

4 Many metal oxides can be reduced to the metal by carbon monoxide. The equation for the reduction of magnesium oxide is given below.

$$MgO(s) + CO(g) \rightarrow Mg(s) + CO_2(g)$$

The conditions under which reactions will occur can be predicted using enthalpy and entropy changes. The entropies of the substances involved in this reaction are shown in the table.

Substance	MgO (s)	CO (g)	Mg (s)	CO$_2$ (g)
Entropy/J K^{-1}mol^{-1}	26.9	197.7	32.7	213.7

(i) Suggest a reason why the entropies of carbon monoxide and carbon dioxide are much higher than those of magnesium and magnesium oxide. [1]

(ii) Calculate the entropy change in this reaction. [1]

(iii) The enthalpy change, ΔH, for the reduction of magnesium oxide is 318.0 kJ mol^{-1}. Calculate the minimum temperature at which this reduction could occur. [3]

5 Tin is an element in Group 4. At low temperatures, tin exists as its grey form. At higher temperatures, the white form is stable. The change can be represented by the equation:

$$Sn(grey) \rightarrow Sn(white) \quad \Delta H^\theta = 1.92 \text{ kJ mol}^{-1}$$

The standard entropy values are 44.8 J K^{-1} mol^{-1} for grey tin and 51.5 J K^{-1} mol^{-1} for white tin.

(i) Calculate the minimum temperature needed to cause grey tin to change to white tin. [3]

(ii) During Napoleon's disastrous campaign in Russia from June to December in 1812 the tin buttons on his infantry's uniforms disintegrated. Suggest a reason why this might have happened. [1]

3.8

1 Nitrogen monoxide, NO, can be formed in small amounts when a mixture of nitrogen and oxygen is exposed to strong heat.

$$N_2 (g) + O_2 (g) \rightleftharpoons 2NO (g)$$

(a) Write the expression for the gaseous equilibrium constant, K_p, for this reaction. [1]

(b) At a temperature of 1500 K, K_p has a value of 1.0×10^{-5}. Calculate the partial pressure (in atm) of nitrogen monoxide, NO, present at equilibrium if the partial pressures of nitrogen and oxygen at equilibrium are each 1.2 atm. [2]

(c) At a temperature of 1100 K, K_p has a value of 4.0×10^{-8}. State, giving your reasoning, whether the reaction to form nitrogen monoxide is exothermic or endothermic. [1]

2 Phosphorus(V) chloride vapour dissociates according to the equation

$$PCl_5(g) \rightleftharpoons PCl_3(g) + Cl_2(g)$$

(a) Giving your reasons, state whether the dissociation of $PCl_5(g)$ will be greater at high pressure or at low pressure. [2]

(b) Write the expression for the equilibrium constant, K_p, for the reaction. [1]

(c) At 150 °C, K_p has the value 2.88×10^{-2} atm. If the equilibrium pressures due to $PCl_3(g)$ and $Cl_2(g)$ are each 5.00×10^{-2} atm, calculate the equilibrium pressure due to $PCl_5(g)$.

3 As solids do not affect the position of equilibrium, for the solution equilibrium

$$MgCO_3(s) \rightleftharpoons Mg^{2+}(aq) + CO_3^{2-} (aq)$$

the simplest expression for the equilibrium constant, K_c, can be written

$$K_c = [Mg^{2+}(aq)][CO_3^{2-} (aq)]$$

(i) Given that the solubility of $MgCO_3$ at 20 °C is 3.16×10^{-3} mol dm^{-3}, state the molar concentrations of magnesium ions, $Mg^{2+}(aq)$, and carbonate ions, CO_3^{2-} (aq), in a saturated $MgCO_3$ solution. [1]

(ii) Hence calculate the value of K_c at 20°C. [1]

(iii) The the free energy change, ΔG, for this change is +28.2 kJ mol^{-1}. Giving your reasons, state whether the value of K_c is consistent with the value of the free energy change, ΔG. [1]

(iv) By applying Le Chatelier's Principle to the chemical equation above, and giving your reasons, state the effect on the solubility of magnesium carbonate of adding sodium carbonate to the solution. [1]

4 Nitrogen dioxide, NO_2, exists in dynamic equilibrium with dinitrogen tetroxide, N_2O_4.

$$2NO_2(g) \rightleftharpoons N_2O_4 \quad \Delta H = -57.2 \text{ kJ mol}^{-1}$$

(i) Write an expression for the equilibrium constant, K_p, for this reaction. [1]

(ii) State and explain the effect of increasing the temperature on the value of K_p. [2]

(iii) At a temperature of 373 K, the partial pressure of a pure sample of NO_2 was 3.00×10^5 Pa. When the mixture was allowed to reach equilibrium, the partial pressure of the remaining NO_2 was 2.81×10^5 Pa. Calculate the value of K_p, stating its units. [3]

5 Aqueous solutions of sodium iodide become yellow in the presence of oxygen due to the slow production of iodine.

One suggested reason for this is that a low concentration of hydrogen ions in the solution produces iodine according to the equation below.

$$4H^+(aq) + 4I^-(aq) + O_2(aq) \rightleftharpoons 2I_2(aq) + 2H_2O(l)$$

Use Le Chatelier's principle to suggest a reagent that you could add, apart from water, to decrease the amount of yellow iodine present. Explain your choice. [2]

6 Hydrogen reacts with iodine in a reversible reaction.

$$H_2(g) + I_2(g) \rightleftharpoons 2HI(g)$$

An equilibrium was established at 300 K, in a vessel of volume 1 dm^3, and it was found that 0.311 mol of hydrogen, 0.311 mol of iodine and 0.011 mol of hydrogen iodide were present.

(i) Write the expression for the equilibrium constant in terms of concentration, K_c. [1]

(ii) Calculate the value of K_c at 300 K. [1]

(iii) What are the units of K_c, if any? [1]

(iv) Equilibria of H_2, I_2 and HI were set up at 500 K and 1000 K and it was found that the numerical values of K_c were 6.25×10^{-3} and 18.5×10^{-3} respectively. Use these data to deduce the sign of ΔH for the forward reaction. Explain your reasoning. [3]

7 A flask containing an initial mixture of 0.100 mol of ethanoic acid and 0.083 mol of methanol was kept at 25 °C until the following equilibrium had been established.

$$CH_3COOH + CH_3OH \rightleftharpoons CH_3COOCH_3 + H_2O \qquad \Delta H = -3\,kJ\,mol^{-1}$$

The ethanoic acid present at equilibrium required 32.0 cm^3 of a 1.25 mol dm^{-3} solution of sodium hydroxide for complete reaction.

(i) Write an expression for the equilibrium constant, K_c, giving the units, if any. [2]

(ii) Calculate the number of moles of ethanoic acid present at equilibrium. [1]

(iii) Calculate the value of the equilibrium constant, K_c, for this reaction. [2]

(iv) State, giving a reason, what happens to the value of the equilibrium constant, K_c, if the temperature is increased. [1]

3.9

1 (a) Ethanoic acid, CH_3COOH, is a **weak acid**.

(i) Explain the meanings of **weak** and **acid** in this context. [2]

(ii) Write an expression for the **acid dissociation constant**, K_a, for ethanoic acid. [1]

(iii) A solution of ethanoic acid has a pH of 4. Calculate the hydrogen ion concentration, $[H^+]$, in this solution. [1]

(b) Explain why a mixed solution of ethanoic acid and sodium ethanoate behaves as a buffer solution. [3]

2 In living systems, enzymes that enable biochemical reactions to take place can function only within a narrow pH range. An important buffer system in human beings is the carbonate buffer, consisting of carbonic acid and its conjugate base, the hydrogencarbonate ion.

$$H_2CO_3(aq) \rightleftharpoons H^+(aq) + HCO_3^-(aq)$$

(K_a for carbonic acid $= 4.5 \times 10^{-7}$ mol dm^{-3} at body temperature)

(a) Write an expression for the dissociation constant, K_a, for the acid. [1]

(b) Define the term pH. [1]

(c) Calculate the pH of blood in a person, given that at body temperature: [3]

$[H_2CO_3] = 1.85 \times 10^{-3}$ mol dm^{-3} \qquad $[HCO_3^-] = 2.09 \times 10^{-2}$ mol dm^{-3}

(d) State the purpose of a buffer solution. [1]

(e) Explain how an aqueous solution of ethanoic acid and sodium ethanoate can act as a buffer solution when a small amount of acid or alkali is separately added to it. [3]

3 The pH of an aqueous lithium hydroxide solution at 298K is 11.5. Calculate the concentration, in mol dm^{-3}, of hydroxide ions in this solution. [3]

[The ionic product of water, K_w, is 1.00×10^{-14} mol^2 dm^{-6} at 298K]

4 A 25.0 cm^3 sample of aqueous chloroethanoic acid, $CH_2ClCOOH$, of concentration 0.100 mol dm^{-3}, was titrated against aqueous sodium hydroxide solution from a burette.

$$CH_2ClCOOH + NaOH \rightarrow CH_2ClCOONa + H_2O$$

(a) Chloroethanoic acid is a weak acid with acid dissociation constant, K_a, having a value 1.30×10^{-3} mol dm^{-3}.

(i) Write an expression for K_a for chloroethanoic acid, $CH_2ClCOOH$. [1]

(ii) Define the term pH. [1]

(iii) Calculate the pH of aqueous chloroethanoic acid solution of concentration 0.100 mol dm^{-3}. [2]

(b) The diagram below shows the change in pH for part of the titration.

(i) Enter a cross on the diagram to show the pH at the start of the titration. [1]

(ii) From the graph, determine the pH at the equivalence-point of the titration. [1]

(iii) From the graph, determine the volume of sodium hydroxide solution added at the end-point. [1]

(iv) Using the concentration of the aqueous chloroethanoic acid given, calculate, to an appropriate number of significant figures, the concentration of the sodium hydroxide solution in mol dm^{-3}. [2]

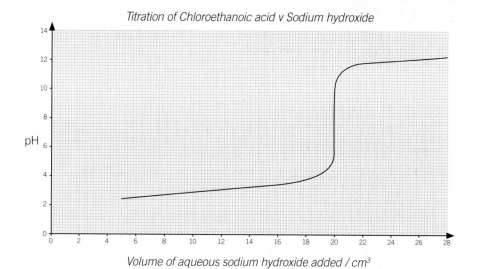

Titration of Chloroethanoic acid v Sodium hydroxide

Volume of aqueous sodium hydroxide added / cm³

(v) Giving a reason, state which of the following indicators would be suitable for this titration. [2]

Indicator	pH range
Methyl orange	3.2 to 4.4
Bromothymol blue	6.0 to 6.7
Phenolphthalein	8.2 to 10.0

5 **(a)** The diagram shows the variation of the ionic product of water, K_w, with temperature.

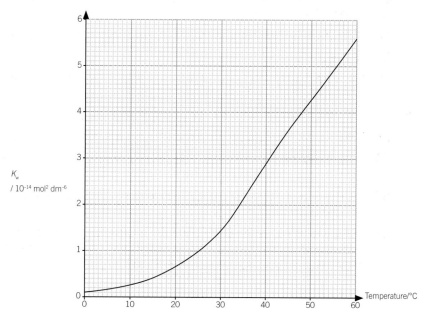

(i) Give the expression for the ionic product of water, K_w. [1]

(ii) By reference to the diagram, and giving your reasoning, state whether the ionisation of water is an exothermic or an endothermic process. [1]

(iii) Use the diagram to determine the value (mol² dm⁻⁶) of K_w at 50°C. [1]

(iv) Hence calculate [H⁺] and the pH of pure water at 50°C. [2]

(b) The diagram below shows how pH changes during the course of a titration when hydrochloric acid of concentration 0.100 mol dm^{-3} is added from a burette to 25.0cm^3 of aqueous ammonia.

$$NH_3(aq) + HCl(aq) \rightarrow NH_4Cl(aq)$$

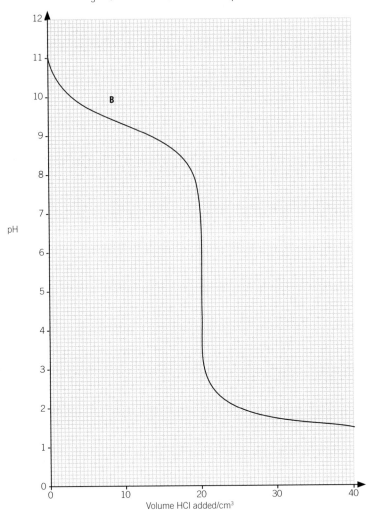

(i) Calculate, to **two** significant figures, the concentration of the aqueous ammonia solution. [3]

(ii) Explain why a buffering effect occurs in the region of the curve marked with the letter **B**, where a mixture of NH$_3$(aq) and NH$_4$Cl(aq) is present. [3]

(iii) Giving your reasoning, state which of the following indicators would be suitable for the titration of ammonia against hydrochloric acid. [2]

Indicator	pH range
Methyl orange	3.2 to 4.4
Bromothymol blue	6.0 to 6.7
Phenolphthalein	8.2 to 10.0

6 Chlorine produces a range of oxoacids, including chloric(I) acid, HOCl, and chloric(VII) acid, HClO$_4$. Chloric(I) acid is considered to be a weak acid whilst chloric(VII) acid is considered to be a strong acid.

(i) What is meant by the term strong acid? [1]

(ii) Write an expression for the acid dissociation constant, K_a, of chloric(I) acid, HOCl. [1]

(iii) The pH of a solution of chloric(I) acid of concentration 0.100 mol dm^{-3} was found to be 4.23. Calculate the concentration of hydrogen ions in this solution. [2]

(iv) Using the information from part (iii), calculate the value of the acid dissociation constant, K_a, for chloric(I) acid. [2]

(v) When the weak acid HOCl reacts with the strong base sodium hydroxide it forms the salt sodium chlorate(I), NaOCl. Suggest a pH value for a solution of NaOCl, giving a reason for your answer. [2]

7 (a) State what is meant by a Lowry–Brønsted acid. [1]

(b) Define pH. [1]

(c) David and Peter were discussing acids and bases. David said that you could decide whether an acid was strong or weak by measuring the pH of the acid solution. He said that the strong acid would have a lower pH. Peter said that he felt that the strength of the acid was not the only factor that affected pH. Discuss the factors that affect pH. [4]

(d) Methanoic acid is a weak acid.

(i) Write the expression for the acid dissociation constant, K_a, of methanoic acid. [1]

(ii) Calculate the pH of 0.10 mol dm^{-3} methanoic acid. [3]

For methanoic acid, HCOOH, the value of the acid dissociation constant, K_a, is 1.75×10^{-4} mol dm^{-3}.

(e) It is important to maintain the pH of some materials within a small range.

(i) What name is given to a system designed to maintain pH within a small range? [1]

(ii) The pH of a shampoo is maintained within a small range by using a weak acid, RCOOH, and its sodium salt, RCOONa. Explain how this mixture maintains pH within a small range. [3]

8 (a) Write an expression for the ionic product of water, K_w, giving its units, if any. [2]

(b) (i) The value for K_w at 298 K is 1.0×10^{-14}. Explain why the pH of pure water at this temperature has a value of 7. [2]

(ii) Calculate the pH of the final solution if 10 cm^3 of 0.10 mol dm^{-3} hydrochloric acid is added to 990 cm^3 of pure water. [2]

(c) Calculate the pH of a solution which is 0.010 mol dm^{-3} with respect to ethanoic acid and 0.020 mol dm^{-3} with respect to sodium ethanoate at 298 K. [3]

[K_a for ethanoic acid = 1.78×10^{-5} mol dm^{-3} at 298 K]

Unit 4

Overview
Organic chemistry and analysis

4.1 Stereoisomerism p114

- The distinction between structural isomerism and optical isomerism and the two types of stereoisomerism
- Common terms used in optical isomerism
- Recognising the features present in organic formulae that lead to optical isomerism
- The effect of enantiomers on plane polarised light

4.3 Alcohols and phenols p125

- The methods of forming primary and secondary alcohols from halogenoalkanes and carbonyl compounds
- The reactions of primary and secondary alcohols with hydrogen halides, ethanoyl chloride and carboxylic acids
- The acidity of phenol and its reactions with bromine and ethanoyl chloride
- The test for phenols using aqueous iron(III) chloride

4.2 Aromaticity p118

- The structure and bonding in benzene and other arenes
- The resistance to addition reactions shown by aromatic compounds such as benzene
- The mechanism of electrophilic substitution, such as in the nitration, halogenation and Friedel–Crafts alkylation of benzene, as the characteristic reaction of arenes
- The interaction between benzene and substituent groups, as exemplified by the increase in C–Cl bond strength in chlorobenzene when compared to an alkene

4.4 Aldehydes and ketones p134

- The formation of aldehydes and ketones by the oxidation of primary and secondary alcohols respectively
- How aldehydes and ketones may be distinguished by their relative ease of oxidation using Tollens' reagent and Fehling's reagent
- The reduction of aldehydes and ketones using sodium tetrahydridoborate(III)
- The mechanism of nucleophilic addition, such as in the addition of hydrogen cyanide to ethanal and propanone
- The reaction of aldehydes and ketones with 2,4-dinitrophenylhydrazine and its use in testing for a carbonyl group and the identification of specific aldehydes and ketones
- The triiodomethane (iodoform) test and its use in identifying $CH_3C=O$ groups or their precursors

4.5 Carboxylic acids and their derivatives

p140

- The relative acidity of carboxylic acids, phenols, alcohols and water
- The formation of carboxylic acids by the oxidation of alcohols and aldehydes
- The reduction of carboxylic acids using $LiAlH_4$
- The formation of aromatic carboxylic acids by the oxidation of methyl side-chains
- The decarboxylation of carboxylic acids
- The conversion of carboxylic acids to esters and acid chlorides and the hydrolysis of these compounds
- The conversion of carboxylic acids to amides and nitriles
- The formation of nitriles from halogenoalkanes and hydroxynitriles from aldehydes
- The hydrolysis of nitriles and amides
- The reduction of nitriles using $LiAlH_4$

4.7 Amino acids, peptides and proteins

p158

- The general formulae and classification of α-amino acids
- The amphoteric and zwitterionic nature of amino acids and their effect on melting temperatures and solubility
- The combination of α-amino acids to form dipeptides
- The formation of polypeptides and proteins
- The basic principles of primary, secondary and tertiary protein structure
- The essential role of proteins in living systems, for example, as enzymes

4.6 Amines

p150

- The formation of primary aliphatic amines from halogenoalkanes and nitriles
- The formation of aromatic amines from nitrobenzenes
- The basicity of amines
- The ethanoylation of primary amines using ethanoyl chloride
- The reaction of primary amines (aliphatic and aromatic) with cold nitric(III) acid
- The coupling of benzenediazonium salts with phenols and aromatic amines
- The role of the –N=N– chromophore in azo dyes
- The origin of colour in terms of the wavelengths of visible light absorbed

4.8 Organic synthesis and analysis

p165

- Synthesis of organic compounds by a sequence of reactions
- Principles underlying the techniques of manipulation, separation and purification used in organic chemistry
- Distinction between condensation polymerisation and addition polymerisation
- How polyesters and polyamides are formed
- Use of melting temperature as a determination of purity
- Use of high resolution ^1H NMR spectra (alongside the other spectral data specified in 2.8) in the elucidation of organic molecules
- Use of chromatographic data from TLC/paper chromatography, GC and HPLC to find the composition of mixtures

4.1
Stereoisomerism

Molecules of organic compounds often contain a large number of atoms. For example, a molecule of the explosive TNT, $C_6H_2(CH_3)(NO_2)_3$, has 21 atoms from four different elements, and a molecule of sucrose, $C_{12}H_{22}O_{11}$, has 45 atoms. Even in the simpler molecule having a molecular formula C_2H_6O, the atoms can be arranged to give ethanol, C_2H_5OH or bonded together with a central oxygen atom to give methoxymethane, CH_3OCH_3. Compounds that have the same molecular formula but are bonded differently are called structural isomers. There is another type of isomerism where differences arise because of the position the atoms take up in space. We call this stereoisomerism. In the first year of this course, we have met *E-Z* isomerism and we now look at another form of stereoisomerism, optical isomerism.

Content

You should be able to demonstrate and apply knowledge and understanding of:

- How stereoisomerism is distinct from structural isomerism and that stereoisomerism encompasses *E-Z* isomerism and optical isomerism.

- The terms chiral centre, enantiomer, optical activity and racemic mixture.

- Optical isomerism in terms of an asymmetric carbon atom.

- The effect of an enantiomer on plane polarised light.

The distinction between structural isomerism and stereoisomerism, and the two types of stereoisomerism

YOU SHOULD KNOW › › ›

› › › the difference between structural isomerism and stereoisomerism

› › › that E-Z isomerism can occur with alkenes

Structural isomers are compounds that have the same molecular formula but differ in their arrangement of atoms. One of the simplest types is chain isomerism, where the chains are straight or branched.

$$CH_3CH_2CH_2CH_2CH_3$$

pentane

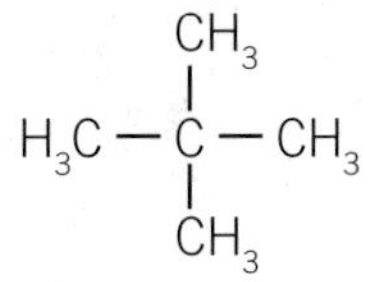

$$H_3C - \underset{\underset{CH_3}{|}}{\overset{\overset{CH_3}{|}}{C}} - CH_3$$

dimethylpropane

If the compounds contain a functional group then this may be at a different position on the chain.

$$CH_3CH_2CH_2OH \qquad\qquad CH_3CH(OH)CH_3$$

propan-1-ol   propan-2-ol

The compounds may have the same molecular formula but a different functional group is present. For example, both cyclohexanol (a secondary alcohol) and hexanal (an aldehyde) have the molecular formula $C_6H_{12}O$.

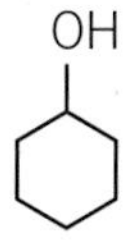

cyclohexanol

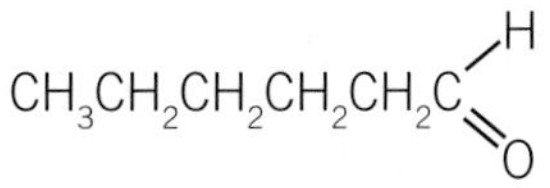

$$CH_3CH_2CH_2CH_2CH_2C\overset{\overset{H}{\diagup}}{\underset{\underset{O}{\diagdown}}{}}$$

hexanal

One form of stereoisomerism is *E-Z* isomerism. Stereoisomerism occurs where the isomers have the same shortened formula but have a different arrangement of the atoms in space. *E-Z* isomerism is studied during the first year of this course. This type of isomerism is shown in alkenes. Dichloroethene can have both chlorine atoms bonded to the same carbon atom or each carbon atom can be bonded to one chlorine atom.

$$H_2C = CCl_2 \qquad\qquad ClHC = CHCl$$

1,1-dichloroethene   1,2-dichloroethene

These two compounds are structural isomers. However, 1,2-dichloroethene can be bonded so that each chlorine is opposite each other or both atoms are on the same side of the double bond.

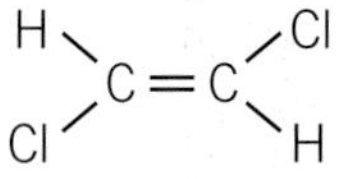

$$\underset{Cl}{\overset{H}{\diagdown}} C = C \underset{H}{\overset{Cl}{\diagup}} \qquad\qquad \underset{H}{\overset{Cl}{\diagdown}} C = C \underset{H}{\overset{Cl}{\diagup}}$$

(*E*)-1,2-dichloroethene 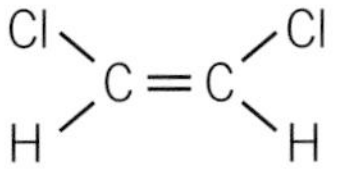   (*Z*)-1,2-dichloroethene

The π bond restricts rotation about the double bond and, as a result, 1,2-dichloroethene exists in two different forms, called *E-Z* isomers.

The other type of stereoisomerism is called optical isomerism and occurs where the two isomers have different effects on plane polarised light.

Knowledge check

The displayed formula of methylcyclobutane is shown below.

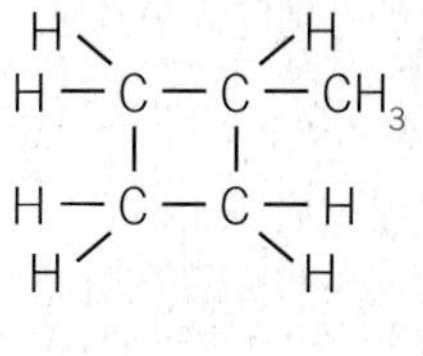

$$H-\overset{\overset{\displaystyle H}{|}}{C}-\overset{\overset{\displaystyle H}{|}}{C}-CH_3$$
$$H-\overset{\underset{\displaystyle H}{|}}{C}-\overset{\underset{\displaystyle H}{|}}{C}-H$$

Give the displayed formula of another compound that has the same molecular formula.

Stretch & Challenge

Give the displayed formula of two isomers whose molecular formula is C_4H_8O but which contain different functional groups.

Knowledge check

Citronellal is a lemon-scented oil that is used in perfumery.

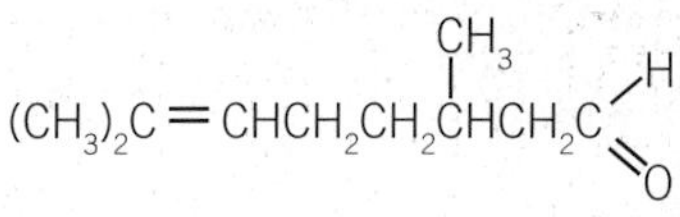

$$(CH_3)_2C = CHCH_2CH_2\overset{\overset{CH_3}{|}}{C}HCH_2C\overset{\overset{H}{\diagup}}{\underset{\underset{O}{\diagdown}}{}}$$

State whether citronellal exists as *E-Z* isomers giving a reason for your answer.

▼ **Study point**

For *E-Z* isomerism to occur the atoms/groups bonded to the carbon atoms at each end of the carbon to carbon double bond, need to be different. 1,1-Dichloroethane has two atoms the same bonded to each carbon atom of the double bond and so does not exist as *E-Z* isomers. The atoms/groups do not have to be the same at either side of the double bond. Both

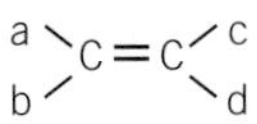

$$\underset{b}{\overset{a}{\diagdown}} C = C \underset{d}{\overset{c}{\diagup}} \quad \text{and} \quad \underset{c}{\overset{a}{\diagdown}} C = C \underset{d}{\overset{b}{\diagup}}$$

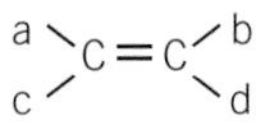

have E-Z isomers.

Key Terms

A **chiral centre** is an atom in a molecule that is bonded to four different atoms or groups.

Enantiomers are non-superimposable mirror image forms of each other that rotate the plane of polarised light in opposite directions.

Optical activity occurs in molecules that possess chiral centre(s). These molecules rotate the plane of polarised light.

A **racemic mixture** is an equimolar mixture of both enantiomers that produces no overall rotation of plane polarised light.

 Extra Help

Carbon atoms that have multiple bonds cannot act as chiral centres as they cannot be bonded to four other atoms or groups. As a result these compounds do not have a chiral centre.

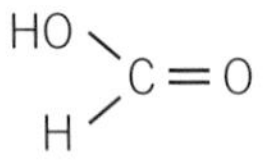

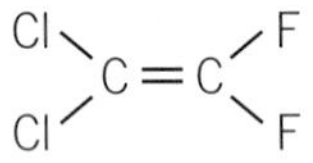

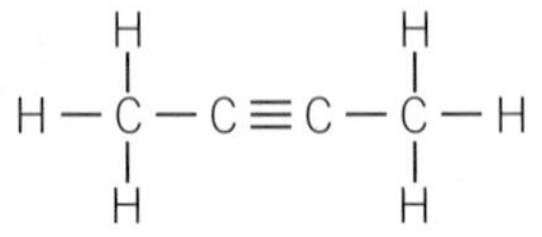

Some terms used in optical isomerism

Chiral centre

A **chiral centre** is an atom that is bonded to four different groups or atoms. This is often a carbon atom and we call this a chiral carbon atom. In older books these chiral carbon atoms were called asymmetric carbon atoms. The four different atoms or groups bonded to this chiral centre can be bonded in two different ways, which are mirror images of each other.

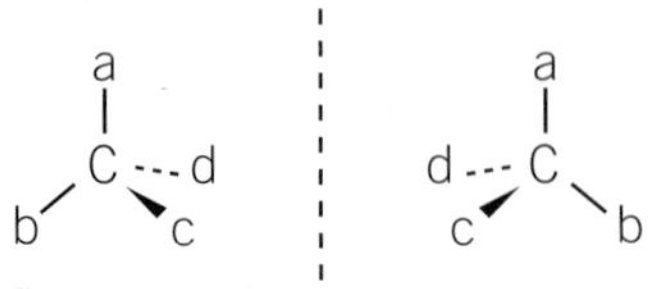

The dotted lines go backward into the page and the wedge shaped lines come out of the page towards you. A common example of a compound with a chiral centre is butan-2-ol, $CH_3CH_2CH(OH)CH_3$.

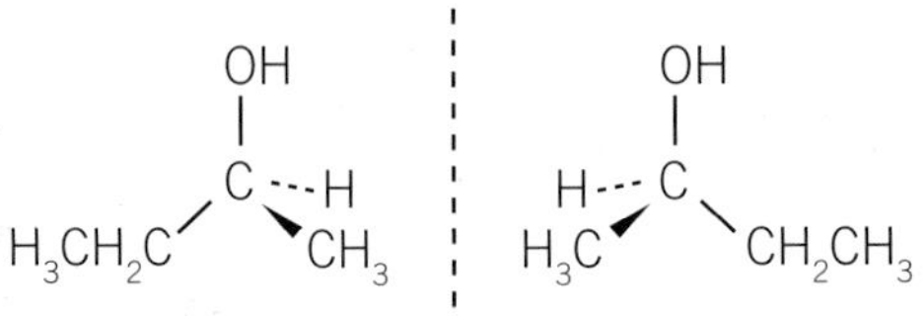

Enantiomer

Enantiomers are stereoisomers that are non-superimposable mirror image forms of each other. These can also be called optical isomers. If a compound contains two or more chiral centres it is possible to have stereoisomers that are not mirror image forms of each other. These are called diastereoisomers, but are not within the scope of this specification. However, you should be able to identify chiral centres within this type of molecule. The diagram shows the formula of butane-1,2-diol with the chiral centres indicated by asterisks.

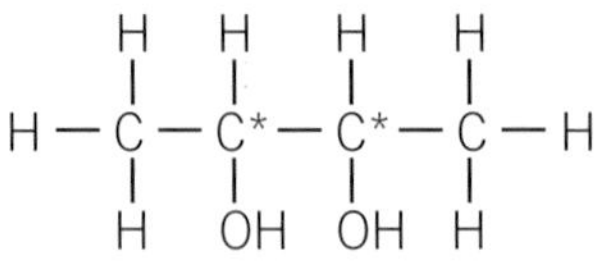

 **Stretch & Challenge**

The formula of 1,3-dichloropropan-2-ol is

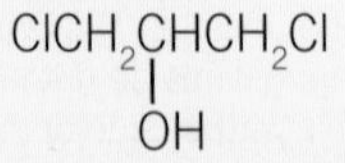

$$CICH_2CHCH_2Cl$$
$$\quad\quad |$$
$$\quad\quad OH$$

Give the displayed formula of another isomer of formula $C_3H_6Cl_2O$ that has a chiral centre.

Optical activity

Optical activity occurs in molecules with chiral centres. Light consists of waves that are vibrating in all planes. If light is passed through a polarising filter (P) (e.g. a piece of Polaroid), the light that emerges is vibrating in one plane only. This light is called plane polarised light. If a solution of an enantiomer (R) is placed in a beam of plane polarised light, the beam is rotated. The instrument used to measure the amount of rotation is called a polarimeter.

The extent to which the plane of polarised light is rotated depends on:

- The particular enantiomer

- The concentration of the enantiomer in the solution

- The length of the tube containing the solution through which the light passes

- The frequency of the light source used and the temperature also need to be considered.

An enantiomer may rotate the plane of polarised light to the right (+) or to the left (−). Equal amounts of each enantiomer in a solution produce no overall rotation since the rotation effects cancel each other out. This mixture results from external compensation, as the effect is caused by two different compounds. This equimolar mixture is called a **racemic mixture.**

The painkiller ibuprofen was first made in 1961.

Ibuprofen contains a chiral centre and is sold as a racemic mixture. Since biological systems usually respond to one enantiomer in the required way rather than the other, there is a danger that the 'unwanted' form could have serious and unwanted side effects. Separation of the two enantiomers (called resolution) would be difficult and expensive. When ibuprofen is taken, one of the enantiomers is much more biologically active than the other but fortunately the less active form is converted by an enzyme in the body into the other, more active enantiomer.

Knowledge check 3

Explain why a racemic mixture can be described as an equimolar mixture or as a mixture containing equal amounts of both enantiomers.

Knowledge check 4

Malic acid occurs in unripe apples. Its systematic name is 2-hydroxybutanedioic acid. Write the displayed formula for malic acid and identify any chiral centre present in its formula.

Knowledge check 5

Explain why the unsaturated acid that has the formula $CH_3(CH_2)_7CH=CH(CH_2)_7COOH$ exists as E-Z isomers.

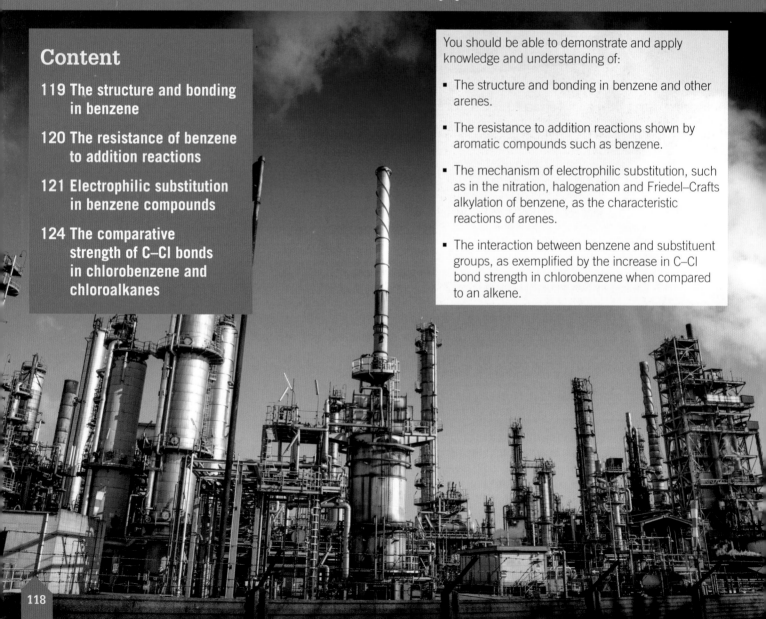

Unit 4

4.2 Aromaticity

The first year of this course includes work on aliphatic and alicylic compounds. Aliphatic compounds are traditionally classed as compounds where the carbon atoms form open chains, rather than rings. Alicyclic compounds do have a ring structure but they react as if they are aliphatic compounds. In the second year of this course, aromatic compounds are introduced. The word 'aromatic' comes from the Latin word 'aroma' meaning fragrance. Not all aromatic compounds have a fragrant smell but they do all contain an aromatic ring system. The simplest aromatic compound is benzene, which has the formula C_6H_6.

Content

You should be able to demonstrate and apply knowledge and understanding of:

- The structure and bonding in benzene and other arenes.

- The resistance to addition reactions shown by aromatic compounds such as benzene.

- The mechanism of electrophilic substitution, such as in the nitration, halogenation and Friedel–Crafts alkylation of benzene, as the characteristic reactions of arenes.

- The interaction between benzene and substituent groups, as exemplified by the increase in C–Cl bond strength in chlorobenzene when compared to an alkene.

The structure and bonding in benzene and other arenes, and their resistance to addition reactions

In 1825 Michael Faraday isolated a colourless flammable liquid from whale oil, whilst obtaining a suitable gas for street lighting.

Michael Faraday.

YOU SHOULD KNOW › › ›

› › › the structure and bonding in benzene

› › › why benzene is resistant to addition reactions

Knowledge check **6**

Look at the Kekule structure of benzene below.

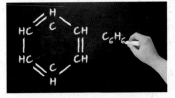

Why might it lose a mark in the examination?

He found that this flammable liquid had the empirical formula CH. Nine years later the liquid, now called benzene, was found to have a relative molecular mass of 78 and the molecular formula C_6H_6. Later workers found that benzene was present in coal tar, from which it was obtained for many years. In 1865 Kekule suggested that the structure of benzene was a six-membered ring, containing alternating single and double carbon-to-carbon bonds.

Unfortunately, the Kekule model for the structure of benzene does not explain some of benzene's reactions. For example, it should react as an alkene and easily undergo addition reactions, such as the reaction with aqueous bromine, where the bromine is decolourised. However, it does not react in this way. To explain this discrepancy, Kekule proposed that benzene had two forms and suggested that one form changed to the other so quickly that an approaching molecule would have no time to react with it by addition.

▲ August Kekule

Knowledge check **7**

Choose the correct statement about the structure of benzene.

(a) Each carbon atom is bonded to two hydrogen atoms and one carbon atom.

(b) The C–C–C bond angle is 120°.

(c) The C=C bond length is longer than the C–C bond length.

(d) The smaller the resonance energy, the more stable the molecule.

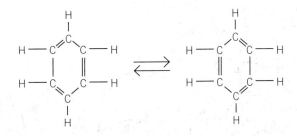

 Stretch & Challenge

Ethene reacts with cold dilute aqueous potassium manganate(VII) to produce ethane-1,2-diol, CH_2OHCH_2OH. Suggest why benzene cannot react in a similar way to give the diol shown below.

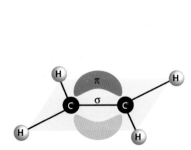

If benzene existed as the Kekule forms above then there would be two different bond lengths between carbon atoms in the molecule. In the early 20th century, x-ray crystallography showed that each carbon-to-carbon bond was the same length at 0.140 nm. This distance is between a carbon-to-carbon double bond at 0.135 nm and a carbon-to-carbon single bond at 0.147 nm.

When cyclohexene is hydrogenated the energy released is 120 kJ mol^{-1}.

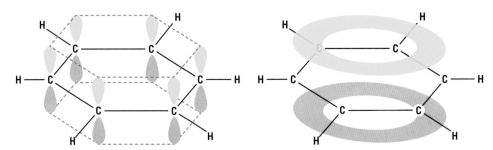

$$+ H_2 \longrightarrow \qquad \Delta H = -120 \text{ kJ mol}^{-1}$$

If benzene existed as the Kekule structure and all three double bonds are hydrogenated, then the enthalpy change would be −360 kJ mol^{-1}. However, when benzene is fully hydrogenated the enthalpy change is −208 kJ mol^{-1}.

This is 152 kJ mol^{-1} less than expected, suggesting that benzene is more stable than the Kekule structure, and it suggests that the Kekule structure is incorrect. This difference in energy values is called the resonance energy.

The delocalised bonding model of benzene

Modern studies of benzene have shown that it is a planar molecule and that the angles between three adjacent carbon atoms are 120°. In an ethene molecule, C_2H_4, each carbon atom is bonded to two hydrogen atoms and a carbon atom by sigma (σ) bonds. The remaining outer p electrons of each carbon atom, overlap above and below the plane of the molecule, giving a localised pi (π) orbital.

In benzene each carbon atom is bonded to two other carbon atoms and a hydrogen atom by sigma bonds. The fourth outer shell electron of a carbon atom is in a 2p orbital, above and below the plane of the carbon atoms. These p-orbitals overlap to give a delocalised electron structure, above and below the plane of carbon atoms. This delocalised electron π structure is often represented by a circle inside the ring hexagon.

ethene

Compounds containing a single benzene ring represent the simplest type of aromatic system but there are a number of other aromatic ring systems, some with fused sides. These include naphthalene and anthracene. There are also aromatic compounds whose rings also contain atoms other than carbon, for example pyridine, C_5H_5N.

naphthalene   anthracene   pyridine

If benzene underwent an addition reaction, the process would disrupt the stable delocalised electron system and the resulting product would be less stable. Benzene can be made to react by addition but more forcing conditions are needed. We have already seen that benzene can be hydrogenated to give cyclohexane but the reaction needs higher temperatures and a nickel or platinum catalyst. Benzene will also react with chlorine in an addition reaction to give hexachlorocyclohexane, $C_6H_6Cl_6$. This is a radical reaction that needs bright sunlight to be effective. One isomer of formula $C_6H_6Cl_6$, γ-hexachlorocyclohexane, was produced under the trade name of Lindane© and used as an insecticide. The use of Lindane© is now restricted as this toxic material is very persistent in the environment. Benzene generally reacts by substitution reactions where the delocalised system of electrons is retained.

The mechanism of electrophilic substitution, such as in the nitration, halogenation and Friedel–Crafts alkylation of benzene, as the characteristic reactions of arenes

Key Term

An **electrophile** is an electron-deficient species that can accept a lone pair of electrons.

Benzene has a delocalised ring of electrons above and below the plane of the carbon atoms. This area of high electron density makes it susceptible to attack by an **electrophile**. A hydrogen atom (as H⁺) is replaced by the incoming electrophile. This type of reaction mechanism is called electrophilic substitution. To replace a hydrogen atom by an electrophile X, the stability of the ring needs to be disturbed, giving an unstable intermediate (called a Wheland intermediate), which then loses a hydrogen ion, H⁺, in a rapid step.

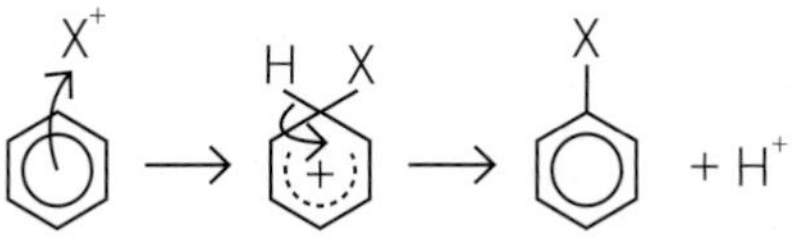

YOU SHOULD KNOW › › ›

››› the mechanism of electrophilic substitution for the nitration, halogenation and Friedel–Crafts alkylation of benzene

intermediate

Nitration

In a nitration reaction a hydrogen atom is replaced by a nitro group, NO_2. The electrophile is the nitryl cation (or nitronium ion), NO_2^+, and this is produced by the reaction of concentrated nitric acid and concentrated sulfuric(VI) acids (sometimes called a nitrating mixture). The nitryl cation reacts with benzene giving nitrobenzene, $C_6H_5NO_2$, as the organic product.

Extra Help

In the nitration of benzene, the hydrogensulfate anion acts as a base by removing a proton from the intermediate. It is the lone pair of electrons on an oxygen atom that is the lone pair donor.

$$HNO_3 + 2H_2SO_4 \rightleftharpoons NO_2^+ + H_3O^+ + 2HSO_4^-$$

one mechanism for the nitration is

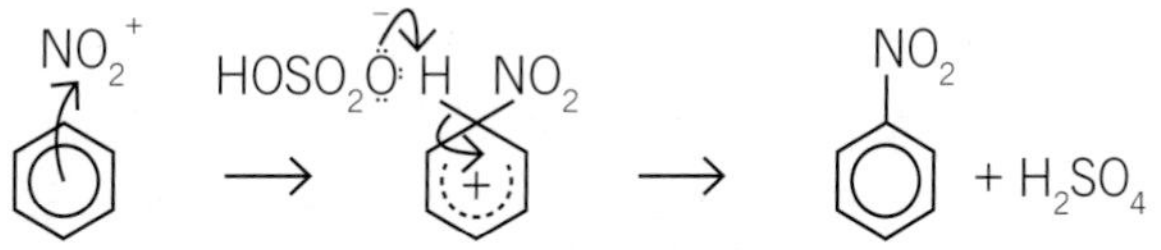

the overall reaction is

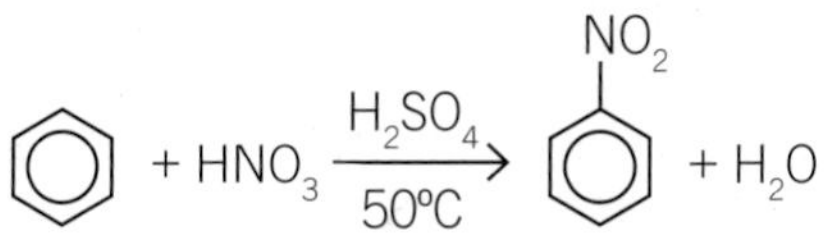

Nitrobenzene is a yellow liquid that is reduced to phenylamine, $C_6H_5NH_2$, by using tin metal and hydrochloric acid.

If the temperature of nitration exceeds 50°C then some 1,3-dinitrobenzene is also produced.

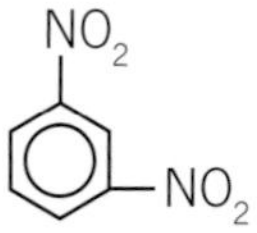

121

Stretch & Challenge

Benzene reacts with sulfuric(VI) acid by electrophilic substitution to give benzenesulfonic acid, $C_6H_6O_3S$, where the sulfur atom is directly bonded to the benzene ring. Deduce the structural formula of benzenesulfonic acid and give the equation for the reaction of benzene with sulfuric(VI) acid to produce this acid.

Halogenation

Benzene and bromine do not react together unless a catalyst such as iron filings, iron(III) bromide or aluminium bromide is present.

$$\text{benzene} + Br_2 \xrightarrow[\text{room temperature}]{Fe/FeBr_3} \text{bromobenzene (Br)} + HBr$$

The π-electron system is not sufficiently nucleophilic to polarise the bromine molecule to any extent to give $Br^{\delta+}-Br^{\delta-}$. In the presence of iron(III) bromide the polarisation of the bromine molecule is more pronounced.

$$\overset{\delta+}{Br}-\overset{\delta-}{Br}\cdots\overset{\delta+}{Fe}\underset{\diagdown Br}{\overset{\diagup Br}{-Br}}$$

! Extra Help

In electrophilic aromatic substitution, the dotted line in the formula of the positively charged intermediate should not extend all the way around the ring. It should not reach the carbon atom at which substitution is occurring.

If iron filings are used then these react with bromine to give iron(III) bromide. One representation of this electrophilic substitution of bromine into the ring is

The role of the iron(III) bromide is catalytic – encouraging greater polarisation of the Br–Br bond so that attack by the ring electrons can occur but being regenerated at the end of the reaction.

Chlorination of benzene can be carried out in a similar way, often using anhydrous aluminium chloride or iron(III) chloride as the catalyst. If an excess of chlorine is used a mixture of 1,2-dichlorobenzene and 1,4-dichlorobenzene is produced.

▼ Study point

When giving a complete equation for the halogenation of benzene, you should also show the other product of the reaction (usually HBr or HCl).

$$\text{benzene} + \text{xs } Cl_2 \xrightarrow{\text{anhydrous } AlCl_3} \text{1,2-dichlorobenzene} + \text{1,4-dichlorobenzene} + HCl$$

In industry the chlorination of benzene is carried out as a continuous process, so that any polychlorination is kept to a minimum.

Chlorobenzene is an important industrial chemical and is nitrated and the nitro-derivatives converted to 2-nitrophenol and 2-nitrophenylamine. The insecticide DDT can be manufactured by the reaction of chlorobenzene with trichloroethanal.

8 Knowledge check

A student was asked to give two reasons how he knew that iron(III) bromide was acting as a catalyst in the bromination of benzene. What do you think he gave as his correct answers?

$$2\ C_6H_5Cl + Cl_3CCHO \xrightarrow{-H_2O} Cl_3C - \underset{\underset{DDT}{\overset{}{\diagdown C_6H_4Cl}}}{\overset{\overset{C_6H_4Cl}{\diagup}}{C}} - H$$

The use of DDT is now heavily restricted because of problems connected with its toxicity, its persistence in the environment and its presence in the food chain.

Friedel–Crafts alkylation

This method provides a way of producing a new carbon-to-carbon bond, giving alkyl derivatives of benzene such as methylbenzene, $C_6H_5CH_3$. The reaction is similar to the halogenation of benzene but uses a halogenoalkane in place of the halogen. Anhydrous aluminium chloride is often used as the catalyst.

Use the equation for the Friedel–Crafts alkylation of benzene and 1-chloropropane to suggest the formula of the major organic product when benzene reacts with 1-chloro-3-methylbutane.

$$\text{benzene} + CH_3CH_2Cl \xrightarrow{AlCl_3} \text{(ethylbenzene, } CH_2CH_3) + HCl$$

One problem with this reaction is that the introduction of an alkyl group onto the ring activates the ring towards further alkylation. As a result the product may also contain 1,2- and 1,4-diethylbenzenes. To reduce the chance of any polyalkylation, the halogenoalkane is added slowly to the benzene and the catalyst. Another problem that may occur is that a primary carbocation formed during the reaction may rearrange to a secondary carbocation.

Give the systematic name of the choroalkane that will react with benzene to give

$$\text{e.g. } CH_3CH_2\overset{+}{C}H_2 \longrightarrow CH_3\overset{+}{C}HCH_3$$

The reaction of 1-chloropropane with benzene gives mainly (1-methylethyl)benzene rather than 1-propylbenzene as the organic product.

$$\text{benzene} + CH_3CH_2CH_2Cl \xrightarrow{AlCl_3} \begin{cases} \text{propylbenzene } CH_2CH_2CH_3 \\ \text{(1-methylethyl)benzene } H_3C\underset{CH}{\diagdown}CH_3 \end{cases}$$

Acid chlorides, such as ethanoyl chloride, also react with benzene in a similar Friedel–Crafts reaction, giving a ketone.

$$\text{benzene} + CH_3C\overset{O}{\underset{Cl}{\diagdown}} \longrightarrow \text{benzene}-C\overset{O}{\underset{CH_3}{\diagdown}} + HCl$$

An important industrial process that uses a Friedel–Crafts style reaction is the manufacture of phenylethene (styrene), $C_6H_5CH=CH_2$.

$$\text{benzene} + CH_2=CH_2 \xrightarrow[AlCl_3]{HCl} \text{benzene}-CH_2CH_3 \xrightarrow[630°C]{ZnO} \text{benzene}-CH=CH_2$$

Stretch & Challenge

Compound M contains both aliphatic and aromatic C–Cl bonds. On heating with aqueous sodium hydroxide, it gives a new compound of formula $C_7H_3Cl_5O$. Deduce the structural formula of compound M, giving reasons for your answer.

9 **Knowledge check**

A sample of 1-bromo-4-(bromomethyl)benzene was heated under reflux with aqueous sodium hydroxide. Give the displayed formula of the most likely organic product.

The comparative strength of C–Cl bonds in chlorobenzene and chloroalkanes

Chloroalkanes such as 1-chlorohexane, react with aqueous sodium hydroxide on heating under reflux, giving hexan-1-ol as the main organic product.

$$CH_3(CH_2)_4\,CH_2Cl + NaOH \longrightarrow CH_3(CH_2)_4CH_2OH + NaCl$$

The mechanism for this nucleophilic substitution reaction is

$$CH_3(CH_2)_4 - \overset{\overset{\displaystyle H}{|}}{\underset{\underset{\displaystyle H}{|}}{C}} \overset{\delta^+}{} \overset{\delta^-}{Cl} \quad \underset{\ddot{O}^- - H}{} \longrightarrow CH_3(CH_2)_4 - \overset{\overset{\displaystyle H}{|}}{\underset{\underset{\displaystyle H}{|}}{C}} - \ddot{O} - H + \ddot{Cl}^-$$

Benzene tends to react by electrophilic substitution. It has little tendency to react with nucleophiles, as these would be repelled by the stable π-system of electrons.

The bond energies and bond lengths of aliphatic and aromatic carbon-to-chlorine bonds are shown in the table.

Bond	Bond length / nm	Bond energy / kJmol^{-1}
aliphatic C — Cl	0.177	346
aromatic C — Cl	0.169	399

The stronger (and shorter) bond between carbon and chlorine in chlorobenzene results from a non-bonding p electron pair on chlorine overlapping with the ring π-system of electrons. The resulting bond needs much more energy to be broken and is stronger that an aliphatic C–Cl bond. Forcing conditions are therefore needed to produce phenol from chlorobenzene.

$$\underset{}{\text{Cl—C}_6\text{H}_5} \xrightarrow[\text{300°C/increased pressure}]{\text{NaOH(aq)}} \underset{}{\text{HO—C}_6\text{H}_5} + \text{NaCl}$$

This reaction is not an environmentally viable method of producing phenol commercially. In industry phenol is generally made from (1-methylethyl)benzene (cumene). This method has the advantage that propanone is a useful co-product of the reaction.

4.3
Alcohols and phenols

Unit 4

An introduction to the chemistry of the alcohols is part of the AS
course and is studied in Topic 2.7. Alcohols contain the –OH group
bonded to a carbon atom and these are studied to a greater depth
in this section. The A2 course provides an introduction to aromatic
chemistry and this section also considers phenols where an –OH
group is bonded directly to a benzene ring.

You should be able to demonstrate and apply knowledge
and understanding of:

- The methods of forming primary and secondary alcohols
  from halogenoalkanes and carbonyl compounds.

- The reactions of primary and secondary alcohols with
  hydrogen halides, ethanoyl chloride and carboxylic acids.

- The acidity of phenol and its reactions with bromine and
  ethanoyl chloride.

- The test for phenols using aqueous iron(III) chloride.

Content

Key Term

Nucleophiles are ions or compounds possessing a lone pair of electrons that can seek out a relatively positive site (often a δ+ carbon atom). Common nucleophiles include $^-$OH, $^-$CN and NH_3.

Stretch & Challenge

Laevulinic acid, $CH_3COCH_2CH_2COOH$, is easily obtained by heating fructose or glucose with concentrated hydrochloric acid. Write the formula of the organic compound produced when laevulinic acid reacts with an aqueous solution of $NaBH_4$.

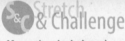

Stretch & Challenge

Name the alcohol produced when

is reduced by lithium tetrahydridoaluminate(III).

Stretch & Challenge

0.200 mole of 2-bromobutane, $CH_3CH_2CHBrCH_3$, is refluxed with potassium hydroxide dissolved in a 50:50 ethanol/water mixture.

(i) Give the structural formula of the two alkenes produced.

(ii) The actual yield of butan-2-ol is 0.095 mole. Calculate the percentage yield of butan-2-ol.

(iii) What should be done to increase the yield of butan-2-ol?

Forming primary and secondary alcohols

The difference between primary and secondary alcohols is that primary alcohols have no more than one carbon atom directly bonded to the carbon of the C–OH group. Secondary alcohols have two carbon atoms bonded to the carbon atom of the C–OH group. All primary alcohols contain the $-CH_2OH$ group whereas all secondary alcohols contain the $-CH(OH)$ group. There are also tertiary alcohols, e.g. 2-methylpropan-2-ol, $(CH_3)_3COH$.

propan-1-ol
primary

pentan-3-ol
secondary

phenylmethanol
primary

cyclohexanol
secondary

There are two common methods of forming primary and secondary alcohols:

- From halogenoalkanes by a substitution reaction

- By reducing aldehydes, ketones or carboxylic acids.

From a halogenoalkane

This reaction is carried out by refluxing together the halogenoalkane and an **aqueous** solution of an alkali (usually sodium or potassium hydroxide).

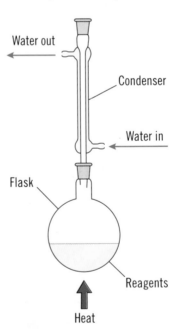

For example, butan-1-ol can be produced from 1-bromobutane.

$$CH_3CH_2CH_2CH_2Br + NaOH \rightarrow CH_3CH_2CH_2CH_2OH + NaBr$$

The products of the reaction have to be separated. The organic reactant and the product, butan-1-ol are both liquids but have different boiling temperatures (100°C and 118°C respectively). Fractional distillation can be used to separate butan-1-ol from unreacted 1-bromobutane.

! Extra Help

The term 'carbonyl compound' in this section refers to aldehydes, ketones and carboxylic acids, and not to esters or acid chlorides. Only the reduction of aldehydes and ketones is required for the A2 course.

▼ **Study point**

When giving an equation for the reduction of a carboxylic acid with lithium tetrahydridoaluminate(III) you must not forget that water is also a product of the reaction.

YOU SHOULD KNOW › › ›

››› the two specified methods for preparing primary and secondary alcohols by hydrolysis and reduction

››› the mechanism for the hydrolysis of halogenoalkanes by hydroxide ions

The mechanism of this reaction is nucleophilic substitution where the hydroxide ion (⁻OH) acts as the **nucleophile** and attacks the relatively positive carbon atom (δ+) of the C–Br bond.

$$CH_3 - CH_2 - CH_2 - \overset{\overset{\displaystyle H}{|}}{\underset{\underset{\displaystyle \overset{..}{O} - H}{|}}{C}} - \overset{\delta^+}{\underset{}{}} \overset{\delta^-}{\ddot{Br}} : \longrightarrow CH_3 - CH_2 - CH_2 - \overset{\overset{\displaystyle H}{|}}{\underset{\underset{\displaystyle H}{|}}{C}} - \overset{..}{O} - H$$

$$+ :\ddot{Br}^-$$

In general the rate of the hydrolysis is C–I > C–Br > C–Cl and the yield of primary alcohols is usually higher than the yield of secondary alcohols, as some alkenes are formed in the latter reaction. It is important to remember that if the concentration of the alkali is too high, or an ethanolic solution of the alkali is used then the yield of alkali is reduced as larger amounts of alkenes are formed.

Knowledge check 10

(a) An alcohol has the formula $(C_6H_5)_2CHCH_2OH$. This formula shows that it is a .... alcohol.

(b) Give the formula of the compound formed by the reduction of HOOC–COOH by $Li\,Al\,H_4$.

(c) When a carbonyl compound reacts with $NaBH_4$ the alcohol $CH_3CH(OH)CH_3$ is formed. The name of the carbonyl compound is ....

By the reduction of a carbonyl compound

Both aldehydes and ketones can be reduced to primary and secondary alcohols respectively by using an aqueous solution of sodium tetrahydridoborate(III) (sodium borohydride), $NaBH_4$. In an equation, the reducing agent is often represented in an acceptable way, by using [H].

Knowledge check 11

A ketone is reduced with sodium tetrahydridoborate(III). The number of hydrogen atoms in the molecular formula for the alcohol produced is 6 more than in the starting ketone. State and explain the number of carbonyl groups present in the ketone.

$$CH_3 - \overset{\overset{\displaystyle }{\underset{\underset{\displaystyle O}{||}}{C}}}{} - CH_2 - CH_3 \ + \ 2[H] \longrightarrow CH_3 - \overset{\overset{\displaystyle H}{|}}{\underset{\underset{\displaystyle OH}{|}}{C}} - CH_2 - CH_3$$

butan–2–ol

$$\text{phenylmethanal (benzaldehyde)} + 2[H] \longrightarrow \text{phenylmethanol}$$

Sodium tetrahydridoborate(III) is not powerful enough to reduce carboxylic acids and the stronger reducing agent lithium tetrahydridoaluminate (III) (lithium aluminium hydride or 'lithal'), LiAlH$_4$, dissolved in ethoxyethane can be used instead.

$$\underset{\text{hexane-1,6-dioic acid}}{\overset{O}{\underset{OH}{\diagdown}}C - (CH_2)_4 - C\overset{O}{\underset{OH}{\diagup}}} + 8[H] \longrightarrow \underset{\text{hexane-1-6-diol}}{HOCH_2 - (CH_2)_4 - CH_2OH} + 2H_2O$$

In general the reduction using sodium tetrahydridoborate(III) is a much safer reaction as an excess of lithium tetrahydridoaluminate(III) is difficult to dispose of in an easy way and the solvent ethoxyethane is very flammable. To obtain a good yield of the alcohol an excess of the reducing agent is used. The excess reducing agent can be removed by adding a dilute acid. The organic product needs to be separated from the aqueous mixture. This is carried out using a separating funnel if the alcohol produced is immiscible with water, or separated by adding an organic solvent such as ethoxyethane, by the technique of solvent extraction.

Reactions of primary and secondary alcohols with hydrogen halides, ethanoyl chloride and carboxylic acids

Reaction with hydrogen halides

Halogenoalkanes are produced by reacting primary or secondary alcohols with hydrogen halides. Unfortunately, it is not as simple as this sentence implies. These reactions are generally slow and reversible, and often give poor yields. The most appropriate method depends on which halogen is to be substituted.

Chlorination One method is to pass hydrogen chloride gas into the alcohol in the presence of anhydrous zinc chloride, which acts as a catalyst.

$$CH_3CH_2CH_2CH_2OH \xrightarrow[\substack{ZnCl_2 \\ heat}]{HCl} CH_3CH_2CH_2CH_2Cl$$

The first stage of this process is protonation of the alcohol.

$$CH_3CH_2CH_2CH_2 - \overset{..}{\underset{\underset{H-\overset{..}{Cl}:}{\diagup}}{O}} - H \longrightarrow CH_3CH_2CH_2CH_2 - \overset{+..}{\underset{H}{O}} - H + :\overset{..}{\underset{..}{Cl}}^-$$

Knowledge check

Suggest a two-stage synthesis to make compound B from compound A.

Compound A   Compound B

① Extra Help

If you are asked to give an equation for a reaction in organic chemistry, the formula of all reactants and products should be given. It is sometimes acceptable to put the reacting reagent over the equation arrow. If a small molecule product is lost from the reaction, for example H$_2$O or HCl, this can be shown under the arrow with a minus sign in front.

An alternative method is to react the alcohol with phosphorus(V) chloride.

$$H_3C\!-\!CH.CH_2OH + PCl_5 \longrightarrow H_3C\!-\!CH.CH_2Cl + POCl_3 + HCl$$

1-chloro-2-methylpropane

One problem with this reaction is that phosphorus(V) oxide trichloride, $POCl_3$, is a liquid and needs to be removed from the reaction mixture. If the halogenoalkane has a similar boiling temperature to $POCl_3$, then separation becomes difficult.

A further method is to react the alcohol with sulfur(VI) oxide dichloride (thionyl chloride), $SOCl_2$.

$$\langle\bigcirc\rangle\!-\!CH_2CH_2OH + SOCl_2 \longrightarrow \langle\bigcirc\rangle\!-\!CH_2CH_2Cl + SO_2 + HCl$$

One advantage of this method is that the co-products sulfur(VI) oxide and hydrogen chloride are both gaseous and are easily lost from the reaction mixture, ensuring easier separation.

Bromination The most convenient way of producing a bromoalkane from a primary or secondary alcohol is to carry out an '*in situ*' reaction. In one method, a mixture of the alcohol, potassium bromide and 50% sulfuric(VI) acid is heated. The sulfuric(VI) acid protonates the alcohol and this then reacts with the bromide ions from the potassium bromide. The overall equation for the preparation of 1-bromobutane in this way is

$$CH_3CH_2CH_2CH_2OH + KBr + H_2SO_4 \rightarrow CH_3CH_2CH_2CH_2Br + KHSO_4 + H_2O$$

Iodination The usual method is to warm damp red phosphorus and iodine together to form phosphorus(III) iodide, PI_3, which then reacts with alcohol present.

$$2P + 3I_2 \rightarrow 2PI_3$$

$$3CH_3CH_2CH_2OH + PI_3 \rightarrow 3CH_3CH_2CH_2I + H_3PO_3$$

Reaction with ethanoyl chloride

An alcohol reacts rapidly with ethanoyl chloride giving an **ester**. During this reaction misty fumes of hydrogen chloride are seen. This method gives a better yield of an ester than using a carboxylic acid, as the reaction is not reversible. However, the cost of acid chlorides means that this is not a cost-efficient process in industry.

$$H_3C\!-\!\underset{H_3C}{\overset{H}{C}}\!-\!OH + CH_3C\overset{O}{\underset{Cl}{=}} \longrightarrow CH_3C\overset{O}{\underset{O-C(CH_3)_2}{\underset{|}{H}}} + HCl$$

1-methylethyl ethanoate

Reaction with carboxylic acids

Primary and secondary alcohols react with carboxylic acids to give esters.

alcohol + carboxylic acid $\longrightarrow$ ester + H_2O

Stretch & Challenge

In an experiment to make 2-bromopentane, pentan-2-ol was reacted with potassium bromide and 50% sulfuric acid. The yield of pentan-2-ol was lower than expected. Mass spectrometry showed the presence of two hydrocarbon products, both of which had a relative molecular mass of 70. Suggest structural formulae for these two hydrocarbons and explain how they are obtained as side-products in this reaction.

Stretch & Challenge

State the name of the alcohol that reacts with ethanoyl chloride to give the ester whose formula is

Key Term

An **ester** always contains a

$-C\overset{O}{\underset{O-}{=}}$ group.

Extra Help

The displayed formulae of esters are generally written 'backwards' with the 'acid' part first but they can be written as the name suggests. For example

$$CH_3\!-\!C\overset{O}{\underset{O-CH_2CH_3}{=}}$$

is the formula for ethyl ethanoate and so is

$$CH_3CH_2O\!-\!C\overset{O}{\underset{CH_3}{=}}$$

Extra Help

In the fractional distillation of an ester mixture where sulfuric acid is used as the catalyst, the sulfuric acid is left in the distillation flask. Some carboxylic acid may distil over with the ester and this is neutralised by the addition of sodium hydrogencarbonate.

Link Link to the esterification of carboxylic acids, page 145 and AS Section 2.7.

Stretch & Challenge

Butane-1,4-dioic acid reacts with an excess of methanol. Give the **empirical** formula of the resulting ester.

---

13 Knowledge check

A student reacted a primary alcohol **A** with ethanoic acid. The mass spectrum of the ester produced showed a molecular ion at m/z 130. State the name of the primary alcohol **A**.

---

14 Knowledge check

An ester, containing one ester group, contains 36.4% by mass of oxygen. Show that the ester could be ethyl ethanoate.

Stretch & Challenge

Write the name and structural formula of the ester that is isomeric with ethanoic acid.

---

15 Knowledge check

The molecular formula of an ester is $C_6H_{12}O_2$. This ester is produced from an alcohol whose molecular formula is C_3H_8O. Write a displayed formula for the ester.

YOU SHOULD KNOW › › ›

››› the different methods needed to replace the hydroxide group in an alcohol by a particular halogen

››› how to produce esters from an alcohol and an acid chloride or a carboxylic acid

---

The reaction is reversible and eventually the mixture will reach a position of equilibrium. To increase the yield of the ester, a little concentrated sulfuric(VI) acid is added to the mixture of the alcohol and the carboxylic acid and the mixture is heated under reflux. The products can then be distilled and the ester collected at its boiling temperature. The distillate generally consists of the ester and water, together with a little unreacted alcohol and carboxylic acid. Many esters are immiscible with water and the distillate often consists of two layers. A separating funnel is used to extract the ester, which is then shaken with sodium hydrogencarbonate solution to remove any remaining carboxylic acid. The ester is then dried with anhydrous calcium chloride, which reacts with any remaining alcohol. The ester can then be redistilled to give a pure product.

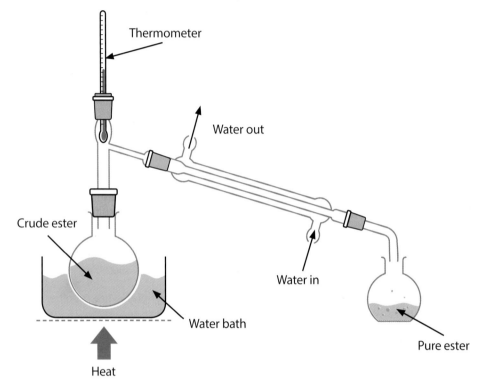

1-Butyl ethanoate can be made in this way from butan-1-ol and ethanoic acid.

Many esters occur naturally and are extensively used in the cosmetic industry as components of perfumes. Esters also have important uses as solvents, for example in nail varnish.

The acidity of phenol and its reactions with bromine and ethanoyl chloride

The acidity of phenol

Phenols are aromatic compounds where –OH groups are bonded directly to a benzene ring

phenol

thymol
(2-isopropyl-5-methylphenol)

'PCMX'
the active ingredient in 'Dettol'©
(4-chloro-3,5-dimethylphenol)

The reactivity of phenols is quite different from that of alcohols. This is partly because one of the lone pairs of the oxygen atom can overlap with the delocalised π system to form a more extended delocalised system. As a result the C–O bond in phenols is shorter and stronger than in an alcohol. This makes C–O bond fission in a phenol harder than C–O bond fission in an alcohol. This extended delocalisation creates a higher electron density in the ring and makes the ring structure more susceptible to attack by electrophiles. Phenols are much more acidic than alcohols. This means that phenol is a stronger acid than ethanol but a considerably weaker acid than ethanoic acid. The ionisation of phenol gives the phenoxide ion, $C_6H_5O^-$.

$$\text{⬡—OH} + H_2O \rightleftharpoons \text{⬡—O}^- + H_3O^+$$

Delocalisation of the negative charge on this ion gives added stability to the phenoxide anion. Phenol itself is not very soluble in water, owing to the –OH group being a small part of a largely hydrophobic molecule. It does dissolve readily in aqueous sodium hydroxide giving a solution of sodium phenoxide.

$$\text{⬡—OH} + NaOH \longrightarrow \text{⬡—O}^- Na^+ + H_2O$$

This is an example of phenol reacting as an acid, losing a proton to the aqueous hydroxide ion present from the sodium hydroxide. The presence of substituents on the benzene ring affects the acidity of phenol. The pK_a of the active component in Dettol© is similar to that of phenol but the pK_a of 2,4-dinitrophenol at 4.30 shows its greater acidity, due to the presence of the two nitro groups.

Although phenol is a weak acid it is not strong enough to react with sodium carbonate or sodium hydrogencarbonate to produce carbon dioxide. A simple test to distinguish between a simple aliphatic acid, such as ethanoic acid, and phenol is to add sodium carbonate solution. The ethanoic acid will react to give bubbles of carbon dioxide but phenol will not.

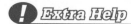

Extra Help

pKa is a term that is used to show how much a compound is dissociated into its anion and hydrogen ions.

$$R - OH_{(aq)} \rightleftharpoons RO^-_{(aq)} + H^+_{(aq)}$$

Stretch & Challenge

The table shows the pK_a of some phenols.

Phenol	pKa
2,4,6–trichlorophenol	6.0
4–nitrophenol	7.2
2–methylphenol	10.2

State which compound(s) are stronger acids than phenol, giving a reason for your choice.

Extra Help

When testing for phenol using aqueous bromine, the usual method is to add aqueous bromine dropwise to the phenol solution. The bromine is at first decolourised and then when more bromine is added, a white precipitate of 2,4,6-tribromophenol is seen. If phenol was added to aqueous bromine, it would be more difficult to see the immediate decolourisation of the bromine.

Stretch & Challenge

Explain why 2,4,6-tribromophenol shows only two separate singlet signals in its ¹H NMR spectrum.

Stretch & Challenge

Phenol reacts with dilute nitric acid to give 2-nitrophenol and 4-nitrophenol in yields of 70% and 30% respectively. Suggest two reasons that may explain this ~2:1 proportion of products.

16 Knowledge check

Aspirin
(2-ethanoyloxybenzenecarboxylic acid)

can be produced by reacting 2-hydroxybenzenecarboxylic acid (salicylic acid) with ethanoic anhydride. Describe, using a chemical test, how you would show that no remaining salicylic acid was present as an impurity in the sample of aspirin.

YOU SHOULD KNOW ›››

››› the relative acidity of phenols, alcohol and carboxylic acids

››› that phenols will react with aqueous bromine and with aqueous iron(III) chloride and that these reactions can used as tests for the presence of an –OH group directly bonded to benzene ring

The reaction of phenol with bromine

The presence of an –OH group bonded directly to a benzene ring activates the ring to attack by electrophiles. Each position is activated towards attack but the 2-, 4- and 6- positions are activated to a greater extent. As a result an incoming substituent is likely to replace a hydrogen atom at one, or more, of these positions. For example, when phenol is treated with dilute nitric acid, both 2- and 4-nitrophenol are formed.

When phenol reacts with bromine, the increased electron density in the ring polarises the bromine molecules giving $Br^{\delta+}- Br^{\delta-}$. Aqueous bromine (bromine water) reacts with phenol to produce a white precipitate of 2,4,6-tribromophenol.

Since aqueous bromine is an orange solution and the products of the reaction are a colourless solution and a white precipitate, the orange colour disappears – 'bromine is decolourised'. This reaction can be used as a test for phenol. This result is different from the reaction of bromine with an alkene, as the reaction with phenol results in the decolourisation of bromine without the additional formation of a white precipitate. The mechanism for this reaction with phenol is electrophilic substitution where the electrophile is $Br^{\delta+}$. Bromine reacts with water to give some HOBr and HBr

$$Br_2 + H_2O \rightleftharpoons H - \overset{\delta^-}{O} - \overset{\delta^+}{Br} + HBr$$

but the concentration of $Br^{\delta+}$ from HOBr is very small as the position of equilibrium lies well to the left.

If the 2,4 or 6- positions of a phenol are already blocked by a substituent, the bromine generally substitutes in the remaining 2,4 or 6- positions. For example, 2-methylphenol gives 4,6-dibromo-2-methylphenol,

whereas 3-methylphenol gives 2,4,6-tribromo-3-methylphenol.

In 2,4-dinitrophenol only the 6-position is free for substitution in this way and 6-bromo-2,4-dinitrophenol is the product.

The reaction of phenol with ethanoyl chloride

Alcohols and phenols can react as nucleophiles by the use of their oxygen lone pairs. However, the delocalisation of an electron pair from the oxygen atom in a phenol means that it is more difficult for a phenol to react as a nucleophile, e.g. in a reaction with a carboxylic acid to give an ester. As a result carboxylic acids are not suitable reagents to make an ester with phenol, even the reaction of phenol with ethanoyl chloride is quite slow at room temperature.

A base, such as pyridine, C_5H_5N, can be added to speed up this reaction. The pyridine reacts with the hydrogen chloride co-product to give pyridinium chloride, $C_5H_5NH^+Cl^-$. Ethanoyl chloride is an expensive reagent and ethanoic anhydride is often used in preference.

If phenol is reacted with a less reactive acyl chloride, such as benzoyl chloride, C_6H_5COCl, then aqueous conditions can be used as the acyl chloride is only slowly hydrolysed by water. In this reaction phenol is added to aqueous sodium hydroxide and the mixture shaken.

Testing for phenols with aqueous iron(III) chloride

Phenol will react with iron(III) chloride to produce a purple colour in the aqueous solution. The colour is produced by a complex being formed between the two reagents. Any compound that contains an –OH bond group bonded directly to a benzene ring will give a brightly coloured complex when reacted with iron(III) chloride – generally these are purple, blue or green in colour.

4.4
Aldehydes and ketones

Aldehydes and ketones are carbonyl compounds (containing a C=O bond). Other organic compounds, such as carboxylic acids and esters, also contain a carbonyl group but in a ketone the carbonyl group is bonded directly to two carbon atoms, rather than oxygen atoms. In an aldehyde the carbonyl group is bonded to a hydrogen atom, and to another hydrogen atom or a carbon atom. Aldehydes and ketones are common in nature and have important domestic and industrial uses. It is the polar nature of this carbonyl bond that makes aldehydes and ketones react in a different way to the alkenes, which contain a C=C bond.

Content

You should be able to demonstrate and apply knowledge and understanding of:

- The formation of aldehydes and ketones by the oxidation of primary and secondary alcohols respectively.

- How aldehydes and ketones may be distinguished by their relative ease of oxidation using Tollens' reagent and Fehling's reagent.

- The reduction of aldehydes and ketones using sodium tetrahydridoborate(III).

- The mechanism of nucleophilic addition, such as in the addition of hydrogen cyanide to ethanal and propanone.

- The reaction of aldehydes and ketones with 2,4-dinitrophenylhydrazine and its use in testing for a carbonyl group and the identification of specific aldehydes and ketones.

- The triiodomethane (iodoform) test and its use in identifying $CH_3C=O$ groups or their precursors.

The structure and naming of aldehydes and ketones

Both aldehydes and ketones contain the polar $C^{\delta+}=O^{\delta-}$ group. This occurs because oxygen in this bond has a greater electronegativity, leaving the carbon atom slightly electron deficient. The double bond comprises a σ-bond, and a π-bond above and below the plane of the sigma bond, caused by p-p orbital overlap, as in an alkene. In an aldehyde, the carbon atom of the carbonyl group bonds to at least one hydrogen atom. An aldehyde has the suffix -al at the end of the name and a ketone ends in -one.

methanal   propanal   benzaldehyde (benzenecarbaldehyde)

A ketone has the carbonyl carbon atom directly bonded to two other carbon atoms.

propanone   phenylethanone   1,5–dichloropentan–3–one

Aldehydes and ketones are very common in both flora and fauna. For example the Pacific sea slug *Navanax intermis* excretes an alarm pheromone that contains Navenone B.

Navenone B

Formation by the oxidation of alcohols

Some alcohol chemistry has been studied during the first year of this course and this included their oxidation. The usual oxidising agent is acidified potassium (or sodium) dichromate, shown as [O] in an equation. Primary alcohols are oxidised to an aldehyde and then, on further oxidation, to a carboxylic acid. The orange colour of aqueous dichromate(VI) ions becomes green as Cr^{3+}(aq) ions are produced.

$$CH_3CH_2OH + [O] \longrightarrow CH_3 - C{\overset{H}{\underset{O}{}}} + H_2O$$

$$CH_3 - C{\overset{H}{\underset{O}{}}} + [O] \longrightarrow CH_3 - C{\overset{OH}{\underset{O}{}}}$$

Knowledge check 18

A double bond (C=C) can be hydrogenated to produce a C–C single bond. What reagent is used to carry out this reaction?

Knowledge check 19

Look at the formula of the sea slug pheromone, Navenone B. If the C=C bonds in this compound are fully hydrogenated, state the molecular formula of the product.

Knowledge check 20

Cyclohexanol is oxidised by acidified dichromate to cyclohexanone. Complete the equation for this reaction.

$+ [O] \longrightarrow$

Stretch & Challenge

(a) Describe a test given by compound E to show that it is an aldehyde.

$$HO - CH_2CH_2CH_2C{\overset{H}{\underset{O}{}}}$$

Compound E

(b) Give the structural formula of another isomer of $C_4H_8O_2$ that will not undergo the reaction that you have described for the isomer in (a).

A secondary alcohol is similarly oxidised to a ketone.

$$\begin{array}{c} CH_3 \\ \diagdown \\ C \\ \diagup \diagdown \\ CH_3 OH \end{array} \begin{array}{c} H \end{array} + [O] \longrightarrow \begin{array}{c} CH_3 \\ \diagdown \\ C = O + H_2O \\ \diagup \\ CH_3 \end{array}$$

Under normal conditions a ketone cannot be further oxidised by this method. Acidified potassium manganate(VII) can also be used as the oxidising agent – the purple colour of the manganate(VII) ion is lost and a colourless solution containing aqueous manganese(II) ions remains. If an aldehyde is required then this must be removed from the reaction mixture before further oxidation to the carboxylic acid can occur. One common method when producing the aldehyde, is to add the oxidising agent slowly to the alcohol.

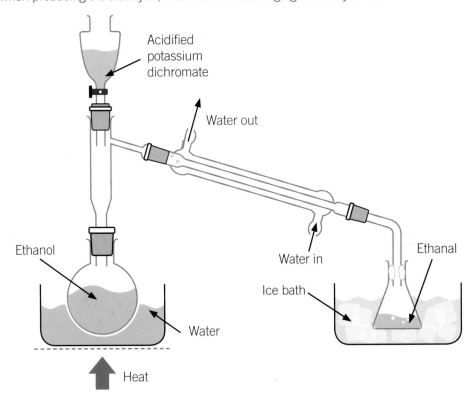

The temperature and rate of addition are controlled so that ethanal vapour reaches the top of the column, which then condenses to be collected in a cooled flask.

Distinguishing between aldehydes and ketones

Aldehydes can be further oxidised to carboxylic acids, but the further oxidation of ketones is more difficult. If a mild oxidising agent is added to an aldehyde, then the aldehyde will be oxidised, and the oxidising agent itself is reduced. Several simple tests show whether a compound is an aldehyde or a ketone. One of these tests uses Tollens' reagent (sometimes called ammoniacal silver nitrate). It is made by adding aqueous sodium hydroxide to silver nitrate solution until a brown precipitate of silver(I) oxide is formed. Aqueous ammonia is then added until the silver(I) oxide just redissolves. The suspected aldehyde is then added to this reagent and the tube is gently warmed in a beaker of water. If the compound is an aldehyde, a silver mirror coats the inside of the tube as the Ag+ ions are reduced to silver. Less soluble aldehydes, like benzaldehyde, are reluctant to react in this way. A ketone will not reduce Tollens' reagent.

Another mild oxidising agent that will react with an aldehyde (but not a ketone) is Fehling's reagent. This test also shows the presence of an aldehyde group in reducing sugars such as glucose. This test was first developed by the German chemist Hermann von Fehling in 1849. The reagent is freshly prepared by mixing together two solutions, Fehling's A and Fehling's B. Fehling's A is an aqueous solution of copper(II) sulfate. Fehling's B is an aqueous solution of potassium sodium tartrate, which is made alkaline with sodium hydroxide. On mixing the two solutions a deep blue solution containing a complex copper(II) ion is produced. If an aldehyde is added to this deep blue solution and the mixture warmed in a water bath, then the aldehyde reduces the complex copper(II) ions and the deep blue solution is replaced by an orange-red precipitate of copper(I) oxide.

Fehling's solution decomposes easily and so the two solutions are mixed when needed. Benedict's reagent is a similar reagent containing a complex copper(II) ion and is similarly reduced to copper(I) oxide. This solution has the advantage that it is stable and is safer to use, as it is less alkaline. The test using these solutions is effective in identifying aliphatic aldehydes but it does not react with aromatic aldehydes such as benzaldehyde (C_6H_5CHO).

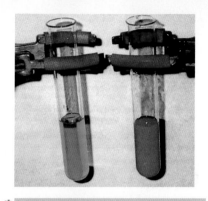

YOU SHOULD KNOW › › ›

› › › the separate tests given by aldehydes but but not ketones

⟨**Link**⟩ Preparation of alcohols by reduction page 127.

The reduction of aldehydes and ketones

Aldehydes and ketones can be reduced to primary and secondary alcohols respectively. The reducing agents used are sodium tetrahydridoborate(III), $NaBH_4$, or lithium tetrahydridoaluminate(III), $LiAlH_4$. Of these two reagents, $NaBH_4$ is preferred as it is safer and can be used in aqueous conditions. In writing equations to show this reduction it is acceptable to use [H] to represent the formula of the reducing agent.

YOU SHOULD KNOW › › ›

› › › that aldehydes and ketones can be reduced by reducing agents such as $NaBH_4$ and $LiAlH_4$

$$\underset{O}{\overset{H}{=}}CCH_2CH_2CH_2C\underset{O}{\overset{H}{=}} + 2[H] \longrightarrow HOCH_2CH_2CH_2CH_2CH_2OH$$

More details of this reaction are seen in Topic 4.3 on alcohols.

Nucleophilic addition reactions of aldehydes and ketones

Aldehydes and ketones contain a polar carbonyl bond, $C^{\delta+}=O^{\delta-}$. The relatively electron-deficient carbon atom can be attacked by nucleophiles, such as a cyanide ion, ^-CN. The reaction of propanone with hydrogen cyanide is an example of this reaction.

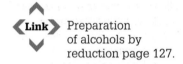

$$\underset{H_3C}{\overset{H_3C}{>}}C=O + H-C\equiv N \longrightarrow \underset{H_3C}{\overset{H_3C}{>}}C\underset{C\equiv N}{\overset{OH}{<}}$$

2-hydroxy-2-methylpropanenitrile

In practice, the reaction is not as straightforward as the equation suggests. Hydrogen cyanide is a very weak acid and the concentration of cyanide ions present is relatively low.

$$H-C\equiv N \rightleftharpoons H^+_{(aq)} + {}^-C\equiv N:_{(aq)}$$

The reaction depends on the initial attack of cyanide ions on propanone. The reaction mixture contains propanone together with aqueous sodium or potassium cyanide, which provide a source of cyanide ions. Sulfuric acid is then slowly added to the stirred mixture. The mechanism for this reaction is described as nucleophilic addition, as it involves attack by the nucleophile ⁻CN and the overall addition of HCN across the C=O bond.

This reaction is important as it forms a method for extending the length of the carbon chain. Hydrolysis of the hydroxynitrile produced by this addition, by refluxing with a dilute acid, gives a hydroxyacid.

2–hydroxy–2–methylpropanoic acid

PRACTICAL CHECK

The identification of an aldehyde or ketone by their reaction with 2,4-dinitrophenylhydrazine is a **specified practical task**.

The identification of aldehydes and ketones using 2,4-dinitrophenylhydrazine

Many common aldehydes and ketones are liquids at room temperature and pressure. The identification of a suspected aldehyde or ketone can be carried out by finding its boiling temperature but some of the boiling temperatures are too similar to each other or are too low or too high, and this makes identification difficult. If an aldehyde or ketone reacts with a suitable reagent to give a solid with a definite melting temperature within an acceptable temperature range, then it makes identification easier. One reagent that is used to produce a suitable solid is 2,4-dinitrophenylhydrazine, $C_6H_3(NO_2)_2NHNH_2$. This material is dissolved in an acid to give a solution called Brady's reagent. Mixing with a suspected aldehyde or ketone gives an orange-red solid, which is filtered off and purified. The formation of this precipitate indicates that the starting material is an aldehyde or ketone. The melting temperature of the purified product (a 2,4-dinitrophenylhydrazone) is taken and compared with a table of known values, to identify the aldehyde or ketone present. This process is called 'making a derivative' or 'derivatisation'.

The mechanism of this reaction is outside the scope of this specification but the reaction proceeds by the nucleophilic attack by a nitrogen lone pair of electrons on the carbonyl carbon atom followed by the elimination of a water molecule. This mechanism is described as nucleophilic addition-elimination. This is sometimes called a **condensation** reaction. The melting temperatures for some 2,4-dinitrophenylhydrazones are shown in the table.

YOU SHOULD KNOW › › ›

››› that many aldehydes and ketones are liquids with low boiling temperatures and that a solid derivative is made to help identify them

Compound	Formula	Boiling temperature /°C	Melting temperature of 2,4–dinitrophenylhydrozone /°C
propanone	CH_3 \ $C=O$ / CH_3	56	187
butanone	CH_3CH_2 \ $C=O$ / CH_3	80	111
pentan–2–one	$CH_3CH_2CH_2$ \ $C=O$ / CH_3	102	143
pentan–3–one	CH_3CH_2 \ $C=O$ / CH_3CH_2	102	156

The identification of aldehydes and ketones in this way is traditionally called a 'wet' method. The use of GC/MS (gas chromatography/mass spectrometry) and NMR has made the identification of these compounds an easier and quicker process.

The triiodomethane (iodoform) reaction

Triiodomethane (traditional name 'iodoform'), CHI_3, is a yellow solid that has some uses as an antiseptic. The formation of this yellow solid is used to identify the presence of a $CH_3C=O$ group (sometimes called a methyl carbonyl group), or a $CH_3CH(OH)$ group in a molecule. The organic compound is warmed with a colourless solution of iodine in aqueous sodium hydroxide ('alkaline iodine') or alternatively with an aqueous mixture of potassium iodide and sodium chlorate(I),NaOCl. These reagents are sometimes represented by I_2/NaOH and I^-/OCl$^-$. This reaction is not completely restricted to carbonyl compounds that contain this grouping. For example, the reaction is also given by ethanol, this is because the reagent used is an oxidising mixture and will oxidise the $CH_3CH(OH)$ grouping in ethanol to ethanal, which contains a $CH_3C=O$ group.

An equation for the reaction of propanone with alkaline iodine is

$$CH_3COCH_3 + 3I_2 + 4\,NaOH \longrightarrow CHI_3 + CH_3COO^-Na^+ + 3NaI + 3H_2O$$

However, the reaction is more complicated than the equation implies and a number of side reactions also occur.

Knowledge check 21

The formula of a 2,4-dinitrophenylhydrazone of a ketone is

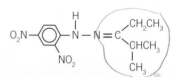

State the name of the starting ketone.

Knowledge check 22

Which of these compounds will undergo the triiodomethane reaction?

(a) Hexan-2-one ✓

(b) Cyclohexanone ✓

(c) 1-Phenylethanol ✶

(d) 2-Methylpropan-2-ol ✗

YOU SHOULD KNOW ›››

››› the test for methyl ketones and their precursors

! Extra Help

Common compounds that undergo the triiodomethane reaction include ethanol, ethanal, propan–2-ol, propanone, butanone, butan-2-ol and phenylethanone.

Among compounds that can be distinguished because they do **not** undergo the triiodomethane reaction are methanol, propan-1-ol and propanal.

4.5
Carboxylic acids and their derivatives

Carboxylic acids contain a –COOH group, where the carbon atom of a C=O group is also bonded to an O–H group. Many carboxylic acids are familiar substances, for example, ethanoic acid is the active ingredient in vinegar, citric acid in lemons and malic acid in apples. The –OH group present in a carboxylic acid can be replaced by chlorine, giving an acid chloride, which, in turn, can be converted to an amide where the –OH group has been replaced by an –NH$_2$ group. Derivatives of carboxylic acids also include esters where the –OH group has been replaced by an –OR group.

Content

You should be able to demonstrate and apply knowledge and understanding of:

- The relative acidity of carboxylic acids, phenols, alcohols and water.

- The formation of carboxylic acids by the oxidation of alcohols and aldehydes.

- The reduction of carboxylic acids using LiAlH$_4$.

- The formation of aromatic carboxylic acids by the oxidation of methyl side-chains.

- The decarboxylation of carboxylic acids.

- The conversion of carboxylic acids to esters and acid chlorides and the hydrolysis of these compounds.

- The conversion of carboxylic acids to amides and nitriles.

- The formation of nitriles from halogenoalkanes and hydroxynitriles from aldehydes.

- The hydrolysis of nitriles and amides.

- The reduction of nitriles using LiAlH$_4$.

The structure and naming of carboxylic acids

All carboxylic acids contain at least one –COOH group. The carbon atom or atoms in this group(s) is counted in the carbon chain when they are named. Thus propanoic acid is CH_3CH_2COOH rather than $CH_3CH_2CH_2COOH$ (which has a three carbon **alkyl** chain but is named butanoic acid). If other functional groups are present in the acid then they are named as derivatives of the parent acid.

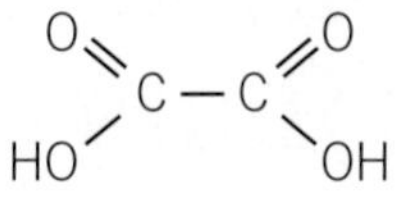

ethanedioic acid

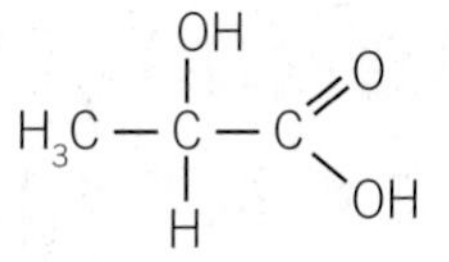

2–hydroxypropanoic acid

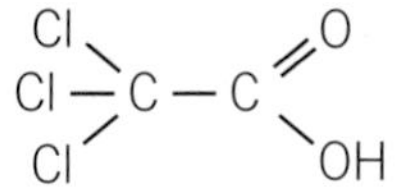

trichloroethanoic acid

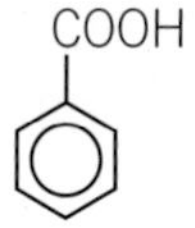

benzoic acid
(benzenecarboxylic acid)

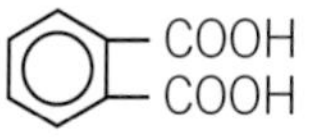

benzene–1,2–dicarboxylic acid

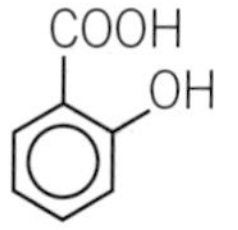

2–hydroxybenzenecarboxylic acid

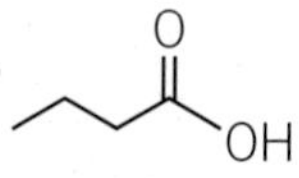

butanoic acid

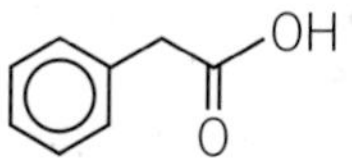

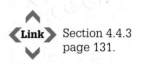

phenylethanoic acid

> **YOU SHOULD KNOW ›››**
>
> ››› how to name carboxylic acids if you are given the formula and vice versa

> **Knowledge check 23**
>
> Give the skeletal formulae of:
>
> (a) 2-methylbutanoic acid
>
> (b) 2-hydroxypropanoic acid
>
> (c) hexane-1,6-dioic acid.

Acidity of carboxylic acids

Carboxylic acids are weak acids and the extent of their ionisation in aqueous solution is very small.

$$CH_3COOH_{(aq)} + H_2O_{(l)} \rightleftharpoons CH_3COO^-_{(aq)} + H_3O^+_{(aq)}$$

At 25°C in an aqueous solution of ethanoic acid of concentration 0.1 mol dm^{-3} only about 0.4% of the acid is dissociated into ions. Carboxylic acids are, however, stronger acids than most phenols. In general the relative order of acidity is

carboxylic acids > phenols > water / alcohols

Link Section 4.4.3 page 131.

> **Knowledge check 24**
>
> Name the carboxylic acid that is reduced to give an unbranched alcohol of formula $C_5H_{12}O$.

This relative difference in acidity can be shown by their reaction with sodium hydrogencarbonate solution. Only carboxylic acids are strong enough acids to produce colourless bubbles of carbon dioxide gas. The presence of other substituent groups may markedly alter the acidity of the carboxylic acid or phenol. Substituting one of the hydrogen atoms in ethanoic acid, giving chloroethanoic acid, $ClCH_2COOH$, increases the dissociation of the acid into ions one hundred times. Trichloroethanoic acid, Cl_3CCOOH, is a relatively strong acid. Similarly, chlorophenols and nitrophenols are stronger acids than phenol itself.

25 Knowledge check

Give the balanced equation for the oxidation of phenylmethanol, $C_6H_5CH_2OH$, to benzoic acid, C_6H_5COOH, using [O] to represent the formula of the oxidising agent.

! Extra Help

Aldehydes can be oxidised by milder oxidising agents. These include Tollens' reagent and Fehling's reagent. The organic product of these reactions is the carboxylic acid anion, as the reaction is carried out in basic conditions. These reactions are discussed further in the aldehydes and ketones section.

Link Section 4.4.4 page 137.

The formation of carboxylic acids by the oxidation of alcohols and aldehydes

Primary alcohols can be oxidised firstly to aldehydes and then, on further oxidation to carboxylic acids.

Acidified potassium dichromate can be used as the oxidising agent and this turns from orange $Cr_2O_7^{2-}$ ions to green Cr^{3+} ions as the oxidation of the alcohol proceeds. Another oxidising agent that can be used is alkaline potassium manganate(VII) solution, and this turns from a purple solution containing MnO_4^- ions, to a brown-black sludge of manganese(IV) oxide as it is reduced by the alcohol. Aldehydes are more volatile than the corresponding carboxylic acid and they should not be allowed to escape from the refluxing reaction mixture, to ensure that further oxidation proceeds to the carboxylic acid. Secondary alcohols are oxidised to ketones and any further oxidation to a carboxylic acid does not occur in this way.

The reduction of carboxylic acids

Carboxylic acids are relatively stable compounds and their reduction to a primary alcohol requires the use of the powerful reducing agent lithium tetrahydridoaluminate(III), $LiAlH_4$. This reagent reacts violently with water and the reduction is carried out using the solvent ethoxyethane. Sodium tetrahydridoborate(III), $NaBH_4$, is a milder reducing agent and, although it will reduce both aldehydes and ketones, will not reduce a carboxylic acid.

The equation for this reduction can be shown using [H] as representing the reducing agent lithium tetrahydridoaluminate(III).

S&C Stretch & Challenge

State the reagent(s) used to carry out the oxidation reactions below.

$$CH_3C\!\!\diagup^{\displaystyle O}_{\displaystyle OH} + 4[H] \longrightarrow CH_3CH_2OH + H_2O$$

$$O=C(H)-CH_2-C(=O)OH \xrightarrow{LiAlH_4} HO-CH_2(H)-CH_2-CH_2(H)-OH$$

propane–1,3–diol

$$\xrightarrow{NaBH_4}$$

$$HO-CH_2(H)-CH_2-C(=O)OH$$

3–hydroxypropanoic acid

Making aromatic carboxylic acids

An aromatic carboxylic acid must have the acid group directly bonded to the benzene ring.

benzenecarboxylic acid   4–methylbenzenecarboxylic acid   (4–hydroxymethyl) benzenecarboxylic acid

The oxidation of a primary alcohol or aldehyde using acidified potassium dichromate or acidified potassium manganate(VII) solutions produces the carboxylic acid.

$$\xrightarrow{2[O]} + H_2O$$

Another method is to oxidise a methyl side chain. One way of doing this is to heat the compound with alkaline potassium manganate(VII) solution.

This represents the overall equation. The initial product is the sodium/potassium salt of benzenecarboxylic acid. The reaction mixture is then acidified, producing the acid itself. Another product of the reduction is a brown-black sludge of manganese(IV) oxide. Some benzaldehyde is also produced. Benzenecarboxylic acid is the end product of this oxidation, irrespective of the length of the carbon side chain. For example, ethylbenzene also produces benzenecarboxylic acid.

Extra Help

When benzenecarboxylic acid (benzoic acid) is produced by oxidising methylbenzene with alkaline potassium manganate(VII) solution, followed by subsequent acidification, a practical problem is the separation of the solid carboxylic acid from the brown-black sludge of manganese(IV) oxide. One method is to heat the mixture, when the carboxylic acid dissolves. The mixture is filtered hot and the filtrate is then allowed to cool, when white crystals of benzenecarboxylic acid (benzoic acid) are produced.

Stretch & Challenge

Hydrogen, in the presence of a nickel catalyst, is another reducing agent that will reduce aldehydes and ketones to primary and secondary alcohols respectively. Carboxylic acids cannot be reduced in this way. Unsaturated acids can, however, be reduced by hydrogen, in the presence of a nickel catalyst, to give the corresponding saturated acid. For example stearic acid can be produced by reducing oleic acid.

$$CH_3(CH_2)_7CH=CH(CH_2)_7COOH$$

$$\xrightarrow[Ni]{H_2} CH_3(CH_2)_{17}COOH$$

The reduction of an unsaturated aldehyde by hydrogen and nickel will give the corresponding primary alcohol.

$$CH_3CH=CHC(=O)(H) \xrightarrow[Ni]{H_2}$$

$$CH_3CH_2CH_2CH_2OH$$

Stretch & Challenge

Benzene-1,2-dicarboxylic acid is obtained by oxidising a hydrocarbon with alkaline potassium manganate(VII) solution. The hydrocarbon contains 89.1% by mass of carbon. Use this information to suggest a displayed formula for the hydrocarbon.

143

26 Knowledge check
State the name of the carboxylic acid that produces propane when it is strongly heated with soda lime.

27 Knowledge check
The mass of 0.40 mol of an amide RCONH$_2$ (where R is an alkyl group) is 29.2g. Deduce the displayed formula of the amide.

28 Knowledge check
Give the name of the nitrile that has the formula

$$H_3C - \underset{\underset{CH_3}{|}}{\overset{\overset{CH_3}{|}}{C}} - C \equiv N$$

29 Knowledge check
A student suggested that either potassium cyanide or sodium cyanide can be used to react with 1-bromobutane to produce pentanenitrile. Explain why this suggestion is correct.

! Extra Help
In decarboxylation reactions where soda lime is used, either the acid or its salt (usually the sodium salt) can be used. Although this seems a useful method for reducing the overall carbon chain length, the reaction is complicated and yields are often poor and a number of side products are also obtained.

Stretch & Challenge
State the name of the acids whose calcium salts, on heating, produce (a) pentan-3-one and (b) 1,7-diphenylheptan-4-one.

Decarboxylation of carboxylic acids

The removal of carbon dioxide from a compound is called decarboxylation. As carbon dioxide is an acidic oxide, it will react with a base. In decarboxylation reactions, the compound generally used is soda lime. This is a mixture that is largely calcium hydroxide, together with a little sodium/potassium hydroxide. The material absorbs both carbon dioxide and water but remains as a solid.

$$Ca(OH)_{2(s)} + CO_{2(g)} \longrightarrow CaCO_{3(s)} + H_2O$$

In a decarboxylation reaction, the organic acid or its sodium salt is heated with soda lime. A hydrocarbon is produced that contains one less carbon atom in the chain than the starting material. This is one of the methods for reducing the length of the carbon chain (descending the homologous series). The equation for decarboxylation using soda lime can be represented using calcium hydroxide, calcium oxide or sodium hydroxide.

$$CH_3COOH + Ca(OH)_2 \longrightarrow CH_4 + CaCO_3 + H_2O$$

In these reactions, the organic product is an alkane or an arene.

Decarboxylation also occurs if the calcium salt of the acid is heated in the absence of soda lime. A ketone is the product. However, in this reaction the chain length is increased from a derivative of the two carbon ethanoic acid to a ketone containing three carbon atoms.

$$(CH_3COO)_2Ca \xrightarrow{\text{heat}} CH_3 - \overset{\overset{O}{\|}}{C} - CH_3 + CaCO_3$$

Calcium benzenecarboxylate (benzoate) is similarly decarboxylated on heating, producing diphenylmethanone.

$$(C_6H_5COO)_2Ca \longrightarrow C_6H_5COC_6H_5 + CaCO_3$$

Decarboxylation reactions also occur if the salts of dicarboxylic acids are heated with soda lime. For example, disodium pentanedioate produces propane.

$$Na^+OOC - CH_2 - CH_2 - CH_2 - COO^-Na^+ + 2NaOH \longrightarrow CH_3 - CH_2 - CH_3 + 2Na_2CO_3$$

Substituted aromatic carboxylic acids can also be decarboxylated in a similar way by heating them with soda lime.

Esters and acid chlorides and the hydrolysis of these compounds

Making esters from carboxylic acids and their hydrolysis

Carboxylic acids can be converted to esters by heating the carboxylic acid with an alcohol in the presence of a little sulfuric acid, which initially protonates the carboxylic acid.

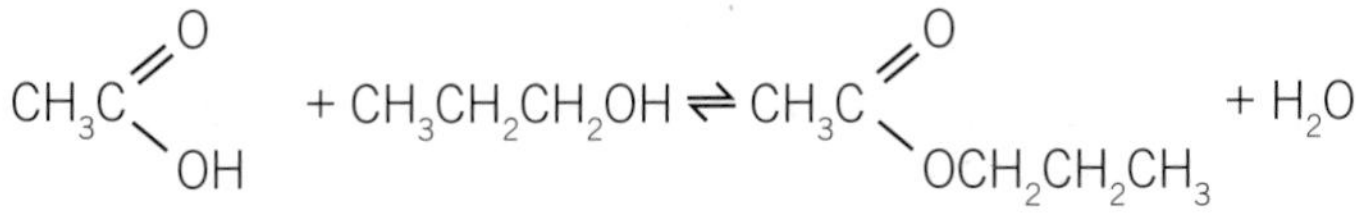

$$CH_3C\overset{O}{\underset{OH}{<}} + CH_3CH_2CH_2OH \rightleftharpoons CH_3C\overset{O}{\underset{OCH_2CH_2CH_3}{<}} + H_2O$$

Experiments using methanol, with some oxygen atoms being the ^{18}O isotope, have shown that the ester contains all the ^{18}O oxygen atoms that were originally in the methanol. It is the acid's –OH group that is lost, rather than the –OH group from the alcohol.

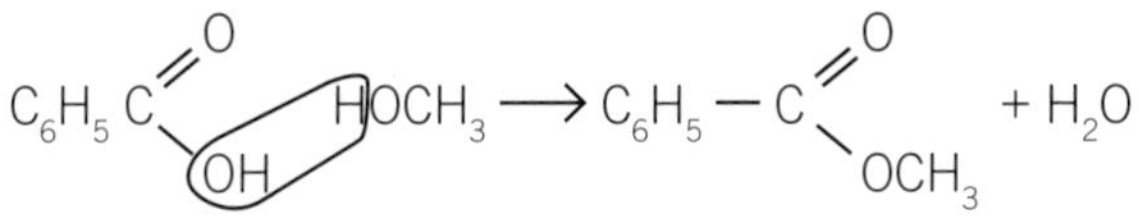

$$C_6H_5C\overset{O}{\underset{OH}{<}} HOCH_3 \rightarrow C_6H_5-C\overset{O}{\underset{OCH_3}{<}} + H_2O$$

Experimental details of ester preparation are discussed in the alcohol section of this book.

Esterification is a reversible reaction and the hydrolysis of esters can be carried under basic or acidic conditions. In hydrolysis using basic conditions the ester is heated to reflux with aqueous sodium hydroxide and the mixture is then acidified to produce the carboxylic acid.

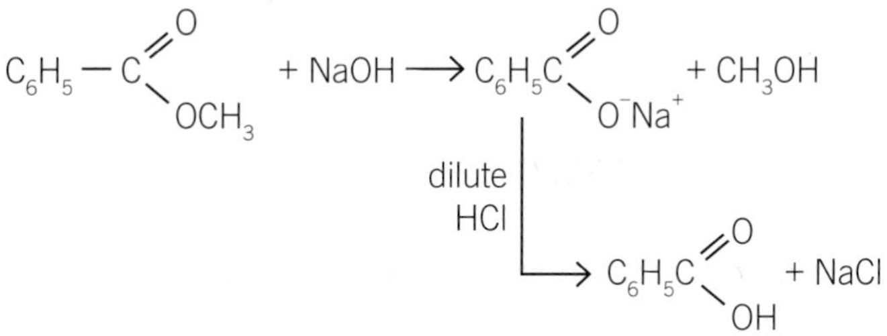

$$C_6H_5-C\overset{O}{\underset{OCH_3}{<}} + NaOH \rightarrow C_6H_5C\overset{O}{\underset{O^-Na^+}{<}} + CH_3OH$$

dilute HCl

$$\rightarrow C_6H_5C\overset{O}{\underset{OH}{<}} + NaCl$$

The rate of hydrolysis depends on the particular ester and the concentration of alkali used. Soap making is a process of the hydrolysis of esters of the trihydric alcohol glycerol (propane-1,2,3-triol). A simplified equation for the hydrolysis of glyceryl esters is

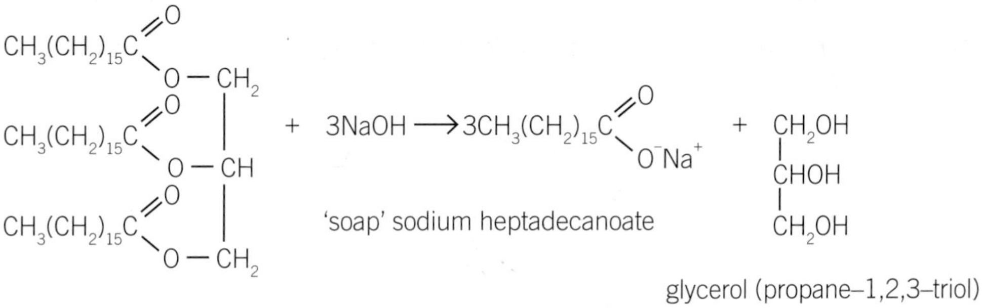

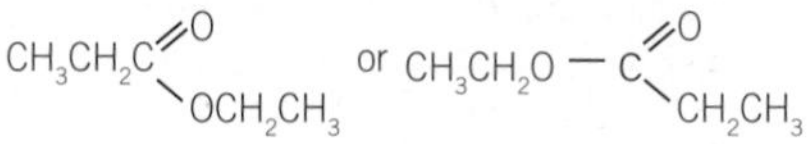

$$\begin{array}{c}CH_3(CH_2)_{15}C\overset{O}{\underset{O-CH_2}{<}}\\ CH_3(CH_2)_{15}C\overset{O}{\underset{O-CH}{<}}\\ CH_3(CH_2)_{15}C\overset{O}{\underset{O-CH_2}{<}}\end{array} + 3NaOH \rightarrow 3CH_3(CH_2)_{15}C\overset{O}{\underset{O^-Na^+}{<}} + \begin{array}{c}CH_2OH\\ |\\ CHOH\\ |\\ CH_2OH\end{array}$$

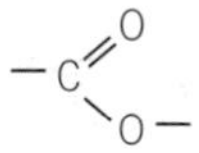

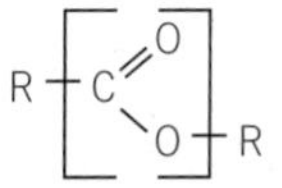

'soap' sodium heptadecanoate

glycerol (propane–1,2,3–triol)

In practice, the three carboxylic acid groups of the glyceryl ester are often different from each other.

Making acid chlorides from carboxylic acids and the hydrolysis of these compounds

To make an acid chloride from a carboxylic acid, the –OH group of the acid needs to substituted by a –Cl atom. Acid chlorides are reactive compounds and are easily hydrolysed if water is present, and a method of production is needed that excludes water. The reagents that can be used for this reaction include phosphorus trichloride, phosphorus pentachloride and sulfur dichloride oxide, $SOCl_2$.

$$3CH_3COOH + PCl_3 \rightarrow 3CH_3COCl + H_3PO_3$$

$$CH_3COOH + PCl_5 \rightarrow CH_3COCl + POCl_3 + HCl$$

$$CH_3COOH + SOCl_2 \rightarrow CH_3COCl + SO_2 + HCl$$

The method that uses phosphorus trichloride produces small quantities of organic compounds of phosphorus. If phosphorus pentachloride is used then phosphorus trichloride oxide, $POCl_3$, is also produced and needs to be separated from the acid chloride. The third method, using sulfur dichloride oxide is often preferred as both the co-products, sulfur dioxide and hydrogen chloride are gases.

In an acid chloride, the carbonyl carbon atom is electron deficient ($\delta+$) as it is bonded to the more electronegative chlorine and oxygen atoms. As a result, acid chlorides are very susceptible to attack by nucleophiles, such as the oxygen atoms in water and alcohols and the nitrogen atoms in ammonia and amines.

(reaction scheme showing $CH_3C(=O)Cl$ reacting with:)
- $H_2O \rightarrow CH_3C(=O)OH + HCl$
- $CH_3OH \rightarrow CH_3C(=O)OCH_3 + HCl$
- $NH_3 \rightarrow CH_3C(=O)NH_2 + HCl$ — ethanamide
- $CH_3CH_2NH_2 \rightarrow CH_3C(=O)N(H)-CH_2CH_3 + HCl$ — N–ethylethanamide

The reaction between smaller molecule acid chlorides such as ethanoyl chloride and water is very vigorous, forming the carboxylic acid and hydrogen chloride. One representation of the mechanism for the hydrolysis is

(mechanism diagram of ethanoyl chloride hydrolysis)

$$H_3C-C \rightarrow H_3C-C \rightarrow H_3C-C(=O)OH + H^+/Cl^- \rightarrow HCl$$

Benzoyl chloride, C_6H_5COCl, reacts with water much more slowly and its reactions can be carried out in aqueous conditions, whereas the use of ethanoyl chloride needs a fume cupboard and anhydrous conditions.

Amides and nitriles from carboxylic acids

Carboxylic acids, such as ethanoic acid, react with ammonia to give the ammonium salt of the acid. When this salt is heated, water is lost and the amide is produced.

$$CH_3COOH \underset{\underset{-CO_2}{(NH_4)_2CO_3}}{\overset{NH_3}{\rightleftharpoons}} CH_3COONH_4 \xrightarrow{heat} CH_3C\overset{O}{\underset{NH_2}{\diagdown}} + H_2O$$

ethanamide

A better method is to heat the acid or its ammonium salt with urea at 120°C.

$$CH_3C\overset{O}{\underset{OH}{\diagup}} + H_2N-\overset{O}{\overset{\|}{C}}-NH_2 \longrightarrow CH_3C\overset{O}{\underset{NH_2}{\diagdown}} + CO_2 + NH_3$$

urea

Amides can be dehydrated by heating with phosphorus(V) oxide, P_4O_{10}, giving the corresponding nitrile.

$$CH_3C\overset{O}{\underset{NH_2}{\diagup}} \xrightarrow[\underset{-H_2O}{heat}]{P_4O_{10}} CH_3C \equiv N$$

When naming nitriles it is important to remember that the carbon atom of the nitrile group is counted as part of the carbon chain. For example, CH_3CH_2CN is propanenitrile but CH_3CH_2Br is bromoethane. Benzonitrile has the formula C_6H_5CN.

Formation of nitriles and hydroxynitriles

Formation of nitriles from halogenoalkanes

Nitriles can be made from halogenoalkanes by their reaction with potassium cyanide using an alcohol-water mixture as solvent.

$$CH_3(CH_2)_3CH_2Br + KCN \longrightarrow CH_3(CH_2)_3CH_2CN + KBr$$

1–bromopentane   hexanenitrile

This is a nucleophilic substitution reaction where the cyanide ion acts as the nucleophile.

$$CH_3(CH_2)_3\overset{H}{\underset{H}{\overset{|}{\underset{|}{C}}}}\overset{\delta^+}{-}\overset{\delta^-}{Br} \longrightarrow CH_3(CH_2)_3\overset{H}{\underset{H}{\overset{|}{\underset{|}{C}}}}-C \equiv N + Br^-$$

Chlorobenzene will not react with cyanide ions as the ring carbon atoms are not susceptible to nucleophilic attack.

Knowledge check 31

Write the displayed formula of the amide that will produce phenylethanenitrile when it is heated with phosphorus(V) oxide.

Knowledge check 32

A straight chain alkyl nitrile, R–CN, contains 14.4% by mass of nitrogen. Find the displayed formula of the nitrile.

⚠ Extra Help

When writing the formula of the cyanide ion, make sure that the negative charge is located on the carbon atom. This means that the carbon atom has a lone pair of electrons and has used three electrons in the triple bond to the nitrogen atom.

‹Link› Nucleophilic addition reactions of aldehydes and ketones pages 137–138.

Formation of hydroxynitriles from aldehydes and ketones

An aldehyde and some simple ketones will react with hydrogen cyanide in the presence of sodium or potassium cyanide to produce a hydroxynitrile.

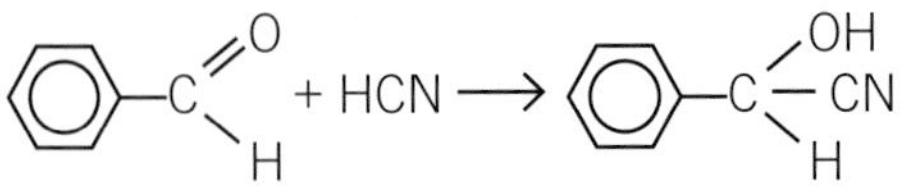

$$C_6H_5-C(=O)H + HCN \longrightarrow C_6H_5-C(OH)(CN)H$$

The mechanism of this reaction has been discussed under aldehydes and ketones.

33 Knowledge check

Complete the equation for the reaction of this acid chloride with water.

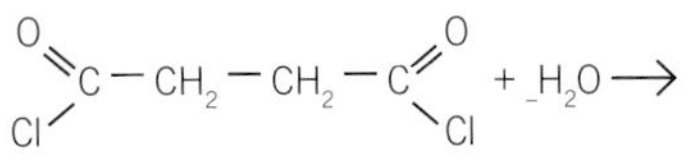

$$ClC(=O)-CH_2-CH_2-C(=O)Cl + \_\ H_2O \longrightarrow$$

Hydrolysis of nitriles and amides

The hydrolysis of nitriles

When heated under reflux with a dilute acid, a nitrile is hydrolysed, giving a carboxylic acid.

$$CH_3CH_2CN \xrightarrow{\ H_2SO_{4(aq)}\ } CH_3CH_2COOH$$

The nitrogen of the cyanide group becomes an ammonium group. If aqueous sulfuric acid is used, the nitrogen-containing product is a solution of ammonium sulfate. The hydrolysis can also be carried out heating the nitrile under reflux with an alkali, for example sodium hydroxide, giving the anion of the carboxylic acid. Acidification of the mixture produces the carboxylic acid.

The hydrolysis of amides

When an amide is heated under reflux with a base such as aqueous sodium hydroxide, the amide is hydrolysed as the carbon to nitrogen bond is broken, producing ammonia gas.

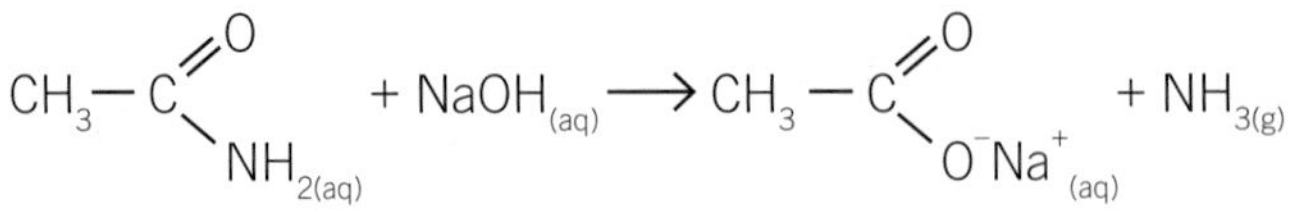

$$CH_3-C(=O)NH_{2(aq)} + NaOH_{(aq)} \longrightarrow CH_3-C(=O)O^-Na^+_{(aq)} + NH_{3(g)}$$

sodium ethanoate

A similar reaction occurs if an N-substituted amide is hydrolysed, giving an amine as one of the products.

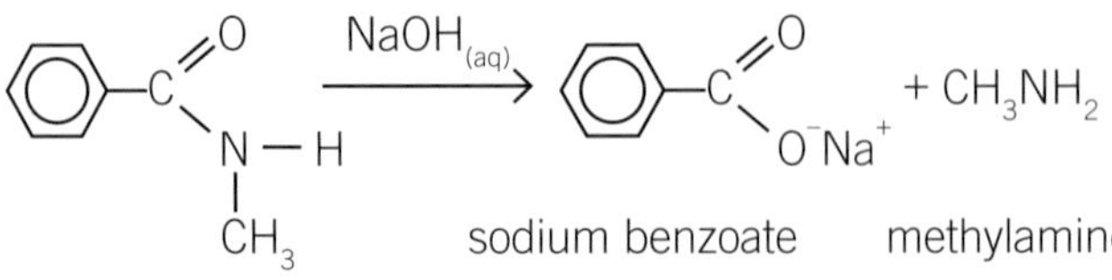

$$C_6H_5-C(=O)N(H)(CH_3) \xrightarrow{\ NaOH_{(aq)}\ } C_6H_5-C(=O)O^-Na^+ + CH_3NH_2$$

sodium benzoate   methylamine

YOU SHOULD KNOW ›››

››› that primary alcohols are oxidised to aldehydes and then to carboxylic acids

››› that lithium tetrahydridoaluminate(III) (and not sodium tetrahydridoborate(III)) is necessary to reduce a carboxylic acid

››› that esters can be hydrolysed using either aqueous alkalis (for example NaOH) or aqueous acids (for example HCl)

››› the reagents used to hydrolyse both amides and nitriles to carboxylic acids

Reduction of nitriles

Warming a nitrile with a solution of lithium tetrahydridoaluminate(III) in ethoxyethane will reduce a nitrile to a primary amine.

$$CH_3CH_2C \equiv N \xrightarrow[\text{ethoxyethane}]{LiAlH_4} CH_3CH_2CH_2NH_2$$
propylamine

'Hydrolysis' means decomposition by water, but in many reactions hydrolysis is carried out using aqueous sodium hydroxide or dilute hydrochloric or sulfuric acids, leading to a faster reaction.

Other reducing agents that can be used include hydrogen and a nickel catalyst, and sodium metal/ethanol. The formation of a nitrile, followed by its reduction, produces compounds with longer carbon chains.

The reduction of a nitrile with lithium aluminium hydride is generally the preferred method as yields are higher. These other reducing agents produce the secondary amine as a by-product.

$$CH_3CH_2C \equiv N \xrightarrow[\text{ethanol}]{\text{sodium}} CH_3CH_2CH_2NH_2 + (CH_3CH_2CH_2)_2 NH$$

Aromatic nitriles such as benzonitrile are similarly reduced by lithium aluminium hydride.

The boiling temperature of benzonitrile and phenylmethylamine are very similar and separation of the product by distillation is not possible. Primary amines, such as phenylmethylamine, are bases (see page 153), and if hydrochloric acid is added to reaction mixture, phenylmethylamine will react with the acid to form a water soluble salt from which the free amine can be obtained by adding an alkali. Phenylmethylamine, unlike benzonitrile, is soluble in water. Therefore another separation method is to extract the reaction products with water, into which the amine would dissolve.

Hydroxynitriles (see page 138) can be similarly reduced by lithium aluminium hydride. For example, 2-hydroxypropanenitrile is reduced to 1-aminopropan-2-ol,

which contains a chiral centre (see page 116). 2-Hydroxypropanenitrile, is similarly reduced to 1-amino-2-methylpropan-2-ol, which does not contain a chiral centre.

4.6 Amines

Primary amines are organic compounds that contain an $-NH_2$ group bonded directly to an alkyl or aryl group, giving $R-NH_2$. They can be considered as derivatives of ammonia, NH_3, where one of the hydrogen atoms has been substituted by an $-R$ group. Substitution of the remaining hydrogen atoms gives a secondary amine, R_2NH and a tertiary amine, R_3N. The nitrogen atom in amines retains the lone pair of electrons, allowing amines to react as bases, by electron pair donation. Amines are very reactive compounds and can take part in reactions where the C–N bond is broken to give, for example, alcohols and phenols. They can also react where the C–N bond is retained, giving, for example, compounds with peptide linkages and azo dyes.

Content

You should be able to demonstrate and apply knowledge and understanding of:

- The formation of primary aliphatic amines from halogenoalkanes and nitriles.
- The formation of aromatic amines from nitrobenzenes.
- The basicity of amines.
- The ethanoylation of primary amines using ethanoyl chloride.
- The reaction of primary amines (aliphatic and aromatic) with cold nitric(III) acid.
- The coupling of benzenediazonium salts with phenols and aromatic amines.
- The role of the –N=N– chromophore in azo dyes.
- The origin of colour in terms of the wavelengths of visible light absorbed.

The structure and naming of amines

All amines contain a nitrogen atom bonded directly to a carbon atom of an alkyl or aryl group. If this nitrogen atom is bonded to only one carbon atom, the compound is called a primary amine. Secondary amines have the nitrogen atom bonded directly to two carbon atoms and if the nitrogen atom is bonded directly to three carbon atoms then it is a tertiary amine. The longest carbon chain is used to name the amine with the number of carbon atoms indicated in the usual way and -amine is used as the suffix.

$CH_3CH_2CH_2CH_2NH_2$

butylamine

$CH_3CH_2CHNH_2$
$\quad\quad\quad |$
$\quad\quad\quad CH_3$

1–methylpropylamine

Aromatic amines have the nitrogen atom bonded directly to the benzene ring.

methylamine

phenylamine

dimethylamine

triethylamine

cyclohexylamine

2–aminoethanol

$HO-CH_2-CH_2-NH_2$

N–methylphenylamine

$H_2N-CH_2(CH_2)_4CH_2-NH_2$

hexane–1,6–diamine

Formation of primary aliphatic amines

Making primary aliphatic amines from halogenoalkanes

The reaction of a halogenoalkane with ammonia using a water/ethanol solvent produces an amine.

$$CH_3CH_2CH_2Br + NH_3 \longrightarrow CH_3CH_2CH_2NH_2 + HBr$$

This is a simplified picture as, if the mixture is warmed, ammonia gas is lost from the mixture, reducing the yield. Some methods of preparation use the reactants in a sealed tube, which is gently heated. Generally, an excess of ammonia is used. This is to react with the acidic gas hydrogen bromide, to give ammonium bromide. If an excess of the halogenoalkane is used, then further substitution can occur giving a secondary amine, in this example dipropylamine.

Knowledge check 34

Give the systematic names of

$CH_3(CH_2)_4NH_2$

$H_2N-CH_2-CH_2-NH_2$

Knowledge check 35

Write the displayed formula of

(a) 4-ethylphenylamine

(b) 2-methylpropylamine.

Stretch & Challenge

Write the displayed formula of a compound $C_7H_{10}N_2$ that contains both aliphatic and an aromatic primary amine groups.

YOU SHOULD KNOW ›››

››› how to name simple amines

››› how to write the displayed formula of simple amines, given their names

››› that the formulae of all primary amines contain the $-NH_2$ group

Key Term

An **aromatic primary amine** must have the $-NH_2$ group directly bonded to the benzene ring.

YOU SHOULD KNOW ›››

››› that it is the polar C–Br bond that leads to nucleophilic substitution

$C_6H_5CH_2NH_3^+Br^-$

36

Knowledge check

Explain why the reaction between 1-chloropropane and methylamine is described as nucleophilic substitution.

37

Knowledge check

Write the shortened formula of the amine salt that is produced when 2-phenylethylamine reacts with hydrogen bromide.

38

Knowledge check

Write the equation for the reaction of methylammonium bromide with hydroxide ions.

39

Knowledge check

A student made butane-1,4-diamine by reducing a nitrile with lithium tetrahydridoaluminate(III). Write the displayed formula of the nitrile.

Link ➤ Reduction of nitriles page 149.

Stretch & Challenge

An intermediate in the preparation of phenylamine, using tin and hydrochloric acid in the laboratory is $(C_6H_5NH_3)_2SnCl_6$. This compound is decomposed by heating it with an alkali. Complete and balance the equation for this reaction.

$(C_6H_5NH_3)_2SnCl_6 + \_NaOH \longrightarrow$

$$CH_3CH_2CH_2NH_2 + CH_3CH_2CH_2Br \longrightarrow (CH_3CH_2CH_2)_2NH + HBr$$

This further reaction occurs because the amine, like ammonia, reacts as a base and attacks the $\delta+$ carbon atom of the C–Br bond. This type of mechanism is called nucleophilic substitution.

Depending on the conditions used, the usual product is not the free amine but its salt.

$$CH_3CH_2CH_2NH_2 + HBr \longrightarrow CH_3CH_2CH_2^+NH_3\ Br^-$$

propylammonium bromide

Propylammonium bromide is a substituted ammonium bromide (NH_4Br), with one of the hydrogen atoms replaced by a propyl group. If an ammonium salt is heated with a base, ammonia is produced. Similarly, when propylammonium bromide is heated with aqueous sodium hydroxide, propylamine is obtained.

$$CH_3CH_2CH_2^+NH_3Br^- + NaOH \longrightarrow CH_3CH_2CH_2NH_2 + NaBr + H_2O$$

Making primary aliphatic amines from nitriles

Nitriles can be reduced with a suitable reducing agent. The usual reducing agent is lithium tetrahydridoaluminate(III) (represented as [H] in the equation) dissolved in ethoxyethane as solvent.

$$CH_3CH_2CHC \equiv N + 4[H] \longrightarrow CH_3CH_2CHCH_2NH_2$$
$$\quad\quad\quad |\qquad\qquad\qquad\qquad\quad |$$
$$\quad\quad\quad CH_3 \qquad\qquad\qquad\qquad CH_3$$

2–methylbutylamine

This reaction has been discussed in the section on aldehydes and ketones.

Formation of aromatic amines from nitrobenzenes

Benzene is not easily attacked by nucleophiles such as ammonia, as the ring electrons repel nucleophiles, but are attracted to electrophiles. Phenylamine, $C_6H_5NH_2$, is made by the reduction of nitrobenzene. A general equation for this reduction is

$$\langle \bigcirc \rangle -NO_2 + 6[H] \longrightarrow \langle \bigcirc \rangle -NH_2 + 2H_2O$$

The traditional reducing agent for this reaction is tin metal and hydrochloric acid. After the initial fast reaction is over the mixture is heated to 100°C for thirty minutes. The product at this stage is not phenylamine but contains a complex tin(IV) salt of formula

$(C_6H_5NH_3)_2SnCl_6$. After cooling the mixture, aqueous sodium hydroxide is added to decompose the salt into phenylamine, sodium chloride and tin(IV) oxide. The mixture is then steam distilled to produce a distillate containing phenylamine and water. The immiscible phenylamine is separated, dried to remove traces of water, and then redistilled to produce pure phenylamine (boiling temperature 185°C). This method from tin and hydrochloric acid is usually a laboratory preparation. Making phenylamine commercially requires the use of more economical reducing agents. These include hydrogen and a nickel catalyst, or iron and hydrochloric acid. Derivatives of nitrobenzene can be reduced in a similar way.

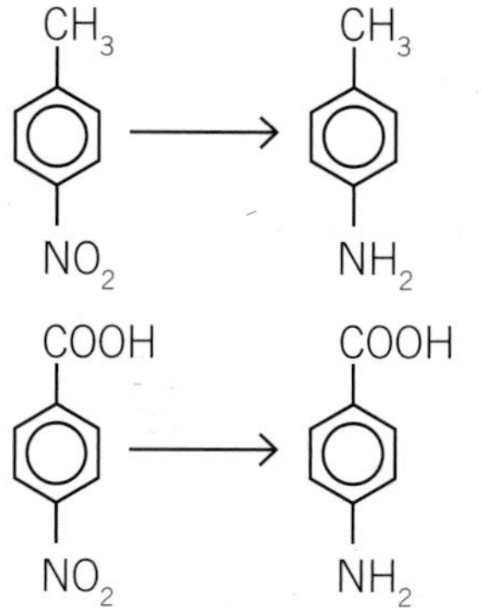

Basicity of amines

Amines, like ammonia, have a lone pair of electrons on the nitrogen atom. These can be used to accept a proton by means of a coordinate bond.

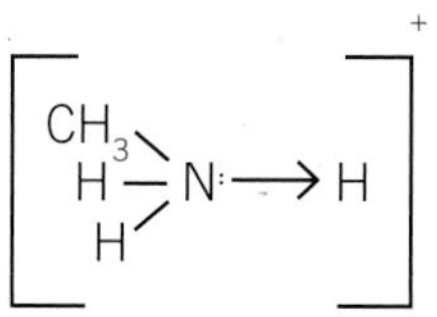

methylammonium ion

The basic nature of amines can be shown by the reaction of 'smaller' amines with water.

$$CH_3NH_2 + H_2O \rightleftharpoons \left[CH_3NH_3 \right]^+ + {}^-OH$$

Amines are weak bases and the equilibrium position of this equation is well to the left – a strong smell of 'fishy ammonia' indicates that free methylamine is present in the solution. The pH of an aqueous solution of methylamine of concentration 0.1 mol dm^{-3} is about 11.8, whereas an ammonia solution of the same concentration has a pH of about 11.1. Methylamine and other alkylamines are stronger bases than ammonia because the alkyl groups 'push' electrons slightly towards the nitrogen atom, making it more δ– when compared with ammonia. Phenylamine is a much weaker base than ammonia or alkylamines as the nitrogen lone pair of electrons becomes, to a certain extent, part of the delocalised π system, and this makes the nitrogen relatively less δ–. Phenylamine is, however, more susceptible to electrophilic ring substitution than benzene because of this nitrogen lone pair effect. Although the –NH$_2$ group of amines can hydrogen bond with water, phenylamine is only slightly soluble in water because of the hydrophobic effect of the benzene ring. Phenylamine, like alkylamines, will react with acids forming salts.

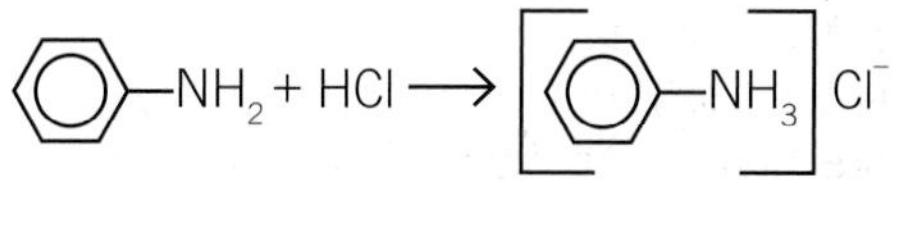

phenylammonium chloride

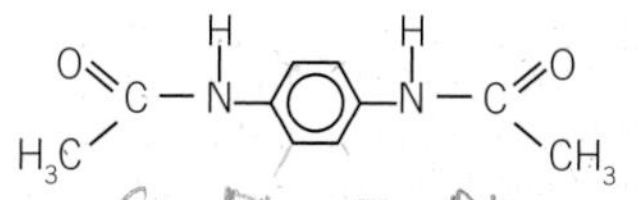

Ethanoylation of primary amines

▼ **Study point**

The reaction of a primary amine with an acid chloride is a method of producing a peptide linkage in a molecule.

The nitrogen lone pair enables amines to react as nucleophiles. They attack the $\delta+$ carbon atom of the carbonyl group in an acid chloride.

$$CH_3 - NH_2 + CH_3C \overset{\overset{\delta-}{O}}{\underset{Cl}{\diagdown}} \longrightarrow CH_3 - N\overset{H}{\underset{\underset{O}{\overset{\|}{C}}-CH_3}{\diagdown}} + HCl$$

N-methylethanamide

The organic product is N-methylethanamide. The letter 'N' means that the methyl group is bonded to the nitrogen atom. This compound is an N-substituted derivative of ethanamide, CH_3CONH_2. Phenylamine reacts in a similar way to produce N-phenylethanamide.

YOU SHOULD KNOW ›››

››› that the peptide linkage is –C(O)–N(H)– and is found in amides, peptides and proteins

The $-\overset{H}{\underset{|}{N}} - \overset{O}{\underset{\|}{C}} -$ is known as a peptide linkage or peptide bond and is also present in peptides, polypeptides and proteins. Polyamides such as Nylon, also contain this linkage. A familiar compound that contains the peptide linkage is the painkiller Paracetamol.

▼ **Study point**

Nitric(III) acid is unstable and made when needed, It can be written as HNO_2 or HONO.

Reaction of primary amines with cold nitric(III) acid

(42) **Knowledge check**

4-Propylphenylamine was treated with sodium nitrate(III) and aqueous hydrochloric acid at 5 °C and the mixture heated to produce 4-propylphenol.

The yield of 4-propylphenol was 0.14 mole, which represented a yield of 70%. Calculate the mass of 4-propylphenylamine used in this experiment.

Nitric(III) acid (or nitrous acid), HNO_2, is an unstable compound and is made when required by the reaction of a dilute acid (eg HCl) on sodium nitrate(III) (nitrite), $NaNO_2$.

$$NaNO_2 + HCl \longrightarrow HNO_2 + NaCl$$

A primary aliphatic amine reacts with nitric(III) acid with the evolution of nitrogen gas. One equation for this reaction this

$$R - NH_2 + HNO_2 \longrightarrow R - OH + N_2 + H_2O$$

Stretch & Challenge

The formula of the diazonium ion can be written as $R–N_2^+$ or

$$R - \overset{+}{N} \equiv N:$$

Another way of representing the formula of this ion is to place the positive charge on the other nitrogen atom. Give the formula of this ion, showing the bonding between the two nitrogen atoms and any lone pairs of electrons.

This looks as if it provides a useful route for preparing a primary alcohol from a primary amine. Although the yield of nitrogen is quantitative, the yield of the alcohol is poor. For example, ethylamine only gives a 60% yield of ethanol, whereas propylamine gives 7% of propan-1-ol, 32% of propan-2-ol and 28% of propene amongst other products. These products suggest that a 1-propylcarbocation, $CH_3CH_2CH_2^+$, is formed as an intermediate, which can undergo isomerisation to a 2-propylcarbocation or else lose H^+ to give the alkene. The reaction may initially form an alkyl diazonium ion, $R - \overset{+}{N} \equiv N:$, which then loses nitrogen to give the primary carbocation.

The corresponding reaction with a primary aromatic amine, for example phenylamine, also proceeds via a diazonium intermediate but this is more stable than an alkyldiazonium ion and, if the temperature is between 0°C and 10°C, a solution containing the benzenediazonium ion is produced.

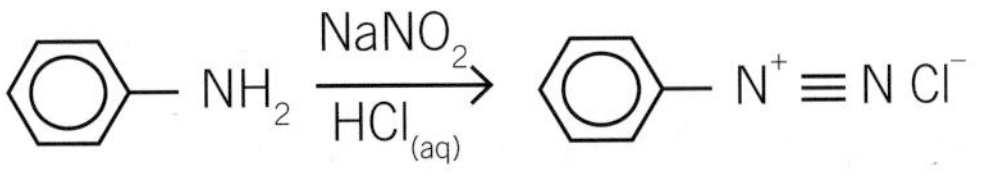

benzenediazonium chloride

If aqueous sulfuric acid is used in place of hydrochloric acid, the intermediate is benzenediazonium hydrogensulfate rather than benzenediazonium chloride. Above 10 °C, decomposition of the benzenediazonium compound occurs, giving phenol.

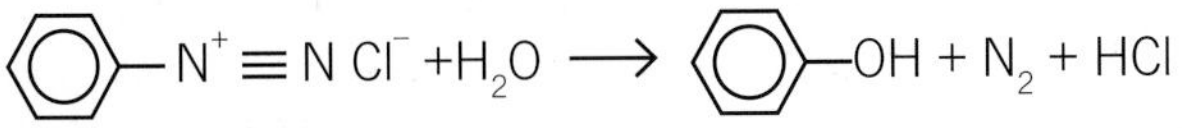

If the reaction is performed at temperatures below 0°C the production of the benzenediazonium compound is too slow.

Coupling reaction of benzenediazonium salts

Benzenediazonium compounds are very reactive compounds and can be used as intermediates in the formation of many other compounds. In the formation of phenol from benzenediazonium chloride, the nitrogen atoms are lost as nitrogen gas as the unstable ion decomposes. Below 10°C benzenediazonium compounds react with phenols and aromatic amines to produce compounds where the –N=N– azo group is retained. The benzenediazonium ion is a weak electrophile and will bond, via electrophilic substitution, with aromatic compounds where the ring has been activated by the presence of –OH or $–NH_2$ groups. The resulting compound is highly coloured, generally yellow, orange or red, and is called an **azo dye**. This reaction is often called a coupling reaction and is carried out in alkaline solution. Coupling often occurs at the 4-position but can occur at the 2-position relative to the –OH or NH_2 group.

(4–phenylazo)phenol

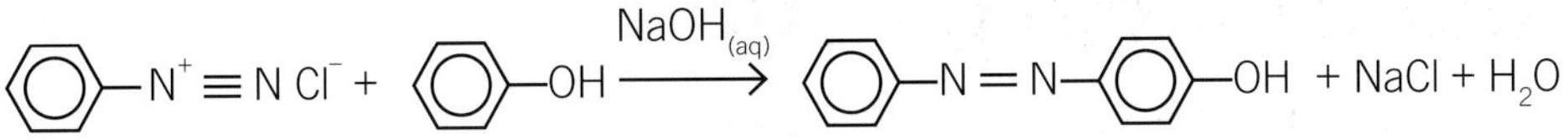

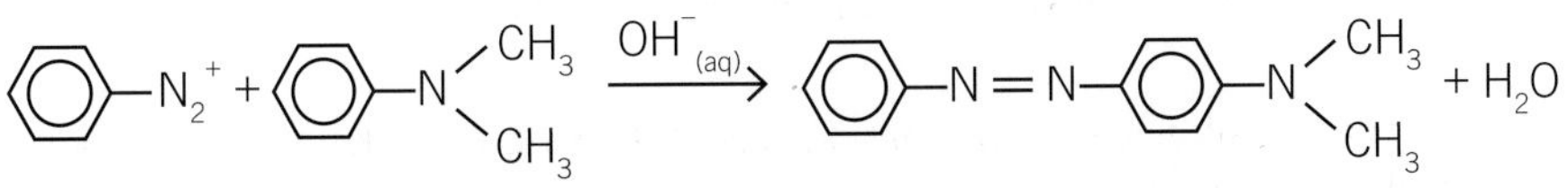

Coupling can also occur with other aromatic systems, for example with naphthalene-2-ol.

naphthalen-2-ol

(1–phenylazo)naphthalen-2-ol

This azo dye forms as red solid and is used under the name Sudan 1. It has been used to colour curry powder but its use for this purpose in banned in the United Kingdom.

YOU SHOULD KNOW ›››

- ››› that aromatic primary amines can have reactions in which the nitrogen is lost
- ››› that aromatic primary amines also have reactions in which the nitrogen atom is retained

Key Term

An **azo dye** contains the grouping Ar–N=N–Ar where Ar is an aromatic ring system.

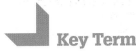

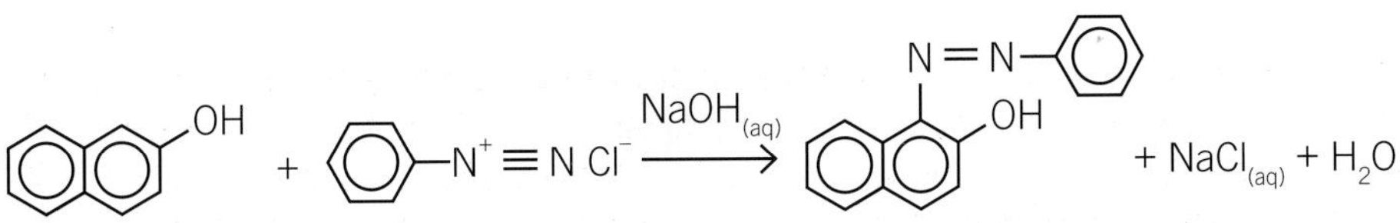

Stretch & Challenge

An azo dye has the formula

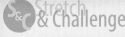

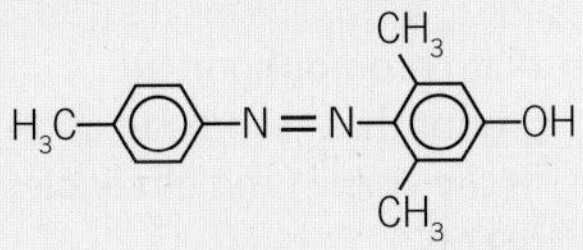

Give the systematic names of the aromatic amine and the phenol used to produce this azo dye in a diazotisation reaction.

The role of the –N=N– chromophore in azo dyes and the origin of colour in terms of the wavelengths absorbed

A **chromophore** is a structural unit in a molecule that is primarily responsible for the absorption of radiation of a certain wavelength, generally in the visible or ultraviolet region. If the absorption is in the visible region, the colour that is not absorbed is the colour observed. The actual wavelengths of light absorbed depend on other groups present in the molecule.

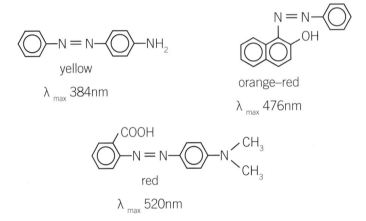

yellow

λ_{max} 384nm

orange–red

λ_{max} 476nm

red

λ_{max} 520nm

43 Knowledge check

The acid-base indicator phenolphthalein in a strongly alkaline solution absorbs in the visible region of the electromagnetic spectrum.

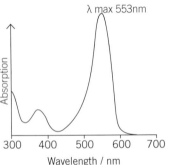

Use the information in this section to show that this alkaline solution of phenolphthalein has a red/violet (magenta) colour.

The intensity of the colour that is observed in solution depends on the concentration of the compound present, and this is the basis of colorimetry. The colour hexagon gives an indication of the colour absorbed and the colour transmitted (not absorbed) when light is shone through the sample.

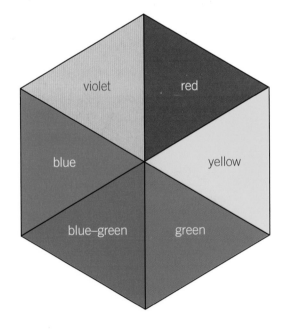

YOU SHOULD KNOW › › ›

› › › that chromophores are groups that absorb radiation in the visible (and ultraviolet) region

For example a solution of Sudan 1 has its maximum visible absorption (λ_{max}) at 476 nm in the blue-green region. The colour opposite blue-green in the hexagon is red, which is the colour of Sudan 1. The approximate wavelength range of the colours is

Colour	Wavelength/nm
Violet	380–430
Blue	430–490
Green	490–560
Yellow	560–580
Orange	580–620
Red	620–750

The visible spectrum of methylene blue is shown below.

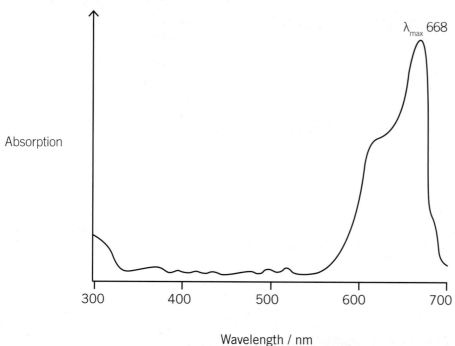

The spectrum shows that its maximum absorption is at 668 nm, which is in the red region of the spectrum. The bluish colour of methylene blue is opposite red in the colour hexagon.

Unit 4

4.7
Amino acids, peptides and proteins

Amino acids, peptides and proteins are naturally occurring nitrogen compounds that form the basis of all living organisms. Amino acids are carboxylic acids that also contain the amino, $-NH_2$, functional group. The condensation of two amino acid molecules gives a dipeptide. Further condensations between amino acid molecules lead to polypeptides and to proteins. This topic also considers the basic ideas behind the primary, secondary and tertiary structure of proteins.

Content

You should be able to demonstrate and apply knowledge and understanding of:

- The general formulae and classification of α-amino acids.

- The amphoteric and zwitterionic nature of amino acids and their effect on melting temperatures and solubility.

- The combination of α-amino acids to form dipeptides.

- The formation of polypeptides and proteins.

- The basic principles of primary, secondary and tertiary protein structure.

- The essential role of proteins in living systems, for example, as enzymes.

General formula and classification of α-amino acids

An α-amino acid has the $-NH_2$ group bonded to the carbon atom that is next to the carboxylic acid group. This carbon atom is called the α-carbon atom. The general formula of these α-amino acids is

$$R - \overset{\displaystyle H}{\underset{\displaystyle NH_2}{\overset{|}{\underset{|}{C}}}} - C\overset{\displaystyle O}{\underset{\displaystyle OH}{}}$$

The simplest α-amino acid is aminoethanoic acid, H_2NCH_2COOH where R = H.
R can also be a simple alkyl group or a carbon-containing group that may also contain an –OH, –SH or another $-NH_2$ or –COOH group. Common α-amino acids have traditional names that continue to be used, especially in biology and biochemistry.

$$H - \overset{\displaystyle H}{\underset{\displaystyle NH_2}{\overset{|}{\underset{|}{C}}}} - COOH$$

aminoethanoic acid
(glycine)

$$H_3C - \overset{\displaystyle H}{\underset{\displaystyle NH_2}{\overset{|}{\underset{|}{C}}}} - COOH$$

2–aminopropanoic acid
(alanine)

$$\bigcirc - CH_2 - \overset{\displaystyle H}{\underset{\displaystyle NH_2}{\overset{|}{\underset{|}{C}}}} - COOH$$

2–amino–3–phenylpropanoic acid
(phenylalanine)

$$HO - CH_2 - \overset{\displaystyle H}{\underset{\displaystyle NH_2}{\overset{|}{\underset{|}{C}}}} - COOH$$

2–amino–3–hydroxypropanoic acid
(serine)

$$HOOC - CH_2 - CH_2 - \overset{\displaystyle H}{\underset{\displaystyle NH_2}{\overset{|}{\underset{|}{C}}}} - COOH$$

2–aminopentanedioic acid
(glutamic acid)

$$HS - CH_2 - \overset{\displaystyle H}{\underset{\displaystyle NH_2}{\overset{|}{\underset{|}{C}}}} - COOH$$

2–amino–3–sulfhydrylpropanoic acid
(cysteine)

Apart from aminoethanoic acid, all α-amino acids contain a chiral centre(s) (shown as *).

$$H_3C - \overset{\displaystyle H}{\underset{\displaystyle NH_2}{\overset{|}{\underset{|}{C^*}}}} - COOH$$

2–aminopropanoic acid
(alanine)

$$H_3C - \overset{\displaystyle H}{\underset{\displaystyle OH}{\overset{|}{\underset{|}{C^*}}}} - \overset{\displaystyle H}{\underset{\displaystyle NH_2}{\overset{|}{\underset{|}{C^*}}}} - COOH$$

2–amino–3–hydroxybutanoic acid
(threonine)

The two optical isomers of 2-aminopropanoic acid (alanine) can be shown as mirror image forms.

YOU SHOULD KNOW ›››

››› how to write the formulae of α-amino acids

››› how to recognise chiral centres in compounds

››› how to write the mirror image forms of α-amino acids

Knowledge check 44

Give the displayed formula of 2-amino-3-methylpentanoic acid.

Stretch & Challenge

Give the molecular formula of the α-amino acid, tryptophan.

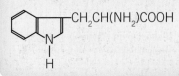

Knowledge check 45

Cystine has the formula

$$HOOC - \overset{H}{\underset{NH_2}{\overset{|}{\underset{|}{C}}}} - \overset{H}{\underset{H}{\overset{|}{\underset{|}{C}}}} - S - S - \overset{H}{\underset{H}{\overset{|}{\underset{|}{C}}}} - \overset{H}{\underset{NH_2}{\overset{|}{\underset{|}{C}}}} - COOH$$

Indicate any chiral centres in the formula of cysteine using an asterisk (*) to indicate a chiral centre.

‹Link› Some terms used in optical isomerism page 116.

Knowledge check 46

Write the formulae of the two mirror image forms of serine (2-amino-3-hydroxypropanoic acid).

Key Term

A **zwitterion** is a dipolar form of an amino acid where the carboxylic acid group loses a proton, becoming COO^- and the amino group gains the proton, becoming $^+NH_3$.

47 Knowledge check

The isoelectric point of proline is 6.3.

Write the displayed formula of the species formed from proline at a pH of 9.0

Stretch & Challenge

Monosodium glutamate (MSG) is used in restaurants as a flavour enhancer for foods.

The isoelectric point of glutamic acid is 3.1. Write the displayed formula of the species in solution at a pH of 13.

Stretch & Challenge

Horses' urine contains hippuric acid.

A sample of hippuric acid is hydrolysed by heating it with aqueous sodium hydroxide. Give the displayed formulae of the two products obtained from this reaction.

48 Knowledge check

Explain how the zwitterion form of glycine suggests that the nitrogen atom cannot exist as a nucleophile.

Amphoteric and zwitterionic nature of α-amino acids and the effect on melting temperature and solubility

α-Amino acids exist as solids at room temperature, whereas similar sized molecules are often liquids or occur as solids with a much lower melting temperature.

aminoethanoic acid
melting temperature 240°C

2–hydroxyethanoic acid
melting temperature 75–80°C

methoxyethanoic acid
melting temperature 8°C
boiling temperature 203°C

The melting temperatures of α-amino acids are much higher than might be expected because they exist as **zwitterions**. A hydrogen ion (H^+) is lost from the carboxylic acid group and gained by the nitrogen atom of the amino group, by use of its lone pair of electrons. The zwitterion formula of aminoethanoic acid is

The ionic nature of zwitterions means that there are strong ionic forces between positive and negative ions and more energy is needed to overcome these forces. As a result, α-amino acids have higher melting temperatures than related covalently bonded compounds. Aminoethanoic acid is described as a neutral amino acid, as the positive and negative charges are balanced out. The zwitterion dipolar form of the amino acid suggests that α-amino acids are soluble in water. The solubility of aminoethanoic acid at 25°C is 25g in 100 cm³ of water, and the solubility of the larger molecule 2-amino-3-phenylpropanoic acid is 3g in 100 cm³ of water. Aqueous solutions of α-amino acids contain zwitterions but the compounds only exist as the zwitterion itself at a certain pH. The value of this pH is called the isoelectric point and the pH value varies depending on the amino acid. The isoelectric point of aminoethanoic acid is at pH 6.0. If the pH is below the value of the isoelectric point then the amino acid acts as a base by accepting a hydrogen ion.

In solutions where the pH is greater than the isoelectric point the amino acid acts as an acid, losing a proton.

Forming dipeptides by combining amino acids together

A dipeptide is formed when two amino acid molecules join together in a condensation reaction, for example using two molecules of aminoethanoic acid.

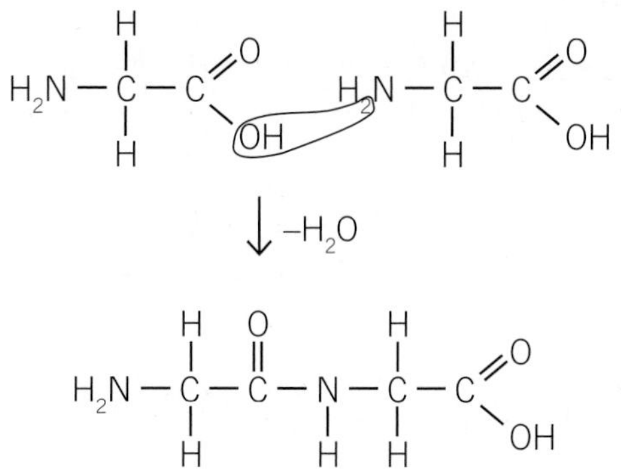

$$\downarrow -H_2O$$

If two different amino acid molecules are used, then two different dipeptides can be formed. For example, if phenylalanine and glycine are used then the two dipeptides are

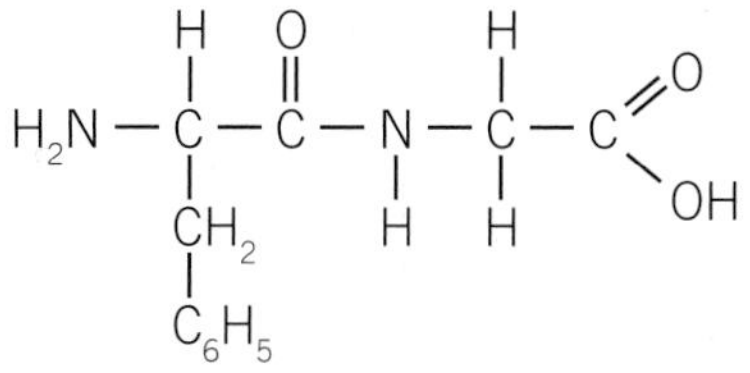

and

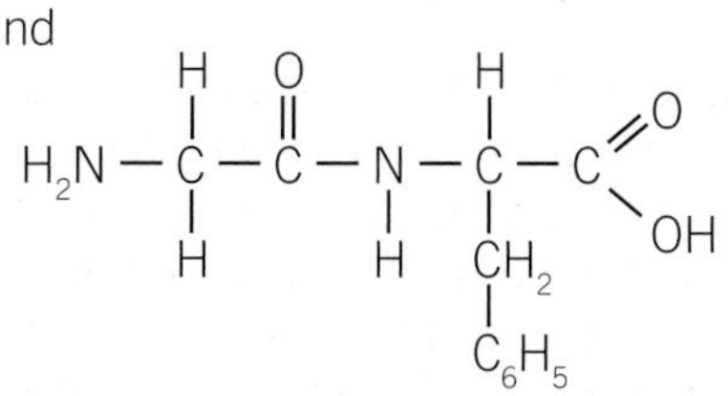

The formation of a dipeptide introduces a peptide linkage (peptide bond, amide linkage)

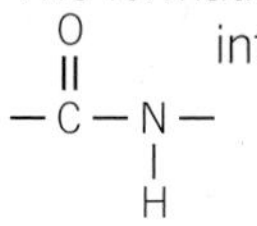

into the condensation product.

One of the artificial sweeteners used in 'diet' carbonated sugar-free drinks is aspartame, which is the methyl ester of the condensation product between phenylalanine and aspartic acid, $HOOC-CH_2-CH(NH_2)COOH$.

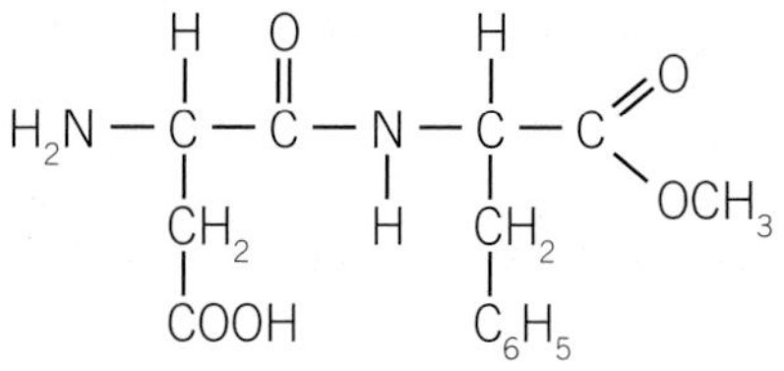

YOU SHOULD KNOW › › ›

››› the reasons for the relative high melting temperature of α-amino acids

››› how to write the conventional and zwitterion formula of α-amino acids

››› the formulae of α-amino acids in acidic and basic solutions

Knowledge check 49

The formula shows the formula of a dipeptide formed between valine, $(CH_3)_2CHCH(NH_2)COOH$ and cysteine, $HSCH_2CH(NH_2)COOH$.

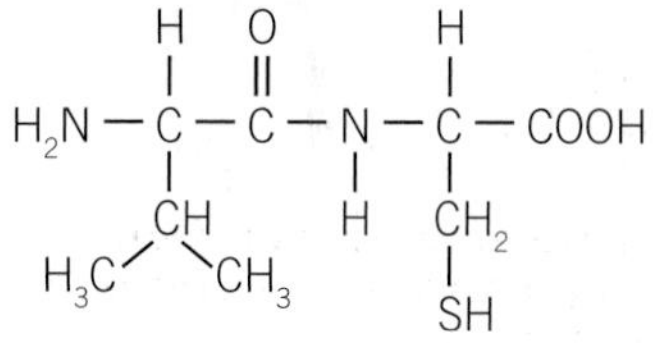

Write the displayed formula of the other dipeptide formed between molecules of these two α-amino acids.

Forming polypeptides and proteins

A polypeptide is a long chain of condensed amino acids joined together by peptide linkages. Part of a polypeptide chain is

$$-N-C-C-N-C-C-N-C-C-N-C-C-$$

Ala   Gly   Phe   Ser

Three letter abbreviations are sometimes used for simplicity when looking at the formula of a polypeptide.

	name	systematic name
Ala	alanine	2–aminopropanoic acid
Gly	glycine	aminoethanoic acid
Phe	phenylalanine	2–amino–3–phenylpropanoic acid
Ser	serine	2–amino–3–hydroxypropanoic acid

Proteins are polypeptides formed by condensing many amino acids together. Human insulin is a protein that consists of two amino acid chains, joined by disulfide bridges (–S–S–). People who have diabetes are not able to produce enough insulin and, as a result, sugar can build up in the blood. If the diabetes cannot be controlled by diet then insulin needs to provided externally, by the use of injections.

Haemoglobin is the oxygen-carrying protein in the blood. The replacement of just one amino acid in its structure can have a profound effect. In sickle cell anaemia a molecule of glutamic acid (2-aminopentane-1,5-dioic acid) is replaced in haemoglobin by a molecule of valine (2-amino-3-methylbutanoic acid). This mutation reduces the oxygen-carrying capacity of haemoglobin but it does provide an increased resistance to malaria.

Human Insulin

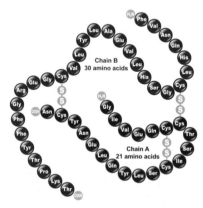

The primary, secondary and tertiary nature of proteins

There are several levels to consider when describing the structure of proteins. The primary structure of a protein has already been discussed – it is the order of amino acids in the chain(s). There are twenty amino acids that can make up polypeptide chains. We obtain, or make in the body, twelve of these but the remaining eight cannot be made in the body and we need to obtain these from the food that we eat. These eight amino acids are called **essential amino acids** and include valine and lysine.

$$H_2N - CH_2 - CH_2 - CH_2 - CH_2 - \underset{\underset{H}{|}}{\overset{\overset{NH_2}{|}}{C}} - COOH \qquad \text{Lysine}$$

The number of possible peptides from these twenty amino acids is enormous. For example, there are 400 possible dipeptides, and 8000 possible tripeptides. The secondary structure of proteins is concerned with how the amino acid chains are arranged. The two commonest arrangements are as an α-helix or as a β-pleated sheet. In an α-helix the polypeptide chain is coiled into a spiral and this shape is maintained by hydrogen bonds between the N–H hydrogen atom of an amide group and the C=O carbonyl oxygen atom of another amide group.

$$C = O \cdots H - N$$

Proteins that have the α-helix structure are found in muscle and in wool. When wool fibres are stretched, the hydrogen bonds are broken but the strong disulfide bonds remain. When the stretching force is removed this hydrogen bonding is restored and the wool resumes its original shape. Keratin is another protein that has the α-helix structure.

The other common arrangement is a β-pleated sheet. The structure is again maintained by hydrogen bonds as before, but the C=O and N—H groups are in different chains. Van der Waals forces are responsible for producing a pleated sheet rather than a flat arrangement.

The tertiary structure of proteins is concerned with the way in which the protein chain is folded. Fibrous proteins have a chain length that is many times its diameter and this type of protein tends to be insoluble in water. Other proteins, including most enzymes, operate in an aqueous environment. Some of these are water soluble but most are colloidal. These proteins are called globular proteins and are roughly spherical in shape. In water these proteins often take up a shape where the polar groups are on the surface of the protein, and lipophilic (fat loving) groups are towards the interior of the structure.

Key Term

Essential amino acids are those α-amino acids that cannot be synthesised in the body and must be supplied through the diet.

Knowledge check **50**

The shortened formula of lysine is shown in the text. Give the systematic name of lysine.

Knowledge check **51**

Explain why hydrogen bonding occurs between a carbonyl group oxygen atom and an amino group hydrogen atom in the α-helix of a protein.

ferritin

The role of proteins in living systems

Enzymes are compounds that catalyse chemical reactions. They can be described as macromolecular biological catalysts and these catalyse over 5000 biochemical reactions. They work like other catalysts, by lowering the activation energy that is necessary for the reaction to take place. Most enzymes are proteins and they work through their unique 3-dimensional structures. The role of enzymes in the body is essential to maintain life. Without them reactions in the body would be rather slow! Amylase is an enzyme that catalyses the hydrolysis of starch into sugars. It is present in human saliva. Rice and potatoes, which are mainly starch, may taste slightly sweet in the mouth as smaller molecule sugars start to be formed from starch.

The use of enzymes in commerce is an important developing area of research. Some examples of the commercial use of enzymes are given in the table.

amylase

52 ▽ **Knowledge check**

In the brewing industry, glucose ($C_6H_{12}O_6$) molecules are broken down by the enzymes from yeast into ethanol and carbon dioxide. Give the equation for this reaction.

Application	Type of enzyme	Mode of action
Laundry	Amylases Lipases Proteases	Removing stains from proteins, starch or fats from clothes
Brewing	Amylases Glucanases Proteases	Hydrolysing polysaccharides and proteins to smaller molecules
Dairy	Rennin	Hydrolyse protein in cheese making

About 150 enzymes have commercial uses. They can operate in aqueous conditions of mild acidity or alkalinity. Enzymes are used in detergents to remove stains from clothes; however, a number of consumers suffer from allergies when handling these detergents or when wearing clothes that have been washed in detergents containing enzymes. In laundry work, amylases degrade starches to water-soluble sugars, lipases hydrolyse fats, and proteases digest proteins. Enzymes also have important uses in the dairy industry where rennin is used to degrade the protein $\varkappa$-casein in cheese making. The hydrophobic product from this degradation is the main component of curd from which cheese is made.

Traditional cheese making

Organic synthesis and analysis

The study of organic chemistry should not just be the learning of the reactions of a number of different compounds. It is also to attain the ability to synthesise a given compound from suitable starting materials, often via a number of stages. When choosing a pathway to the compound, consideration should be given to a number of factors, which include the availability of the reactants, health and safety, cost and yield. Increasingly, attention is being given to 'green' synthetic methods. The evaluation of the chosen method to make the compound is also very important. Another important feature of the work is the qualitative and quantitative analysis of the reactants and products. In the last fifty years, instrumental methods of analysis, particularly NMR and mass spectrometry, have become increasingly important and with the continuing sophistication of these instrumental methods, there seems to less need for the traditional 'wet' methods of analysis.

You should be able to demonstrate and apply knowledge of:

- The synthesis of organic compounds by a sequence of reactions.

- The principles of the techniques of manipulation, separation and purification.

- The distinction between condensation polymerisation and addition polymerisation.

- How polyesters and polyamides are formed.

- The use of melting temperature as a determination of purity.

- The use of high-resolution ^1H NMR spectra in the elucidation of the structure of organic molecules.

- The use of chromatographic data from TLC/paper chromatography, GC and HPLC in finding the composition of mixtures.

Content

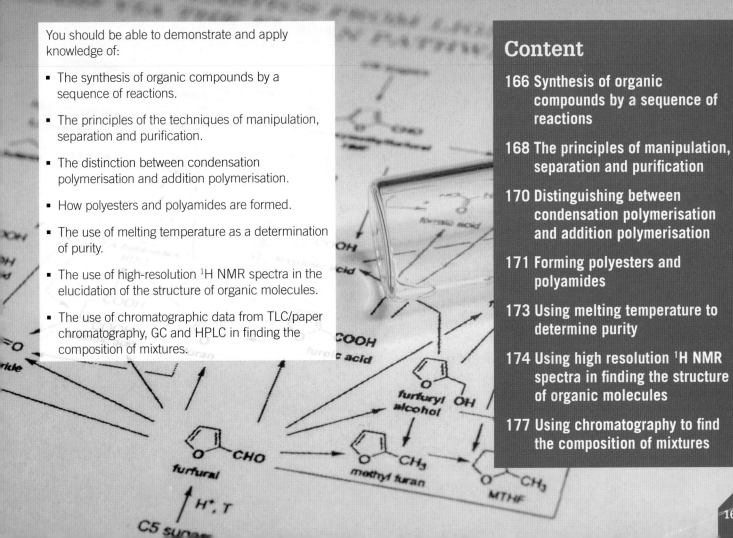

Synthesis of organic compounds by a series of reactions

Making an organic compound by a series of steps is a topic that is challenging for many students at 'A' level. This may be because good problem-solving skills and a sound knowledge of organic chemistry are required. An important point to note when devising a reaction sequence is to see if there is a difference in the number of carbon atoms between the starting compound and the compound required. If there is this difference, then one or more steps must involve a reaction where the length of the carbon chain is altered.

Increase in chain length The reaction of potassium cyanide with a halogenoalkane produces a nitrile, which can be hydrolysed to produce a carboxylic acid. Alternatively, the nitrile can be reduced by lithium tetrahydridoaluminate(III) to give the amine.

$$CH_3CH_2CH_2CH_2Br \xrightarrow{KCN} CH_3CH_2CH_2CH_2C \equiv N$$

1–bromobutane

warm with dilute acid

$LiAlH_4$

$CH_3CH_2CH_2CH_2NH_2$ $CH_3CH_2CH_2CH_2COOH$

pentylamine   pentanoic acid

Another method of lengthening the carbon chain is by the addition of hydrogen cyanide to an aldehyde or ketone, followed by hydrolysis of the hydroxynitrile.

propanal   2–hydroxybutanoic acid

In aromatic systems, a Friedel–Crafts alkylation or acylation reaction can be used to introduce a carbon-containing side chain to a benzene ring.

propylbenzene

phenylethanone

Decrease in chain length Heating an acid or its salt with soda lime (in a decarboxylation reaction) produces an alkane that contains fewer carbon atoms than the starting material.

$$CH_3C \underset{O^-Na^+}{\overset{O}{<}} \xrightarrow[\text{(NaOH)}]{\text{soda lime}} CH_4 + Na_2CO_3$$

YOU SHOULD KNOW › › ›

› › › how to prepare a given compound using a number of stages, which may include a reduction or an increase in the length of the carbon chain

YOU SHOULD KNOW › › ›

› › › the reactions necessary to change the number of carbon atoms in the chain

YOU SHOULD KNOW › › ›

› › › any essential conditions (e.g. a need for increased pressure or the use of a catalyst) that are necessary for a reaction to proceed

53 Knowledge check

Show how 3-phenylpropanoic acid, $C_6H_5CH_2CH_2COOH$, can be made in two steps from 2-bromoethylbenzene, $C_6H_5CH_2CH_2Br$.

54 Knowledge check

State the reagents, lettered **A**, **B** and **C** that are needed to produce benzene from methylbenzene.

! Extra Help

Constructing flow charts for the reactions of the main groups of organic compounds is a very useful way of learning reaction sequences.

Another method is to use the triiodomethane (iodoform) reaction, where a methyl ketone (or its precursor) is treated with alkaline iodine. The products are triiodomethane and the salt of a carboxylic acid that contains one fewer carbon atom than the starting compound.

Flow charts of reactions are a useful way of learning about reaction sequences. A sample one, centred on ethene, is shown. Only the reagents are given, essential conditions have been omitted for clarity.

$$CH_3CH_2CN \xleftarrow{\text{KCN}} CH_3CH_2Br \xrightarrow{\text{NaOH}_{(aq)}} CH_3CH_2OH \xrightarrow{H^+/Cr_2O_7^{2-}} CH_3C\overset{O}{\underset{H}{<}}$$

$$CH_3CH_2COOH \quad\downarrow H_2SO_{4(aq)}$$

$$\downarrow HBr$$

$$CH_2=CH_2 \xrightarrow{Br_2} BrCH_2-CH_2Br$$

$$Pt/Ni \mid H_2$$

$$NaOH_{(aq)} \downarrow$$

$$CH_3-CH_3 \qquad HOCH_2-CH_2OH$$

$$\downarrow H^+/Cr_2O_7^{2-}$$

$$CH_3C\overset{O}{\underset{OH}{<}}$$

$$\downarrow \text{soda lime}$$

$$CH_4$$

Worked example

State the reagents required and any necessary conditions, to prepare benzene from (chloromethyl)benzene, $C_6H_5CH_2Cl$.

This reaction cannot be carried out in one step. It requires a reduction in the length of the carbon chain to give a hydrocarbon as the product. This suggests a decarboxylation reaction, perhaps from benzenecarboxylic acid, C_6H_5COOH, by use of soda lime. A carboxylic acid can be obtained by the oxidation of a primary alcohol. To obtain a primary alcohol from a halogenoalkane requires a hydrolysis reaction using an alkali in aqueous solution. A suggested route is

Knowledge check 55

Devise a route to produce methyl ethanoate from bromomethane.

Knowledge check 56

State the name of a compound used, together with a catalyst, in a Friedel–Crafts reaction to prepare 1,4-diethylbenzene from ethylbenzene.

Stretch & Challenge

An important compound in rose oil is β-damascenone. This has the formula

Give the molecular formula of this compound.

Knowledge check 57

Give the displayed formula of the aldehyde that reacts with hydrogen cyanide/sodium cyanide to give a hydroxynitrile that is then hydrolysed to give compound **P**.

$$CH_3CH_2CH(OH)COOH$$

Compound **P**

PRACTICAL CHECK

A two-step synthesis, including purification and determination of the melting temperature of the product is a **specified practical task**.

PRACTICAL CHECK

Planning a sequence of tests to identify organic compounds from a given list is a **specified practical task**.

Knowledge check 58

Give the name of the compound produced by the decarboxylation of $Na^+{}^-OOC-CH_2-CH_2-CH_2-CH_2-COO^-\,{}^+Na$.

59

Knowledge check

Deduce which one of these compounds will undergo the triiodomethane reaction.

a ⬡—CH₂—CH₂OH

b ⬡—CH(OH)—CH₃

c ⬡—CH₂—CH₂—CH₂—OH

d ⬡—CH(OH)—CH₂—CH₃

60

Knowledge check

State the reagents needed for the reaction sequence.

⬡—CH₂Br →(D) ⬡—CH₂CN →(E)

⬡—CH(OH)—COOH →(F) ⬡—C(=O)—COOH

YOU SHOULD KNOW › › ›

› › › the reasons when the use of fractional distillation is preferable to simple distillation

YOU SHOULD KNOW › › ›

› › › why steam distillation is sometimes the preferred option in the separation of liquids

Stretch & Challenge

Devise a reaction scheme to make 2,4,6-tribromophenol starting from phenylamine.

▼ Study point

Reaction sequences are not really concerned with yield but are only an indication of whether the reaction will work. There may be several different routes that are acceptable but the yield may vary.

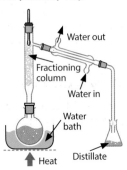

The principles of the techniques of manipulation, separation and purification

Many organic reactions do not go to completion as required and other products may be produced, and some unreacted starting products may remain. An important part of any organic preparation is the separation and purification of the products. When ethyl ethanoate is made from ethanol and ethanoic acid, the reaction products include the required ester, together with water and some unreacted ethanol and ethanoic acid.

$$CH_3CH_2OH + CH_3COOH \rightleftharpoons CH_3COOCH_2CH_3 + H_2O$$

These four compounds are liquids that are **miscible** with each other, but that is not necessarily the case with other reactions. The products may be an insoluble solid, be present in solution or as immiscible liquids. Each of these mixtures of products needs a different method of separation.

Separating miscible liquids If the product does not decompose at or below its boiling temperature and the boiling temperature is not too high, then distillation can be used to separate the product from the other substances present in the reaction mixture. Simple distillation can be used if the boiling temperature of the product differs by a reasonable amount (perhaps 20°C or more) from the boiling temperatures of the other compounds present. It can also be used to separate a volatile liquid from other substances in the mixture that are not volatile.

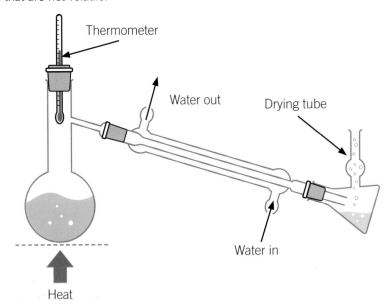

An example is the distillation of 2-chloro-2-methylpropane from its mixture with 2-methylpropan-2-ol and hydrochloric acid.

$$(CH_3)_3COH + HCl \longrightarrow (CH_3)_3CCl + H_2O$$

boiling temperatures   82°C   51°C   100°C

Fractional distillation (shown in the margin) is used if the boiling temperatures are closer together. A fractionating column is used, which enables a more efficient separation of the products to occur.

The separation of ethanol obtained from the fermentation of sugars is more effective if fractional distillation is used. The primary separation of the products present in crude oil (petroleum) is also carried out by fractional distillation. For compounds that decompose just before or at their boiling temperatures, or have very high boiling temperatures, distillation can be carried out under reduced pressures (vacuum distillation) or steam distillation can be used. The reduction in pressure used in vacuum distillation enables compounds to boil at lower temperatures than when distillation occurs at atmospheric pressure. For example, the alkane dodecane, $C_{12}H_{26}$, boils at 216°C under atmospheric pressure (~ 101 kPa) but at 92°C if the pressure is reduced to 1.3 kPa.

Separating immiscible liquids Steam distillation is a very important method in the perfumery industry where essential oils extracted from plants may decompose if heated to their boiling temperatures at atmospheric pressure.

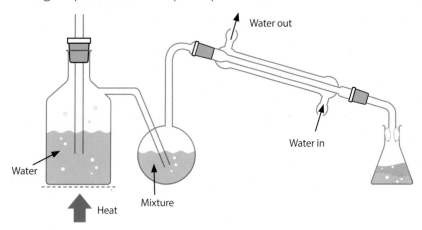

Water out

Water in

Water

Mixture

Heat

Steam is passed into the reaction mixture and the volatile compounds present pass over with steam, and condense in the receiving flask. Rose oil is one of the most widely used oils in the perfume industry. Steam distillation of rose petals gives an oil (containing a number of different compounds) and water from the condensed vapours.

Solvent extraction This is a method that depends on the differing solubility of a compound in two immiscible solvents. For example, iodine is about 90 times more soluble in tetrachloromethane than in water. If tetrachloromethane is added is to an aqueous solution of iodine and mixture shaken, most of the iodine is extracted into the tetrachloromethane layer. The two layers can then be separated using a separating funnel.

Insoluble solid separation Filtration is used to separate the solid from the liquid present. This can be carried using a filter paper and funnel. The use of a fluted filter paper is quicker than the traditional method as the filtrate only needs to travel through one layer of filter paper and the paper only touches the funnel at the folds.

Alternatively, filtration using a Buchner funnel can be used (vacuum filtration).

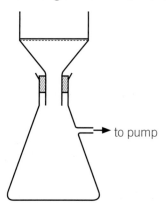

to pump

Once the solid is in the funnel it needs to be washed with an appropriate solvent and dried – in the air, or in a drying oven at a temperature below its melting temperature.

Miscible liquids are completely soluble in each other at all concentrations. An example of this is ethanol and water.

YOU SHOULD KNOW › › ›

› › › the reasons why solvent extraction is carried out

PRACTICAL CHECK

The synthesis of a liquid organic product, including separation using a separating funnel is a **specified practical task**.

Knowledge check 61

Explain why heating under reflux cannot be used to concentrate a solution.

Knowledge check 62

4.25g of butane-1,4-dioic acid (M_r 118) was dissolved in water and an equal volume of the solvent ethoxyethane (immiscible with water) was added and the mixture shaken. The two layers were allowed to separate. The aqueous layer now contained 6×10^{-3} g of the acid. Calculate how many more times the acid is soluble in ethoxyethane, than in water under these conditions.

YOU SHOULD KNOW › › ›

› › › the essential steps for the process of recrystallization

63 Knowledge check

In a reaction to make methyl benzenecarboxylate (boiling temperature 224°C) by esterification, some methanol (boiling temperature 65°C) remained. State, giving a reason, which method of distillation would be the most appropriate to remove this excess of methanol.

PRACTICAL CHECK

The synthesis of a solid organic product, including recrystallisation and the determination of melting temperature is a **specified practical task**.

64 Knowledge check

Propane-1,2,3-triol has a boiling temperature of 290°C at atmospheric pressure (101 kPa) but boils at 167°C under a pressure of 17 kPa.

(a) Give the displayed formula of propane-1,2,3-triol.

(b) Suggest a reason why propane-1,2,3-triol is often purified by using vacuum distillation.

65 Knowledge check

Iodine (I_2) can be extracted from its aqueous solution by the use of tetrachloromethane (CCl_4), which is immiscible with water. I_2 is 90 times more soluble in CCl_4 than it is in water. 100 cm³ of an aqueous solution of iodine contained 0.030g of dissolved iodine. An equal volume of CCl_4 was added and the mixture shaken. The mixture was allowed to separate and the CCl_4 layer removed. Calculate approximately how much iodine remained in the aqueous layer.

66 Knowledge check

The action of nitric acid on an organic acid produced a colourless crystalline product when the mixture was cooled. A yellow solution was also present, which contained traces of impurities. The crystals were filtered and washed with water, in which it was insoluble. State how you could be certain that the solid product was free of impurities.

Soluble solids from solution If the solid is present as a solute in solution then the products are obtained by crystallisation. If the solution should be colourless but is coloured due to the presence of impurities then decolourising charcoal can be used. The solution is boiled with a little decolourising charcoal to remove the colour, and then filtered hot to remove the charcoal that contains the absorbed colour. The filtrate is then concentrated by boiling and cooled. If the solution has been sufficiently concentrated then crystals of the solute appear on cooling. These are filtered off and dried. If no crystals appear on cooling then the solution needs to be made more concentrated. Extra care needs to be taken when concentrating the solution if the solvent is flammable – generally a water bath or some method of electrical heating, for example a hot plate is used. The solute obtained by crystallisation may not be pure and it needs to be recrystallised. The essential steps for this are:

- Dissolve the solute in a minimum volume of hot solvent

- Filter hot, if necessary, to remove insoluble impurities

- Allow to cool

- Filter

- Wash the solid with a small amount of an appropriate solvent

- Dry at a temperature below its melting temperature.

Distinguishing between condensation polymerisation and addition polymerisation

Polymerisation is the joining together of a large number of **monomer** molecules. Alkenes undergo polymerisation when the –C=C– double bond is used to join the monomer units together giving a polymer that now contains only single bonds between carbon atoms in the chain.

$$n \begin{array}{c} H_3C \\ \\ H \end{array} C=C \begin{array}{c} H \\ \\ H \end{array} \longrightarrow \begin{bmatrix} \begin{array}{cc} CH_3 & H \\ | & | \\ C & -C \\ | & | \\ H & H \end{array} \end{bmatrix}_n$$

propene   poly(propene)

Condensation polymerisation occurs when a large number of monomer molecules join together with the loss of small molecules (often water or hydrogen chloride). If two different monomers are used, each one having different functional groups, then small molecules are lost when bonding occurs between them. For example, a condensation polymer is formed when a dicarboxylic acid bonds with a diol.

$$\underset{OH}{\overset{O}{\underset{}{C}}} - (CH_2)_n - \underset{OH}{\overset{O}{C}} \quad HO - \underset{H}{\overset{H}{C}} - (CH_2)_n - \underset{H}{\overset{H}{C}} - OH$$

$$\downarrow -H_2O$$

$$\cdots \overset{O}{\overset{||}{C}} - (CH_2)_n - \overset{O}{\overset{||}{C}} - O - \underset{H}{\overset{H}{C}} - (CH_2)_n - \underset{H}{\overset{H}{C}} - O \cdots$$

$$\cdots N-(CH_2)_n-C-N-(CH_2)_n-C\cdots$$

Knowledge check 67

A section of a polymer is

$$\left[CH_2-(CH_2)_6-\overset{\overset{O}{\|}}{C}-O\right]_n$$

State whether addition polymerisation or condensation polymerisation has occurred when this polymer was made from its monomer(s), giving a reason for your answer.

Condensation polymerisation can also occur between the two different functional groups present in just one type of monomer molecule. For example, using an α,ω-amino acid (i.e. with an amino group $-NH_2$ at one end of the molecule and a carboxylic acid group $-COOH$ at the end of the carbon chain).

It is useful to have some rules for distinguishing between these two types of polymerisation. If:

- The monomer is an alkene, then addition polymerisation occurs.

- No small molecule is lost and the polymer is the only product, then addition polymerisation has occurred.

- The monomer(s) contain functional groups such as $-NH_2$, $-COOH$ or $-OH$ then condensation polymerisation occurs.

- The chain contains the amide link $-C(O)N(H)$ or an ester linkage $-OC(O)-$ then condensation polymerisation has occurred.

- The chain only consists of carbon atoms then addition polymerisation has occurred.

Stretch & Challenge

Write the displayed formula of a repeating section of the addition polymer 'polyacrylonitrile' that is made by polymerising propenenitrile.

Knowledge check 68

Give the displayed formula of the monomer that can be used to make the polyamide, Nylon 8.

How polyesters and polyamides are formed

Polyesters are very important materials that have extensive uses in the production of clothing, packaging and plastic bottles.

The most common polyester is PET, this an abbreviated name of polyethylene terephthalate. The monomer or monomers from which a polyester is made need to have a functional group at each end of the molecule. PET is produced from ethane-1,2-diol and benzene-1,4-dicarboxylic acid (terephthalic acid).

! **Extra Help**

Hexanedioic acid is used in the manufacture of Nylon 6,6. Some of this acid is converted to 1,6-diaminohexane. This is carried out in the following way:

(a) the acid is neutralised with ammonia to produce the ammonium salt of the acid;

(b) the ammonium salt is heated to produce hexane-1,5-dinitrile;

(c) the dinitrile is reduced with hydrogen in the presence of a nickel catalyst.

S&C **Stretch & Challenge**

The starting material for making melamine resins is melamine itself. This is made by heating carbamide (urea).

$$6 \, CO(NH_2)_2 \longrightarrow \text{[melamine]} + 6NH_3 + 3CO_2$$

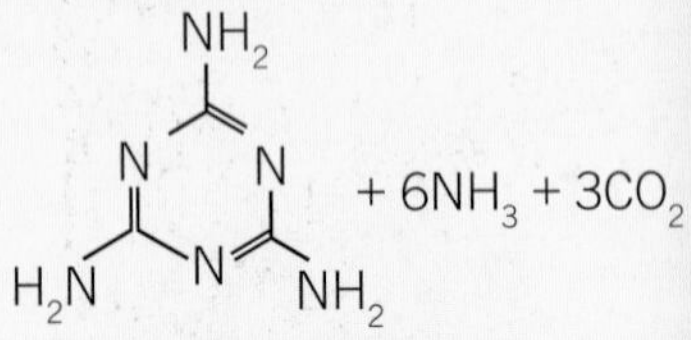

(a) Give the empirical formula of melamine

(b) Calculate the atom economy of this reaction, assuming that melamine is the only useful product.

PET itself is made into synthetic fibres such as Terylene©, either then used by itself or together with natural fibres such as cotton. The polyester is a good insulator and its fibres can be used in the making of blankets and as a filling material for duvets. PET does not easily biodegrade and there is a need for polyesters that will degrade quickly in landfill. One of these is poly(lactic acid), PLA. This polyester has the added advantage that it can be derived from renewable resources such as corn starch or sugar cane. The equation for the polymerisation from 2-hydroxypropanoic acid (lactic acid) is shown below.

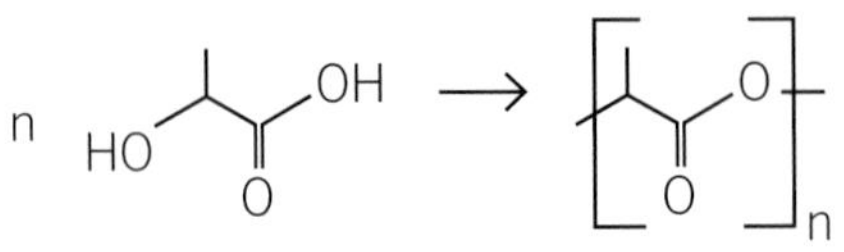

PLA is a polyester that is made from one type of monomer molecule whereas PET requires two different types of monomer molecules.

Polyamides are also a product of condensation polymerisation. The first polyamide, Nylon 6,6 was made in 1935. The starting material can be benzene, which is reduced to cyclohexane and this product is then oxidised, giving cyclohexanol and cyclohexanone. The mixture is then itself oxidised to hexanedioic acid.

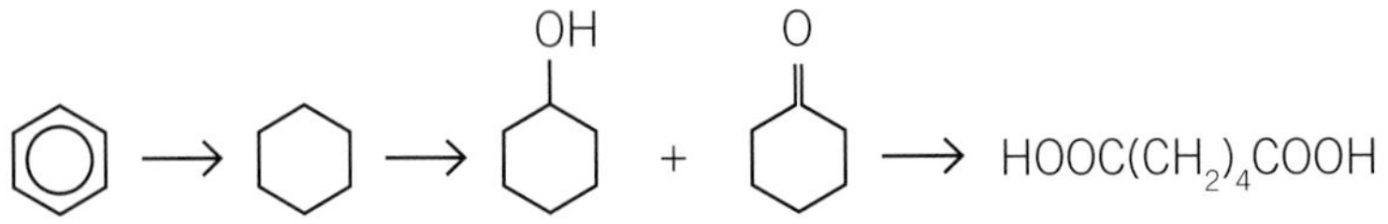

Some of the hexanedioic acid is converted to hexane-1,6-diamine, which is combined with hexanedioic acid.

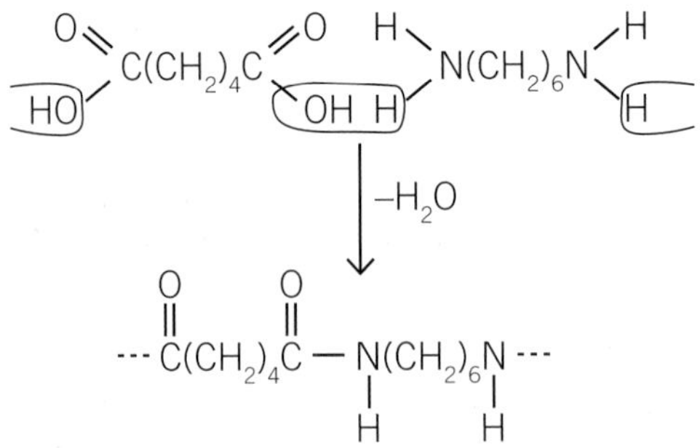

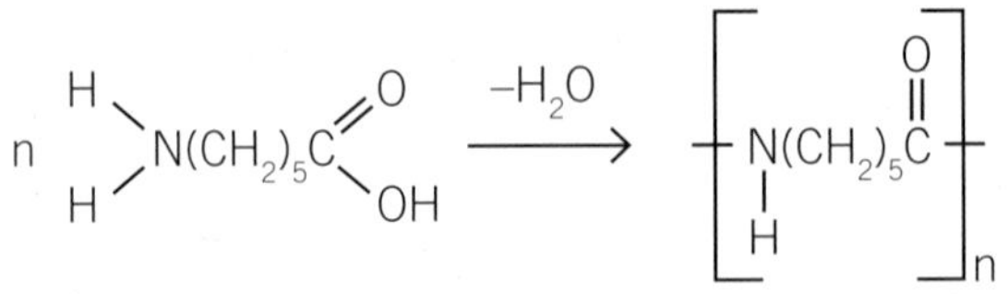

The product is named Nylon 6,6 because each of the two monomers has six carbon atoms. Another polyamide, Nylon 6, was developed in Germany in 1939. Although Nylon 6 is derived from the six carbon-containing acid, 6-aminohexanoic acid, it is not produced directly from the acid itself. Instead it is produced from caprolactam, which itself is made in several stages from benzene. On treating with water it ring opens and polymerises giving Nylon 6.

Another important polyamide is Kevlar©. This can be produced from benzene-1,4-dioic acid and benzene-1.4-diamine.

Kevlar© has good fire retardant properties and is five times stronger than steel. The compound can be produced as a fibre which is spun into bullet proof vests.

! **Extra Help**

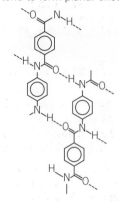

Kevlar© chains are relatively rigid and tend to form planar sheets.

The Kevlar© chains lock together by hydrogen bonding between the carbonyl group oxygen of one chain and the N–H hydrogen atom of another chain. This leads to a relatively rigid sheet structure with a high tensile strength.

Using melting temperature to determine purity

The melting temperature of a solid is the temperature at which the solid begins to change into a liquid. For many pure substances, the temperature at which this change from a solid to a liquid occurs is quite sharp (within 1°C) and the figure obtained is useful for identification purposes. The melting temperature is affected by the presence of impurities and the values obtained give an indication of the compound's purity. The presence of impurities lowers the expected melting temperature and the compound melts over a range of temperature rather than at a fixed value. For example, a sample of a compound has a sharp melting temperature of 122°C and is suspected to be benzenecarboxylic acid. A little pure benzenecarboxylic acid is mixed with the sample and the melting temperature again taken. If the melting temperature remains at the same temperature, it is likely that the compound is as suggested. However, if the melting temperature is now lower and not sharp, then the original substance was not benzenecarboxylic acid. Aldehydes and ketones often exist as liquids or low melting temperature solids and it is sometimes difficult to obtain an accurate melting temperature for them. The aldehyde or ketone is reacted with 2,4-dinitrophenylhydrazine to give a derivative. These derivatives (2,4-dinitrophenylhydrazones) are usually orange-red solids that have a melting temperature that is easier to measure. The melting temperature of the 2,4-dinitrophenylhydrazone can be compared with a table of melting temperatures to identify the starting aldehyde or ketone.

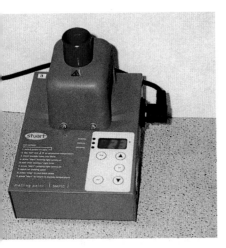

The melting temperature of the compound can be found using an electrical heating method.

Alternatively, the melting temperature can be found using a heating bath method.

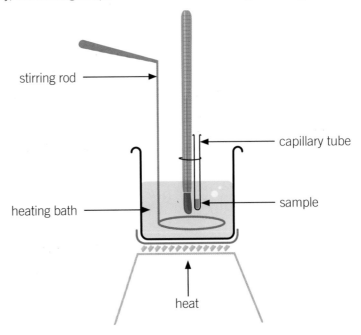

stirring rod

capillary tube

sample

heating bath

heat

A 2–3 mm depth sample is placed in a capillary tube that is attached to a thermometer by a rubber band. The thermometer and capillary tube are placed into a suitable heating bath. Water is used if the melting temperature is likely to be below 100 °C. For melting temperatures above 100 °C, silicone oil or other non-flammable liquid is used. The mixture is gently heated and stirred.

Knowledge check

69

The melting temperature of a pure compound is 158 °C. It is thought that it is either 2-hydroxybenzenecarboxylic acid or 3-chlorobenzenecarboxylic acid, both of which also have the melting temperature of 158 °C. State how you would find out which acid is present as the unknown compound, using a melting temperature method.

Key Term

In NMR spectroscopy the **environment** means the nature of the surrounding atoms or groups in the molecule.

▼ Study point

If the compound contains more than two carbon atoms, the ^{1}H NMR spectrum can become more complicated. In propane ($CH_3CH_2CH_3$) there are eight hydrogen protons. The six CH_3 protons are all in the same environment and the two CH_2 protons are equivalent to each other but in a different environment to the methyl protons. There are two peaks in a low resolution ^{1}H NMR spectrum, reflecting the CH_3 and CH_2 hydrogen protons. These are in a relative peak area ratio of 6:2 (i.e. 3:1) respectively.

Using high resolution ^{1}H NMR in finding the structure of organic molecules

During the first year of this course, you will have studied the use of low-resolution proton magnetic resonance spectroscopy (^{1}H NMR) in the identification of chemical structure. In ethane

ethane   chloroethane

all the hydrogen protons are in equivalent **environments** and only one signal is seen. A hydrogen atom is now replaced by a chlorine atom to produce chloroethane. The hydrogen atoms are now in two environments, the three CH_3 protons are identical but the two CH_2 protons are in a different environment. This gives a low-resolution NMR spectrum showing two peaks with peak areas 3:2, reflecting the protons of the CH_3 and the CH_2 hydrogen atoms.

Dichloroethane, has two isomers 1,2-dichloroethane and 1,1-dichloroethane.

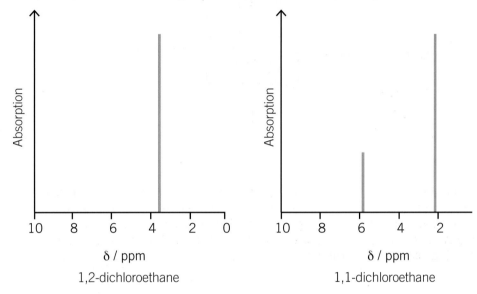

1,2-dichloroethane   1,1-dichloroethane

In 1,2-dichloroethane all the hydrogen protons are in an identical environment and the ^1H NMR spectrum shows a single peak (a singlet) at 3.7δ. However, in 1,1-dichloroethane the four hydrogen protons are in two different environments, one signal is seen at 5.9δ for the $CHCl_2$ hydrogen proton and the other is seen at 2.1δ for the CH_3 hydrogen protons. The peak areas for these two signals occur as a 1:3 ratio respectively.

If the ^1H NMR spectrum of 1,1-dichloroethane is measured using a high resolution spectrometer these two peaks are seen to be split. This splitting occurs because the magnetic environment of a proton or protons in one group is affected by the magnetic environment of neighbouring groups. The high resolution ^1H NMR spectrum of 1,1-dichloroethane shows that both signals are split – one into four peaks (a quartet) and the other into two peaks (a doublet). This process of signal splitting is called **spin-spin coupling**. The process is only considered for hydrogen protons 'on' neighbouring atoms – usually carbon, nitrogen or oxygen. Thus in 1,1,1,2-tetrachloropropane the hydrogen proton on carbon two is affected by the hydrogen protons on carbon three and vice versa.

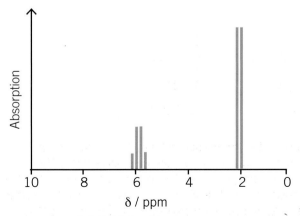

1,1,2,2-tetrachloropropane

However, in 1,1,2,2-tetrachloropropane the hydrogen atoms are not bonded to adjacent carbon atoms and the high resolution ^1H NMR spectrum shows two signals that show no splitting.

70 Knowledge check

The ^1H high-resolution NMR spectrum of a methyl ester consists of a singlet, a doublet and a triplet. The ^{13}C NMR spectrum indicates that there are four distinct environments for the carbon atoms. Suggest a displayed formula for this ester.

71 Knowledge check

Butanedione has the formula

$$H_3C - \overset{\overset{O}{\|}}{C} - \overset{\overset{O}{\|}}{C} - CH_3$$

State what you would see in its ^1H high-resolution NMR spectrum.

▼ **Study point**

In questions involving NMR spectra, you should assume that the magnetic field around ^{13}C nuclei has no effect on the ^1H NMR spectrum of a compound.

If a hydrogen proton bonded to a carbon, nitrogen or oxygen atom has n hydrogen protons bonded to an adjacent carbon, nitrogen or oxygen atom then its single peak will be split into (n + 1) smaller peaks. The table shows some examples of this rule in practice.

compound	hydrogen(s) a		hydrogen(s) b	
	splitting pattern	relative peak area	splitting pattern	relative peak area
$\overset{H^a}{\underset{F}{}}C=C\overset{H^b}{\underset{Br}{}}$	doublet	1	doublet	1
$\overset{a}{C}H_3\overset{b}{C}H_2C \equiv N$	triplet	3	quartet	2
$ClCH_2 \overset{a}{} - \overset{\overset{O}{\|}}{C} - \overset{b}{C}H_3$	singlet	2	singlet	3
$\overset{a}{C}H_3 - C\overset{\nearrow O}{\underset{\searrow H^b}{}}$	doublet	3	quartet	1

Questions may be set where candidates are asked to find the structure of a compound by the use of its ^{13}C NMR spectrum, high-resolution ^1H NMR spectrum, as well as its mass spectrum and its infrared absorption spectrum. In questions, the effect of the magnetic field of ^1H protons on ^{13}C nuclei will not be considered and only decoupled ^{13}C spectra will be provided.

Worked example

A candidate was given the following information about compound **M** and was asked to deduce its displayed formula.

- The infrared spectrum showed an absorption peak at 1718 cm^{-1} but did not show a peak at ~2800 cm^{-1} indicating the C–H bond of an aldehyde group, or an absorption at 1000 – 1300 cm^{-1} that is characteristic of a C–O single bond

- The mass spectrum showed a molecular ion at m/z 86 and significant fragmentation peaks at m/z 71 and 43

- The ^{13}C NMR spectrum showed four distinct environments for carbon atoms

- The high resolution ^1H NMR spectrum of compound **M** gave the spectrum below

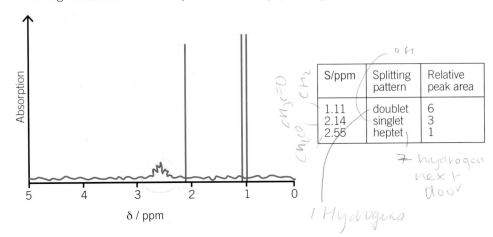

S/ppm	Splitting pattern	Relative peak area
1.11	doublet	6
2.14	singlet	3
2.55	heptet	1

The infrared spectrum shows an absorption peak at 1718 cm^{-1}. This suggests that the compound contains a C=O double bond and therefore could be an aldehyde, ketone, ester or carboxylic acid. The information indicates that it cannot be an aldehyde as there is no absorption at ~2800 cm^{-1}. It is not an ester or a carboxylic acid as the absorption due to a C–O single bond is missing absent. The compound must therefore be a ketone of formula R$_1$–C(O)–R$_2$ where R$_1$ and R$_2$ could be the same group or different groups. The relative molecular mass is 86 as compound **M** has a molecular ion at m/z 86. The fragmentation peak at m/z 71 shows a reduction of 15, indicating the possible loss of a methyl group. The fragment at m/z 43 could indicate a CH$_3$C=O$^+$ or C$_3$H$_7^+$ ion. The ^{13}C NMR spectrum indicates that the carbon atoms are in four different environments. One peak in the ^{1}H NMR spectrum is a singlet – suggesting that there are no hydrogen atoms bonded to the adjacent carbon atom. It is possible that there is a –C(O)CH$_3$ group present in the molecule. This group has 'M_r' 43 and therefore the other alkyl group must also have 'M_r' 43, corresponding to C$_3$H$_7$. A doublet in the ^{1}H NMR spectrum suggests a single hydrogen atom on an adjacent carbon atom. This removal of CH leaves 2 carbon atoms and 6 hydrogen atoms. The ^{1}H NMR spectrum shows a signal at 2.6δ as a heptet. This suggests that there are 6 equivalent hydrogen protons on the adjacent two carbon atoms. This is a characteristic pattern for a 2-propyl group, –CH(CH$_3$)$_2$. This evidence suggests that the compound could be 3-methylbutanone,

which has the molecular formula is C$_5$H$_{10}$O and relative molecular mass 86.

The use of chromatographic data from TLC/paper chromatography, GC and HPLC in the composition of mixtures

Chromatography is a technique that is used to separate substances from a mixture by their slow movement, at different rates, through or over a stationary phase. This technique of separation was developed early in the 20th century and was initially used to separate plant pigments by using a column containing powdered calcium carbonate. In the last hundred years chromatography has been extensively developed so that mixtures of substances can be separated using a number of different methods, which are appropriate to the number and nature of the components present. Although chromatography was originally a qualitative method, it can now be used in a quantitative way and is often used in conjunction with mass spectrometry to identify individual components that are present in the mixture. The emphasis in this topic is finding the composition of mixtures rather than the theory and principle of this technique. A description of the two mechanisms for the separation process – partition and adsorption are not required.

▼ **Study point**

Questions involving gas chromatography often show peak areas. These figures are relative values and not necessarily percentages, unless the sum of the peak areas adds up to 100.

! Extra Help

When deducing a structure from the fragmentation pattern of a mass spectrum, a signal at m/z 29 often indicates a C$_2$H$_5^+$ ion and a signal at m/z 43 may indicate C$_3$H$_7^+$ or CH$_3$CO$^+$ ions.

Stretch & Challenge

The equation shows a dehydration reaction.

(a) State how the infrared red absorption spectrum of the distinguishing peaks for the two compounds differ from each other.

(b) Another product of the dehydration is

Comment on how the ^{13}C NMR spectrum of the two **products** would differ. It is not necessary to consider the position of the signals in the spectrum.

(c) State whether either of the two products could exist as E–Z isomers, explaining your answer.

72 **Knowledge check**

(a) A TLC was taken of a sample of some carboxylic acids. The solvent front distance was measured as 6.9cm and the spot for benzenecarboxylic acid was measured at 4.0cm from the start line. Calculate the R_f value for this acid under these conditions.

(b) A spot was also seen around 5.2cm that appeared to consist of two spots close together. Suggest what should be done to separate the spots caused by these two compounds.

PRACTICAL CHECK

Paper chromatography separation including two-way separation is a **specified practical task**.

Paper chromatography / TLC

In paper chromatography the stationary phase is water trapped in the cellulose fibres of the paper, whereas in TLC the stationary phase is a layer of silica (SiO_2) or aluminium oxide (Al_2O_3) coated onto a plastic or glass plate. The techniques for paper chromatography and TLC are similar. Spots of the starting materials in a suitable solution are placed at the bottom of a piece of chromatography paper or TLC plate, which is then placed in a in a suitable solvent with the initial solvent level below the spots. The solvent front then rises up the paper/plate, separating the mixture into a series of spots. When the solvent front has risen to a suitable level, the paper/plate is removed and dried. The position of the separated spots and the solvent front are noted and the distance that these have risen from the starting line is measured.

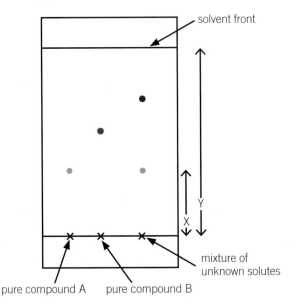

The position of the spots for a known and the unknown solute are then compared, to see if they have travelled the same distance. The R_f value can also be calculated.

$$R_f = \frac{\text{distance moved by spot (x)}}{\text{distance move by the solvent front (y)}}$$

Sometimes the use of a particular solvent does not completely separate the spots. This may be overcome by rotating the dried chromatogram through 90° and then using a different solvent. This technique is called two-way separation.

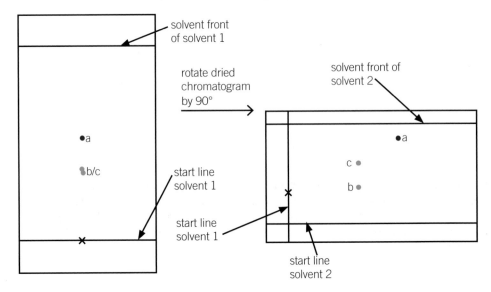

The identification of spots is relatively easy if they are coloured. Sometimes solutes produce colourless spots and the chromatogram is sprayed with a suitable reagent that causes the spots to become coloured. An example of this is to dry a chromatogram containing spots of different amino acids and then spray it with a solution of ninhydrin and then gently warm the paper. Blue-purple spots appear that show the position of the different amino acids. Another method that can be used to show the position of colourless spots is to shine UV light onto the plate. If the separated compounds are fluorescent then they show a colour. Alternatively the plate itself can have a coating of fluorescent materials and then the plate is exposed to UV light. The spots then show up as dark spots on a fluorescent background. Advantages of TLC over paper chromatography are that it is faster and that the thin layer on the plates can be made from a variety of materials. TLC continues to have important uses in forensic science.

Gas chromatography

The most common type of gas chromatography is gas-liquid chromatography (GLC) where a gaseous mixture is passed 'through' liquid particles supported on an unreactive (inert) solid. The gaseous mixture is swept into the column by a carrier gas, which might be hydrogen, helium or argon. The column itself contains fine solid material or is a hollow column whose walls are coated with a solid on which there is a liquid stationary phase. The retention time is the time taken from the sample entering the injection port until it reaches the detector. The efficient separation of the compounds in the mixture depends on a number of factors – these include the volatility of the compound itself, the column temperature, the length of the column and the flow rate of the carrier gas. For similar compounds (for example those in the same homologous series) an important factor in separating the compounds by GLC is their boiling temperatures. Retention times vary enormously because of the factors outlined above and identification by retention time only depends on the conditions being exactly the same. Very often, the separated components of the mixture are led into a mass spectrometer, where a positive identification can be made. This important technique is abbreviated to GC-MS.

The ABE fermentation process is a method of bacterial fermentation that produces propanone (acetone), butan-1-ol and ethanol from starch. The chromatogram shows a typical GC chromatogram of the products from the ABE process.

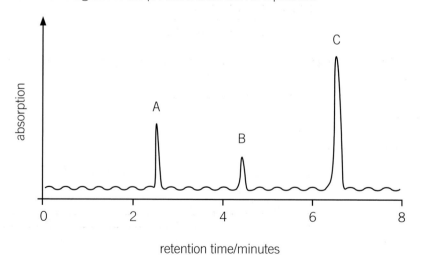

retention time/minutes

Peak **A** represents propanone and peaks **B** and **C** represent ethanol and butan-1-ol respectively. Propanone is less polar than the two alcohols and its lower boiling temperature of 56°C suggests that it will come off the column first. This is followed by ethanol and then butan-1-ol, which have boiling temperatures of 78°C and 117°C respectively.

Knowledge check 73

The diagram shows a gas chromatogram of a mixture of compounds. The figures indicate the peak area of each compound.

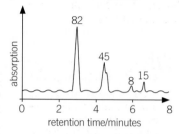

Comment on each of these details about the chromatogram.

(a) The percentage of the largest component present is 82.

(b) If the chromatography was carried out at a different temperature then the relative peak areas would be quite different.

(c) The peak around 4.5 minutes represents two compounds whose retention times are very similar. Separation might occur if a different column was used.

▼ Study point

If components take a long time to reach the detector in GLC, a shorter time might be achieved by increasing the column temperature or by using a different column. If the column temperature is raised too much there might be a risk of decomposition of one or more of the compounds in the mixture and this possibility needs to be considered.

Stretch & Challenge

Ethyl ethanoate and ethanol both have a boiling temperature of 77–78 °C. Explain why it is unlikely that both compounds will have the same retention time when a mixture of these two compounds is injected into a gas chromatograph.

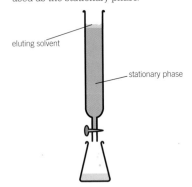

High performance liquid chromatography

In this technique, the column is packed with solid particles (of uniform size) and the mixture sample is dissolved in a suitable solvent. This solution is then forced through the column at a high pressure. High performance liquid chromatography (previously high-pressure liquid chromatography) is generally shortened to HPLC and is a very important method of separation that can be used for compounds that vaporise at high temperatures where they may start to decompose. This method has many applications, for example in testing urine samples of athletes for the presence of banned substances. Another application is in food chemistry, where antioxidants are added to fatty food products, such as margarine and cream cheese to help prevent oxidation. The most common antioxidants include BHA, BHT and various esters of gallic acid. In BHA the $C(CH_3)_3$ group can be in the 2⁻ or 5⁻ positions in the ring.

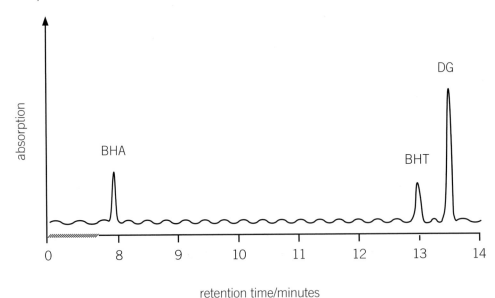

The presence of these antioxidants in food can be detected by HPLC:

retention time/minutes

4.1

1   Butanedioic acid exists as stereoisomers.

  (a)   State what is meant by the term stereoisomers.   [1]

  [handwritten: isomers – same shortened formula diff arrangement of atoms in space]

  (b)   Draw the displayed formula of the two stereoisomers of butanedioic acid, labelling them as the *E*-isomer or the *Z*-isomer.   [2]

  (c)   The *E*-form can be produced from the *Z*-form by heating it in an acidic solution. 0.040 mol of the *Z*-form was heated in aqueous hydrochloric acid for 30 minutes. The yield of the *E*-form was 86%. Calculate the mass of the *E*-form produced.   [3]

  (d)   Compounds that have the molecular formula $C_3H_4Cl_2$ exist as several different non-cyclic isomers. Draw the displayed formulae of the:

   (i)   Two isomers that are *E*–*Z* isomers.   [2]

   (ii)   Two isomers that do **not** show *E*–*Z* isomerism.   [2]

2   (a)   State the meaning of the term enantiomers.   [1]

  [handwritten: non-superimposable mirror images of themselves]

  (b)   Draw the displayed formulae of the two enantiomers of bromochlorofluoromethane, CHBrClF.   [1]

  [handwritten: Br / Cl–C–H / F]

  (c)   The formula of propane-1,2,3-triol can be written

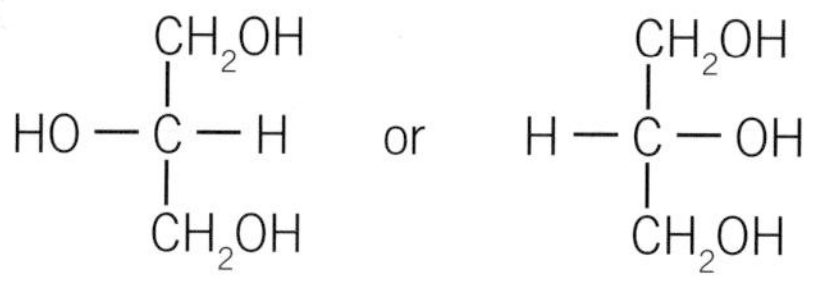

$$HO-\underset{\underset{CH_2OH}{|}}{\overset{\overset{CH_2OH}{|}}{C}}-H \quad or \quad H-\underset{\underset{CH_2OH}{|}}{\overset{\overset{CH_2OH}{|}}{C}}-OH$$

   Explain whether these two formulae are identical or whether propane-1,2,3-triol exists as enantiomers.   [2]

  [handwritten: each carbon has 2 atoms or groups that are same. not]

  (d)   3.50g of an enantiomer of an amino acid is dissolved in 50 cm³ of water. When a sample of this solution is placed in a polarimeter it rotates the plane of polarised light by 15°. What mass of the other enantiomer of this amino acid should be dissolved in the solution to produce a solution that now shows no apparent rotation of the plane of polarised light? Explain your answer.   [2]

3   (a)   Write the displayed formula of butane-2,3-diamine and use an asterisk (*) to indicate any chiral centres that may be present.   [2]

  (b)   Explain why pent-3-en-2-ol exists as four stereoisomers.   [1]

   $CH_3CH = CHCH(OH)CH_3$

  (c)   (i)   Cis-platin is a drug that is used in chemotherapy. This planar platinum complex has the formula

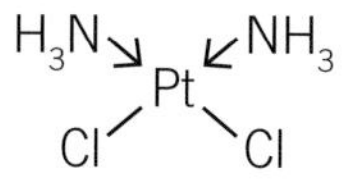

$$\underset{Cl}{\overset{H_3N}{\diagdown}}Pt\underset{Cl}{\overset{NH_3}{\diagup}}$$

      Explain why cis-platin exists as one of two possible stereoisomers.   [1]

   (ii)   The octahedral ion $[Co(NH_3)_4Cl_2]^+$ can exist as two stereoisomers. Draw the displayed formulae of these two stereoisomers.   [2]

4.2

1 (a) (i) Cyclohexane is produced by the reaction of benzene and hydrogen. Give the equation for this reaction. [1]

(ii) The enthalpy change for the reaction in (a) (i) is −208 kJ mol^{-1}. The expected value for this hydrogenation is around −360 kJ mol^{-1} if benzene is considered to be cyclohexa-1,3,5-triene. Explain how the difference between these two figures provides evidence for the greater relative stability of benzene. [2]

(b) X-ray diffraction measurements show that all the carbon to carbon bond lengths in benzene are the same. Explain how this provides evidence for the delocalised electron structure in benzene. [1]

(c) Explain why benzene does not easily react with nucleophiles. [2]

2 The reaction of chlorine with ethene and benzene is represented by the equations below,

Reaction 1

Reaction 2   Reaction 3

(a) Reaction 1 is an addition reaction.

(i) State the type of mechanism involved in this reaction. [1]

(ii) Chlorine is a non-polar molecule. Explain how the first stage of this mechanism is able to occur. [1]

(b) Reaction 2 is also an addition reaction. For the reaction to start, ultraviolet light is necessary. The first stage of this reaction is the dissociation of chlorine into radicals.

(i) What is meant by the term radical? [1]

(ii) Give the equation for this dissociation of chlorine into radicals. [1]

(iii) One product of this reaction is

State the empirical formula of this compound. [1]

(c) (i) Explain the role of the iron(III) chloride, which is used as a catalyst in reaction 3. [1]

(ii) Suggest why the reaction of benzene with iodine monochloride, I–Cl, gives iodobenzene as the main organic product. [1]

3 (a) The equation for the preparation of ethylbenzene from benzene by a Friedel–Crafts reaction is

    (i) State the type of reaction mechanism occurring during this reaction. [1]

    (ii) The yield of ethylbenzene is not 100% as other products are formed. One of these products is a compound that has a molecular formula $C_{10}H_{14}$. Suggest a displayed formula for this compound and a reason for how it might be formed. [2]

(b) Nitrobenzene is generally produced by the nitration of benzene at temperatures below 50°C.

Mr 78   Mr 123

    (i) State the compounds present in the 'nitrating mixture' that is used for this nitration. [1]

    (ii) Give the formula of the electrophile that takes part in this nitration. [1]

    (iii) In an experiment 26.0 g of benzene produced 35.0 g of nitrobenzene. Calculate the percentage yield of nitrobenzene. [2]

    (iv) The nitration of benzene is an exothermic process and if the temperature rises above 50°C, the amount of the co-product 1,3-dinitrobenzene markedly increases. Suggest **two** ways in which the amount of 1,3-dinitrobenzene being produced is kept to a minimum. [2]

4.3

1 **(a)** Propan-2-ol is formed from 2-bromopropane by heating it with aqueous sodium hydroxide.

    (i) State the type of mechanism that occurs in this reaction. [1]

    (ii) Draw the reaction mechanism for this reaction, showing charges and curly arrows where appropriate. [2]

    (iii) State the name of another organic product of this reaction, which is formed particularly if the aqueous solution is concentrated or if it is carried out in an alcoholic solution. [1]

(b) The equation shows the reduction of a ketone by a suitable reducing agent to produce hexane-3,4-diol.

$$CH_3CH_2\overset{\overset{O}{\|}}{\underset{\underset{H}{|}}{C}}-\overset{OH}{\underset{|}{C}}-CH_2CH_3 + 2[H] \longrightarrow CH_3CH_2\overset{OH}{\underset{\underset{H}{|}}{\overset{|}{C}}}-\overset{OH}{\underset{\underset{H}{|}}{\overset{|}{C}}}-CH_2CH_3$$

    (i) State the name of a suitable reducing agent for this reaction. [1]

    (ii) Indicate the position of any chiral centre in the formula of hexane-3,4-diol by the use of an asterisk (*). [1]

    (iii) Hexane-3,4-diol is oxidised by acidified potassium dichromate solution to give propanoic acid as the only organic product. Balance the equation for this reaction. [2]

$$CH_3CH_2\overset{OH}{\underset{\underset{H}{|}}{\overset{|}{C}}}-\overset{OH}{\underset{\underset{H}{|}}{\overset{|}{C}}}-CH_2CH_3 + \_[O] \longrightarrow$$

(iv) Assuming that the organic reactant and product are both colourless, state what you would see during the reaction **(iii)** above. [1]

2 (a) Sulfur dichloride oxide $SOCl_2$, can be used to produce a chloroalkane from an alcohol.

(i) State why $SOCl_2$ is often preferred for this method rather than the use of PCl_3 or PCl_5. [1]

(ii) Give the equation for the reaction of phenylmethanol with sulfur dichloride oxide. [1]

(b) 1-Pentyl ethanoate can be made by reacting pentan-1-ol with either ethanoyl chloride or ethanoic acid.

(i) A student made 1-pentyl ethanoate by reacting together pentan-1-ol and ethanoyl chloride. He started with 20.0 cm^3 of pentan-1-ol (M_r 88) and obtained 25.1 cm^3 of 1-pentyl ethanoate (M_r 130). The density of pentan-1-ol is 0.81 g cm^{-3} and the density of 1-pentyl ethanoate is 0.88 g cm^{-3}. Calculate the percentage yield of the ester. [3]

(ii) Another student made 1-pentyl ethanoate by refluxing together pentan-1-ol and ethanoic acid in the presence of a little sulfuric(VI) acid. The yield obtained was less than the yield obtained by the ethanoyl chloride method. Suggest **two** reasons why this lower yield may have been produced. [2]

3 (a) Three different aqueous solutions are provided. One contains phenol, another contains ethanoic acid and the third one contains propenoic acid, CH_2=CHCOOH. Devise some simple test tube reactions to decide which one is which. [2]

(b) In a practical examination some students were given a sample of the compound whose formula is shown below, dissolved in a suitable solvent.

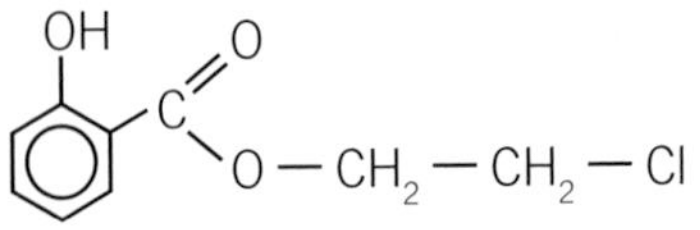

They were asked to show the presence of the phenolic group and chlorine in the 2-chloroethyl group by only using aqueous solutions of iron(III) chloride, sodium hydroxide, dilute nitric(V) acid and silver nitrate. Devise tests to identify these groups and comment on the chemistry involved. [4]

(c) 4-Nitrophenyl benzoate is made by shaking together 4-nitrophenol and benzoyl chloride, C_6H_5COCl, in an alkaline solution.

(i) Explain why it is necessary for the phenol to be dissolved in an alkali for this reaction to occur. [1]

(ii) Give the displayed formula of the ester, 4-nitrophenyl benzoate. [1]

4.4

1 (a) State the name of a reagent that is used to produce ethanal from ethanol. [1]

(b) State the name of a reagent that is used to produce ethanol from ethanal. [1]

2 (a) Fehling's solution can be used to distinguish between aldehydes and ketones.

(i) State what is seen if a little propanal is added to some Fehling's solution and the mixture gently warmed. [1]

      (ii) This reaction shows that propanal (and many other aldehydes) is readily oxidised. State the name of the oxidation product in the reaction in **(i)** above. [1]

  (b) State another test tube reaction that can be used to differentiate between an aldehyde and a ketone, giving the result of the test. [2]

3 **(a)** **(i)** Draw the mechanism of the reaction of hydrogen cyanide with pentan-3-one, showing appropriate charges and curly arrows to represent electron pair movement. [2]

      (ii) The reaction in **(i)** above is described as a nucleophilic addition reaction. Give the formula of the nucleophile taking part and describe why it is described as an addition reaction. [2]

     (iii) The product formed in **(i)** above is now hydrolysed by the use of a dilute acid. Give the displayed formula and the name of this hydrolysis product. [2]

4 'Phorone' is the common name for the unsaturated ketone whose formula is shown below.

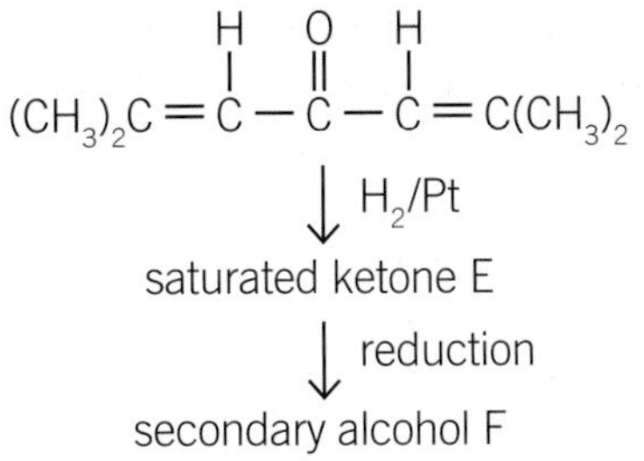

$$(CH_3)_2C = C - C - C = C(CH_3)_2$$

with H, O, H groups shown above the chain

$$\downarrow H_2/Pt$$

    saturated ketone E

$$\downarrow \text{reduction}$$

    secondary alcohol F

  (a) Complete the flow chart, by giving the displayed formula of compounds E and F. [2]

  (b) Explain why the empirical formula for the secondary alcohol, compound F, is the same as its molecular formula. [1]

5 2,4-Dinitrophenylhydrazine is used to identify specific aldehydes and ketones, as it produces crystalline derivatives having sharp melting temperatures. The melting temperatures of the 2,4-dinitrophenylhydrazine derivatives of some ketones are shown in the table.

Ketone	Melting temperature of derivative /°C
Butanone	111
Pentan-2-one	143
Cyclopentanone	146
Propanol	155
Pentan-3-one	156

The melting temperature of a 2,4-dinitrophenylhydrazine derivative of a ketone, known to be one of those in the table, was found to be 150–154°C.

  (a) State, giving a reason, which ketone(s) in the table cannot give a derivative that has a melting temperature of 150–154°C. [2]

  (b) The melting temperature shown does not clearly identify which of the remaining possible ketones has produced the 2.4-dinitrophenylhydrazine derivative. An analysis of the 'unknown' ketone showed that it contained 27.6% of oxygen by mass. Use this information to deduce which of the ketones listed in the table has produced this derivative of melting temperature 150–154°C. [4]

  (c) Suggest why the melting temperature of this derivative is not sharp and it has melted over a range of temperatures. [1]

6 **(a)** State the reagents used and the observation when a positive triiodomethane test is carried out. [2]

(b) State, giving reasons for your answer(s), which of these compounds will undergo a positive triiodomethane test. [2]

Compound A $(CH_3)_3C - \overset{\overset{\displaystyle O}{\|}}{C} - CH_3$

Compound B $CH_3CH_2CH_2 - \overset{\overset{\displaystyle O}{\|}}{C} - CH_2CH_3$

Compound C $CH_3CH_2CH_2CH_2CH_2C \overset{\displaystyle \nearrow O}{\underset{\displaystyle \searrow H}{}}$

Compound D $\square - \overset{\overset{\displaystyle H}{|}}{\underset{\underset{\displaystyle OH}{|}}{C}} - CH_3$

Compound E $CH_3CH_2 - \overset{\overset{\displaystyle O}{\|}}{C} - \overset{\underset{\underset{\displaystyle H}{|}}{}}{C}(CH_3)_2$

4.5

1 **(a)** Ethane-1,2-diol is a sweet-tasting liquid that has been used illegally to sweeten wine. Unfortunately it is very toxic and when swallowed is converted in the body to ethanedioic acid. This acid can also be formed from the diol by the use of acidified dichromate but the yield is poor as some methanal is also formed. Give the equation for oxidation of ethane-1,2-diol to methanal, using [O] to represent the formula of the oxidising agent. You should assume that methanal is the only organic product of the reaction. [1]

(b) Another method for producing ethanedioic acid is to use nitric(V) acid to oxidise sucrose.

(i) Complete the equation below, where the formula of the oxidising agent is represented by [O] and the only other product of the reaction is water. [2]

$C_{12}H_{22}O_{11} + \_[O] \longrightarrow$

(ii) During this oxidation of sucrose some oxopropanedioic acid is produced.

$\underset{HO}{\overset{O}{\diagdown}} C - \overset{\overset{\displaystyle O}{\|}}{C} - C \overset{\displaystyle \diagup H}{\underset{\displaystyle \diagdown OH}{}}$

Write the formula of the compound produced if this acid is completely reduced to its corresponding alcohol by lithium tetrahydridoaluminate (III). [1]

(c) **(i)** Vinegar is an aqueous solution of ethanoic acid that is made by the atmospheric oxidation of a dilute solution of ethanol in the presence of the bacteria *Mycoderma aceti*.

$CH_3CH_2OH + O_2 \longrightarrow CH_3COOH + H_2O$

A sample of vinegar obtained in this way was analysed and found to contain 8% by mass of ethanoic acid in this solution. Calculate the concentration of ethanoic acid in this sample of vinegar in mol dm^{-3}. [2]

(ii) Aqueous solutions of ethanol, phenol and ethanoic acid were placed in separate beakers. You are given some solid sodium hydrogencarbonate and some aqueous bromine. Devise a scheme, using only these materials, to confirm the identity of each solution. [2]

2 An aromatic hydrocarbon has the molecular formula C_8H_{10}. A sample of this hydrocarbon is refluxed for some time with alkaline potassium manganate(VII) solution. After the removal of solid manganese(IV) oxide, the cold colourless solution is acidified with dilute hydrochloric acid, when a white solid is precipitated. The solid is filtered off and dried. This solid is a carboxylic acid whose mass spectrum shows a molecular ion at m/z 122.

(a) Why does the colourless solution need to be acidified? [1]

(b) Why does the white solid appear as a precipitate after acidification? [1]

(c) Explain how the account shows that this reaction is an oxidation and reduction reaction. [2]

(d) Use the mass spectrum data to deduce a possible displayed formula for the carboxylic acid. [2]

(e) Use the information to deduce the name of the aromatic hydrocarbon. [2]

3 (a) State what is meant by decarboxylation. [1]

(b) The sodium salt of 2,4,6-trimethylbenzenecarboxylic acid was heated with soda lime (represented as NaOH). Give the equation for this reaction, showing the displayed formula of the organic product. [2]

(c) The low-resolution NMR spectrum of the organic product was measured. State and explain the number of peaks seen and their relative peak areas. [2]

(d) In another decarboxylation experiment a straight chain hydrocarbon was produced that had a relative molecular mass of 72. Suggest a formula for the sodium salt of the carboxylic acid that produced this hydrocarbon when it was heated with soda lime. [3]

4 The ^{13}C NMR spectrum of an ester showed three separate peaks and its ^1H NMR spectrum showed two peaks, each having the same peak area.

(a) Deduce the displayed formula of the ester. [3]

(b) Give the equation for the formation of this ester from the relevant alcohol and carboxylic acid, stating the catalyst used. [2]

5 Identify the compounds in this reaction sequence. [5]

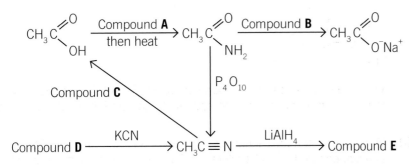

6 You are given some methyl 2-hydroxybenzoate

and are asked to produce a dry sample of 2-hydroxybenzoic acid from it by hydrolysis with aqueous sodium hydroxide. The following details are provided

• methyl 2-hydroxybenzoate is a liquid of boiling temperature 224 °C • the hydrolysis of the ester produces an aqueous solution of sodium 2-hydroxybenzoate • addition of hydrochloric acid to the cold solution of sodium 2-hydroxybenzoate gives a white crystalline precipitate of 2-hydroxybenzoic acid • the melting temperature of the 2-hydroxybenzoic acid is 158°C.

Devise a method for this experiment that will produce dry crystals of 2-hydroxybenzenecarboxylic acid. In your account you should point out any essential details that missing from the outline instructions given. Chemical equations are not required.   [6]

4.6

1 **(a)** Primary aliphatic amines can be formed by reacting together halogenoalkanes and ammonia.

   (i) One method of preparing butylamine is to react 1-bromobutane with ammonia in a sealed tube. Give an equation for this reaction to prepare butylamine.   [1]

   (ii) A student suggested an easier method. He said 'place some 1-bromobutane dissolved in a little alcohol as solvent, in a flask equipped with a reflux condenser. Warm the mixture in a water bath while passing ammonia through it for some time'. State two disadvantages of this method.   [2]

   (iii) Explain why it is likely that the reaction of ammonia with 1-bromobutane will produce 1-butylammonium bromide and draw a mechanism showing how this compound forms.   [3]

   (b) At room temperature some amines exist as gases or volatile liquids and they are more conveniently sold as their salts, for example methylammonium chloride. State how you produce methylamine from its salt methylammonium chloride, using a simple test tube reaction.   [2]

   (c) Use the displayed formulae of propylamine and propanenitrile to explain why they are both soluble in water.   [2]

2 **(a)** In the laboratory phenylamine can be produced by reducing nitrobenzene with tin metal and hydrochloric acid.

   (i) Give the equation for this reaction using [H] to represent the reducing agent.   [1]

   (ii) This method was used to prepare phenylamine: 25g of nitrobenzene was reduced and produced 17g of phenylamine. Calculate the percentage yield of phenylamine.   [2]

(iii) A similar metal-acid reduction was used in industry to produce phenylamine from nitrobenzene but has now been superseded by a vapour stage process. In one method nitrobenzene is reduced by hydrogen, passing the reactants over a metal catalyst at moderate temperatures and at a pressure of 1.3 atmospheres. Suggest an advantage of this vapour phase process over the metal/acid liquid phase process. [1]

(iv) In a newer vapour phase process, phenol and ammonia are passed over a metal oxide catalyst at moderate temperatures and at a pressure of 200 atmospheres.

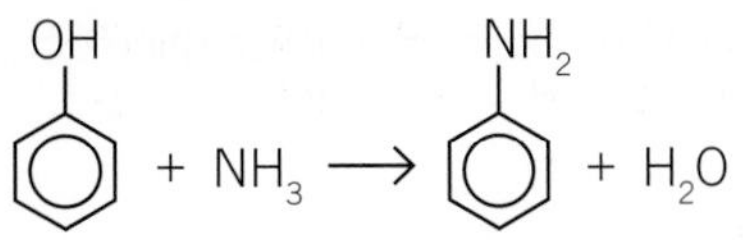

This method has a number of advantages over the process described in **(iii)** but also has a number of disadvantages. Suggest one disadvantage of this newer process. [1]

(b) If an attempt is made to obtain 4-nitrophenylamine by the nitration of phenylamine, a number of other products are produced and the yield is poor. A more satisfactory method to produce 4-nitrophenylamine is to firstly prepare N-phenylethanamide.

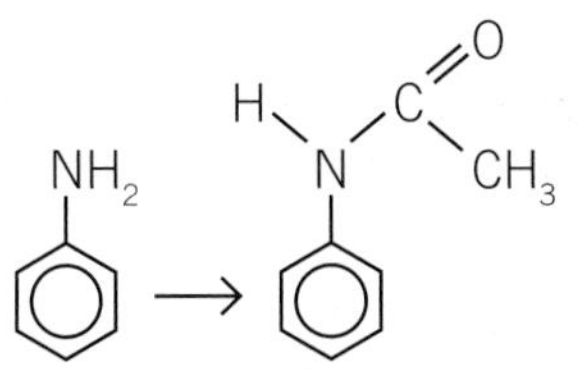

(i) State the reagent that can be used to produce N-phenylethanamide from phenylamine. [1]

(ii) Nitration of N-phenylethanamide gives a mixture of the 2- and 4-isomers.

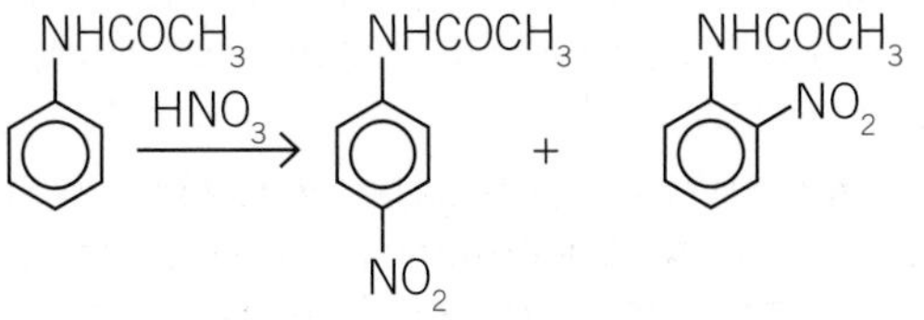

The 2-isomer is soluble in trichloromethane whereas the 4-isomer is insoluble in this solvent. Suggest how you could separate a mixture of these two isomers using trichloromethane or otherwise. [1]

3 The reaction of an aliphatic primary amine with nitric(III) acid gives a poor yield of the alcohol, although the yield of nitrogen gas is quantitative (all the nitrogen present becomes nitrogen).

$$CH_3CH_2NH_2 \xrightarrow{\text{HNO}_2} CH_3CH_2OH + N_2$$

This reaction could be used to find the concentration of an amine present in solution. In an experiment 75 cm^3 of an aqueous solution of ethylamine was treated with an excess of nitric(III) acid. 90 cm^3 of nitrogen, measured at room temperature and pressure was obtained. Calculate the concentration of the ethylamine solution in mol dm^{-3}. [2]

[1 mole of nitrogen gas has a volume of 24.0 dm^3 at room temperature and pressure]

4 (a) Nitric(III) acid reacts with primary aromatic amines at temperature around 5–10°C to give a solution containing the benzenediazonium cation.

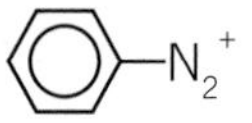

(i) Nitric(III) acid is unstable and is produced when required from sodium nitrate(III) and hydrochloric acid.

$$NaNO_2 + HCl \longrightarrow HNO_2 + NaCl$$

In practice phenylamine is dissolved in hydrochloric acid and a cold solution of sodium nitrate(III) is added. This solution contains benzenediazonium chloride.

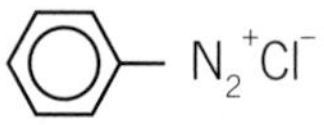

Give the displayed formula of the benzenediazonium ion, showing any appropriate lone pairs of electrons. [1]

(ii) The benzenediazonium chloride solution can react with a phenol or an aromatic amine to produce an azo dye. For example, when it reacts with 3,5-dimethylphenol.

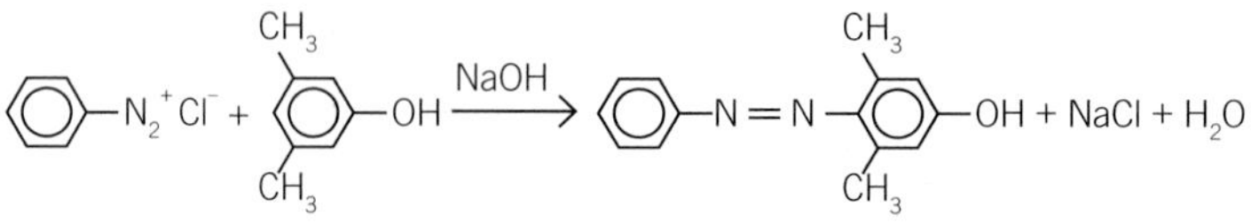

Explain why this reaction is carried out in alkaline solution. [1]

(b) The indicator methyl red has the formula

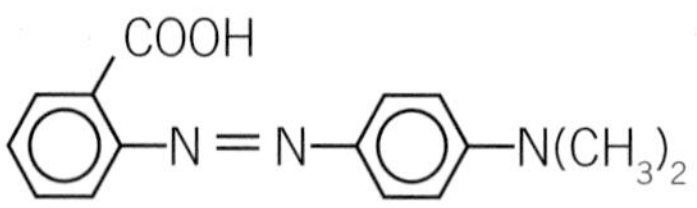

Give the formulae of the primary aromatic amine used, and of the amine that reacts with the diazotised aromatic amine to produce methyl red. [2]

5 Many azo dyes are used as acid-base indicators. The table shows two indicators and the wavelength at which the maximum absorption of visible light occurs.

Indicator	λmax/nm
Methyl Red	410
Thymol Blue	594

The values of some physical constants are

- Planck's constant (h) = 6.63×10^{-34} J s
- Velocity of light (c) = 3.00×10^{8} ms^{-1}
- Avogadro's constant (L) = 6.02×10^{23} mol^{-1}

(a) Calculate the frequency of the light at which methyl red has its maximum absorption. [1]

(b) State which of these two absorption maxima has the highest energy, explaining your answer. [2]

(c) Use your answer to **(a)** to calculate the energy absorbed in kJ mol^{-1}. [2]

(d) Explain, in terms of the light absorbed, why the indicator methyl red is seen as red in white light. [1]

1 **(a)** Give the general formula for an α-amino acid. [1]

(b) Use your answer to (a) to explain why all α-amino acids, except one, contain at least one chiral centre. [2]

(c) 2-Amino-3-phenylbutanoic acid is an α-amino acid. Write the displayed formula of this acid and identify any chiral centre(s) present by the use of an asterisk (*). [2]

2 **(a)** The formula of leucine (2-amino-4-methylbutanoic acid) is

$(CH_3)_2CHCH_2CH(NH_2)COOH$

(i) Write the formula of the zwitterion form of leucine. [1]

(ii) Write the formula of the species formed when leucine is dissolved in a strongly alkaline solution, explaining your answer. [2]

(iii) Explain why the melting temperature of leucine is 293°C, whereas 5-methylhexanoic acid is a liquid at room temperature and pressure. [4]

(iv) The table shows the solubility of some α-amino acids in water.

Amino acid	solubility at 25°C g/100g H_2O
2-aminopropanoic acid	16.7
2-amino-3-methylbutanoic acid	7.1
2-amino-4-methylpentanoic acid	1.0

Deduce and then suggest a reason for the trend in solubility. [2]

(b) Histidine is an α-amino acid. In the body enzymes can decarboxylate histidine, producing histamine, which is responsible for many of the symptoms associated with hay fever.

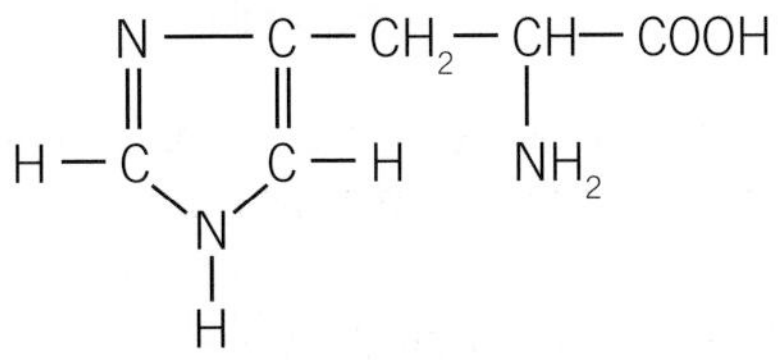

Histidine

Write the displayed formula of histamine. [1]

3 Amino acids are largely neutral substances and therefore unsuitable for use as acids in acid-base titrations using sodium hydroxide. If methanal is also used in the titration then the amino acid will react with sodium hydroxide in a 1:1 molar ratio. In a titration 1.48 g of an unknown α-amino acid was dissolved in a solvent and the solution was made up to 250 cm³. 25.00 cm³ of this solution reacted with 12.65 cm³ of sodium hydroxide of concentration 0.100 mol dm⁻³.

(a) Calculate the relative molecular mass of the α-amino acid. [3]

(b) Use the relative molecular mass found in **(a)** to suggest two displayed formulae for the α-amino acid. [2]

(c) State an instrumental method that would be the most appropriate procedure to decide which of the acids found in **(b)** was the unknown acid, giving a reason for your answer. [2]

4 Dipeptides are formed by the condensation of two amino acid molecules. The formula below shows the formula of a dipeptide formed from two different amino acids.

Write the formula of the other dipeptide formed from these two amino acids. [1]

5 The structure of proteins can be described in different ways. Outline what is meant by the primary, secondary and tertiary structure of proteins. [5]

4.8

1 Study the reaction sequence below and then answer the questions that follow.

(a) Methyl 2-aminobenzoate boils at 256°C under normal atmospheric pressure. Why is it preferable to purify this compound by vacuum distillation before use, rather than using ordinary distillation? [1]

(b) In stage 1 the ester methyl 2-aminobenzoate is hydrolysed by heating with aqueous sodium hydroxide. State why the reaction then needs to be acidified in order to obtain the product shown. [1]

(c) State how nitric(III) acid is produced for use in stage 2. [1]

(d) In stage 3, nitric(V) acid is added to 2-hydroxybenzoic acid and water and the mixture warmed. On cooling, crystals of 2-hydroxy-5-nitrobenzoic acid are produced, together with a yellow solution that contains polynitration products. The mixture is then filtered. How could you tell that the crystals were as pure as possible at this stage? [1]

(e) Give the formula of the azo dye that is produced at the end of stage 5. [1]

(f) (i) The sample of 2-hydroxy-5-nitrobenzoic acid obtained after stage 3 had a melting temperature of 200–215°C. The pure acid has a melting temperature of 230°C. What can you deduce from these figures? Explain your answer. [1]

(ii) A student said that 2-hydroxy-5-nitrobenzoic acid decomposes before its melting temperature. Explain why this statement must be wrong. [1]

(g) The product after stage 3 was recrystallised from ethanol. Outline the stages of this process to obtain pure crystals of the acid. Your answer should include a consideration of health and safety. [5]

2 Some details about compound **N** are given below.

• chemical analysis shows that it contains only carbon, hydrogen and oxygen and the percentage of oxygen is 28.1% by mass • it does not react with Tollens reagent • the mass spectrum shows a molecular ion at m/z 114 and significant peaks at m/z 43, 71 and 99 • it produces a yellow solid when reacted with alkaline iodine solution • the infrared spectrum shows a prominent absorption at 1713 cm^{-1} but no characteristic absorptions for an O–H group or a C–O single bond • the ^{13}C NMR spectrum shows the presence of three distinct carbon environments • the ^{1}H NMR spectrum shows two singlets at 2.19δ and 2.71δ in peak areas of 3:2 respectively • it reacts with 2,4-dinitrophenylhydrazine to give an orange-red solid of melting temperature 257°C

(a) Use all this information to suggest a displayed formula for compound **N**, explaining your reasoning. [6]

(b) Using the information provided, describe a procedure to further confirm the identity of compound **N**. [2]

3 The formula shows a section of a polymer.

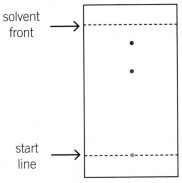

These type of polymers are attracting much attention because they can be produced from carbohydrates such as glucose or starch, using micro-organisms. The polymers are also non-toxic and largely biodegradable.

(a) If this polymer was made by a chemical method, state the name and formula of the monomer. [2]

(b) State the type of polymerisation that occurs when the polymer is made from the monomer and the type of polymer whose formula is shown above. [2]

4 Compound **P** is thought to be diethyl 2-chlorobutanedioate.

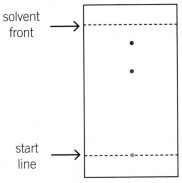

• Describe the ^{1}H NMR spectrum of this compound • Describe the ^{13}C NMR spectrum of this compound • Describe the characteristic infrared absorptions of this compound, stating the bonds identified and their approximate wavenumbers in cm^{-1} • Compound **P** was hydrolysed, producing a Cl$^-$ ion. Describe a test to show the presence of this ion. [6]

5 The thin layer chromatogram (TLC) of a mixture of phenols is shown below.

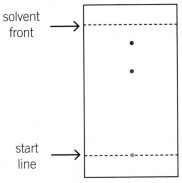

(a) The phenol spots in the chromatogram were colourless and the spots were made to be visible by the use of the locating agent, diazotised 4-aminobenzenesulfonic acid.

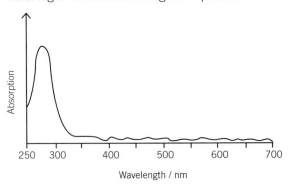

State the type of compound produced in this locating process. [1]

(b) Use the table to state which phenols are present in the mixture, showing your working. [2]

Phenol	R_f
2,5-dihydroxybenzoic acid	0.45
2-hydroxybenzoic acid	0.58
3,4-dihydroxybenzoic acid	0.63
1,3-dihydroxybenzene	0.86

(c) It was suspected that 3,4,5-trihydroxybenzoic acid was also present but that this had given a colourless spot, even when the locating agent was used. Suggest what might be done about this problem. [1]

(d) Write the displayed formula of 3,4,5-trihydroxybenzoic acid. [1]

(e) 3,4,5-Trihydroxybenzoic acid has its maximum absorption at 271nm in the ultra violet region of the electromagnetic spectrum.

State and explain the colour of the compound when seen in sunlight. [2]

Practical examination ⌐ Unit 5

All chemistry examinations need some assessment of practical skills. In Unit 5 candidates are given the opportunity to demonstrate their skill, knowledge and understanding in relation to practical techniques and their ability to evaluate experimental data. The unit comprises two tasks to be carried out individually under controlled conditions. One task is an experimental task that carries 30 marks and the other is a short written paper of one hour duration that also carries 30 marks. The total mark for Unit 5 counts 10% of the total mark for the 'A' level award. Both tasks for Unit 5 are marked externally by the WJEC, with some marks being awarded by teachers for the direct assessment of practical skills.

You are given an aqueous solution of ammonium benzoate. Describe how you would obtain pure dry crystals of benzoic acid from this solution. Benzoic acid is soluble in hot water but nearly insoluble in cold water.

Sample answer Add hydrochloric acid to the solution and stir. Continue adding the acid until no more benzoic acid precipitates as a white solid. Filter and wash the acid with cold water. Recrystallise the acid by adding it to a minimum volume of hot water. Cool to room temperature, filter and dry the crystals at a temperature below the melting temperature of the acid.

An aqueous solution contains methanoic acid and ethyl ethanoate. Devise a method to obtain pure ethyl ethanoate from the aqueous solution. Use this information to help you in your answer. • Potassium methanoate is insoluble in ethoxyethane • Methanoic acid and ethyl ethanoate are soluble in ethoxyethane • Ethoxyethane and water are immiscible • Ethoxyethane boils at 35 °C • Ethyl ethanoate boils at 77 °C.

Sample answer Add aqueous potassium hydroxide to the cold mixture to neutralise the methanoic acid, producing potassium methanoate. Add ethoxyethane and shake the mixture in a separating funnel. Allow the layers to separate. Run off and dry the ethoxyethane layer. Evaporate off the ethoxyethane to leave ethyl ethanoate, which can be distilled if necessary.

Practical examination

Practical work is carried out throughout the 'A' level course and this will enable learners to think independently, and to use and apply scientific methods and practices. There will also be opportunities to develop their numeracy skills and mathematical ideas in a practical context. This may include graph work, the analysing of data and consideration of the margins of error, accuracy and precision. Another important skill is the development of research skills, both online and offline. The ability to correctly cite sources of information is an important feature of this research work. The examination for Unit 5 gives candidates an opportunity to demonstrate the skills that they have gained during the two years of the course. Obviously in an examination lasting only a few hours there is not the time for a comprehensive review of the skills obtained. The specification lists those practical techniques to be gained by learners, together with some suggested practical exercises to illustrate these techniques. The examination board has published a set of sample assessment materials that shows the type of exercises that could be set during the practical and written assessment of this unit. The specimen practical examination asks candidates to analyse tablets for their aspirin content. This is carried out by hydrolysing a known mass of aspirin tablets using an excess of aqueous sodium hydroxide. The excess sodium hydroxide present is found by titration with a standard solution of sulfuric acid. The concentration of the sodium hydroxide solution used is also found by a titration with this standard acid.

The specimen one hour written paper consists of questions written in a practical context. These include an enthalpy of neutralisation question and a question involving reaction rates at a certain temperature and also at different temperatures (using the Arrhenius equation). Also included in the paper is a question about pH changes during neutralisation. An organic question is also included where candidates are given known compounds in unlabelled bottles and ask to devise tests to decide which one is which. This style of question is often successfully answered with the aid of a flow diagram. Instrumental techniques such as NMR and IR absorption spectroscopy could be used to confirm the results obtained.

You are given four liquids, in bottles without labels – they are propan-1-ol, methyl ethanoate, propanone and propanoic acid. Using only their infrared absorption spectra to help you decide which one is which.

Sample answer • Propan-1-ol → O–H peak at 2500–3500 cm^{-1}, C–O absorption at 1000–1300 cm^{-1} no C=O absorption • Methyl ethanoate → C=O peak at 1650–1750 cm^{-1} and C–O absorption at 1000–1300 cm^{-1}, no O–H absorption • Propanone → C=O peak at 1650–1750 cm^{-1}, no C–O or O–H absorption • Propanoic acid → C=O peak at 1650–1750 cm^{-1}, C–O peak at 1000–1300 cm^{-1} and O–H peak at 2500–3500 cm^{-1}.

Five different aqueous solution are provided in unlabelled bottles. They contain ethanol, propanone, propanal, ethanamide and ethylamine. Devise simple tests that will identify which solution is which.

Sample answer Add Universal Indicator solution to samples of each solution. Only ethylamine will give a reaction and turn the indicator to blue, showing that it's a base. Add 2,4-dinitrophenylhydrazine reagent (Brady's reagent) to samples of the remaining four solutions. Propanal and propanone will give orange precipitates. Add Tollens' reagent to samples of these two liquids and gently warm. Propanal will give a silver mirror and propanone will not. Two solutions remain. Add aqueous sodium hydroxide to samples of these remaining solutions and warm. Ethanamide will produce ammonia gas – turns red litmus paper to blue. The remaining solution must be ethanol.

Unit 3

1 **1** OXIDATION $Mg (s) \rightarrow Mg^{2+} (aq)+ 2e$
REDUCTION $Fe^{2+} (aq) + 2e \rightarrow Fe (s)$

   2 OXIDATION $Zn (s) \rightarrow Zn^{2+} (aq)+ 2e$
REDUCTION $2H^+ (aq) + 2e \rightarrow H_2 (g)$

2

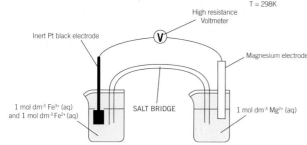

3

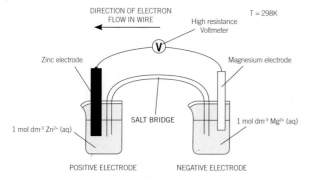

EMF = 1.60V

4 OXIDISING AGENTS: Na^+, I_2, MnO_4^-
REDUCING AGENTS: Cu, Cl^-, Mg
Order of decreasing oxidising power = MnO_4^-, I_2, Na^+.

5 **(a)** $2Fe^{3+} + Zn \rightarrow 2Fe^{2+} + Zn^{2+}$

   (b) $Cu + Cl_2 \rightarrow CuCl_2$

6 **(a)** Yes it is feasible as the EMF for the reaction is +0.76V, and positive values represent feasible reactions.

   (b) No it is not feasible as the EMF for the reaction would be negative, which is not feasible.

7 **(a)** $2ClO_4^- + 16 H^+ + 14 e \rightarrow Cl_2 + 8H_2O$

   (b) $MnO_4^- + 4H^+ + 3e \rightarrow MnO_2 + 2H_2O$

8 $2MnO_4^- + 5C_2O_4^{2-} + 16 H^+ \rightarrow 2Mn^{2+} + 10 CO_2 + 8H_2O$

9 Moles manganate (VII) in each titration = $23.30 \times 0.0200 \div 1000 = 4.66 \times 10^{-4}$ moles.

Reacting ratio 1:5 so moles iron in the 25.0 cm^3 = 2.33×10^{-3} moles.

Moles iron in original 250 cm^3 = 2.33×10^{-2} moles

Mass of iron = $2.33 \times 10^{-2} \times 55.8 = 1.300g$

Percentage of iron = 1.300 / 1.740 × 100 = 74.7%

10 Acting as a base: $ZnO + 2HCl \rightarrow ZnCl_2 + H_2O$

    Acting as an acid: $ZnO + 2NaOH + H_2O \rightarrow Na_2[Zn(OH)_4]$

11

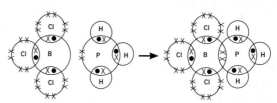

12 The standard electrode potential for Cl_2/Cl^- is much more positive than that for I_2/I^-. This means that chlorine is a stronger oxidising agent than iodine, so chlorine can oxidise iodide to form iodine.

    $Cl_2 + 2I^- \rightarrow 2Cl^- + I_2$

13 $H_2SO_4 + 6HI \rightarrow S + 3I_2 + 4H_2O$
$H_2SO_4 + 8HI \rightarrow H_2S + 4I_2 + 4H_2O$

14 Ti: $1s^2 2s^2 2p^6 3s^2 3p^6 3d^2 4s^2$

    V: $1s^2 2s^2 2p^6 3s^2 3p^6 3d^3 4s^2$

    Fe: $1s^2 2s^2 2p^6 3s^2 3p^6 3d^6 4s^2$

15 Cr^{3+} : $1s^2 2s^2 2p^6 3s^2 3p^6 3d^3$

    Mn^{2+}: $1s^2 2s^2 2p^6 3s^2 3p^6 3d^5$

    Fe^{2+}: $1s^2 2s^2 2p^6 3s^2 3p^6 3d^6$

    Fe^{3+}: $1s^2 2s^2 2p^6 3s^2 3p^6 3d^5$

    Cu^{2+}: $1s^2 2s^2 2p^6 3s^2 3p^6 3d^9$

    Zn^{2+}: $1s^2 2s^2 2p^6 3s^2 3p^6 3d^{10}$

16 The water ligands cause the d-orbitals into three of lower energy and two higher energy. Electrons can move from lower to higher energy level by absorbing specific frequencies of light. These correspond to the energy gap (E=hf). The light not absorbed is the colour seen, so this complex is green as it absorbs all other colour apart from green.

17 The d-orbitals in the Zn^{2+} ion are full, so electrons cannot move between energy levels and therefore cannot absorb light energy.

18 Either $[Cu(H_2O)_6]^{2+}$ (aq) + $2OH^- \rightarrow Cu(OH)_2 + 6H_2O$ or
$Cu^{2+} + 2OH^- \rightarrow Cu(OH)_2$

19 (a) Second order   UNITS: $mol^{-1}\ dm^3\ s^{-1}$

    (b) First order   UNITS: s^{-1}

    (c) First order   UNITS: s^{-1}

    (d) First order   UNITS: s^{-1}

    (e) Third order

20 Rate = $k[H_2O_2][I^-]$

    $k = 2.8 \times 10^{-2}\ mol^{-1}\ dm^3\ s^{-1}$

21 (a) $C_2H_4 + Br_2 \rightarrow$ products

    (b) $I_2 \rightarrow$ products

    (c) $H_2O_2 + I^- + H^+ \rightarrow$ products

22 Rate constant at 300K = $0.0345 \div 0.100 = 0.345\ s^{-1}$

    Frequency factor = $A = k\ /\ e^{-(Ea/RT)} =$
0.345 / $e^{-(42000/8.314 \times 300)} = 7.10 \times 10^6$

    Rate constant at 320K = $0.989\ s^{-1}$

    Rate = $k \times$ [concentration] = $0.989 \times 0.150 =$
$0.148\ mol\ dm^{-3}\ s^{-1}$

23 Enthalpy of solution

    = Enathlpy of lattice breaking + Enthalpy of hydration
$(Ca^{2+} + 2 \times Cl^-)$

    = $2237 - (1650) - (2 \times -364)$

    = $-141\ kJ\ mol^{-1}$

The calcium chloride will be soluble in water as the process of dissolving is exothermic.

24 (a) $Cu(g) \rightarrow Cu^+(g)$

    (b) $Cl_2(g) \rightarrow 2Cl(g)$

    (c) $\frac{1}{2}\ O_2(g) \rightarrow O(g)$

    (d) $2Na^+(g) + O^{2-}(g) \rightarrow Na_2O(s)$

    (e) $F(g) + e \rightarrow F^-(g)$

25 $C_6H_{14}(l) + 9\frac{1}{2}\ O_2(g) \rightarrow 6CO_2(g) + 7H_2O(l)$

    Entropy change = $6 \times S(CO_2) + 7 \times S(H_2O) - 9.5 \times S(O_2)$
           $- S(hexane)$

           = $1284 + 490 - 1947.5 - 204$

           = $-377.5\ J\ K^{-1}\ mol^{-1}$

26 Reaction 1: $K_c = \dfrac{[H^+]^2[CO_3^{2-}]}{[H_2CO_3]}$

    Reaction 2: $K_c = \dfrac{[NH_4OH]}{[NH_4^+][OH^-]}$

    Reaction 3: $K_c = \dfrac{[HCl][HOCl]}{[H_2O][Cl_2]}$

    Reaction 4: $K_c = \dfrac{[FeNCS^{2+}]}{[Fe^{3+}][NCS^-]}$

27 Reaction 1: $K_p = \dfrac{P_{SO_3}^2}{P_{SO_2}^2 \times P_{O_2}}$

    Reaction 2: $K_p = \dfrac{P_{CO} \times P_{H_2}^3}{P_{CH_4} \times P_{H_2O}}$

    Reaction 3: $K_p = \dfrac{P_{HI}^2}{P_{H_2} \times P_{I_2}}$

    Reaction 4: $K_p = \dfrac{P_{CO} \times P_{Cl_2}}{P_{COCl_2}}$

    Reaction 5: $K_p = \dfrac{P_{PCl_3} \times P_{Cl_2}}{P_{PCl_3}}$

28

	Fe^{3+} (aq)	+	NCS^- (aq)	$\rightleftharpoons$	$FeNCS^{2+}$ (aq)
Start (mol dm^{-3})	0.2		0.2		0
At equilibrium	0.05		0.05		0.15

To make 0.15 $FeNCS^{2+}$, 0.15 Fe^{3+} and 0.15 NCS^- are needed which leaves 0.05 of each of the reactants. (1 mark)

$K_c = \dfrac{[FeNCS^{2+}]}{[Fe^{3+}][NCS^-]}$ (1 mark)

$K_c = \dfrac{0.15}{0.05 \times 0.05} = 60\ mol^{-1}\ dm^3$

29 At the start the partial pressures of H_2 and I_2 are 50500 Pa each.

To form 37500 Pa HI then half this amount of H_2 and I_2 must react = 18750 Pa, leaving 50500 − 18750 = 31750 Pa of H_2 and I_2.

$K_p = \dfrac{P_{HI}^2}{P_{H_2} \times P_{I_2}} = 37500^2\ /\ 31750^2 = 1.40$ (no units)

30 (a) pH = $-\log_{10}(0.2) = 0.70$

    (b) pH = $-\log_{10}(0.03) = 1.52$

    (c) pH = $-\log_{10}(10^{-9}) = 9$

    (d) pH = $-\log_{10}(3 \times 10^{-11}) = 10.52$

31 (a) $[H^+] = 10^{-pH} = 1\ mol\ dm^{-3}$

    (b) $[H^+] = -10^{-pH} = 2 \times 10^{-3}\ mol\ dm^{-3}$

    (c) $[H^+] = -10^{-pH} = 5 \times 10^{-7}\ mol\ dm^{-3}$

    (d) $[H^+] = -10^{-pH} = 3.16 \times 10^{-11}\ mol\ dm^{-3}$

    (e) $[H^+] = -10^{-pH} = 1 \times 10^{-14}\ mol\ dm^{-3}$

32 $K_a = [H^+][ClO^-] / [HClO]$

$K_a = [H^+][CN^-] / [HCN]$

33 As temperature increases, Le Chatelier's principle suggests the equilibrium will shift in the endothermic reaction. If K_w increases this means the equilibrium shifts to the right. The forward reaction must therefore be endothermic, with a positive enthalpy change.

34 So $[H^+]^2 = K_a \times [CH_3COOH]$

1 **(a)** $[H^+]^2 = 1.7 \times 10^{-5} \times 0.5 = 8.5 \times 10^{-6}$
$[H^+] = 2.9 \times 10^{-3}$
$pH = -\log (2.9 \times 10^{-3}) = 2.54$

(b) $[H^+]^2 = 1.7 \times 10^{-5} \times 2 = 3.4 \times 10^{-5}$
$[H^+] = 5.8 \times 10^{-3}$
$pH = -\log (2.9 \times 10^{-3}) = 2.23$

(c) $[H^+]^2 = 1.7 \times 10^{-5} \times 0.01 = 1.7 \times 10^{-7}$
$[H^+] = 4.12 \times 10^{-4}$
$pH = -\log (2.9 \times 10^{-3}) = 3.38$

2 **(a)** $[H^+]^2 = 2.9 \times 10^{-8} \times 1 = 2.9 \times 10^{-8}$
$[H^+] = 1.703 \times 10^{-4}$
$pH = 3.77$

(b) $[H^+]^2 = 2.9 \times 10^{-8} \times 0.5$
$[H^+] = 1.204 \times 10^{-4}$
$pH = -\log (1.204 \times 10^{-4}) = 3.92$

(c) $[H^+]^2 = 2.9 \times 10^{-8} \times 5 = 1.45 \times 10^{-7}$
$[H^+] = 3.808 \times 10^{-4}$
$pH = 3.42$

3 Ethanoic acid is stronger as it has the larger K_a value (a less negative power indicates a larger number).

35 Using $K_a = \dfrac{[H^+][A^-]}{[HA]}$

where the two terms on the top are equal, we simply need to obtain $[H^+]$ from pH.

(a) For HB, $[H^+] = 10^{-pH} = 0.001258$
so $K_a = 0.001258^2 \div 0.5 = 3.16 \times 10^{-6}$

(b) For HC, $[H^+] = 10^{-pH} = 6.310 \times 10^{-3}$
so $K_a = (6.310 \times 10^{-3})^2 \div 1 = 4 \times 10^{-5}$ mol dm^{-3}

(c) For HD, $[H^+] = 10^{-pH} = 3.16 \times 10^{-4}$
so $K_a = (3.16 \times 10^{-4})^2 \div 0.5 = 2 \times 10^{-7}$ mol dm^{-3}

36 Since $K_w = [H^+] \times [OH^-] = 1 \times 10^{-14}$ mol^2 dm^{-6},
$[H^+] = (1 \times 10^{-14}) \div [OH^-]$.

(a) $[H^+] = (1 \times 10^{-14}) \div 1 = 1 \times 10^{-14}$
$pH = -\log (1 \times 10^{-14}) = 14$

(b) $[H^+] = (1 \times 10^{-14}) \div 0.2 = 5 \times 10^{-14}$
$pH = -\log (5 \times 10^{-14}) = 13.3$

(c) $[H^+] = (1 \times 10^{-14}) \div 0.05 = 2 \times 10^{-13}$
$pH = -\log (2 \times 10^{-13}) = 12.7$

(d) $[H^+] = (1 \times 10^{-14}) \div 0.003 = 3.33 \times 10^{-13}$
$pH = -\log (3.33 \times 10^{-13}) = 11.5$

37 To work out the pH of a buffer solution, we can use K_a expression to derive:

$[H^+] = K_a \times [ACID] \div [SALT]$

Then we can use $pH = -\log [H^+]$ to work out the pH of the buffer.

(a) $[H^+] = 1.7 \times 10^{-5} \times [0.20] \div [0.10] = 3.4 \times 10^{-5}$
$pH = -\log (3.4 \times 10^{-5}) = 4.47$

(b) $[H^+] = 1.7 \times 10^{-5} \times [0.20] \div [0.40] = 8.5 \times 10^{-6}$
$pH = -\log (8.5 \times 10^{-6}) = 5.07$

(c) $[H^+] = 1.7 \times 10^{-5} \times [1] \div [0.2] = 8.5 \times 10^{-5}$
$pH = -\log (8.5 \times 10^{-5}) = 4.07$

(d) $[H^+] = 1.6 \times 10^{-2} \times [0.20] \div [0.10] = 0.032$
$pH = -\log (0.032) = 1.49$

38 Ammonia is a weak base and sulfuric acid is a strong acid so the salt should have an acidic pH e.g. pH 6. This is because the ammonium sets up an equilibrium where H^+ ions are lost increasing $[H^+]$ and decreasing pH.

Unit 4

4.1

1

2 Citronellal does not exist as *E-Z* isomers as the left carbon atom of the carbon-to-carbon double bond is bonded to two groups that are the same.

3 Enantiomers have the same molecular formula and hence the same relative molecular mass. Therefore equal 'amounts' will contain the same number of moles of each enantiomer.

4

5 Although each carbon atom of the carbon-to-carbon double bond is bonded to a hydrogen atom, one carbon atom is also bonded to a $CH_3(CH_2)_7-$ group whereas the other carbon atom is bonded to a $-(CH_2)_7COOH$ group.

4.2

6 The formula of benzene has a ring made up of five carbon atoms and a hydrogen atom.

7 The correct statement is (b). Each benzene atom is bonded to two carbon atoms and a hydrogen atom, and therefore (a) is wrong. Statement (c) is also wrong as multiple bonds between carbon atoms are shorter than carbon to carbon single bonds. As the value of the resonance energy increases, the stability of the molecule also increases.

8 The student said that the mechanism showed that iron(III) bromide was 'regenerated' at the end of the reaction and that, without the presence of iron(III) bromide, the reaction was very slow.

9 CH_2OH

Br

4.3

10 (a) Primary

(b) $HOCH_2-CH_2OH$

(c) Propanone

11 Every time that a ketone group is reduced, the resulting molecule has gained two more hydrogen atoms as a secondary alcohol group is produced. If the product has gained six more hydrogen atoms than the starting ketone, then the original compound had three ketone carbonyl groups.

12 Compound **A** (4-chlorocyclohexanone) should be heated under reflux with aqueous sodium hydroxide, to produce 4-hydroxycyclohexanone. This is then reduced with aqueous sodium tetrahydridoborate(III) to give compound **B** cyclohexane-1,4-diol.

13 The relative molecular mass of the 'ethanoate part' of the ester, CH_3COO, is 59. The M_r of the alkyl group is $130 - 59 = 71$; this could be C_5H_{11}. As the question states that it is a primary alcohol, the primary alcohol could be pentan-1-ol, 3-methylbutan-1-ol or 2,2-dimethylpropan-1-ol.

14 Ethyl ethanoate has the formula $CH_3COOCH_2CH_3$. This compound has M_r of 88. The percentage of oxygen in this compound is $32/88 \times 100 = 36.4$.

15

or

16 Salicylic acid contains a phenol group as an OH group is bonded directly to the benzene ring. Aspirin does not contain this phenolic group. If a few drops of iron(III) chloride are added to a solution of aspirin, then a purple colour will be seen if any salicylic acid remains.

17 CH_2OH OCH_3

and

4.4

18 Hydrogen, using a nickel or platinum catalyst

19 $C_{16}H_{24}O$

20

21 2-Methylpentan-3-one

22 Hexan-2-one, this contains a $CH_3C=O$ group

1-Phenylethanol this contains a $CH_3CH(OH)$ group

4.5

23 (a)

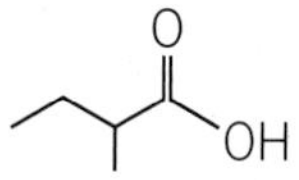

(b)

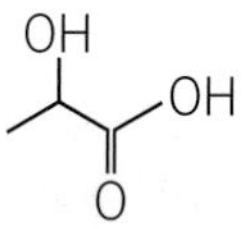

(c)

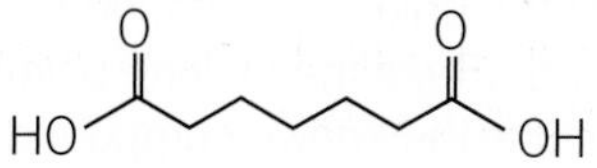

24 Pentanoic acid

25

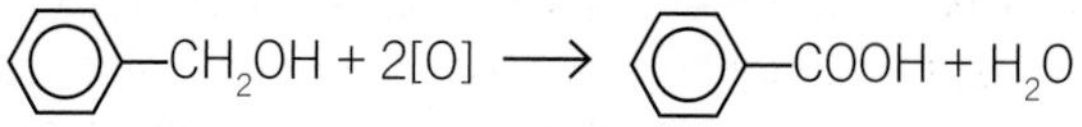

$\bigcirc$—CH$_2$OH + 2[O] $\rightarrow$ $\bigcirc$—COOH + H$_2$O

26 Butanoic acid

27 0.40 mol $\rightarrow$ 29.2 g 1 mol $\rightarrow$ 73g

M_r 'CONH$_2$' $\rightarrow$ 44 M_r 'R' = 73 – 44 = 29

R = C$_2$H$_5$ Amide is CH$_3$CH$_2$C(O)NH$_2$

28 2,2-dimethylpropanenitrile

29 The nucleophile is the cyanide ion, $^-$CN. Both potassium cyanide and sodium cyanide produce cyanide ions in solution.

30 C$_3$H$_5$O$_2$

31

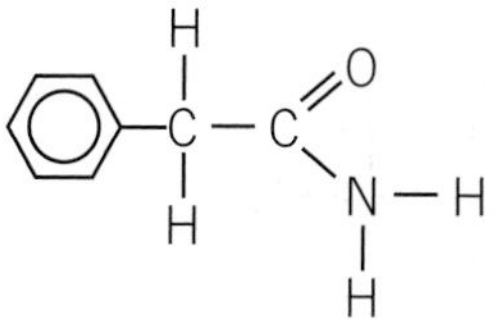

32 CH$_3$CH$_2$CH$_2$CH$_2$CH$_2$C$\equiv$N

33

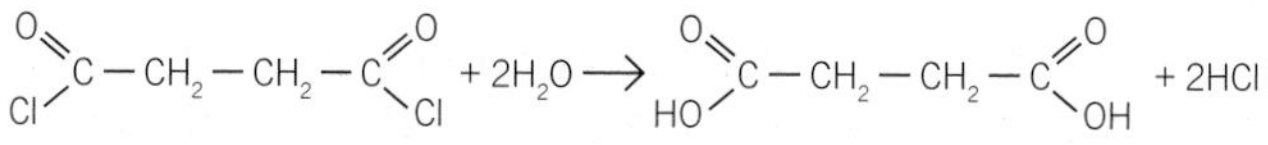

4.6

34 (a) Pentylamine

(b) Diphenylamine

(c) Ethane-1,2-diamine

35 (a)

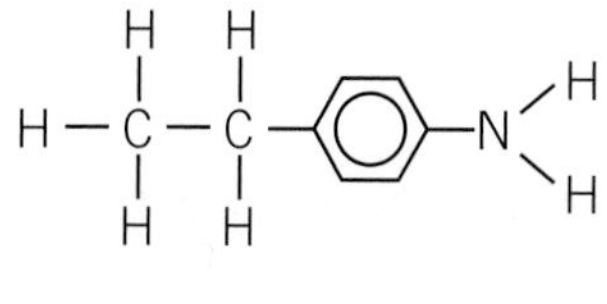

(b)

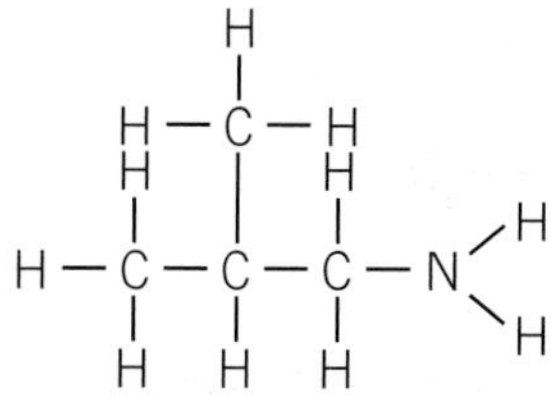

36 The carbon-to-chlorine bond is polarised C$^{\delta+}$–Cl$^{\delta-}$ and the $\delta+$ carbon atom attracts a lone pair of electrons from the nitrogen atom of the amine.

37 C$_6$H$_5$CH$_2$CH$_2$NH$_3^+$ Br$^-$

38 CH$_3$NH$_3^+$Br$^-$ + OH$^-$ $\rightarrow$ CH$_3$NH$_2$ + H$_2$O + Br$^-$

39

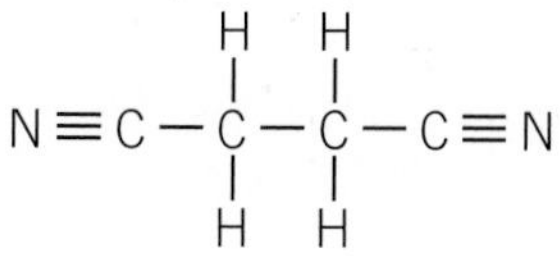

40 (a) C$_2$H$_5$NH$_3^+$ Cl$^-$

(b) C$_6$H$_5$NH$_3^+$HSO$_4^-$

41 C$_5$H$_6$NO

42 27g

43 Phenolphthalein in alkaline solution has λ_{max} at 553nm, in the green region. Using the colour hexagon this is opposite red-violet and this is the colour that is seen.

4.7

44

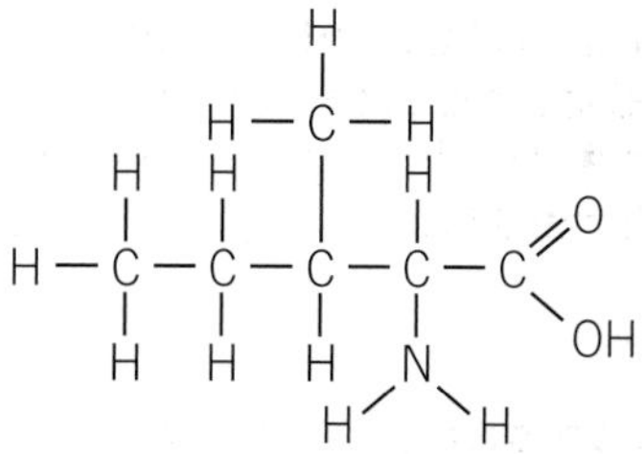

45

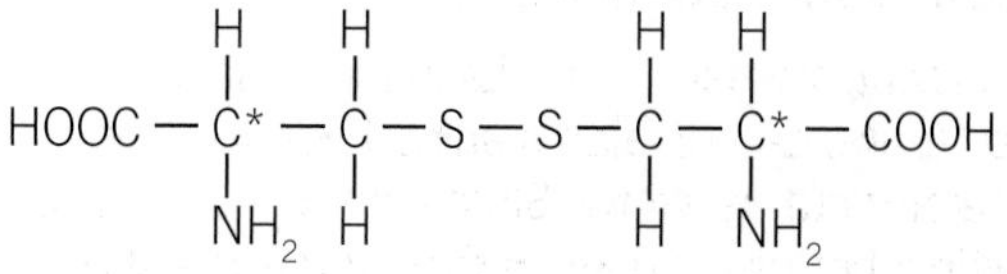

46

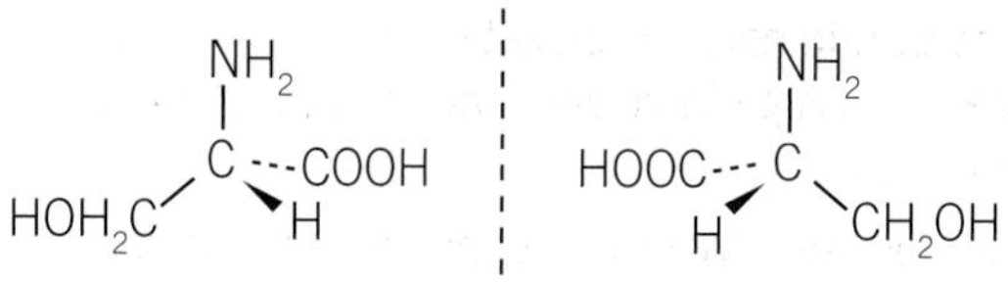

47

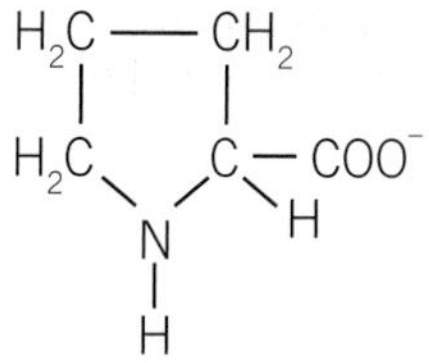

48 The zwitterion form $^+$NH$_3$CH$_2$COO$^-$ has used the lone pair of electrons on the nitrogen atom to bond the hydrogen ion, H$^+$, and there is now no lone pair of electrons for nucleophilic attack.

49

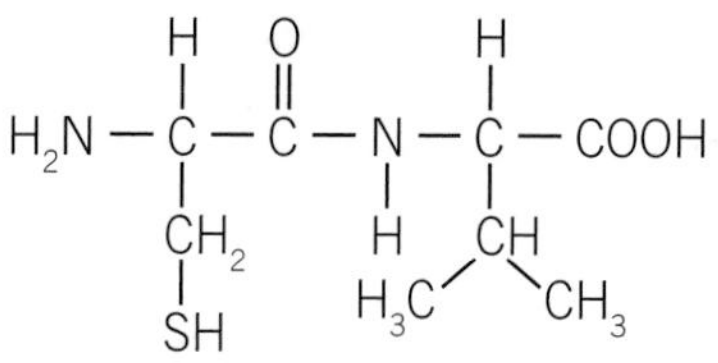

50 2,6-Diaminohexanoic acid

51 There is attraction between the δ– oxygen atom of the $C^{\delta+}= O^{\delta-}$ group and the δ+ hydrogen atom of the $N^{\delta-}- H^{\delta+}$ group.

52 $C_6H_{12}O_6 \longrightarrow 2C_2H_5OH + 2CO_2$

4.8

53

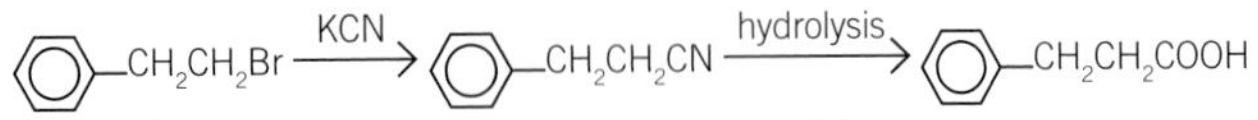

54 **A** Alkaline potassium manganate(VII) solution

B (Dilute) hydrochloric acid

C Soda lime

55

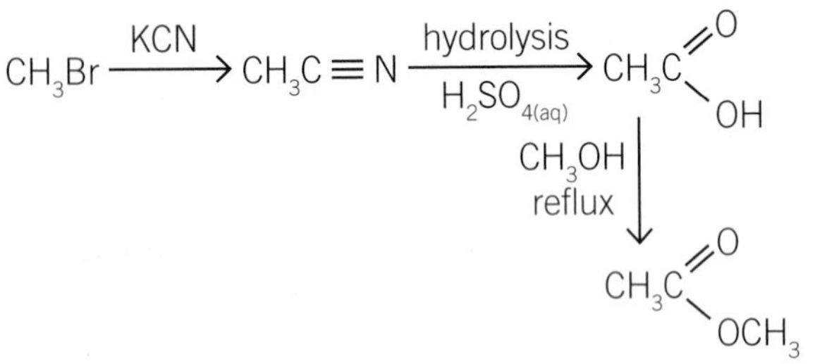

56 Bromoethane/chloroethane/iodoethane

57

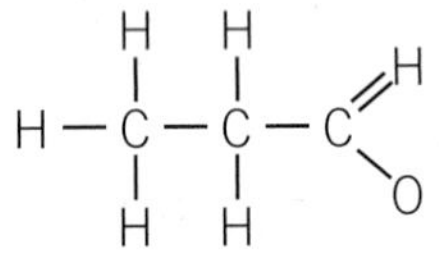

58 Butane

59 Compound (b)

60 **D** Potassium cyanide or sodium cyanide

E Aqueous sulfuric acid / hydrochloric acid

F Acidified potassium dichromate

61 No solvent is lost by evaporation, the concentration remains the same.

62 4.25/118 = 0.036 mol of acid At the end 0.006 mol is in the aqueous layer. Therefore in ethoxyethane there is 0.030 mol. It is 5 times more soluble in ethoxyethane.

63 Simple distillation should suffice, as the boiling temperatures are very far apart.

64 **(a)**

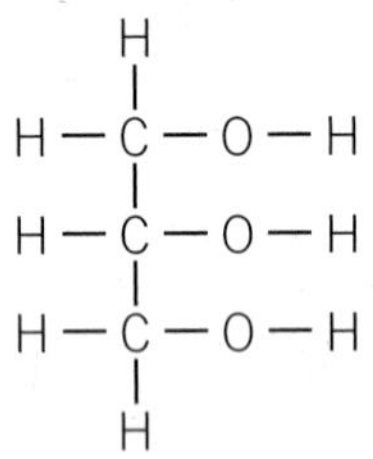

(b) It may start to decompose if it is distilled at its boiling temperature under normal atmospheric pressure. Consideration should be given as to whether the lower temperature used during vacuum distillation **may** be more cost effective.

65 About 3×10^{-4} g

66 When the washing water is no longer yellow.

67 The compound is a polyester and it is likely that water has been eliminated during the polymerisation process – it is condensation polymerisation.

68

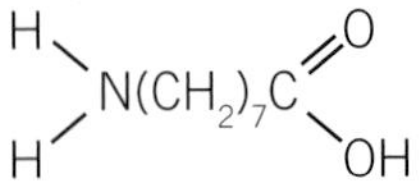

69 Mix equal quantities of the unknown compound and one of the known compounds. Take the melting point – if it remains at 158°C then it is the known compound used. If the melting temperature is now lower, the unknown compound is the other carboxylic acid.

70

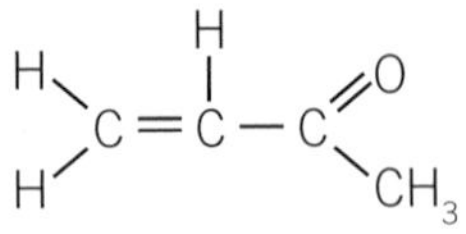

71 A single peak as all its hydrogen atoms are in identical environments.

72 **(a)** 0.58

(b) Use a different solvent or use two-way chromatography.

73 **(a)** The total peak area is 150. The percentage of the largest component is 54.7.

(b) The proportion of components in the mixture is not affected by running the procedure at a different temperature.

(c) A column that is packed with a different material might well effect a separation of these two compounds.

Unit 3

3.1

1 Oxidation is the loss of electrons. (1)

2 The oxidation state of iron has changed from +2 to +3 so it has been oxidised / The Fe^{2+} ion loses an electron so it has been oxidised. (1)

The oxidation state of the chlorine has changed from 0 to –1 so it has been reduced / Each chlorine atom has gained an electron so they have been reduced. (1)

3 The bromine molecule is the oxidising agent as it has taken electrons from the Na, oxidising the sodium atom. (1)

4 The standard hydrogen electrode has an inert platinum electrode in a 1 mol dm^{-3} solution of H^+ ions with hydrogen gas at a pressure of 1 atm, bubbled over it at a temperature of 298K. (1 for substances and 1 for conditions.) (2)

5 The standard electrode potential is the EMF measured on a high resistance voltmeter when a half-cell containing all solutions at 1 mol dm^{-3} concentration and all gases at 1 atm pressure is connected to the standard hydrogen electrode at a temperature 298K. (1 for apparatus and 1 for conditions.) (2)

6 A salt bridge completes the circuit without allowing the solutions to mix. (1)

7 **(a)** 1 mark for reagents in both cells; 1 mark for conditions (must refer to each at least once); 1 mark for salt bridge and high resistance voltmeter.

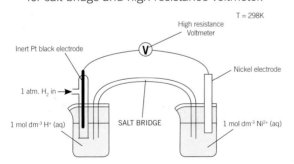

(b) The electrons flow from the standard hydrogen electrode to the nickel half-cell. (1)

(c) The nickel electrode is the positive electrode. (1)

8 **(a)** Fe (s) (1)

(b) 0.19 V (1)

(c) Fe, Ni, H_2, Cu (1)

(d) A reaction should occur as the standard electrode potential for the Nickel half-cell is more negative than that for the copper half-cell, which means that the nickel will be oxidised and the copper ions will be reduced.

OR A reaction should occur as the EMF for the reaction of Cu^{2+} with Ni is +0.59 V. A positive EMF means that the reaction is feasible. (2)

(e) Acid contains H^+ ions that should corrode Ni as the standard electrode potential for the Nickel half-cell is more negative than that for the hydrogen half-cell, which means that the nickel will be oxidised and the hydrogen ions will be reduced.

OR A reaction should occur as the EMF for the reaction of H^+ with Ni is +0.25 V. A positive EMF means that the reaction is feasible. (2)

9 **(a)** Oxidation states of iron are 0 at the start and +2 at the end so the iron is being oxidised.

Oxidation state of oxygen in O_2 is 0 at the start and –2 at the end so the O_2 is being reduced.

(b) The standard electrode potential of the iron half-cell is more negative than the oxygen half-cell so the iron can be oxidised by oxygen. (1)

The standard electrode potential of the silver half-cell is more positive than the oxygen half-cell so the silver cannot be oxidised by oxygen. (1)

10 Advantage: Energy is released more efficiently by a fuel cell than by combustion / greater percentage of energy in fuel is converted to useful energy / Use of hydrogen means that no CO_2 or no greenhouse gases are released.

Disadvantage: Production of hydrogen uses fossil fuels and this process does not transfer all energy from fossil fuel into hydrogen/ Production of hydrogen releases CO_2 or greenhouse gases.

11 **(a)** EMF = 1.33 – 0.77 = 0.56V [1]

(b) An inert metal to provide electrical connection to the solutions (no metal present in either half-equation) [1]

(c)

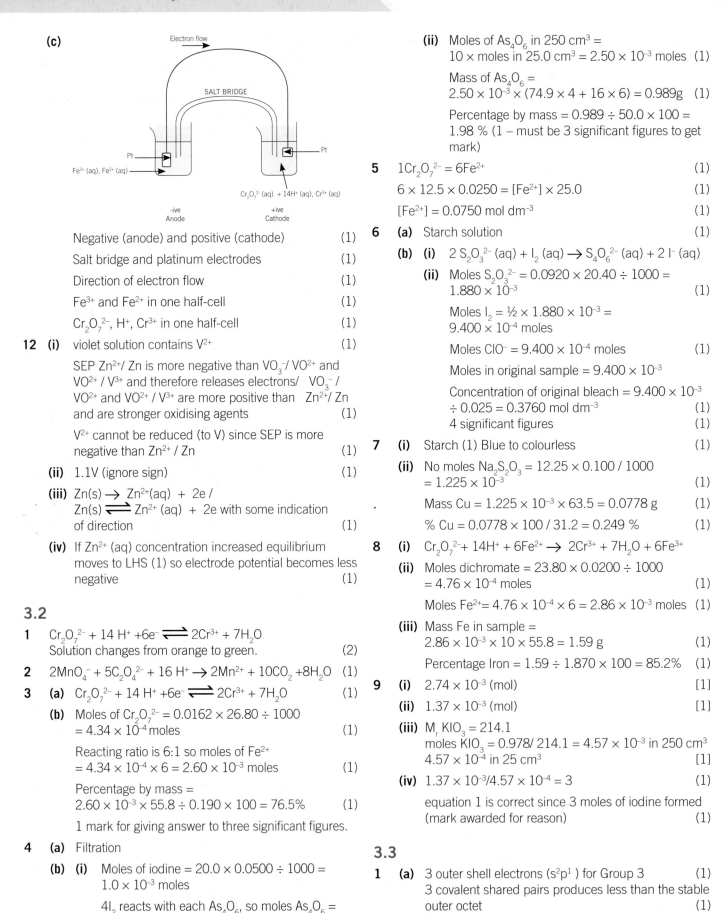

Negative (anode) and positive (cathode) (1)

Salt bridge and platinum electrodes (1)

Direction of electron flow (1)

Fe^{3+} and Fe^{2+} in one half-cell (1)

$Cr_2O_7^{2-}$, H^+, Cr^{3+} in one half-cell (1)

12 (i) violet solution contains V^{2+} (1)

SEP Zn^{2+}/Zn is more negative than VO_3^-/VO^{2+} and VO^{2+}/V^{3+} and therefore releases electrons/ VO_3^-/VO^{2+} and VO^{2+}/V^{3+} are more positive than Zn^{2+}/Zn and are stronger oxidising agents (1)

V^{2+} cannot be reduced (to V) since SEP is more negative than Zn^{2+}/Zn (1)

(ii) 1.1V (ignore sign) (1)

(iii) $Zn(s) \rightarrow Zn^{2+}(aq) + 2e$ /
$Zn(s) \rightleftharpoons Zn^{2+}(aq) + 2e$ with some indication of direction (1)

(iv) If $Zn^{2+}(aq)$ concentration increased equilibrium moves to LHS (1) so electrode potential becomes less negative (1)

3.2

1 $Cr_2O_7^{2-} + 14\,H^+ + 6e^- \rightleftharpoons 2Cr^{3+} + 7H_2O$
Solution changes from orange to green. (2)

2 $2MnO_4^- + 5C_2O_4^{2-} + 16\,H^+ \rightarrow 2Mn^{2+} + 10CO_2 + 8H_2O$ (1)

3 (a) $Cr_2O_7^{2-} + 14\,H^+ + 6e^- \rightleftharpoons 2Cr^{3+} + 7H_2O$ (1)

(b) Moles of $Cr_2O_7^{2-} = 0.0162 \times 26.80 \div 1000$
$= 4.34 \times 10^{-4}$ moles (1)

Reacting ratio is 6:1 so moles of Fe^{2+}
$= 4.34 \times 10^{-4} \times 6 = 2.60 \times 10^{-3}$ moles (1)

Percentage by mass =
$2.60 \times 10^{-3} \times 55.8 \div 0.190 \times 100 = 76.5\%$ (1)

1 mark for giving answer to three significant figures.

4 (a) Filtration

(b) (i) Moles of iodine $= 20.0 \times 0.0500 \div 1000 = 1.0 \times 10^{-3}$ moles

$4I_2$ reacts with each As_4O_6, so moles $As_4O_6 = 1.00 \times 10^{-3} \div 4 = 2.50 \times 10^{-4}$ moles

(ii) Moles of As_4O_6 in 250 cm³ =
$10 \times$ moles in 25.0 cm³ $= 2.50 \times 10^{-3}$ moles (1)

Mass of As_4O_6 =
$2.50 \times 10^{-3} \times (74.9 \times 4 + 16 \times 6) = 0.989$g (1)

Percentage by mass $= 0.989 \div 50.0 \times 100 = 1.98$ % (1 – must be 3 significant figures to get mark)

5 $1Cr_2O_7^{2-} = 6Fe^{2+}$ (1)

$6 \times 12.5 \times 0.0250 = [Fe^{2+}] \times 25.0$ (1)

$[Fe^{2+}] = 0.0750$ mol dm⁻³ (1)

6 (a) Starch solution (1)

(b) (i) $2\,S_2O_3^{2-}(aq) + I_2(aq) \rightarrow S_4O_6^{2-}(aq) + 2\,I^-(aq)$

(ii) Moles $S_2O_3^{2-} = 0.0920 \times 20.40 \div 1000 = 1.880 \times 10^{-3}$ (1)

Moles $I_2 = \frac{1}{2} \times 1.880 \times 10^{-3} = 9.400 \times 10^{-4}$ moles

Moles $ClO^- = 9.400 \times 10^{-4}$ moles (1)

Moles in original sample $= 9.400 \times 10^{-3}$

Concentration of original bleach $= 9.400 \times 10^{-3} \div 0.025 = 0.3760$ mol dm⁻³ (1)
4 significant figures (1)

7 (i) Starch (1) Blue to colourless (1)

(ii) No moles $Na_2S_2O_3 = 12.25 \times 0.100 / 1000 = 1.225 \times 10^{-3}$ (1)

Mass $Cu = 1.225 \times 10^{-3} \times 63.5 = 0.0778$ g (1)

% $Cu = 0.0778 \times 100 / 31.2 = 0.249$ % (1)

8 (i) $Cr_2O_7^{2-} + 14H^+ + 6Fe^{2+} \rightarrow 2Cr^{3+} + 7H_2O + 6Fe^{3+}$

(ii) Moles dichromate $= 23.80 \times 0.0200 \div 1000 = 4.76 \times 10^{-4}$ moles (1)

Moles $Fe^{2+} = 4.76 \times 10^{-4} \times 6 = 2.86 \times 10^{-3}$ moles (1)

(iii) Mass Fe in sample =
$2.86 \times 10^{-3} \times 10 \times 55.8 = 1.59$ g (1)

Percentage Iron $= 1.59 \div 1.870 \times 100 = 85.2\%$ (1)

9 (i) 2.74×10^{-3} (mol) [1]

(ii) 1.37×10^{-3} (mol) [1]

(iii) $M_r\ KIO_3 = 214.1$
moles $KIO_3 = 0.978 / 214.1 = 4.57 \times 10^{-3}$ in 250 cm³
4.57×10^{-4} in 25 cm³ [1]

(iv) $1.37 \times 10^{-3}/4.57 \times 10^{-4} = 3$ (1)

equation 1 is correct since 3 moles of iodine formed (mark awarded for reason) (1)

3.3

1 (a) 3 outer shell electrons (s^2p^1) for Group 3 (1)
3 covalent shared pairs produces less than the stable outer octet (1)

(b) Phosphorus can undertake octet expansion so can form species with more than 8 outer shell electrons (1)
Nitrogen has no available d-orbitals so cannot expand its octet / is limited to 8 outer shell electrons. (1)

2 Amphoteric – exhibits both acidic behaviour and basic behaviour (1)
description of Al_2O_3 reacting with acid e.g dissolves in dilute hydrochloric acid AND description of Al_2O_3 reacting with base e.g dissolves (on warming) in (excess) sodium hydroxide (1)
equation for each
$Al_2O_3 + 6HCl \rightarrow 2AlCl_3 + 3H_2O$ (1)
$Al_2O_3 + 2NaOH + 3H_2O \rightarrow 2NaAl(OH)_4$ (1)

3 Oxidation state +2 becomes more stable (1)
CO_2 more stable than CO, but PbO more stable than PbO_2 (1)
Inert pair effect – the two s electrons become more stable as the group is descended. (1)

4 **(a)** e.g. $PbO_2 + 4HCl \rightarrow PbCl_2 + Cl_2 + 2H_2O$ (1)
(b) e.g. $Pb(OH)_2 + 2H^+ \rightarrow Pb^{2+} + 2H_2O$ (as a base) and
e.g. $Pb(OH)_2 + 2OH^- \rightarrow [Pb(OH)_4]^{2-}$ as an acid. (1)
(c) e.g. $CuO + CO \rightarrow Cu + CO_2$ /
$Fe_2O_3 + 3CO \rightarrow 2Fe + 3CO_2$ (1)

5 CCl_4 and water : no reaction / immiscible liquids / two layers (1)
$SiCl_4$ and water : violent / highly exothermic reaction / acid solution / gas effervescence / white solid formed / cloudy (Any two points for 1)
Because of octet expansion / d orbitals available, Si is subject to attack by water but C is not. (1) [3]

6 BN and C can both adopt the same hexagonal structure:
BN and C are isoelectronic (or equivalent statement) [1]
(Both) can form three (trigonal) bonds with one unbonded p-orbital [1]
(Can show appropriate diagram(s))
Both BN and C exhibit lubricating properties:
Both BN and C have a layer structure [1]
Weak van der Waals forces between layers allow slippage of the layers [1]
C is an electrical conductor but BN is an insulator at room temperature:
Any two from:
In C, delocalisation of electrons (between the unbonded p-orbitals) allows conduction of electricity. [1]
Unlike C, in BN each N has a full unbonded p-orbital whereas each B has an empty unbonded p-orbital. [1]
In BN, N is more electronegative than B, so electron density not evenly spread. [1]

7 • NaCl: steamy gas / bubbles (1)
• NaI: steamy gas /smell of rotten eggs / purple vapour or brown solution or black solid / yellow solid (1 mark for 2 observations)
• NaCl: $NaHSO_4$, HCl / NaI: $NaHSO_4$ / HI / I_2 / H_2S / SO_2 / S / H_2O (1 mark for 2 products; 2 marks for 4 products)
• Iodide is easier to oxidise / iodide is a stronger reducing agent than chloride (1)

8 **(i)** $Fe_2O_3 + 3CO \rightarrow 2Fe + 3CO_2$ (1)
(ii) Fe oxidation state goes from +3 to 0 / so it is reduced (1)
OR C (not CO) oxidation state goes from +2 to +4 / so it is being oxidised. (1)
(iii) Stable oxidation state of (C is +4 whilst) Pb is +2 (1)
due to the inert pair effect becoming more significant down the group. (1)

9 **(a)** **(i)** Oxidising agent [1]
(ii) A = lead(II) chloride / $PbCl_2$ (1)
B = chlorine / Cl_2 (1)
(iii) $[Pb(OH)_6]^{4-}$ / $[Pb(OH)_4]^{2-}$ / $Na_4[Pb(OH)_6]$, etc. [1]
(iv) Yellow [1]
(v) $PbO + 2HNO_3 \rightarrow Pb(NO_3)_2 + H_2O$ [1]
(b) **(i)** Each C atom covalently bonded to three other C atoms forming layers (1)
Layers held together by weak intermolecular forces (1)
BN is isoelectronic with C so it forms similar structures (1)
Graphite conducts electricity since electrons are delocalised but in BN, each N has a full unbonded p-orbital and each B has an empty unbonded p-orbital so it does not conduct electricity (Accept electrons are not delocalised in BN so it does not conduct electricity) (1)
(ii) Wear-resistant coatings/catalyst support/for mounting high power electronic components / drills in industry / cutting instruments (1)

3.4

1 **(a)** **(i)** Chromium metal, Cr $1s^22s^22p^63s^23p^63d^54s^1$ (1)
(ii) Cr^{3+} ion $1s^22s^22p^63s^23p^63d^3$ (1)
(b) 3d orbitals split by water ligands (1)
(in an octahedral field) three d-orbitals have lower energy, two have higher energy (1)
electrons absorb (visible) light energy to jump from lower level to higher level (1)
colour is that due to the remaining / non-absorbed frequencies (appropriate diagrams are acceptable alternatives) (1)

2 Electronic structure: $1s^22s^22p^63s^23p^63d^{10}$ (1)
Cu^+ has full 3d orbitals. (1) [2]
(ii) **I.** $[Cu(H_2O)_6]^{2+}$ octahedral (1) blue (1)
$[CuCl_4]^{2-}$ tetrahedral (1) yellow or green [4]
II. Complexes consist of a Cu^{2+} ion surrounded by ligands (1)
that form coordinate bonds with it. (1)

3 (a)

3d   4s

Ar [↑][↑][↑][↑][↑] [ ]

(b)

(accept either type)

(c) The ligand splits the d orbitals into 2 higher levels and 3 lower levels. (1)
As an electron is promoted from a lower to a higher level, energy is absorbed (1)
from the visible spectrum. The colour seen is the unabsorbed colours (1)

(d) Brown/yellow/red precipitate (1)
that is insoluble in excess of the sodium hydroxide solution (1)

$Fe^{3+} + 3OH^- \rightarrow Fe(OH)_3$ (1)

4 (a) (i) Iron $1s^2 2s^2 2p^6 3s^2 3p^6 3d^6 4s^2$
(or equivalent 'electrons in boxes') (1)

(ii) Iron(II) cation $1s^2 2s^2 2p^6 3s^2 3p^6 3d^6$
(or equivalent 'electrons in boxes') (1)

(b) 3d and 4s electrons involved (in bonding)
3d and 4s levels very similar in energy OR similar ionisation energies / different numbers of electrons can be removed.
Energy released in bonding is sufficient to balance the energy needed to ionise each electron.
(Any 2 points from three × (1)) [2]

(c) Dative covalent / coordinate covalent bonding (1)

Lone pair of electrons (on O atom) in water bonds to metal ion d-orbitals (1)

5 (i) Blue (1) precipitate (1)

(ii) $Cu^{2+} + 2OH^- \rightarrow Cu(OH)_2$ or
$CuSO_4 + Ca(OH)_2 \rightarrow Cu(OH)_2 + Ca SO_4$ (1)

6 (a) (i) Transition metals have partially filled d-orbitals (in atom or ion) [1]

(ii) Iron and copper have partially filled d-orbitals in their ions, zinc does not [1]

(b) • Ligands cause d-orbitals to split

• into 2 higher energy/ 3 lower energy

• Electrons absorb light (frequencies) to move to higher energy level

• Colour seen is colour transmitted/reflected/not absorbed

• Copper(II) complexes absorb red /orange/yellow/ all colours except blue.
[MAX 4 marks from points above]

• Different ligands cause different splittings / different ΔE.

• Copper(I) ion has full d-orbitals.

• So electrons cannot move to upper energy levels. [OVERALL MAX 6]

7 (i) +2 [1]

(ii) co-ordinate/ dative (covalent) [1]

(iii) pink is $[Co(H_2O)_6]^{2+}$ and blue is $[CoCl_4]^{2-}$ (1)
(ligand is) Cl^- (1)
(addition of HCl sends) equilibrium to RHS (1) [3]

(iv) $[Co(H_2O)_6]^{2+}$ shown as octahedral
[with attempt at 3D] (1)
$[CoCl_4]^{2-}$ shown as tetrahedral/ square planar (1) [2]

3.5

1 (a) Rate-determining step is the slowest step which limits the rate of reaction (1)

Stage 1 is the rate determining step since the reactant molecules match up with the rate equation $(2NO_2)$ (1)

(b) (i) First order with respect to NO_2 (1)
First order with respect to CO (1)
Rate equation Rate = $k[NO_2][CO]$ (1)

(ii) k = 4.48×10^{-2} (1)
Units $mol^{-1} dm^3 s^{-1}$ (1)

(iii) $NO_2(g) + CO(g) \rightarrow$ Any specified intermediates

2 (a) Rate = $k[O_3]^2$ (1)

Order (2) is the power to which the concentration (of O_3) is raised (1)

(b) Rate = $3.4 \times 10^{-5} \times (0.023)^2$ (1)
= 1.8×10^{-8} mol $dm^{-3} s^{-1}$ (1) [2]

(c) Catalysts provide a different route (1)
of lower activation energy (1) [2]

3 (a) (i) Rate of change of concentration with time. (1)

(ii) x = 1 / first order (1)
y = 1 / first order (1)

(iii) Hydrochloric acid is a catalyst (1)
as it affects the rate but is not used up during the reaction. (1)

(b) (i) Rate = $k[CH_3COOCH_3][HCl]$
k= 1.12×10^{-3} (1)
Units = mol $^{-1}$ $dm^3 s^{-1}$

(ii) Mechanism 2 (1) As it contains one molecule of ester and one acid in the rate-determining step.

4 **(i)** Rate = 0.0020 / 17.5 = 1.14×10^{-4} mol dm^{-3} min^{-1}
(or 1.90×10^{-6} mol dm^{-3} s^{-1})

Value 1 mark, units 1 mark

(ii) Follow the decrease in brown colour due to the Br$_2$ / use a colorimeter (1)

Reference to the measurement of time (1)

(iii) Br$_2$(aq) zeroth order (1)
CH$_3$COCH$_3$(aq) first order (1)

(iv) **I** As the pH increases the rate of reaction decreases (1)

II When pH increases by one unit, [H$^+$] decreases by a factor of ten, as does the rate, so must be first order (or equivalent statement) (1)

III A catalyst (as more H$^+$ speeds the reaction up without being in the equation) (1)

IV Rate = k [CH$_3$COCH$_3$] [H$^+$] (1)

Units of k are mol^{-1} dm^3 min^{-1} (1)

5 **(a)** When concentration doubles, rate doubles (1)
Therefore first order or rate is proportional to concentration (must give reason to obtain this mark) (1)

Alternative approaches:
Calculate k for each and show that all values are the same; Calculate k for one concentration and use to calculate other values.

(b) k = Rate ÷ [N$_2$O$_5$]
e.g. k = 3.00×10^{-5} ÷ 4.00×10^{-3} (1)
= 7.50×10^{-3} (1)
must be 3 significant figures; Units = s^{-1} (1)

(c) Rate-determining step must have one N$_2$O$_5$ molecule as reactant. (1)

Mechanism A matches this rate equation (1)
need reason to get this mark

6 **(i)** The experiments show that both the concentrations of iodide and persulfate have doubled (1)
therefore the initial rate should increase four times
$4 \times 8.64 \times 10^{-6} = 3.46 \times 10^{-5}$ (1)

(ii) Rate = k [S$_2$O$_8^{2-}$] [I$^-$] (1)
Therefore k = 8.64×10^{-6} ÷ (0.0400 × 0.0100) (1)
= 0.0216 (1)
mol^{-1} dm^3 s^{-1} (1)

(iii) In the rate equation one S$_2$O$_8^{2-}$ ion reacts with one I$^-$ ion. The rate-determining step therefore has to have 1 mole of each reacting, as (only) seen in step 1 (1)

7

	[NH$_4^+$(aq)]/mol dm^{-3}	[NO$_2^-$(aq)]/mol dm^{-3}	Initial rate/mol dm^{-3}s^{-1}
1	0.200	0.010	4.00×10^{-7}
2	**0.100**	0.010	2.00×10^{-7}
3	0.200	**0.030**	1.20×10^{-6}
4	0.100	0.020	4.00×10^{-7}

(1 mark for each correct answer) (3)

(ii) 2×10^{-4} (1)
mol^{-1} dm^3 s^{-1} (1)

(iii) No change (1)

(iv) If temperature is increased rate increases (1)
and since concentrations do not change the rate constant must increase (or similar) (1)

8 **(a)** Second order as the units of the rate constant are those of a second order reaction (1)

(b) **(i)** Activation energy is the minimum amount of energy required for a collision to be successful/ for particles to react.

(ii) k = A × e$^{-(Ea/RT)}$ so A = k / e$^{-(Ea/RT)}$ (1)
Insert relevant values:
A = 3×10^7 / e$^{-(23000/8.314 \times 350)}$ = 8.124×10^{10} (1)
mol^{-1} dm^3 s^{-1} (1)

(iii) k = A × e$^{-(Ea/RT)}$ = 8.124×10^{10} × e$^{-(23000/8.314 \times 400)}$
= 8.06×10^7 (mol^{-1} dm^3 s^{-1})

(c) **(i)** k = A × e$^{-(Ea/RT)}$ = 8.124×10^{10} × e$^{-(11500/8.314 \times 350)}$
= 1.56×10^9 (mol^{-1} dm^3 s^{-1})

(ii) Catalysts can increase the rate more than temperature; (1)
Increasing temperature requires much more energy which is expensive/releases greenhouse gases; (1)
Increasing the temperature of reversible reactions can decrease the yield. (1) [ANY TWO]

3.6

1 **(a)** Energy change for ½ H$_2$ (g) → H (g) = ½ × 436
= 218 kJ mol^{-1} (1)

$\Delta_f H^\theta$ NaH = 107 kJ mol^{-1} + 218 kJ mol^{-1} + 496 kJ mol^{-1} − 72 kJ mol^{-1} − 806 kJ mol^{-1}
(2 marks, 1 mark if one enthalpy term has the incorrect sign)
= −57 kJ mol^{-1} (1)

(b) NaH is more stable than the elements as the enthalpy of formation is negative.

2 $\Delta_f H = \Delta_{at} H$Cu + I.E. Cu + $\Delta_{at} H$F$_2$ + E.A. F + $\Delta_{lat\ form} H$ CuF$_2$ (1)
Doubling value for forming 2F and 2F− (1)
(These marks can be obtained from Born–Haber cycle)
$\Delta_f H$ CuF$_2$ = 339 + 2705 + 158 − 696 − 3037 (1)
$\Delta_f H$ CuF$_2$ = −531 kJ mol^{-1} (1)

3 **(a)** −705 (kJ mol^{-1}) (2 marks, 1 if sign incorrect).

(b) hydration and lattice **breaking** (1)

4 **(i)** atomisation of magnesium / vaporisation of magnesium

(ii) increased ratio positive charge on nucleus: number of electrons

(iii) is positive because the (negative) electron is repelled by negative species

(iv) lattice enthalpy is −3835(kJ mol^{-1}) numerical value (1)
negative sign (1)

3.7

1 Reaction is feasible if entropy overall increases / Feasible if Gibbs free energy is negative (1)

Although enthalpy change is positive, entropy increases when ions are freed into solution. (1)

2 (a) $\Delta H = -393.5 - 601.7 + 1095.8 = +100.6$ kJ mol^{-1} (1)

(b) The entropy increases because a gas is formed by the reaction and gases have higher entropies than solids. (1)

(c) $\Delta G = \Delta H - T\Delta S$ (1)

$\Delta G = 0$ when reaction becomes feasible, so T = $\Delta H/\Delta S$ (1)

Need consistent units so $\Delta S = 0.1748$ kJ mol^{-1} K^{-1} (1)
T = 100.6 / 0.1748 = 576 K (1)

3 (i) $\Delta H = 2 \times \Delta H (H_2O) + \Delta H (CO_2) - \Delta H(CH_3OH)$
$= 2 \times -286 + (-394) -(-239)$ (1)
$= -727$ kJ mol^{-1} (1)

(ii) Entropy of (methanol) gas is higher than liquid (1)

So entropy change will be more negative (1)

(iii) $\Delta G = -727 - (298 \times -81/1000) = -703$ kJ mol^{-1} (1)

Negative ΔG means reaction is feasible. (1)

4 (i) gases are more random/ have more disorder / move more freely and therefore have a higher entropy (1)

(ii) $\Delta S = 21.8$ (JK^{-1}mol^{-1}) (1)

(iii) $\Delta G = \Delta H - T\Delta S$ (1)

ΔG must be $-$ve if reaction to be spontaneous/ to calculate T make $\Delta G = 0$ (1)

0 = 318000 – T 21.8 so T = 14587/14600 (K) (1)

5 (i) $\Delta G = \Delta H - T\Delta S$ ($\Delta G = 0$ for reaction to be spontaneous) (1)
T = 1.92 ÷ 0.0067 (1)
T = 286.6 K (1)

(ii) Changes in temperature (above or below 286.6 K) caused the tin to change form making it unstable (and causing it to disintegrate) (1)

3.8

1 (a) $K_p = \dfrac{(pNO)^2}{(pN_2)(pO_2)}$

(b) (b) p NO = $\sqrt[2]{K_p \times (pN_2) \times (pO_2)}$ (1)

p NO = 3.79×10^{-3} atm (1)

(c) K_p decreases with decrease in temperature / K_p increases with increase in temperature, so must be endothermic (1)

2 (a) The forward dissociation reaction leads to an increase in the number of moles of gas (1)

So (by Le Chatelier's Principle) the dissociation of PCl_5(g) will be greater at low pressure. (1)

(b) $Kp = (pPCl_3)$x (pCl$_2$)÷ (pPCl$_5$) (1)
(There must be some indication of pressure. Square brackets not acceptable).

(c) pPCl$_5$ = $5.00 \times 10^{-3} \times 5.00 \times 10^{-3} \div 2.88 \times 10^{-2}$ (1)
= 8.68×10^{-2} atm (1 if value and units correct)

3 (i) [Mg^{2+}(aq)] = [CO$_3{}^{2-}$(aq)] = 3.16×10^{-3} mol dm^{-3} (1)

(ii) $K_c = [3.16 \times 10^{-3}]^2 = 1.0 \times 10^{-5}$ mol^2 dm^{-6} (1)

(iii) Yes, they are consistent, because as ΔG was positive (and the reaction would not occur spontaneously), K_c must have a very small value. (1)

(iv) Adding extra carbonate ions would push the equilibrium to the left, decreasing the solubility. (1)

4 (i) $K_p = \dfrac{P_{N_2O_4}}{P_{NO_2}^2}$ (1)

(ii) Increasing temp shifts equilibrium to left / favours endothermic reaction (1)
so value of K_p is decreased. (1)

(iii) PN$_2$O$_4$ = 9.5×10^3 Pa (1)
$K_p = 9.5 \times 10^3 \div (2.81 \times 10^5)^2 = 1.20 \times 10^{-7}$ (1)
Units = Pa^{-1} (1)

5 E.g. add a small 'amount' of an alkali / sodium hydroxide / NaOH / OH$^-$ ions (1)
this would remove / react with hydrogen ions giving water, shifting the position of equilibrium to the left (removing iodine) (1)

6 (i) $K_c = $ [HI]^2 / [H$_2$][I$_2$] must be square brackets (1)

(ii) $K_c = 0.011^2 / 0.311^2 = 1.25 \times 10^{-3}$ (1)

(iii) K_c has no units (1)

(iv) when temperature increases K_c increases (1)
this means equilibrium has moved to RHS / increasing temperature favours endothermic reaction (1)

therefore ΔH for forward reaction is +ve (1)

7 (i) $K_c = $ [CH$_3$COOCH$_3$][H$_2$O] / [CH$_3$COOH][CH$_3$OH] (1)
No units (1)

(ii) moles = $1.25 \times 32.0 \div 1000 = 0.04(0)$ (1)

(iii) [CH$_3$COOH] = 0.04, therefore 0.06 used in reaction and [CH$_3$COOCH$_3$] = 0.06, [H$_2$O] = 0.06 and [CH$_3$OH] = 0.083 – 0.06 = 0.023 (1)
$K_c = 0.06 \times 0.06 / 0.04 \times 0.023 = 3.91$ (1)

(iv) Value of K_c decreases since the equilibrium shifts to the left / the forward reaction is exothermic (1)

3.9

1 (a) (i) **Weak** Only slightly / partially dissociated (1)
Acid Produces H$^+$ ions (in solution) (1)

(ii) $K_a = \dfrac{[H^+][CH_3COO^-]}{[CH_3COOH]}$

(iii) 1.0×10^{-4} / 0.00010 mol dm^{-3}

(b) The equilibrium
$CH_3COOH \rightleftharpoons CH_3COO^- + H^+$ is present (1)

The CH_3COO^- / CH_3COONa reacts with any acid /
Equilibrium shifts to left to remove added H^+ (1)

The CH_3COOH reacts with any alkali added / Alkali
removes H^+ and the equilibrium shifts to the right to
replace H^+ lost (1)

2 (a) $K_a = \dfrac{[HCO_3^-][H^+]}{[H_2CO_3]}$

(b) $pH = -\log[H^+]$ (1)

(c) Rearrange equation to
$[H^+] = \dfrac{Ka \times [H_2CO_3]}{[HCO_3^-]}$ (1)

$[H^+] = 3.98 \times 10^{-8}$ (1)

$pH = -\log 3.98 \times 10^{-8} = 7.4$ (1) [3]

(d) Keeps pH constant (when small amounts of acid or
alkali are added). [1]

(e) Solution contains a large amount of CH_3COOH and
CH_3COO^- ions. (Accept correct equations) (1)

When an acid is added, the CH_3COO^- ions react
with the H^+ ions, removing them from solution and
keeping the pH constant. (1)
When an alkali is added the CH_3COOH reacts with
the OH^- ions, removing them from solution and
keeping the pH constant. (1)
(Accept answer in terms of equilibrium between
dissociated and undissociated acid molecules)

3 $[H^+] =$ antilog $-11.5 = 3.16 \times 10^{-12}$ mol dm^{-3} (1)
$[OH^-] = 1.00 \times 10^{-14} \div 3.16 \times 10^{-12}$ (1)
$= 3.16 \times 10^{-3}$ mol dm^{-3} (1)

4 (a) (i) $K_a = \dfrac{[CH_2ClCOO^-][H^+]}{[CH_2ClCOOH]}$

(ii) $pH = -\log[H^+]$

(iii) $[H^+]^2 = 1.3 \times 10^{-3} \times 0.1$
$[H^+] = 0.0114$ mol dm^{-3} (1)
$pH = 1.94$

(b) (i) Cross at pH 1.9 and volume 0 cm^3

(ii) 7.8 ± 0.2

(iii) $20.0 + 0.1$ cm^3

(iv) 0.125 mol dm^{-3} (1)
Three significant figures (1)

(v) Bromothymol blue and phenolphthalein (1)
Indicator range lies on vertical part of curve. (1)

5 (a) (i) $K_w = [H^+][OH^-]$ (1)

(ii) Equilibrium constant increases with
temperature, so must be an endothermic
process. (1)

(iii) $K_w = 4.3 \times 10^{-14}$ (mol^2 dm^{-6}) (1)

(iv) $[H^+] = 4.3 \times 10^{-14} = 2.07 \times 10^{-7}$ mol dm^{-3}
(allow 2.1) (1)
$pH = -\log (2.07 \times 10^{-7}) = 6.7$ (1)

(b) (i) End point = 20.0 cm^3 (*allow* 20 cm^3) (1)
$[NH_3] \times 25.0 = 0.100 \times 20.0$
(1 mark for setting up equation)
$[NH_3] = 0.080$ mol dm^{-3}
(must be two significant figures) (1)

(ii) $NH_4^+ \rightleftharpoons NH_3 + H^+$ / conjugate acid and
base mixture (1)
NH_3 reacts with added acid to form NH_4^+ (1)
NH_4^+ dissociates as H^+ reacts with added
alkali (1)

(iii) Methyl red (1)
(*any additional indicators treated as right /
wrong*)
pH range lies on the steep part of the curve (1)

6 (i) (Almost) completely dissociates to release H^+. (1)

(ii) $K_a = [H^+][ClO^-] / [HOCl]$ (1)

(iii) $[H^+] = 10^{-pH}$ OR $pH = -\log [H^+]$ (1)
$[H^+] = 5.88 \times 10^{-5}$ mol dm^{-3} (1)

(iv) $K_a = [H^+][ClO^-] / [HOCl] = (5.88 \times 10^{-5})^2 / 0.100$ (1)
$= 3.46 \times 10^{-8}$ (mol dm^{-3}) (1)

(v) pH above 7 (up to 10) (1)
OCl^- in equilibrium with HOCl / OCl^- will remove
H^+ from solution (1)

7 (a) an acid is a proton / H^+ donor (1)

(b) $pH = -\log[H^+]$ / negative log of hydrogen ion
concentration (1)

(c) a low pH corresponds to a high concentration of H^+ (1)

a strong acid is totally dissociated whilst a weak acid
is partially dissociated (1)
need to consider concentration (of acid solution) as
well as strength of the acid (1)
a concentrated solution of a weak acid could have a
lower pH than a dilute solution of a strong acid (1)

(d) (i) $K_a = [HCOO^-][H^+] / [HCOOH]$ (1)

(ii) $1.75 \times 10^{-4} \times 0.1 = x^2$ (1)
$x = 4.183 \times 10^{-3}$ (1)
$pH = 2.38$ (1)

(e) (i) buffer [1]

(ii) $RCOOH \rightleftharpoons RCOO^- + H^+$ and $RCOONa \rightarrow$
$RCOO^- + Na^+$ (1)

added H^+ removed by salt anion/ $A^- + H^+ \rightarrow$
HA (1)

added OH^- removed by acid/ $OH^- + HA \rightarrow$
$A^- + H_2O$ (1)

8 (a) $K_w = [H^+][OH^-]$ (1)
Units = mol^2 dm^{-6} (1)

(b) (i) In pure water $[H^+] = [OH^-]$ or $[H^+] = \sqrt{1.0 \times 10^{-14}}$ (1)
$pH = -\log 10^{-7} = 7$ (1)

(ii) Final volume of solution is 1000 cm³ so acid has been diluted by a factor of 100 so final concentration of acid is 0.001 or moles acid
$$= 0.1 \times 10 = 0.001 \quad (1)$$
$$pH = -\log 0.001 = 3 \quad (1)$$

(c) $K_a \times [SALT] = [H^+] \times [ACID]$

$1.78 \times 10^{-5} \times 0.01 = [H^+] \times 0.02$ (1)

$[H^+] = 8.90 \times 10^{-6}$ (1)

$pH = 5.05$ allow 5 or 5.1   (1)

Unit 4

4.1

1 (a) Stereoisomers are species that have the same structural formula but have a different arrangement of the atoms / groups in space. (1)

(b)

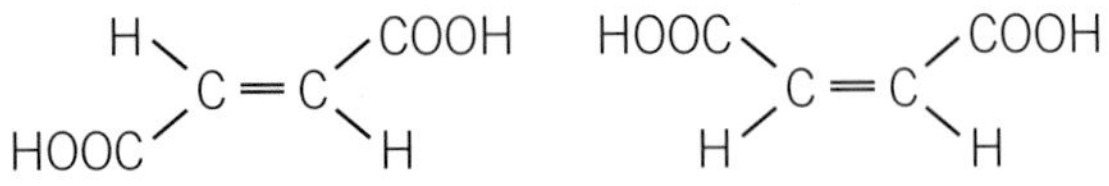

E-form   Z-form   (2)

(c) The mole ratio is 1:1, therefore the theoretical yield of the E-form is 0.040 mol. (1)

The relative molecular mass of the acid is 116 and the theoretical mass is 4.64g (1)

but only 86% is converted into the E-form, therefore the mass produced is 86 × 4.64 /100 = 3.99g (1)

(d) (i)

(2)

(ii)

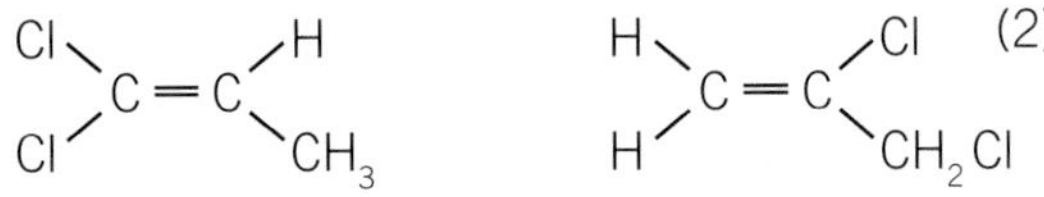

(2)

2 (a) Enantiomers are non-superimposable mirror image forms of each other. (1)

(b) (1)

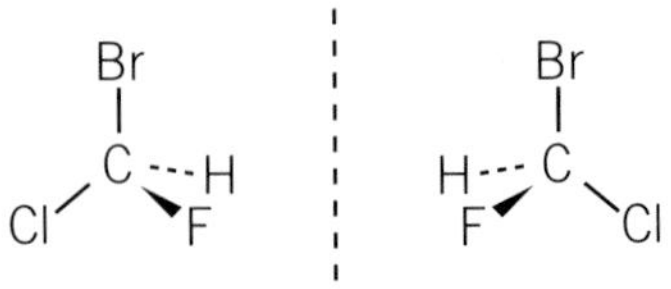

(c) Each carbon atom has two atoms or groups that are the same, therefore it does not exist as enantiomers. (1)

The formulae are simply different ways of showing the formula of the same compound. (1)

(d) One enantiomer will rotate the plane of polarised light clockwise and the other enantiomer will rotate it anticlockwise. For no apparent rotation the molar concentration of each enantiomer needs to be the same. Since the relative molecular mass of each enantiomer is the same, the required mass is the same (1)
therefore 3.50g is needed. (1)

3 (a) (2)

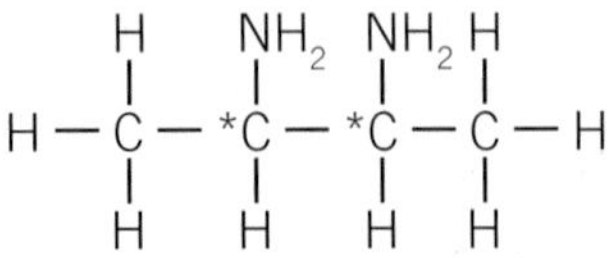

(b) Pent-3-en-2-ol has E-Z isomers and a chiral centre on the *CH(OH)CH₃ carbon atom. There are therefore 2 enantiomers for each of the E- and Z- isomers. (1)

(c) **(i)** A structure could exist where the two NH_3 groups (or the chlorine atoms) are opposite each other. (1)

(ii)

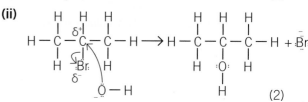

(2)

4.2

1 **(a)** **(i)**

$$\text{(benzene)} +3H_2 \longrightarrow \text{(cyclohexane)}$$

(1)

(ii) The difference between the two values is called the resonance energy. The lower figure suggests that benzene is more stable than expected, as more energy is needed to overcome the delocalised electron ring system. (2)

(b) If benzene had the Kekule structure of alternating double and single carbon-to-carbon bonds there would be two different bond lengths, for a C=C bond and a greater bond length for a C–C bond. In the delocalised structure all carbon-to-carbon bond lengths are the same. (1)

(c) A nucleophile has a lone pair of electrons and seeks out sites that are electron deficient. The delocalised π electron structure of benzene is electron rich and is more attractive to electrophiles rather than nucleophiles. (2)

2 **(a)** **(i)** Electrophilic addition (1)

(ii) The double bond is electron rich and polarises an approaching chlorine molecule, $Cl^{\delta+}$- $Cl^{\delta-}$. The relative electron deficient end of the Cl-Cl bond is the then attacked by a lone pair from the carbon-to-carbon double bond. (1)

(b) **(i)** An atom or group that has an unpaired electron. (1)

(ii) $Cl_2 \longrightarrow 2Cl\cdot$ (1)

(iii) C_3H_5Cl (1)

(c) **(i)** It is used to polarise the chlorine molecule into $Cl^{\delta+}- Cl^{\delta-}$, so that the molecule can be attacked by the ring electrons. (1)

(ii) Iodine monochloride is polarised $I^{\delta+}- Cl^{\delta-}$. The nucleophile from the ring will attack the more electron-deficient iodine atom of the iodine monochloride molecule. (1)

3 **(a)** **(i)** Electrophilic substitution (1)

(ii)

$$\text{(benzene ring with } C_2H_5 \text{ substituents)}$$

The presence of the ethyl group that is already present activates the ring towards further 'electrophilic attack'. (2)

(b) **(i)** Concentrated nitric(V) and sulfuric(VI) acids (1)

(ii) NO_2^+ (1)

(iii) 78g (1 mol) of benzene → 123g (I mol) of nitrobenzene
1g of benzene → 123/78g of nitrobenzene
26 g of benzene → 123 × 26/78g of nitrobenzene = 41g (theoretical yield)
% Yield = 35 × 100/41 = 85 (2)

(iv) Use a cold water / ice bath to maintain the temperature below 50°C.
Slow addition of benzene to ensure that sudden temperature rises do not occur (2)

4.3

1 **(a)** **(i)** Nucleophilic substitution (1)

(ii)

$$\text{(nucleophilic substitution mechanism)} \quad + \bar{B}r$$

(2)

(iii) Propene (1)

(b) **(i)** Sodium tetrahydridoborate(III) or lithium tetrahydroaluminate(III), or hydrogen and nickel catalyst (1)

(ii) (1)

$$CH_3CH_2 - \overset{OH}{\underset{H}{C^*}} - \overset{OH}{\underset{H}{C^*}} - CH_2CH_3$$

(iii)

$$CH_3CH_2 - \overset{OH}{\underset{H}{C}} - \overset{OH}{\underset{H}{C}} - CH_2CH_3 +3[O] \longrightarrow 2CH_3CH_2C\overset{O}{\underset{OH}{}} + H_2O$$

(2)

(iv) The colour of the solution changes from orange to green. (1)

2 **(a)** **(i)** The co-products are gaseous and easily lost from the reaction mixture. This is not the case when using the either of the phosphorus halides as liquid co-products are formed. (1)

(ii)

$$\text{(benzene ring)}-CH_2OH + SOCl_2 \longrightarrow \text{(benzene ring)}-CH_2Cl + SO_2 + HCl$$

(1)

(b) **(i)** 1 mol of pentan-1-ol gives 1 mol of ester
Mass of pentan-1-ol = 20.0. × 0.81 = 16.2 g
Moles of pentan-1-ol = moles of ester = 16.2/88 = 0.184
Mass of ester expected = 0.184 × 130 = 23.9 g
Actual mass of ester obtained = 25.1 × 0.88 = 22.1 g
% Yield = 22.1 × 100/23.9 = 92 (3)

(ii) The reaction reaches equilibrium and does not go to completion
Some ester was lost during separation as water is a product rather than gaseous hydrogen chloride. (2)

3 (a) Method 1
Add sodium hydrogencarbonate to a sample of each solution. The two solutions that effervesce are the two carboxylic acids, ethanoic acid and propenoic acid. The remaining liquid must be a solution of phenol. Add aqueous bromine to a sample of the two acids. Bromine will only be decolourised by the sample that is propenoic acid. The remaining solution must be aqueous ethanoic acid.

Method 2
Add aqueous bromine to samples of all three solutions. The one that does not decolourise the bromine is ethanoic acid. Phenol decolourises bromine and also gives a white precipitate of 2,4,6-tribromophenol. The other solution, containing propenoic acid only decolourises aqueous bromine.

Method 3
Add iron(III) chloride solution to each solution. Only phenol gives a purple colour. Add aqueous bromine to the two remaining solutions. Only propenoic acid will decolourise aqueous bromine. (2)

(b) Add iron(III) chloride solution. A purple colour shows that a phenol is present. Heat the compound with aqueous sodium hydroxide solution. This will hydrolyse the $-CH_2CH_2Cl$ group leaving a $-CH_2CH_2O^-$ anion and a chloride ion. Acidify the product with dilute nitric(V) acid and then add a few drops of aqueous silver nitrate. A white precipitate of silver chloride shows the presence of a chloride ion in the product. (4)

(c) (i) To generate the 4-nitrophenoxide ion, $O_2NC_6H_4O^-$, so that this can attack the relatively δ^+ carbonyl carbon atom of the acid chloride. (1)

(ii)

(1)

4.4

1 (a) Acidified potassium dichromate solution / 'acidified dichromate' / acidified potassium manganate(VII) solution / acidified manganate(VII) solution / acidified potassium permanganate solution (1)

(b) Sodium tetrahydridoborate(III) / sodium borohydride / lithium tetrahydridoaluminate(III) / lithium aluminium hydride (1)

2 (a) (i) The (dark) blue solution turns cloudy as a red-brown precipitate (of copper(I) oxide) is produced. (1)

(ii) Sodium propanoate / propanoic acid (1)

(b) Warm a sample with Tollens' reagent / ammoniacal silver nitrate solution. If an aldehyde is present a silver mirror is seen. (2)

3 (a) (i)

(2)

(ii) The nucleophile is the cyanide ion, ^-CN. It is described as an addition reaction because HCN is added across the C=O double bond. (2)

(iii)

2-ethyl-2-hydroxybutanoic acid (2)

4 (a)

Ketone E

Secondary alcohol F
(2)

(b) Compound **F** only contains one oxygen atom in each molecule, it cannot be made any simpler. (1)

5 (a) Butanone, pentan-2-one and cyclopentanone cannot be the ketone as a melting temperature of the derivative cannot be higher than the text book value. (2)

(b) Propanal $\rightarrow CH_3CH_2CHO \rightarrow C_3H_6O$ M_r 58.1
% oxygen = 16 × 100 / 58.1 = 27.6

Pentan-3-one $\rightarrow CH_3CH_2COCH_2CH_3 \rightarrow C_5H_{10}O$
M_r 86.1
% oxygen = 16 × 100 / 86.1 = 18.6

The unknown ketone is propanal (4)

(c) The derivative is impure – this results in a lower melting temperature than expected and over a wider range. (1)

6 (a) An alkaline solution of iodine / sodium chlorate(I) and potassium iodide solution, a yellow solid is seen. (2)

(b) Compound **A** as this is a methyl ketone / contains a $CH_3C=O$ group

Compound **D** as this contains the $CH_3CH(OH)$ group, a precursor of the $CH_3C=O$ group. (2)

4.5

1 (a)

$$HOCH_2\text{-}CH_2OH + [O] \longrightarrow 2 \quad \overset{H}{\underset{H}{\diagdown}}C=O + H_2O$$
(1)

(b) (i) $C_{12}H_{22}O_{11} + 18[O] \longrightarrow 6HOOC-COOH + 5H_2O$ (2)

(ii)

(1)

(c) (i) 8% is 8g / 100 cm³ solution
therefore 80 g dm⁻³
M_r CH_3COOH is 60
therefore concentration = 80/60 = 1.3 mol dm⁻³   (2)

(ii) Add aqueous bromine to a sample of each solution. Only phenol will decolourise aqueous bromine (and also produce a white precipitate). Add solid sodium hydrogencarbonate to the remaining two solutions. The one that gives an effervescence is ethanoic acid. The remaining solution must be ethanol.   (2)

This could be done in the reverse order of addition.

2 (a) The carboxylic acid is produced as its (soluble) salt (generally the sodium or potassium salt).   (1)

(b) It is not soluble in cold water / solution.   (1)

(c) The oxidation state on manganese goes from +7 in $KMnO_4$ to +4 in MnO_2. A drop in positive oxidation state is reduction. The hydrocarbon has gained oxygen in becoming the acid. Gain of oxygen is oxidation.   (2)

(d) m/z is 122. 'M_r' of COOH is 45, therefore M_r of the R fragment of the acid R–COOH is 122 – 45 = 77. Aromatic compound – this fits C_6H_5. The displayed formula of the acid is therefore

    (2)

(e) The formula is C_8H_{10}. The hydrocarbon must be

Since only one acid group is formed there can only be one alkyl group present. The aromatic hydrocarbon is ethylbenzene.   (2)

3 (a) The removal of 'CO_2' from a compound.   (1)

(b)

    (2)

(c) There are 2 peaks → one for the CH_3 protons and one for the aromatic C–H protons. These peaks are in a relative peak area 9:3 (ie 3:1) since there are 9 methyl protons and 3 aromatic protons.   (2)

(d) It is straight chain hydrocarbon, therefore not aromatic. M_r 72, must be an alkane, hence C_5H_{12}. The acid / anion must have 6 carbon atoms. Perhaps the salt is $CH_3CH_2CH_2CH_2CH_2COO^-Na^+$.   (3)

4 (a) 3 separate carbon environments. Ester must be

Only 2 peaks in the ¹H NMR spectrum, therefore 1 peak for R and 1 peak for R'. Both R and R' can only have one carbon atom each. Formula of the ester is

Each methyl group has three hydrogen protons giving an ¹H NMR spectrum with the same peak areas.   (3)

(b)   (2)

H_2SO_4 is the catalyst

5 Compound **A** → NH_3 / ammonia

Compound **B** → NaOH / sodium hydroxide

Compound **C** → H_2SO_4(aq) / aqueous sulfuric(VI) acid

Compound **D** → eg CH_3Br

Compound **E** → $CH_3CH_2NH_2$ / ethylamine   (5)

6 • Place a sample of the ester and an (excess) of aqueous sodium hydroxide in a flask equipped with a reflux condenser • heat the mixture • for a specified period of time (time is missing from the outline instructions) • allow to cool • add an excess of hydrochloric acid until no more white crystals of the acid precipitate • filter off the white crystalline precipitate • wash the crystals well with cold water • dry the crystals at room temperature / at a temperature below their melting temperature.

5–6 marks

Describes, giving full practical details, how the ester is hydrolysed and dry crystals of the acid are produced.

The candidate constructs a relevant, coherent and logically structured account including all key elements of the indicative content. A sustained and substantial line of reasoning is evident and scientific conventions and vocabulary are used accurately throughout.

3–4 marks

Describes, giving the main practical details, how the hydrolysis is carried out and the acid is isolated.

The candidate constructs a coherent account including most of the key elements of the indicative content. Some reasoning is evident in the linking of key points and use of scientific conventions and vocabulary is generally sound

1–2 marks

Describes some details of how the hydrolysis is carried out and the acid isolated.

The candidate attempts to link at least two relevant points from the indicative content. Coherence is limited by omission and/or inclusion of irrelevant material. There is some evidence of appropriate use of scientific conventions and vocabulary.

0 marks

The candidate does not make any attempt or give an answer worthy of credit.

4.6

1 **(a) (i)** $CH_3CH_2CH_2CH_2Br + NH_3 \longrightarrow CH_3CH_2CH_2CH_2NH_2 + HBr$ (1)

   (ii) Passing ammonia gas into a warm sample of 1-bromobutane in an open system would result in the loss of ammonia gas.
   An excess of 1-bromobutane is (initially) present – this may lead to the formation of the secondary and/or tertiary amines, reducing the yield of butylamine. (2)

   (iii) An amine has a lone pair of electrons on the nitrogen atom and will act as a base removing hydrogen as H^+ from hydrogen bromide, giving 1-butylammonium bromide.

(3)

   (b) Heat with aqueous sodium hydroxide. (2)

   (c) Both compounds have a lone pair of electrons on their nitrogen atoms that can hydrogen bond with water molecules.

(2)

2 **(a) (i)**
(1)

   (ii) $M_r\ C_6H_5NO_2 \rightarrow 123$ $M_r\ C_6H_5NH_2 \rightarrow 93$
   $123\ g \rightarrow 93\ g$ $25\ g \rightarrow 25 \times 93/123 = 18.9$ (theoretical yield)
   Percentage yield = $17 \times 100/18.9 = 90$ (2)

   (iii) e.g. can be a continuous process rather than a batch process / less separation of products needed (1)

   (iv) e.g. the need to use high pressures etc. (1)

   (b) (i) Ethanoyl chloride / ethanoic anhydride (1)

   (ii) e.g. Dissolve in trichloromethane, stir, filter off the 4-isomer, wash and dry / preparative gas chromatography (1)

3 $24000\ cm^3 \rightarrow 1$ mole
therefore $90\ cm^3 \rightarrow 90/24000 = 0.00375$ mole
equation states 1:1 ratio
therefore 0.00375 mole of ethylamine present in $75\ cm^3$
Concentration of ethylamine = $0.00375 \times 1000/75$
= $0.05\ mol\ dm^{-3}$ (2)

4 **(a) (i)**
or (1)

   (ii) A product of this reaction is HCl, this is removed by the alkali as NaCl. (1)

   (b)
and (2)

5 **(a)** $c = f/\lambda$ $f = c/\lambda = 3.00 \times 10^8 / 410 \times 10^{-9} = 7.32 \times 10^{14}$ Hz (1)

   (b) $E = hf$ therefore $E = hc/\lambda$
   the lower the wavelength the higher the energy, methyl red has the higher energy. (2)

   (c) $E = hf$
   $E = 6.63 \times 10^{-34} \times 7.32 \times 10^{14} = 4.85 \times 10^{-19}$ J (per molecule)
   therefore per mole = $4.85 \times 10^{-19} \times 6.02 \times 10^{23}$
   = $292160 = 292\ kJ\ mol^{-1}$ (2)

   (d) Red is the colour not absorbed / 'wavelength' at the other end of the visible spectrum is absorbed leaving red / blue is absorbed leaving red (1)

4.7

1 **(a)** $R-CH(NH_2)COOH$ (1)

   (b) If the 'R' group is hydrogen, then the central carbon atom is bonded to two hydrogen atoms, and this carbon atom cannot be a chiral centre. If the R group is not hydrogen then the central carbon atom has four different groups or atoms bonded to it, and this is a chiral carbon atom. (2)

   (c)
(2)

2 **(a) (i)** $(CH_3)_2CHCH_2CH(\overset{+}{N}H_3)COO^-$ (1)

   (ii) $(CH_3)_2CHCH_2CH(NH_2)COO^-$
   Amines, such as leucine, are largely neutral substances, and can act as acids when they are added to an alkaline solution. The OH^- ion reacts with the H^+ ion of the $^+NH_3$ group, producing an anion and water. (2)

   (iii) There are strong ionic forces between molecules of leucine. More energy is needed to overcome these forces and therefore the melting temperature is high. In 5-methylhexanoic acid the forces between molecules are largely Van der Waal's forces, these are weaker than the ionic forces in the amino acid and the melting temperature is therefore relatively much lower. The stronger intermolecular hydrogen bonding between the oxygen and hydrogen atoms of the carboxylic acid groups is only a small contributor to the intermolecular bonding as the acid groups are a small part of a larger molecule. (4)

(iv) As the chain length increases the solubility decreases. This is because the polar part of the molecule ($\sim\sim\sim\sim\sim\sim^{+}NH_3COO^{-}$) has increasingly less influence as the length of the carbon chain increases. (2)

(b)

$$N \underset{\parallel}{\overset{}{\rule{2em}{0.4pt}}} C \overset{}{\rule{1em}{0.4pt}} CH_2CH_2NH_2$$

(structure of a substituted imidazole: ring with N=C and C=N, H—C and C—H, N—H at bottom, side chain CH₂CH₂NH₂) (1)

3 (a) Number of moles of sodium hydroxide used
= 0.100 × 12.65 / 1000
= 1.265 × 10⁻³

Since mole ratio is 1:1 the number of moles of the amino acid in 25.00 cm³ of the solution is also 1.265 × 10⁻³.   Mass of acid used = 1.48 g

∴ Moles in 250 cm³ = 1.265 × 10⁻²

Therefore M_r of the acid = 1.48 / 1.265 × 10⁻² = 117 (3)

(b) Acid has the formula R–CH(NH₂)COOH where the 'M_r' of the CH(NH₂)COOH group is 45 + 13 + 16 = 74. Therefore the 'M_r' of the R group is 43. This corresponds to C_3H_7 and this could be

$$CH_3-CH_2-CH_2-\underset{\underset{NH_2}{|}}{\overset{\overset{H}{|}}{C}}-COOH \quad \text{or} \quad CH_3-\underset{\underset{H}{|}}{\overset{\overset{CH_3}{|}}{C}}-\underset{\underset{NH_2}{|}}{\overset{\overset{H}{|}}{C}}-COOH \quad (2)$$

(c) Use ¹³C NMR The acid CH₃CH₂CH₂CH(NH₂)COOH will give 5 peaks as there five discrete carbon environments. The acid (CH₃)₂CHCH(NH₂)COOH will give four peaks as there are four discrete carbon environments.
OR
Use the mass spectrum. The fragmentation pattern for each acid will be different. (2)

4 (1)

$$HO-\langle\text{benzene ring}\rangle-\underset{\underset{COOH}{|}}{\overset{\overset{H}{|}}{C}}-\underset{}{\overset{\overset{H}{|}}{N}}-\overset{\overset{O}{\parallel}}{C}-\underset{\underset{CH_3}{|}}{\overset{\overset{H}{|}}{C}}-NH_2$$

5 The primary structure is the sequence of amino acids making up the protein chain. The secondary structure is concerned with how the amino acids chains are arranged, this could be as an α-helix or as a β-pleated sheet. The arrangement is held together by hydrogen bonds between the carbonyl oxygen atoms of an amide group and the N–H hydrogen atoms in another amide group. These would be in the same spiral chain for an α-helix and between the atoms in different chains for a β-pleated sheet structure. The tertiary structure is concerned with how the protein chain(s) are folded. (5)

4.8

1 (a) The temperature is too high for safe ordinary distillation / some decomposition may occur at this temperature. (1)

(b) Hydrolysis produces the sodium salt of the carboxylic acid, this needs to be acidified to replace $\sim\sim\sim\sim\sim O^{-}Na^{+}$ by $\sim\sim\sim\sim\sim OH$. (1)

(c) By adding sodium nitrate(III) / NaNO₂ to dilute hydrochloric acid / HCl. (1)

(d) Wash until there is no more yellow colour in the filtrate. (1)

(e) (1)

$$\underset{}{\overset{COOH}{\langle\text{ring}\rangle}}-N=N-\langle\text{ring}\rangle-OH$$

(f) (i) It must be impure as it melts at a lower temperature than expected and over a range. (1)

(ii) The compound has a sharp precise melting temperature. (1)

(g) Warm the ethanol in a water bath (not directly heated). Add the impure acid until no more will dissolve. Filter, if necessary (away from flames). Allow to cool. Filter and dry. (5)

2 (a) Indicative content

• The M_r is 114 and since the % of oxygen is 28.1, the number of oxygen atoms is 32/2 = 2 • The infrared spectrum shows the presence of a carbonyl C=O group but not a carboxylic acid group COOH, therefore the compound must be an aldehyde or a ketone • It cannot be an ester as there is no C–O single bond present • Tollens' test is negative, therefore it is not an aldehyde and must be a ketone • It reacts with 2,4-dinitrophenylhydrazine, strongly suggesting a ketone • This evidence suggests that two C=O groups are present, as there are two oxygen atoms in a molecule of the compound • The reaction with iodine suggests that a CH₃C=O group may be present (not CH₃(OH), as there is no O–H bond in the compound) • the mass spectrum fragment at m/z 43 suggests CH₃C⁺=O, the fragment at m/z 71 may be due to CH₃COCH₂CH₂⁺ and that at m/z 99 may be due to CH₃COCH₂CH₂C⁺O • Three distinct peaks in the ¹³C NMR spectrum, and the ¹H NMR having two singlets suggests three carbon atoms with no hydrogen atoms bonded to adjacent carbon atoms.
• The δ values in the ¹H NMR spectrum suggest hydrogen protons bonded to a carbon atom next to a carbonyl C=O group The compound may be hexane-2,5-dione.

$$H-\underset{\underset{H}{|}}{\overset{\overset{H}{|}}{C}}-\overset{\overset{O}{\parallel}}{C}-\underset{\underset{H}{|}}{\overset{\overset{H}{|}}{C}}-\underset{\underset{H}{|}}{\overset{\overset{H}{|}}{C}}-\overset{\overset{O}{\parallel}}{C}-\underset{\underset{H}{|}}{\overset{\overset{H}{|}}{C}}-H$$

5–6 marks

Considers every point and deduces correct information from the deductions, arrives at a logically reasoned structure for compound **N**.

The candidate constructs a relevant, coherent and logically structured account including all key elements of the indicative content. A sustained and substantial line of reasoning is evident and scientific conventions and vocabulary are used accurately throughout.

3–4 marks

Considers most of the points and obtains correct information from the deductions. Makes an attempt at giving a structure for compound **N**.

The candidate constructs a coherent account including most of the key elements of the indicative content. Some reasoning is evident in the linking of key points and use of scientific conventions and vocabulary is generally sound.

1–2 marks

Considers some of the points and obtains some correct deductions from them.

The candidate attempts to link at least two relevant points from the indicative content. Coherence is limited by omission and/or inclusion of irrelevant material. There is some evidence of appropriate use of scientific conventions and vocabulary.

0 marks

The candidate does not make any attempt or give an answer worthy of credit.

(b) Take the melting temperature of the 2,4-dinitrophenylhydrazine derivative of hexane-2,5-dione and see if it has a value at / close to 257°C. Make a mixture of the 2,4-dinitrophenylhydrazine derivatives of the unknown compound and hexane-1,5-dione and see if the temperature varies from 257°C. (2)

3 (a)

4-Hydroxybutanoic acid (2)

(b) Condensation polymerisation
Polyester (1)

4 Indicative content

• The ^{1}H NMR spectrum confirms the identity of the two ethyl groups present as a quartet (CH_2) and a triplet (CH_3). The CHCl and CH_2 are seen as a triplet (CHCl) and and a doublet (CH_2). • The ^{13}C NMR spectrum shows 6 separate peaks indicating 6 discrete environments – for the carbon of the ester methyl groups, for the carbon of the CH_2 alkyl ester group, for the carbonyl oxygen atom (next to CHCl and the ester group), for the carbonyl

oxygen atom (next to CH_2 and the ester ethyl groups), for the carbon atom of the CHCl group, for the carbon atom of the CH_2 group.
• The infrared spectrum shows characteristic absorptions for the C=O bond at around 1650 to 1750 cm^{-1}, for the C–O single bond at around 1000 to 1300 cm^{-1} and for the C–Cl bond at 650 to 800 cm^{-1}. • To identity the chloride anion, add aqueous silver nitrate to the acidified (HNO_3) mixture. A white precipitate (of silver chloride) soluble in excess aqueous ammonia is seen.

5–6 marks

Considers every point in detail, giving correct conclusions for the structure provided.

The candidate constructs a relevant, coherent and logically structured account including all key elements of the indicative content. A sustained and substantial line of reasoning is evident and scientific conventions and vocabulary are used accurately throughout.

3–4 marks

Considers most of the points required and gives mostly accurate responses but the account is lacking in some of the details needed.

The candidate constructs a coherent account including most of the key elements of the indicative content. Some reasoning is evident in the linking of key points and use of scientific conventions and vocabulary is generally sound.

1–2 marks

Considers some of the points required but there is a general lack of detail in the responses.

The candidate attempts to link at least two relevant points from the indicative content. Coherence is limited by omission and/or inclusion of irrelevant material. There is some evidence of appropriate use of scientific conventions and vocabulary.

0 marks

The candidate does not make any attempt or give an answer worthy of credit.

5 (a) Azo dye (1)

(b) The lower spot has R_f value 2.0/3.2 = 0.63 and this corresponds to 3,4-dihydroxybenzoic acid.

The top spot has R_f value 2.7/3.2 = 0.84 and this corresponds to 1,3-dihydroxybenzene. (2)

(c) Use another locating agent to produce a coloured spot. (1)

(d) (1)

(e) The compound will be seen as white (if solid) / colourless (if in a solution) as no absorption occurs in the visible region of the electromagnetic spectrum. (1)

Index

W

Z